Perspectives on Workplace Communication and Well-Being in Hybrid Work Environments

Alexandre Duarte
CECS, Universidade do Minho, Portugal

Patrícia Dias
Universidade Católica Portuguesa, Portugal

Teresa Ruão
Universidade do Minho, Portugal

José Gabriel Andrade
Universidade do Minho, Portugal

A volume in the Advances in Human Resources Management and Organizational Development (AHRMOD) Book Series

IGI Global
PUBLISHER of TIMELY KNOWLEDGE

Published in the United States of America by
IGI Global
Business Science Reference (an imprint of IGI Global)
701 E. Chocolate Avenue
Hershey PA, USA 17033
Tel: 717-533-8845
Fax: 717-533-8661
E-mail: cust@igi-global.com
Web site: http://www.igi-global.com

Library of Congress Cataloging-in-Publication Data

Names: Duarte, Alexandre, editor. | Dias, Patrícia, DATE- editor. | Rução, Teresa, DATE- editor. | Andrade, José Gabriel, editor.
Title: Perspectives on workplace communication and well-being in hybrid work environments / edited by Alexandre Duarte, Patrícia Dias, Teresa Rução, José Gabriel Andrade.
Description: Hershey, PA : Business Science Reference, [2023] | Includes bibliographical references and index. | Summary: "The world is facing the Covid-19 pandemic for over two years now. Daily life changed dramatically, and social distancing and remote working has become the "new normal". Several countries, as is the case of Portugal, underwent multiple lockdown periods during which many work activities became hybrid or completely remote. Research about how people are facing these challenges, conducted in different geographies, point to common findings and concerns. First, the pandemic has enhanced inequalities regarding income, access to digital technology, learning, working and even wellbeing and affection. Second, the pandemic has taken a toll on the mental health of many people, with anxiety and depression being the most common consequences. Finally, the use of digital technologies, for fun, for learning, for social relations but also for working has increased significantly. In addition, after the first lockdown, many people didn't fully go back to their pre-pandemic routines, having maintained a more frequent and intense use of digital technologies, which has been reinforced by a second period of lockdown and remote working. At the same time, many workers are suffering from "digital fatigue" and struggle to self-regulate their life/work balance, as the permanent digital connection to work is reinforced and they struggle with blurred borders concerning privacy, leisure, or rest. In this context, it is vital to research about how organizations reinvented themselves to cope with the Covid-19 pandemic and understanding which of the reactive workplace communication practices and improvised solutions were considered advantageous and persisted in a post-pandemic setting. In addition, it is relevant to understand the perspective of the workers and to assess how these changes in their workplace (physical and/or virtual) communication (both formal and informal) impacted their wellbeing. This book aims, therefore, to realize how workers are coping with these new workplace communication practices, the advantages and disadvantages of these changes, emergent needs, and how organizations can reinvent themselves in order to promote the wellbeing and happiness of their members"-- Provided by publisher.
Identifiers: LCCN 2022060067 (print) | LCCN 2022060068 (ebook) | ISBN 9781668473535 (hardcover) | ISBN 9781668473542 (paperback) | ISBN 9781668473559 (ebook)
Subjects: LCSH: Flexible work arrangements. | Telecommuting. | Work environment. | Organizational change. | Organizational effectiveness.
Classification: LCC HD5109 .P47 2023 (print) | LCC HD5109 (ebook) | DDC
331.25/72--dc23/eng/20221215
LC record available at https://lccn.loc.gov/2022060067
LC ebook record available at https://lccn.loc.gov/2022060068

This book is published in the IGI Global book series Advances in Human Resources Management and Organizational Development (AHRMOD) (ISSN: 2327-3372; eISSN: 2327-3380)

British Cataloguing in Publication Data
A Cataloguing in Publication record for this book is available from the British Library.

For electronic access to this publication, please contact: eresources@igi-global.com.

Advances in Human Resources Management and Organizational Development (AHRMOD) Book Series

Patricia Ordóñez de Pablos
Universidad de Oviedo, Spain

ISSN:2327-3372
EISSN:2327-3380

Mission

A solid foundation is essential to the development and success of any organization and can be accomplished through the effective and careful management of an organization's human capital. Research in human resources management and organizational development is necessary in providing business leaders with the tools and methodologies which will assist in the development and maintenance of their organizational structure.

The **Advances in Human Resources Management and Organizational Development (AHRMOD) Book Series** aims to publish the latest research on all aspects of human resources as well as the latest methodologies, tools, and theories regarding organizational development and sustainability. The **AHRMOD Book Series** intends to provide business professionals, managers, researchers, and students with the necessary resources to effectively develop and implement organizational strategies.

Coverage

- Upward Feedback
- Change Management
- Executive Education
- Compliance
- Personnel Retention
- Organizational Learning
- Workplace Discrimination
- Executive Compensation
- Recruitment Process
- Process Improvement

IGI Global is currently accepting manuscripts for publication within this series. To submit a proposal for a volume in this series, please contact our Acquisition Editors at Acquisitions@igi-global.com or visit: http://www.igi-global.com/publish/.

The Advances in Human Resources Management and Organizational Development (AHRMOD) Book Series (ISSN 2327-3372) is published by IGI Global, 701 E. Chocolate Avenue, Hershey, PA 17033-1240, USA, www.igi-global.com. This series is composed of titles available for purchase individually; each title is edited to be contextually exclusive from any other title within the series. For pricing and ordering information please visit http://www.igi-global.com/book-series/advances-human-resources-management-organizational/73670. Postmaster: Send all address changes to above address.

Titles in this Series

For a list of additional titles in this series, please visit: www.igi-global.com/book-series

Female Entrepreneurship as a Driving Force of Economic Growth and Social Change
Ana Dias Daniel (Universidade de Aveiro, Portugal) and Cristina Fernandes (Universidade da Beira Interior, Porugal)
Business Science Reference • © 2023 • 241pp • H/C (ISBN: 9781668476697) • US $250.00

Diversity, Equity, and Inclusion Efforts of Businesses in Rural Areas
Shashi Bala (V.V. Giri National Labour Institute, India) and Puja Singhal (National Centre for School Leadership (NIEPA), ndia)
Business Science Reference • © 2023 • 310pp • H/C (ISBN: 9781668468784) • US $225.00

Socio-Economic Disparities, Vulnerable Communities, and the Future of Work and Entrepreneurship
JoAnn Denise Rolle (Medgar Evers College, City University of New York, USA) and Micah Crump (Medgar Evers College, City University of New York, USA)
Business Science Reference • © 2023 • 335pp • H/C (ISBN: 9781668469903) • US $240.00

Developing Diversity, Equity, and Inclusion Policies for Promoting Employee Sustainability and Well-Being
Sónia P. Gonçalves (ISCSP, Universidade de Lisboa, Portugal) Paula Cristina Nunes Figueiredo (Universidade Lusófona, Portugal) Eduardo Luis Soares Tomé (ULHT, Universidade Lusófona, Portugal) and José Baptista (ISCSP, Universidade de Lisboa, Portugal)
Business Science Reference • © 2023 • 333pp • H/C (ISBN: 9781668441817) • US $240.00

Valuing People and Technology in the Workplace Ethical Implications and Imperatives for Success
Claretha Hughes (University of Arkansas, USA)
Business Science Reference • © 2023 • 367pp • H/C (ISBN: 9781668453216) • US $205.00

Talent Acquisition and Retention Strategies in Global Startups
Neetima Agarwal (Symbiosis International University, India) Leo Paul Dana (Kingston University, UK) and Sujata Khandai (Amity University, India)
Business Science Reference • © 2023 • 305pp • H/C (ISBN: 9781668475140) • US $250.00

Strategic Human Resource Management in the Hospitality Industry A Digitalized Economic Paradigm
Kannapat Kankaew (Suan Sunandha Rajabhat University, Thailand)
Business Science Reference • © 2023 • 309pp • H/C (ISBN: 9781668474945) • US $250.00

IGI Global
PUBLISHER of TIMELY KNOWLEDGE

701 East Chocolate Avenue, Hershey, PA 17033, USA
Tel: 717-533-8845 x100 • Fax: 717-533-8661
E-Mail: cust@igi-global.com • www.igi-global.com

Table of Contents

Detailed Table of Contents

Wellbeing is a multidimensional concept that can be seen as balance between the psychological, social, and physical resources that an individual owns and his psychological, social, and physical challenges. Despite digital technologies becoming widespread and deeply rooted in our daily lives, there is increasing interest in debating the benefits and downsides they bring, not only in the personal life but also in the professional environment. This chapter explores the definition, dynamics, and strategies of wellbeing in the workplace, especially within the digital context, and suggests best practices for a good balance between personal and professional lives.

This study aims to analyse the relationship between internal communication and organizational performance. It was carried out at Natixis in Portugal, a company in the banking sector, which structured and outlined an organised, original, and creative internal communication strategy in record time during COVID-19. Quantitative research was carried out through a survey questionnaire of 160 Natixis employees so that we may have a perception of the impacts of a well-designed internal communication strategy on the employees of this company. The results show that the original and creative communication strategy used by the company made a positive contribution to the employees' organisational performance, also contributing to the establishment of interpersonal relationships between employees, even at a distance, and the feeling of belonging and identification with the organisation under study. Overall, the results of this study provide a better understanding of the role of internal communication in organisations and how essential it is.

This chapter explores the mental health challenges faced by journalists through a review of existing literature and a brief survey of journalists in Brazil. The study suggests that more research is needed on the mental health of journalists and calls for preventive measures such as mental health training in journalism schools and news organizations, as well as identifying and addressing the root causes of mental health issues in the industry. The chapter also highlights various strategies and best practices for journalists to maintain their mental well-being, including techniques for managing stress, establishing boundaries between work and personal life, and seeking support from colleagues. The study emphasizes that addressing the mental health challenges faced by journalists is important for the well-being of individual journalists and the quality of journalism and its role in serving society. The study concludes that, by promoting mental health practices and awareness, the journalism industry can improve the lives of its professionals and better serve the public.

In the wake of the pandemic, a new working model known as the "hybrid model" has emerged, combining the advantages and disadvantages of both "on-site" and "work from home" cultures to create a balance between the two worlds. This study conducts an in-depth survey of the merits and demerits of diverse working cultures among employees at various hierarchy levels in different industry sectors. Based on the assortment of over 350 white-collar employees working across India in the cultures mentioned earlier, it has been observed that the hype of the hybrid is justified. The study discovered that the majority of the workforce favors the hybrid model, providing the perfect balance between work and personal life. However, this new blend needs to have a better cognizance and acceptance from both the employer and the employee perspectives. The insights would set a benchmark for companies and employees to develop a plan of action.

The growing investment and interest of leading brands in the applicability of digital transformation strategies seeks to respond to the high expectations of a consumer profile that is progressively more informed and consequently more detailed. Consumers, as we know them today, demand effective monitoring in their relationship with brands, adapted to each profile, increasingly based on a digital universe. The level of connectivity registered by customers demonstrates the adoption of an always-on behavior in line with the lifestyle and pace of life of the majority. This chapter intends to explore the impact and influence of technology on the consumer experience in physical stores of brands in the luxury sector, as well as identify technological and digital trends that contribute to a more interesting and successful relationship between consumers and the staff that accompanies them.

work strategies in the Radio Renascença during the Corona Virus pandemic. In this context, there are identified internal communication antecedents and technological processes which enabled the station's teleworking. To carry out this research, semi-structured interviews were conducted with several radio presenters and producers, the channel's director and deputy director, and the sound engineer chief. Further information followed the participant observation method since it came from the author's personal experience, since she worked for 16 years.

The chapter aims to highlight how the theme of mental health has become a relevant agenda for Brazilian professionals in organizational communication and public relations, and who work in agencies, since the pandemic caused by COVID-19. After successive disruptions in areas of digital technology, microbiology has also shown itself capable of revolutionizing habits and ways of working in society. Time management, priority management, and hybrid work are now considered fundamental among communicators. Through a qualitative exploratory methodology, the chatper includes in-depth interviews, a multiple-question questionnaire, and an interview with the Brazilian Association of Communication Agencies. The research is also supported by a multidisciplinary bibliographic and documental base.

The chapter focuses on how advertising agencies organised hybrid work and developed well-being strategies for employees during the pandemic timespan (2020-2022) in Romania. It starts with an overview of academic perspective on hybrid work organization in companies. Then it unfolds the issue of well-being and the features of work in advertising agencies (flexibility, creativity, innovation). The chapter also presents several transformations brought by the COVID-19 pandemic to work organization in Romania. The second part analyzes the findings of 14 semi-structured interviews with advertising professionals from Romania. The findings show that some companies started the process of adaptation to hybrid work before the pandemic, while others implemented strategies for remote work during the lockdown. Online and hybrid work generated work-life imbalance because of the blurring lines between personal and professional space and time. Companies' management focused on rapid solutions for improving internal communication and for increasing adaptation to online/hybrid work.

The crisis of COVID-19 has resulted in pharmaceutical organizations moving towards new communication strategies with some launching new business models to survive and reach their target audience that in turn were layered onto, and dramatically accelerated, long-standing trends such as digitization and sustainability. In many ways, the changes in healthcare professionals and patient behavior are an acceleration of digital trends that were in motion before the pandemic hit. Pharma companies are experiencing a

Preface:

Workplace Communication in Hybrid Environments

The world faced the COVID-19 pandemic for more than two years. Daily life has changed dramatically, and social distancing and working remotely have become the "new normal". Several countries have experienced multiple periods of isolation during which many work activities have become hybrid or completely remote. Since then, digital communication is developing not a virtual world, but a real virtuality integrated with other forms of interaction in an increasingly "hybridized" everyday life.

As we write this presentation, we are dealing with this time of post-coronavirus pandemic crisis that has also affected brands, organizations, and institutions, without having encountered an effective model to deal with this new reality. The current situation exposes the impact of living in an increasingly digitally connected world.

Research about how people are coping with these challenges, conducted in different countries, point out common findings and concerns. First, the pandemic has increased inequalities in income, access to digital technology, learning, work, and even well-being and affection. Second, the pandemic has had an impact on many people's mental health, with anxiety and depression being the most common consequences. Finally, the use of digital technologies, for fun, for learning, for social relationships, but also for work, has increased significantly. Moreover, after the first lockdown, many people have not completely returned to their pre-pandemic routines but have maintained a more frequent and intense use of digital technologies, which has been reinforced by a second period of lockdown and remote working. At the same time, many workers suffer from "digital fatigue" and struggle to self-regulate as the permanent digital connection to work becomes established, blurring boundaries regarding privacy, leisure, or rest. It is in this context that we present this book on how organizations reinvented themselves to deal with the COVID-19 pandemic consequences, looking to understand which of the reactive workplace communication practices and makeshift solutions were deemed advantageous and persisted in a post-pandemic scenario. Furthermore, it is relevant to comprehend the workers' perspective and assess how these changes in communication (physical and/or virtual) in their workplace (both formal and informal) have affected their well-being. This book therefore aims to understand how workers are coping with these new workplace communication practices, the advantages and disadvantages of these changes, emerging needs, and how organizations can reinvent themselves to promote the well-being and happiness of their members.

With this line of study in mind, the editors of this book have shared several research questions about the design and use of Information and Communication Technologies in workplace environments. There are many challenges in analyzing, prototyping, evaluating, and developing digital plans and services to provide information and communication to either internal or external audiences.

To rise to these challenges, we need both social and technological approaches to communication strategies. Thus, the aim of the book *Perspectives on Workplace Communication and Well-Being in Hybrid Work Environments* is to provide an in-depth review of research related to the concepts and theories around topics such as Organizations and Communication, Digitalization, Connectivity, and Interactivity, among others. We aim to contribute to an improvement of the understanding of Digital Communication in Organizations. In order to do so, this book brings together different approaches that explore the impact of the COVID-19 pandemic on communication in the workplace, focusing specifically on internal communication, mapping new communication practices, and assessing their consequences, notably on the well-being of workers, who are coping with these changes. The book combines a scientific exploration of these ongoing changes, as we transition to a post-COVID-19 world, with a collection of examples and best practices that help different organizations to support their members through these transformations and nurture their well-being.

This book contains 13 chapters that analyze several key issues related to virtualization processes in organizations and the growth of digital ecosystems, while discussing the challenges and opportunities of those phenomena for the development of organizational structures and communication practices during and after COVID-19 pandemic.

The first chapter, "Digital Wellbeing in the Workplace Environment: Definition, Dimensions, Strategies, and Best Practices," presents wellbeing as a multidimensional concept, which can be seen as a balance between the psychological, social, and physical resources that an individual possesses, and the psychological, social, and physical challenges one faces, by making an overview of the referred concepts and connecting them in an organizational communication perspective.

The second chapter, "Linking Internal Communication and Organizational Performance During the COVID-19 Pandemic," discusses the relationship between internal communication and organizational performance. It was carried out at Natixis in Portugal, a company in the banking sector, which structured and outlined an organized, original, and creative internal communication strategy in a record time during COVID-19.

Chapter 3, "Reporting and Feeling: Considerations on the Mental Health of Journalists During the Pandemic," presents the mental health challenges faced by journalists, through a review of existing literature and a brief survey of journalists in Brazil.

The chapter "The Hype of the Hybrid on Work Culture Compatibility" promotes a reflection on a new work model known as the "Hybrid Model," combining the advantages and disadvantages of "On-Site" and "Work from Home" cultures to create a balance between the two worlds.

Chapter 5, "The Luxury Stores of the Future: The Impact of Technology on the Relationship Between Consumers and the Brand's Staff," presents the growing investment and interest of leading brands in the applicability of digital transformation strategies that seeks to meet the high expectations of a progressively more informed and, consequently, more detailed consumer profile.

Chapter 6, "Is Internal Communication a 'Bet on the Right Horse' on the Path for Promoting Employees' Eco-Friendly Behavior? The Mediator Role of Organizational Green Culture," presents the guidelines of the "Sustainable Development Goals" (SDGs) which are a key area of development for contemporary organizations. The commitment towards the development of internal organizational policies with the alignment of the SDGs clearly invites the adoption of employee-oriented environmentally friendly actions, in which the role of Internal Communication policies and practices should be discussed.

"Spillover Stress From 'The Great Resignation' in the United States: Broken Cross-Departmental Dependencies," is the seventh chapter. The authors examine the repercussions of stress following the so-called "Great Resignation" in the United States after the COVID-19 pandemic.

The eighth chapter, "Inside Out-Radio Being Radio Outside the Studio: Renaissance's Communication During the First Wave of COVID-19", proposes a reflection on how radio had to rethink its strategies and resort to new technologies and digital devices to continue its broadcast.

Chapter 9, "The Post-COVID-19 Communicator: What Makes the Professional's Head in New Times?" presents a project that intends to highlight how the topic of mental health has become a relevant agenda for Brazilian professionals in organizational communication and public relations offices and agencies, since the COVID-19 pandemic.

The next chapter, "Hybrid Work Organization and Well-Being Strategies in Advertising Agencies During the COVID-19 Pandemic," explores the topic of how advertising agencies have organized hybrid work and develop well-being strategies for workers during the pandemic period (2020-2022) in Romania.

Chapter 11 is "Reimagining Communication in Pharmaceutical Industry in the Next Normal," which aims to reflect on how the COVID-19 crisis made pharmaceutical organizations move towards new communication strategies with some new business models in order to survive and reach their target audience.

Chapter 12 presents "Communication and Coordination Issues in Managing Distributed Scrum Teams" by analyzing software development companies that have been progressively feeling the need to migrate their traditional development processes to agile environments.

Finally, the last chapter, "The Growth of Cyberbullying at Workplace After COVID-19: The Problems of New Forms of Communication," aims to explain the role of internal communication in organizations as one of the fundamental pillars for their proper development.

Throughout the 13 chapters, the book highlights the relevance of organizational communication strategies and practices to give employees information, direction, and support in a post-COVID-19 world. In a crisis situation, employees face pressures and challenges as they deal with unexpected disruption in their routine working conditions with a high level of uncertainty. In fact, the COVID-19 emergency had a great impact on individual and collective health, but also on working processes. The mandatory remote working and the constant use of technology for employees raised different implications related to technostress and psycho-physical disorders. In such a period of crisis and changes, the role of organizational communication was quite important for reestablishing mental balance and confidence in the system, and by reorganizing new working processes.

After the pandemic many of these organizational practices continued, leading to a technological addiction and an information overload, and this environment can bring once again confusion, uncertainty, worries, fear, stress, or anxiety to organizational members. However, communication is pointed out in the chapters of this book as the core of organizational reconstruction in the search for a new equilibrium in the post-pandemic world.

Alexandre Duarte
Universidade Nova de Lisboa, Portugal

Patrícia Dias
Universidade Católica Portuguesa, Portugal

Teresa Ruão
CECS, Universidade do Minho, Portugal

José Gabriel Andrade
CECS, Universidade do Minho, Portugal

Chapter 1
Digital Wellbeing in the Workplace Environment:
Definition, Dimensions, Strategies, and Best Practices

Alexandre Duarte
https://orcid.org/0000-0002-2665-864X
Universidade Nova de Lisboa, Portugal

Patrícia Dias
Universidade Católica Portuguesa, Portugal

ABSTRACT

Wellbeing is a multidimensional concept that can be seen as balance between the psychological, social, and physical resources that an individual owns and his psychological, social, and physical challenges. Despite digital technologies becoming widespread and deeply rooted in our daily lives, there is increasing interest in debating the benefits and downsides they bring, not only in the personal life but also in the professional environment. This chapter explores the definition, dynamics, and strategies of wellbeing in the workplace, especially within the digital context, and suggests best practices for a good balance between personal and professional lives.

WHY IS WELLBEING IMPORTANT?

According to Scaria et al. (2020), despite it's a concept that was "addressed thousands of years ago, starting with Plato, Socrates, Epicurus and Aristotle" (p. 4), the word "wellness" appeared for the first time written in English in 1654, as opposite of "illness" (that combines "ness" to "ill"), by adding "ness" to "well", and therefore, designating the state of being well, or the absence of disease. Although it's early origins, the concept only gained momentum from the 80's of the last century with the growth of the idea that wellness should be more about promoting health instead of just preventing diseases.

DOI: 10.4018/978-1-6684-7353-5.ch001

Wassell and Dodge (2015) stated that wellbeing is a multidimensional concept, that can be seen as balance between the resources (psychological, social, and physical) that an individual possesses, versus his psychological, social, and physical challenges. To the authors, several factors contribute to wellbeing, namely physical health, happiness, work-life balance, work environment, social support, education, and security, all each item with different levels of resources and challenges (p. 97).

For Mary Brandt (2020), the ultimate reason why take care of wellbeing is so important is to prevent four kinds of losses: personal, institutional, societal, and the meaning and purpose. In personal losses, the author includes physical health, healthy lifestyle, mental health, relationships, employment, and life. On the Institutional perspective, includes losses of employees, productivity, and customer satisfaction, quality, and safety. All these losses are relevant in the environmental workplace at several levels. By losing any of the referred components in the personal life, the balance of the worker is affected and its consequences often leading to profound losses for institutions and, in the end, to society as a whole. Finally, the misalignment of core values between the individual and the company, also known as person-organization (PO) misfit, besides the deviant behaviors, as well as increasing turnover intentions and lower performance, also affects employees' performance, job satisfaction or organizational commitment (Brown et al., 2020), and many times results in loss of meaning and purpose, that means loss of a life well-lived.

Besides that, one cannot assume that wellbeing in workplace is always connected to work-based situations, as many times employees are experiencing individual conflicts related to their own private lives, as family, health, social, financial, or community issues, among others, that influences their life balance. This way, even in the work environment, wellbeing needs to be contextualized in a holistic standpoint, encompassing all aspects of the worker's life (Cvenkel, 2020).

Another unavoidable aspect is the increasing use of technology in the workplace. This reality helped, in most cases, to improve working efficiency and reduced physical human effort, increasing therefore the living conditions of the employees, but it was also a generator of anxiety and stress (McClure, 2018). As stated by Griep et al. (2021), in the actual economic context, the increasing use of technology made the boundaries between private and working life being every day more blurred, giving rise to the need of understand and study the wellbeing in the digital context.

WHAT IS DIGITAL WELLBEING?

Throughout history, technological development has always aroused polarized reactions between enthusiasm for progress and the expectation of improved quality of life, and reluctance, criticism or even rejection based on the fear of negative effects or nostalgia in the face of imminent change. In Communication Sciences, the relationship between human beings, society and technology has been discussed between technological determinism and social constructivism, between media panics and technological optimism (Fuglsang, 2001). However, the most contemporary approaches are based on the recognition of a constant and intricate dynamic between the affordances that each new technology provides and stimulates (Gibson, 1979), and the appropriation that each user makes of them (Silverstone & Haddon, 1996). This dynamic has been studied and questioned from perspectives and contributions that cross risks and benefits, and that seek to understand how each of us can participate in the digital world in a conscious, informed, responsible, critical, and beneficial way.

Most of the scientific studies on this theme focus on children and young people, who are considered more vulnerable to the risks posed by the digital world. The work of Sonia Livingstone, in collaboration with many other colleagues, even from other scientific areas, resulted in the proposal of the defense of the digital rights of children and young people based on three Ps: Participation, Protection and Provision (Livingstone & Helsper, 2010). Children and young people have the right to participate in the digital world, and to benefit from the various opportunities it has to offer, both in terms of learning and personal development. However, because they have not yet developed all the skills that allow them to have sufficient media literacy for a responsible, informed, and critical use of digital technologies, they also have the right to be protected from the risks they are exposed to online, among which are the protection of their privacy and the fight against their commercial exploitation. The paradox that the protection that adults wish to give children and young people often results in their participation in the digital world being prohibited or restricted is overcome through the third pillar. Children and young people must be provided, throughout their development and education, with the knowledge and skills necessary to become aware, capable, and responsible agents in the digital world, capable of autonomous participation that is beneficial to each and everyone.

However, as digital technologies became widespread and deeply rooted in our daily lives, there is increasing interest in debating the benefits and downsides they bring, not only to children and young people, but to all users. In fact, the negative dimension of digital media stands out when we consider frequent and intense use. For example, the permanent contact provided by digital technologies, combined with the access to an endless amount of content and stimuli, generates a feeling of overload, of inability to pay attention to everything at the same time, of excessive spending of time that is then missing for other activities (Bawden & Robinson, 2020). However, on the other hand, not being connected to the online world also causes anxiety, fear of missing out on important information, anxiety about not knowing what is going on in the world, or simply in our social circle (FOMO - Fear of Missing Out) (Tandon et al., 2021). Today's major digital platforms, all of which operate algorithmically, also play an important role in this process, as they aim to maximize the time users spend on them by offering them content aligned with their online behavior (van Dijck, Poell & de Waal, 2018; Zuboff, 2019). This algorithmic logic has generated not only distrust and discontent regarding privacy and the commercial exploitation of data, but also a certain disenchantment among those who seek knowledge or entertainment but always receive more of the same (Paasonen, 2021).

In the aftermath of the Covid-19 pandemic, there is recent research about the effects of excessive use of digital media, with a significant strand investigating its impact on wellbeing (Nguyen et al., 2021). This period has significantly altered our relationship with digital media and our experience in the digital world. On the one hand, the use of digital technologies has expanded and intensified (Suwana et al., 2020). On the other hand, the consequences of overuse have been experienced, leading even the most enthusiastic to recognize digital fatigue and to give redoubled importance to the non-digital dimension of their lives (Sharma et al., 2021). On a more general level, the Covid-19 pandemic, and especially the lockdown periods, have had a strong impact on physical and mental health, and have provoked deep reflection on how each person lives his or her life, and on the pursuit of happiness and wellbeing (Talevi et al., 2020). Among adults, new models of remote or hybrid work have emerged that are here to stay (Nagel, 2020), as well as phenomena such as quiet quitting (Formica & Sfodera, 2022), which reflect a search for a better work-life balance, for purpose, for personal development, and for greater wellbeing (Kim et al, 2022).

In this context, the concept of digital wellbeing has recently gained track both in academic literature and in society in general. The World Health Organization (WHO) states that "digital wellbeing is the ability to maintain a healthy balance between the use of technology and other aspects of daily life, and to use technology in a way that promotes physical, mental, and social wellbeing" (WHO, 2020, n.d.). This definition points to the fact that digital wellbeing is, at the same time, a particularization of the general concept of wellbeing, one that concerns our relationship with technology, but one with a generalized impact on all the other dimensions of wellbeing.

Thus, to fully comprehend the concept of digital wellbeing, it is necessary to consider in the light of the general conceptualization of wellbeing. Looking at the academic literature on the topic, it is unanimous in acknowledging that the search for wellbeing is intrinsic to the human nature (Huta & Ryan, 2010). However, different approaches to wellbeing can be found since the Ancient Greek philosophy. These can be summarized in two opposing perspectives: hedonism, which conceptualizes wellbeing as brief moments when one experiences pleasure and/or happiness; and the eudemonic conceptualization, according to which wellbeing is a pursuit to fulfilling one's true potential throughout life (Henderson & Knight, 2012). More recent contributions on this debate have argued that the hedonistic and the eudemonic approaches are not opposing but instead complementary (Henderson & Knight, 2012).

Attempting to break down further the concept of wellbeing, the literature mentions its physical and mental dimensions (McCullough et al., 2000), and discusses numerous factors that can impact such dimensions, positively or negatively. According to Ryff (1989), self-acceptance, positive relations with others, autonomy, environmental mastery, purpose in life, and personal growth contribute to psychological wellbeing. In addition, Keyes (1998) argued that a social dimension of wellbeing should be considering, considering that human beings live integrated in social institutions and communities. Thus, social integration, social acceptance, social contribution, social actualization and social coherence are key for wellbeing.

Thus, the concept of digital wellbeing is also multifaceted, encompassing the physical, mental, emotional, and social dimensions of the self, but focusing on one's relationship with digital media (Keyes, 2005). It can be described as an optimal state of one's relationship with digital technologies, in a way that affords a sense of satisfaction, purpose, fulfillment and happiness (Twenge et al., 2021).

In the core of the concept of digital wellbeing is individual agency and accountability. Searching for digital wellbeing is an active process, through which each user manages their relationship with digital technologies in a way that supports and promotes their purposes and values, and consequently their wellbeing, and minimizes possible harms or risks (Rosen et al., 2019). Fornells-Ambrojo et al. (2020) emphasize the notion of finding a balance between the desired benefits that digital media afford and the undesired negative impacts that digital media also cause.

In the face of the downsides of digital technologies, particularly of their excessive use, trends of digital disconnection (Satchel & Dourish, 2009), and even an activist rejection of the digital (Portwood-Stacer, 2013), started to emerge. These trends gained renewed strength in the aftermath of the Covid-19 pandemic, a period that highlighted both the importance and usefulness of digital media, and the negative outcomes of their excessive use (Nguyen et al., 2021). Thus, digital disconnection gained track as a strategy for coping with these negative outcomes. However, the literature on digital wellbeing highlights that the concept does not propose a radical rupture with the digital world, but rather the development of the necessary literacy and skills for finding a positive place in it (Kim & Lee, 2019). This view is, of course, disseminated by the main digital platforms, which, attempting to minimize the backlash against its algorithmic structure and addictive nature, which supports their business model, became promoters of digital wellbeing. For example, Google states that "digital wellbeing is the ability to use technology in a way that enhances our lives, rather than detracting from it" (Google, 2022, p. n.d.).

Dimensions of Digital Wellbeing: Individual, Social, Organizational

In the previous chapter, we have established that the concept of digital wellbeing is complex and multifaceted, referring to how one's relationship with digital technologies reflects upon the physical, mental, emotional, and social dimensions of one's wellbeing (Keyes, 2005).

Another way of approaching this construct is considering Brofenbrenner's (1979) ecological theory of the child's development. This theoretical construct considers concentric circles that surround the individual, in which one undergoes a complex socialization process, and influence one's development in a fluid and ongoing dynamic. Thus, the concept of digital wellbeing, despite being recent, has been studied from different points of view or approaches, namely, the individual, the social, and the organizational (study/work).

On an individual level, research has focused on mapping the diversity of practices that are emerging to manage one's relationship with digital technologies, ranging from radical disconnection to masterful self-regulation (Nguyen et al., 2021). In general, these strategies include, to some extent, mindfulness practices applied to self-regulating the use of digital media (Fornells-Ambrojo et al., 2020), learning how to set boundaries regarding digital practices (Kim & Lee, 2019), and practicing self-care, thus committing to healthy habits such as sleeping well, exercising regularly, eating well, socializing, and taking some time away from digital technologies (Lee & Robbins, 2019). Furthermore, research has identified specific aspects of individual wellbeing that are particularly affected by digital practices, namely sleep time and quality (Cain & Gradisar, 2010; Sampasa-Kanyinga & Lewis, 2016), cognitive aspects such as focus, attention span, memory and sense of control over one's life (Kirschner & Karpinski, 2010; Alzahrani & Alghamdi, 2016), aspects of physical health such as sedentarism, obesity and bad postures (Chinapaw et al., 2010) and aspects of mental health such as anxiety, stress and depression (Twenge et al., 2018; Rosen et al., 2019). Research has also explored which strategy works best for whom attempting to find correlations between individual features such as age, gender, socioeconomic status, and personality traits, among others, and the strategies that are efficient in promoting digital wellbeing. In fact, different individuals have different degrees of vulnerability to the negative effects of excessive digital media use, and diverse in how easily (or difficultly) they adopt strategies and practices that promote digital wellbeing. For example, Rosen et al. (2019) identified neuroticism and anxiety as personality traits that enhance one's susceptibility to the negative effects of excessive digital practices. After exploring correlations between several individual traits and the efficiency of diverse digital wellbeing strategies, Sassenberg et al. (2019) conclude that there is no one-size-fits-all approach to digital wellbeing and that effective strategies must be tailored and personalized.

Social Networking Sites (SNS) are intrinsically social, and they are one of the digital activities to which users dedicate more time to (Duarte & Dias, 2021). Therefore, their weight on the social dimension of wellbeing is considerable and has been investigated. For example, Rosen et al. (2013) found that peer pressure is a significant predictor of excessive use of digital media, followed by social anxiety, being its most common expression FOMO (Fear Of Missing Out). Social comparisons have also been highlighted by Fardouly et al. (2015) as a factor that can impact wellbeing either positively or negatively. Individuals tend to constantly compare themselves to others, to assess their position in social groups and where they stand regarding social norms. Upwards social comparisons can be beneficial, as we can look up to role models that inspire us to act and reach goals. On the contrary, downward social comparisons can be detrimental to our wellbeing by making us feel unsatisfied with our image, our lifestyle, our achievements, thus leading to low self-esteem, anxiety, and depression. Media discourse, that is, the main messages spread by media outlets, can also reflect positively or negatively on digital wellbeing, in the sense that they can promote increased or decreased use of digital media. For example, media discourses around productivity and an implicit obligation to be constantly connected and available, as well as pressure to be successful, lead to increased use of digital media, and consequently to a feeling of overwhelmness, to stress and anxiety. Additionally, media discourses that promote digital media as locus for success, social validation and self-worth lead to excessive use and are related to mental health issues such as depression or eating disorders (Lin et al., 2019). On the other hand, media discourses about negative effects of excessive use of digital media and the dangers that these may hold, such as addiction, cyberbullying, privacy invasion, pedophilia, or digital frauds, can lead to a decrease in social media use, while at the same time increasing stress and anxiety (Reinecke & Trepte, 2014). However, Grieve et al. (2013) have found that digitally mediated social relationships can have a positive impact on digital wellbeing, as they are a source of support and can afford a sense of belonging to a group, as well as feeling esteemed and valued. Looking at the social dimensions of digital wellbeing, most studies point to negative impacts on social skills and social relationships. Twenge et al. (2018), for example, report that excessive use of digital media is correlated with a decrease in face-to-face interaction, which can lead to feeling isolated and lonely. In this sense, Wang et al. (2019) found that excessive digital media use is detrimental for the ability to be empathic, and Lin et al. (2019) found that it can have a negative impact on social and emotional development, decreasing pro-social behavior.

As strategy for promoting digital wellbeing in this social dimension, apart from seeking to engage in offline social activities, several studies (Kim & Lee, 2019; Twenge et al., 2020) point to the cultivation of positive online relationships and upward social comparisons, that can make digital users feel more socially supported, integrated in online communities, connected to others with whom they share affinities, and ultimately esteemed, and loved.

Focusing on the organizational dimension, the Covid-19 pandemic was a powerful accelerator of digital transformation processes in a huge diversity of organizations worldwide (Cennamo & Santoro, 2020). New working modalities emerged and disseminated, generally described as hybrid or remote working models, and organizations are learning how to cope with digital wellbeing (Bondarouk & Ruel, 2021). Allen (2017) presents a discussion of the advantages and disadvantages of hybrid and remote work models for workers. On the one hand, hybrid and remote work afford flexibility and autonomy, they facilitate the work-life balance by allowing convenient work schedules, it is possible to work from anywhere (if there are digital equipment and internet connection available) and it may be easier to focus without interruptions from colleagues. On the other hand, the lack of face-to-face communication can cause more communication problems and ultimately lead to social isolation and loneliness, there is a risk of privacy invasion when it comes to work supervision, and it has been reported to be very difficult to maintain healthy boundaries between work and other dimensions of life, as well as disconnecting from work and resting.

Taking this overview as departure point, we can look into specific impacts on digital wellbeing. First, the easy access and constant availability to digital resources at home, in the light of organizational discourses, cultures and leaderships which pressure towards success and productivity, can lead to excessive use of digital technologies – and even to addiction and compulsive behavior (Kooij et al., 2021), to a sense of being overloaded (Nikolova & Devinney, 2021), to difficulties in managing work and time (Chen et al.,

2021), to difficulties in reaching a work-life balance (Premeaux et al., 2021), and ultimately to burnout and technostress (Bakker, 2021; Liang et al., 2021). Another important effect is the increase of social isolation and a lack of social support in hybrid or remote working environments. For example, Smith and Anderson (2019) have found that remote workers experience a sense of disconnection regarding their colleagues and organization, which can impact their wellbeing. Another hot topic is privacy and data security (Bhattacharya et al., 2020; Barsham & Al-Zoubi, 2021). On the side of organizations, hybrid and remote work pose risks, such as workers using personal devices and networks, or sharing devices with other family members, which increases the risks for data breaches and cyberattacks. Additionally, it is more difficult to monitor the performance of employees. The reverse side of this coin is that personal data or workers is exposed online, and they can be more easily targeted by online advertising or even frauds. Also, workers are more exposed to privacy invasion from supervisors, and even to cyberbullying and online harassment (Holt & Munday, 2020).

However, many of these negative outcomes can be mitigated by using adequate digital tools, by complying to laws and regulations (e.g. the General Data Protection Regulation), and by promoting digital wellbeing in organizations. For example, Meske et al. (2021) discuss how hybrid and remote work can increase distraction and make it difficult to focus, or the reverse, depending on the work environment that was created in the home.

Thus, research on digital wellbeing is unanimous that it must be nurtured and fostered. Next, we present an overview of general strategies for the promotion of digital wellbeing.

Strategies for Digital Wellbeing: From Disconnection to Self-Regulation

Strategies for reaching an optimized or maximized state of digital wellbeing take many forms. They can take the form of "detox" or "rest" periods, after which users resume all their digital routines (Nguyen et al., 2021). Even though more recent definitions of digital wellbeing, particularly those promoted by digital platforms themselves, do not accept digital disconnection as a strategy that may lead to increased digital wellbeing (Google, n.d.), in practice, some users are resorting to the abandonment of specific platforms or practices, although it rarely materializes as a radical refusal to participate in the digital world (Nguyen et al., 2021).

These experiences have evolved beyond abstinence toward self-regulation. Digital wellbeing has been defined as "a healthy balance between connectivity and disconnection" (van den Abeele, 2021, p. 933), and as this becomes a goal for more and more users, digital platforms themselves have sought to support them in this pursuit, or else lose them. There are several platforms and devices that support users in adopting balanced and healthy digital practices, from timers that help control the time spent online, to usage modes that prevent disruptions from notifications, to even usage reports that facilitate reflection on how we use our time (Roffarello & de Russis, 2019). Digital wellbeing has become part of the quest for personal development and fulfillment: being able to make a conscious, informed, balanced, and beneficial management of our digital practices is a requirement for becoming the best version of ourselves. However, the literature on the subject admits that this concept is subjective and dynamic. The media diet that provides the greatest digital wellbeing varies from person to person and may vary at different times in the same person's life. It is "an optimal and dynamic balance between the advantages and disadvantages of digital connectivity, as well as time spent online and offline" (van den Abeele, 2021, p. 945). Assessing when one reaches this goal depends on an introspective self-assessment that is made by each individual, in cognitive and affective terms, of his or her journey towards digital wellbeing. And this journey is influenced by multiple factors concerning each technological device or platform, each user, and their social, cultural, economic, political and media context, which in most cases exert high pressure for permanent connectivity (Buchi, 2021). Digital wellbeing has been conceptualized as the resumption of control over digital practices, as an act of self-determination that requires the development of self-regulation skills (Cecchinato et al., 2019).

The literature on digital wellbeing agrees that there are no one-size-fits-all solutions, but instead a set of flexible and adaptable strategies, resources, and techniques, based on the most recent scientific knowledge on the subject and on implementation experiences, which can be tailored to develop skills such as media literacy, critical thinking skills, and self-regulation (Gui, Fasoli & Carradore, 2017), among others, essential for the promotion of digital wellbeing.

Digital Wellbeing Practices: What Organizations Can Do for Their Collaborators (and for Themselves)

From a historical point of view, the workplace has usually been seen as productivity-oriented, with little concerns on the employee's wellbeing (Cvenkel, 2020). Nevertheless, this paradigm is changing in the last years, especially due the emerging environmental critique of modern consumer society. For Carlisle et al. (2009) wellbeing is a collateral casualty of modernity, because of the economic, social, and cultural changes that we're facing in the Western society, consequence of the materialistic and individualistic culture. This fact is especially relevant when we look into how youngsters are dealing with all these changes. The next generation will decide their future careers by its contribution to society and will measure the success of their professional development based on the change they will be able to create (USC, 2022, p.36). In this context, the wellbeing they'll create to their lives and to society should be taken in consideration in the strategic decisions of organizations. Another unavoidable aspect is the growing adoption of technology in all levels of our daily lives, and also in the professional context. Griep et al. (2021) analyzed the impact of technology in the workplace to try to understand potential advantages and disadvantages of (1) telework, (2) automation in the workplace, and (3) algorithmic management. Regarding telework, although some positive consequences such as increasing performance, and a potential work-life balance, a significant proportion of employees refer a negative social consequence, especially in terms of social and/or professional isolation. We suggest that a levelheaded politic between physical and remote work should be implemented, as well as do not overload the employees with work, allowing the balance between private and professional worlds. In third place, it is suggested to create and decide a teleworking policy based on a shared discussion with the workers.

About automation in the workplace, the authors highlight the importance of, when implementing new technologies, not overlook the human aspect. This means that, before making that decision, organizations should assess their workers' needs to ensure the best possible PO fit.

Finally, the algorithmic management. Once employees generally don´t have a positive reaction to its use in the workplace, the design of an algorithmic system should be done by adequately explain it and demonstrating sensitivity and empathy with the workers. This way the organization guarantees the involvement and good-will of the collaborators.

The impulse on digital transformation and hybrid or remote work models brought about by the Covid-19 pandemic highlighted both benefits and downsides of the intensification of the presence of digital technologies in work activities. On the one hand, they can increase productivity, comfort, and facilitate work-life balance. But on the other hand, recent studies have attested increased risk of blurring of borders between work and personal life, of the tendency for digital addiction, of fatigue and burnout (Sianoja, 2019). In the face of these trends, organizations have been struggling to minimize such risks, while harvesting the benefits that digital technologies can propitiate. One of the pathways to do so is promoting the digital wellbeing of workers. Within this scope, some relevant trends are emerging. One is establishing (and committing) to wellbeing policies, particularly focusing on creating boundaries between work and the personal lives of workers, setting, for example, limits for when they should be available for work-related communication, setting working hours and breaks, and discouraging volunteer work during non-working hours. However, it is necessary to find a balance between setting boundaries and affording flexibility and adaptability, which is one of the big advantages of hybrid or remote work (Makiniemi & Kinnunen, 2020). Another idea is that organizations should provide resources and training to support workers in coping with new working processes and practices, such as, for example, training on time management, managing digital distractions and focus, or mindfulness. In addition, digital resource can support self-regulation practices, and they do on an individual level, setting timers for breaks, or limiting the time of use of certain digital platforms, for example. Plus, organizations could also provide mental health resources, mindfulness activities, and counseling services. Finally, encouraging open communication and regular feedback also supports digital wellbeing. These resources and support from organizations should focus on encouraging healthy habits in workers. Examples are taking regular breaks, doing exercise, resting, and engaging in non-digital activities (Laato et al., 2021). Organizations must realize thar promoting the digital wellbeing of workers, encouraging them to be physically and mentally healthy, is the best way of increasing productivity and preventing burnout (Hao, 2018).

Of course, all of these actions must be supported by an adequate organizational culture, one that does not coerce workers to present results regardless of how, and truly values their wellbeing. Makiniemi and Kinnunen (2020) go as far as suggesting that organizations should recognize and reward workers who prioritize their digital (and overall) wellbeing, thus changing radically the mindset of most organizational cultures. However, this new mindset based on the acknowledgement of work-life balance as something that should be promoted and achieved is key not only for preventing risks, but also to increase productivity, and mostly to increase overall happiness, which is reflected in the organizations' ability to attract and retain talent.

In a very interesting chapter called "Why wellbeing, why now?", Hesketh and Cooper (2017) analyzed the evolution of wellbeing in the last years, and how business in general looked to it in the modern era. Concluding that the private corporations were quick to understand how wellbeing impacts productivity, they also argued that leadership approaches and the prevailing culture of an organization impacts performance. The same conclusions were reached by Chen et al. (2020) who stressed the important role of organizational leadership in promoting these changes towards digital wellbeing and nurturing an adequate organizational culture that supports it.

In short, organizational wellbeing, especially in a highly digitized era, must take into account human-friendly decisions that protect human beings while optimizing the quality of work, but also the balance between professional and personal life, performance, and sustainable employability of workers.

REFERENCES

Allen, T. D. (2017). The work-family role interface: A synthesis of the research from industrial and organizational psychology. In A. M. Rossi, J. Meurs, & T. D. Allen (Eds.), *The work-family interface: An introduction* (pp. 3–26). Routledge.

Alzahrani, M., & Alghamdi, N. (2016). The negative effects of social media: Anxiety and cognitive capacity. *Journal of King Saud University - Computer and Information Sciences, 28*(4), 395-400. doi:10.1016/j.jksuci.2015.09.001

Bakker, A. B. (2021). Job crafting and the COVID-19 pandemic: An opportunity for a new normal. *Work, Aging and Retirement*, *7*(1), 23–33. doi:10.1093/workar/waaa027

Barsham, F., & Al-Zoubi, A. (2021). Cybersecurity and data privacy concerns in remote work during the COVID-19 pandemic. *Journal of Cybersecurity and Information Management*, *4*(1), 22–37. doi:10.37380/jcim.2021.4.2

Bawden, D., & Robinson, L. (2020). Information Overload: An Overview. In *Oxford Encyclopedia of Political Decision Making*. Oxford University Press. doi:10.1093/acrefore/9780190228637.013.1360

Bhattacharya, S., Sengupta, S., & Sharma, R. (2020). Privacy and security in the era of remote work: A review and research agenda. *Journal of the Association for Information Science and Technology*, *71*(12), 1419–1435. doi:10.1002/asi.24372 PMID:32427189

Bondarouk, T., & Ruel, H. J. M. (2021). The COVID-19 pandemic as a catalyst for the reinvention of the future of work. *Journal of Business Research*, *122*, 1–8. doi:10.1016/j.jbusres.2020.12.016

Brandt, M. (2020). Why focus on is wellbeing? In E. Kim & B. Lindeman (Eds.), *Wellbeing* (pp. 11–19). Springer., doi:10.1007/978-3-030-29470-0_2

Bronfenbrenner, U. (1979). *The Ecology of Human Development*. Harvard University Press.

Brown, L. W., Manegold, J. G., & Marquardt, D. J. (2020). The effects of CEO activism on employee's person-organization ideological misfit: A conceptual model and research agenda. *Business and Society Review*, *125*(1), 119–141. doi:10.1111/basr.12196

Büchi, M. (2021). Digital well-being theory and research. *New Media & Society*. Advance online publication. doi:10.1177/14614448211056851

Cain, N., & Gradisar, M. (2010). Electronic media use and sleep in school-aged children and adolescents: A review. *Sleep Medicine*, *11*(8), 735–742. doi:10.1016/j.sleep.2010.02.006 PMID:20673649

Carlisle, S., Henderson, G., & Hanlon, P. (2009). 'Wellbeing': A collateral casualty of modernity? *Social Science & Medicine*, *69*(10), 1556–1560. doi:10.1016/j.socscimed.2009.08.029 PMID:19765875

Cecchinato, M. E., Rooksby, J., Hiniker, A., Munson, S., Lukoff, K., Ciolfi, L., Thieme, A., & Harrison, D. (2019, May 2). Designing for digital wellbeing: A research & practice agenda. *Conference on Human Factors in Computing Systems - Proceedings*. https://doi.org/10.1145/3290607.3298998

Cennamo, C., & Santoro, G. (2020). The digital transformation of firms during the COVID-19 pandemic. *Journal of Business Research, 116*, 276–283. doi:10.1016/j.jbusres.2020.07.042

Chen, L., Wang, Y., & Cui, Y. (2020). How do firms promote digital wellness in the workplace? The role of top management support and participative management. *International Journal of Environmental Research and Public Health, 17*(14), 5019. doi:10.3390/ijerph17145019 PMID:32668635

Chen, Y. R., Chen, M. Y., & Chen, C. W. (2021). The effect of remote work on job performance: Evidence from the COVID-19 pandemic. *Sustainability, 13*(15), 8545. doi:10.3390u13158545

Chinapaw, M. J. M., Proper, K. I., Brug, J., van Mechelen, W., & Singh, A. S. (2010). Relationship between young peoples' sedentary behaviour and biomedical health indicators: A systematic review of prospective studies. *Obesity Reviews, 11*(8), 621–632. doi:10.1111/j.1467-789X.2009.00678.x PMID:21438990

Cvenkel, N. (2020). *Well-being in the workplace: governance and sustainability insights to promote workplace health*. Springer Nature. doi:10.1007/978-981-15-3619-9

Duarte, A., & Dias, P. (2021). TikTok: Usos e motivações entre adolescentes em Portugal. *Chasqui, Revista Latinoamericana de Comunicación, 1*(147), 81–103. doi:10.16921/chasqui.v1i147.4419

Fardouly, J., Diedrichs, P. C., Vartanian, L. R., & Halliwell, E. (2018). Social comparisons on social media: The impact of Facebook on young women's body image concerns and mood. *Body Image, 26*, 38–45. doi:10.1016/j.bodyim.2018.06.003 PMID:25615425

Formica, S., & Sfodera, F. (2022). The Great Resignation and Quiet Quitting paradigm shifts: An overview of current situation and future research directions. *Journal of Hospitality Marketing & Management, 31*(8), 899–907. doi:10.1080/19368623.2022.2136601

Fornells-Ambrojo, M., Davenport, T., & Auton, J. (2020). Digital well-being: A comprehensive framework for health and well-being in the digital age. *Internet Interventions : the Application of Information Technology in Mental and Behavioural Health, 21*, 100327. doi:10.1016/j.invent.2020.100327

Fuglsang, L. (2001). Three Perspectives in STS in the Policy Context. In S. Cutcliffe & C. Mitcham (Eds.), *Visions of STS: Counterpoints in Science, Technology, and Social Studies* (pp. 35–49). State University of New York Press.

Gibson, J. J. (1979). *The Theory of Affordances. The Ecological Approach to Visual Perception*. Taylor & Francis.

Google Digital Wellbeing. (n.d.). *What is Digital Wellbeing?* https://bit.ly/2sEOjE0

Griep, Y., Vranjes, I., van Hooff, M. M., Beckers, D. G., & Geurts, S. A. (2021). Technology in the workplace: Opportunities and challenges. In C. Korunka (Ed.), *Flexible Working Practices and Approaches: Psychological and Social Implications* (pp. 93–116). Springer. doi:10.1007/978-3-030-74128-0_6

Grieve, R., Indian, M., Witteveen, K., Tolan, G. A., & Marrington, J. (2013). Face-to-face or Facebook: Can social connectedness be derived online? *Computers in Human Behavior, 29*(3), 604–609. doi:10.1016/j.chb.2012.11.017

Gui, M., Fasoli, M., & Carradore, R. (2017). Digital well-being. Developing a new theoretical tool for media literacy research. *Italian Journal of Sociology of Education*, *9*(1), 155–173. doi:10.14658/pupj-ijse-2017-1-8

Hao, K. (2018). How to Promote Digital Well-being at Work. *Harvard Business Review*. https://bit.ly/3UbkGpC

Henderson, L., & Knight, T. (2012). Integrating the hedonic and eudaimonic perspectives to more comprehensively understand wellbeing and pathways to wellbeing. *International Journal of Wellbeing*, *2*(3), 196–221. doi:10.5502/ijw.v2i3.3

Hesketh, I., & Cooper, C. L. (2017). Why wellbeing, why now? In C. L. Cooper & I. Hesketh (Eds.), *Managing health and wellbeing in the public sector: A guide to best practice* (pp. 19–32). Routledge. doi:10.4324/9781315681344-3

Holt, E., & Munday, I. (2020). Cyberbullying in remote work: The mediating roles of social support and communication frequency. *Journal of Business and Psychology*, *35*(4), 519–533. doi:10.100710869-019-09644-w

Huta, V., & Ryan, R. M. (2010). Pursuing Pleasure or Virtue: The Differential and Overlapping Well-Being Benefits of Hedonic and Eudaimonic Motives. *Journal of Happiness Studies*, *11*(6), 735–762. doi:10.100710902-009-9171-4

Keyes, C. L. M. (1998). Social Well-Being. *Social Psychology Quarterly*, *61*(2), 121–140. doi:10.2307/2787065

Keyes, C. L. M. (2005). Mental illness and/or mental health? Investigating axioms of the complete state model of health. *Journal of Consulting and Clinical Psychology*, *73*(3), 539–548. doi:10.1037/0022-006X.73.3.539 PMID:15982151

Kim, J., Jung, S., Seok, B., & Choi, H. (2022). The Relationship among Four Lifestyles of Workers amid the COVID-19 Pandemic (Work–Life Balance, YOLO, Minimal Life, and Staycation) and Organizational Effectiveness: With a Focus on Four Countries. *Sustainability (Basel)*, *14*(21), 14059. Advance online publication. doi:10.3390u142114059

Kim, J., & Lee, J. (2019). Digital well-being: Concept, measurement, and future directions. In S. S. Sundar (Ed.), *The Oxford handbook of digital well-being* (pp. 3–22). Oxford University Press. doi:10.1093/oxfordhb/9780190932590.013.1

Kirschner, P. A., & Karpinski, A. C. (2010). Facebook and academic performance. *Computers in Human Behavior*, *26*(6), 1237–1245. doi:10.1016/j.chb.2010.03.024

Kooij, D. T., Kanfer, R., Betts, M., & Rudolph, C. W. (2021). Future of work: Implications for individual well-being, organizational performance, and societal prosperity. *Work, Aging and Retirement*, *7*(1), 3–22. doi:10.1093/workar/waaa026

Laato, S., Islam, A. N., Islam, M. N., Whelan, E., & Talukder, S. (2021). What drives unproductive smartphone usage at work? Roles of self-control, autonomy, relatedness, and work engagement. *Sustainability*, *13*(5), 2815. doi:10.3390u13052815

Lee, R. M., & Robbins, S. B. (2019). Digital well-being: A framework for research and practice. In S. S. Sundar (Ed.), *The Oxford handbook of digital well-being* (pp. 23–35). doi:10.1093/oxfordhb/9780190932590.013.2

Liang, Y., Wu, X., Liu, J., & Zhu, L. (2021). How digital technology induces technostress: A review and synthesis of the literature. *International Journal of Information Management*, *57*, 102–282. doi:10.1016/j.ijinfomgt.2020.102282

Lin, L. Y., Sidani, J. E., Shensa, A., Radovic, A., Miller, E., Colditz, J. B., & Primack, B. A. (2018). Association between social media use and depression among US young adults. *Depression and Anxiety*, *35*(9), 818–826. doi:10.1002/da.22714

Lin, L. Y., Sidani, J. E., Shensa, A., Radovic, A., Miller, E., Colditz, J. B., & Primack, B. A. (2019). Association between social media use and empathy among US young adults. *The Journal of Adolescent Health*, *65*(6), 703–711. doi:10.1016/j.jadohealth.2019.06.003

Livingstone, S., & Helsper, E. (2010). Balancing opportunities and risks in teenagers' use of the internet: The role of online skills and internet self-efficacy. *New Media & Society*, *12*(2), 309–329. doi:10.1177/1461444809342697

Mäkiniemi, J. P., & Kinnunen, U. (2020). Promoting digital well-being at work: The roles of job resources and personal resources. *International Journal of Environmental Research and Public Health*, *17*(7), 2516. doi:10.3390/ijerph17072516 PMID:32272647

McClure, P. K. (2018). "You're fired," says the robot: The rise of automation in the workplace, technophobes, and fears of unemployment. *Social Science Computer Review*, *36*(2), 139–156. doi:10.1177/0894439317698637

McCullough, G., Huebner, E. S., & Laughlin, J. E. (2000). Life Events, Self-Concept, and Adolescents' Positive Subjective Well-Being. *Psychology in the Schools*, *37*(3), 281–290. doi:10.1002/(SICI)1520-6807(200005)37:3<281::AID-PITS8>3.0.CO;2-2

Meske, C., Leicht-Deobald, U., & Schütte, M. (2021). The Effects of Home Office on Digital Distraction, Work Engagement, and Exhaustion. *Journal of Business and Psychology*, 1–18. doi:10.100710869-021-09703-x

Nagel, L. (2020). The influence of the COVID-19 pandemic on the digital transformation of work. *The International Journal of Sociology and Social Policy*, *40*(9/10), 861–875. doi:10.1108/IJSSP-07-2020-0323

Nguyen, M. H. (2021). Managing Social Media Use in an "Always-On" Society: Exploring Digital Wellbeing Strategies That People Use to Disconnect. *Mass Communication & Society*, *24*(6), 795–817. doi:10.1080/15205436.2021.1979045

Nikolova, I., & Devinney, T. M. (2021). The long-term effects of COVID-19 on employee well-being: Implications for HRM research and practice. *The Academy of Management Perspectives*, *35*(4), 457–462. doi:10.5465/amp.2021.0184

Paasonen, S. (2021). *Dependent, Distracted, Bored: Affective Formations in Networked Media*. MIT Press. doi:10.7551/mitpress/11903.001.0001

Portwood-Stacer, L. (2013). Media refusal and conspicuous non-consumption: The performative and political dimensions of Facebook abstention. *New Media & Society*, *15*(7), 1041–1057. doi:10.1177/1461444812465139

Premeaux, S. F., Adkins, C. L., & Brasington, D. M. (2021). It's the little things that matter: Remote work and well-being during COVID-19. *Journal of Business and Psychology*, *36*(5), 687–702. doi:10.100710869-021-09790-3

Reinecke, L., & Trepte, S. (2014). Authenticity and well-being on social network sites: A two-wave longitudinal study on the effects of online authenticity and the positivity bias in SNS communication. *Computers in Human Behavior*, *30*, 95–102. doi:10.1016/j.chb.2013.07.030

Roffarello, A. M., & de Russis, L. (2019, May 2). The race towards digital wellbeing: Issues and opportunities. *Conference on Human Factors in Computing Systems - Proceedings*. 10.1145/3290605.3300616

Rosen, L. D., Whaling, K., Carrier, L. M., Cheever, N. A., & Rokkum, J. (2013). The media and technology usage and attitudes scale: An empirical investigation. *Computers in Human Behavior*, *29*(6), 2501–2511. doi:10.1016/j.chb.2013.06.006 PMID:25722534

Rosen, L. D., Whaling, K., Rab, S., Carrier, L. M., & Cheever, N. A. (2019). Is Facebook creating "iDisorders"? The link between clinical symptoms of psychiatric disorders and technology use, attitudes and anxiety. *Computers in Human Behavior*, *84*, 183–190. doi:10.1016/j.chb.2018.02.033

Ryff, C. D. (1989). Happiness Is Everything, or Is It? Explorations on the Meaning of Psychological Well-Being. *Journal of Personality and Social Psychology*, *57*(6), 1069–1081. Advance online publication. doi:10.1037/0022-3514.57.6.1069

Sampasa-Kanyinga, H., & Lewis, R. F. (2016). Sleep duration and screen time among children and adolescents: A systematic review. *Journal of Sleep Research*, *25*(5), 556–567. doi:10.1111/jsr.12436 PMID:27178659

Sassenberg, K., Greving, H., & Fetterman, A. K. (2019). Individual differences in the experience of digital stress. In S. S. Sundar (Ed.), *The Oxford handbook of digital well-being* (pp. 125–138)., doi:10.1093/oxfordhb/9780190932590.013.8

Satchell, C., & Dourish, P. (2009). Beyond the User: Use and Non-Use in HCI. *OZCHI '09: Proceedings of the 21st Annual Conference of the Australian Computer-Human Interaction Special Interest Group: Design: Open 24/7*, 9–16.

Scaria, D., Brandt, M. L., Kim, E., & Lindeman, B. (2020). What is wellbeing? In E. Kim & B. Lindeman (Eds.), *Wellbeing* (pp. 3–10). Springer. doi:10.1007/978-3-030-29470-0_1

Sharma, M. K., Sunil, S., Anand, N., Amudhan, S., & Ganjekar, S. (2021). Webinar fatigue: Fallout of Covid-19. *The Journal of the Egyptian Public Health Association*, *96*(9), 9. Advance online publication. doi:10.118642506-021-00069-y PMID:33861363

Sianoja, M., Syrek, C. J., & Korpela, K. (2019). Digitalization and work–life boundaries. *International Journal of Environmental Research and Public Health*, *16*(19), 3698. doi:10.3390/ijerph16193698 PMID:31581430

Silverstone, R., & Haddon, L. (1996). Design and the Domestication of Information and Communication Technologies: Technical Change and Everyday Life. In R. Silverstone & R. Mansell (Eds.), *Communication by Design. The Politics of Information and Communication Technologies* (pp. 44–74). Oxford University Press.

Smith, M. L., & Anderson, C. M. (2019). From remote to hybrid work: Challenges and opportunities. *Journal of Business and Psychology*, *34*(6), 681–687. doi:10.100710869-019-09640-y

Suwana, F., Pramiyanti, A., Mayangsari, I., Nuraeni, R., & Firdaus, Y. (2020). Digital Media Use of Gen Z During COVID-19 Pandemic. *Jurnal Sosioteknologi*, *19*(3), 327–340. doi:10.5614ostek.itbj.2020.19.3.2

Talevi, D., Socci, V., Carai, M., Carnaghi, G., Faleri, S., Trebbi, E., di Bernardo, A., Capelli, F., & Pacitti, F. (2020). Mental Health Outcomes of the Covid-19 Pandemic. *Rivista di Psichiatria*, *55*(3), 137–144. doi:10.1708/3382.33569 PMID:32489190

Tandon, A., Dhir, A., Almugren, I., AlNemer, G. N., & Mantymaki, M. (2021). Fear of Missing Out (FOMO) among social media users: A systematic literature review, synthesis and framework for future research. *Internet Research*, *31*(3), 782–821. doi:10.1108/INTR-11-2019-0455

Twenge, J. M., Martin, G. N., & Campbell, W. K. (2021). Decreases in psychological well-being among American adolescents after 2012 and links to increased digital media use. *Emotion (Washington, D.C.)*, *21*(6), 1132–1142. doi:10.1037/emo0000927

USC Annenberg Center for Public Relations. (2022). *The future of Corporate Activism.* Global Communication Report. https://annenberg.usc.edu/research/center-public-relations/global-communication-report

van den Abeele, M. M. P. (2021). Digital Wellbeing as a Dynamic Construct. *Communication Theory*, *31*(4), 932–955. doi:10.1093/ct/qtaa024

van Dijck, J., Poell, T., & de Waal, M. (2018). *The Platform Society: Public Values in a Connective World*. Oxford University Press. doi:10.1093/oso/9780190889760.001.0001

Wang, Y., Zhou, Y., Li, S., & Zhang, L. (2019). The effects of digital media on children's empathy: A meta-analysis. *Journal of Educational Computing Research*, *57*(8), 1999–2025. doi:10.1177/0735633118797999

Wassell, E., & Dodge, R. (2015). A multidisciplinary framework for measuring and improving wellbeing. *International Journal of Sciences, Basic and Applied Research*, *21*(2), 97–107.

World Health Organization. (2020). *Digital health.* https://bit.ly/3zl3y73

Zuboff, S. (2019). *The Age of Surveillance Capitalism: The fight for a human future at the new frontier of power*. PublicAffairs.

Chapter 2
Linking Internal Communication and Organisational Performance During the COVID-19 Pandemic

Pedro Pacheco Coelho
Porto School of Accounting and Business (ISCAP), Polytechnic of Porto, Portugal

Orlando Lima Rua
Porto School of Accounting and Business (ISCAP), Polytechnic of Porto, Portugal

ABSTRACT

This study aims to analyse the relationship between internal communication and organizational performance. It was carried out at Natixis in Portugal, a company in the banking sector, which structured and outlined an organised, original, and creative internal communication strategy in record time during COVID-19. Quantitative research was carried out through a survey questionnaire of 160 Natixis employees so that we may have a perception of the impacts of a well-designed internal communication strategy on the employees of this company. The results show that the original and creative communication strategy used by the company made a positive contribution to the employees' organisational performance, also contributing to the establishment of interpersonal relationships between employees, even at a distance, and the feeling of belonging and identification with the organisation under study. Overall, the results of this study provide a better understanding of the role of internal communication in organisations and how essential it is.

INTRODUCTION

Organisations find themselves in extremely competitive environments, the result of their presence in global and constantly changing markets, which, combined with the current economic situation, leads to the need for companies to explore ways of becoming more effective (Corrêa, 2005). One of the resources that enable the differentiation of organisations and, consequently, the gain of competitiveness, is Human Resources. However, it is not enough for organisations to have a set of talented and competent

DOI: 10.4018/978-1-6684-7353-5.ch002

employees. If the communication process is not the most adequate, the company will never be able to maximise the potential of these resources. In an era in which knowledge is rapidly disseminated and shared, knowing how to manage the communication process becomes one of the greatest competitive advantages of companies (Michel, 2013). Thus, internal communication has been gaining increasing importance within organisations to the extent that managing the organisation internally is as relevant as managing the organisation's performance and relationships with the outside (Almeida, 2013).

Alongside this context of organisational changes, a serious worldwide public health situation emerged in 2020, designated by the World Health Organisation (WHO) as the new coronavirus pandemic, which brought unprecedented changes to the world economy and the world of work. One of the many consequences that have redefined the ways of working and the work experience of employees (Workplace, 2021), forcing organisations to rethink their priorities and bringing a series of challenges to be overcome. This scenario tested communication professionals who saw their ability to solve problems and adapt to change in record times highlighted, enabling them to overcome these increased challenges (Knowles, 2020), while producing messages of hope, clarity and unity (Gallagher, 2021).

The objective of this research is to understand and analyse how the satisfaction and motivation of Natixis in Portugal employees are perceived, according to the internal communication actions developed, in face of the current health crisis scenario that we are going through and that had strong implications in the companies' management, and also to understand how the Communication Department reacted to an unexpected crisis. With a view to a better understanding of the effects that this pandemic brought to organisations in the scope of internal communication and organisational performance, this research is a case study of the Communication Department of Natixis in Portugal.

The research question that this study seeks to answer is: *What was the impact of internal communication on employees' organisational performance during the COVID-19 pandemic*?

To this end, the paper is divided into three parts: (1) Theoretical framework, where one seeks to understand and review concepts, namely the function of internal communication, the influence that internal communication can have on employee satisfaction and motivation and, finally, the challenges that internal communication faces in the 21st century, thanks to the COVID-19 pandemic; (2) Methodology, in which the research methodology is presented, based on a quantitative perspective. Data collection is based on the literature review, the completion of an online questionnaire to Natixis employees in Portugal, and the analysis of results. The questionnaire was one of the most important parts that led to the conclusion of this research work; and (3) Discussion and conclusions bring this study to a close, with the results discussion, conclusions, research limitations and proposal for future studies.

THEORETICAL BACKGROUND

Internal Communication

Concept and Evolution

To survive the globalised, technological, and competitive market, and its constant change, it is essential for organisations to adopt an integrated organisational communication policy where internal communication plays a key role. Nowadays it is no longer seen only as an isolated activity, but as essential to the creation of synergies between the organisation and its internal audiences (Pasquale, Neto, and Gomes,

2012). In addition, internal communication requires the creation of an updated and constant communication process, which can be understood without distortions by all the public involved. Cunha (2018) states that a well-planned and structured internal communication policy is vital for any company.

Bussy (2003) explains that for an internal communication policy to be well-planned and structured, it should follow the Stakeholder Theory. This theory states that organisations should treat their employees as key stakeholders of the company, giving priority to their interests. The organisation should, firstly, know how to satisfy, motivate, and involve its internal customer to better meet the needs of the external customer (Pimpão, 2013; Devesa, 2016). Through an elaborate internal communication programme, it is possible to keep employees integrated, motivated, informed and committed to the organisation. Consequently, companies must recognize communication as a management tool.

Brum (2010) believes information to be the best tool available to organisations to achieve organisational objectives and, consequently, to achieve a greater competitive advantage in the market. Businesses must keep their employees well informed to make them true multipliers of their objectives, because a well-informed and oriented internal public will have greater credibility to talk about the organisation with its external public, in other words, the internal public works as a vehicle for the dissemination of the company's image with the external public (Devesa, 2016). Almeida (2013) affirms that a poorly structured and planned internal communication policy will have negative consequences at an external communication level. In this sense, coherence between internal and external communication is essential to acquire effective organisational communication (Devesa, 2016).

As illustrated in Table 1, there is no consensus among authors regarding the definition of internal communication, what should be done with it and who should be responsible for it.

Table 1. Definitions of the concept of internal communication

Author	Definition
Kunsch (2003, p.149)	"Internal communication is a strategic tool for compatibility of the interests of employees and the company, through stimulating dialogue, the exchange of information and experiences and participation at all levels."
Silva (2006, p.13)	"Internal communication is all types of information flow occurring within a company, in an exchange relationship between employees, bosses, departments and all levels that make up the organisation. As a result of this exchange, employees become more motivated and integrated and the flow of information occurs with more clarity and agility".
Curvello (2012, p.183)	"Internal communication encompasses the entire set of actions that the organisation coordinates with the aim of listening, informing, mobilising, educating and maintaining internal cohesion around values that need to be recognised and shared by all and that can contribute to building a good public image".
Clemen (2015, p.54)	"Internal communication is one of the main processes for conveying to the internal public the strategies, objectives and values of the company's strategies, objectives and values to the internal public.".
Cunha (2018, p.41)	"Internal communication is the main process in any organisations and the main responsible for sharing information and knowledge, and through which it is possible to create inter-relationships in organisations".
Oliveira (2021, p.63)	"Internal communication is a multidisciplinary area positioned between the disciplines of marketing, public relations and human resources.".

Source: Own elaboration.

Although each author presents a different concept of internal communication, all of them describe internal communication according to two dimensions: instrumental and strategic. Therefore, it is fundamental to differentiate between these two dimensions. The first refers to the means and instruments used by the organisation during the communication process with its internal audience and, the second considers internal communication as a strategic tool of the organisation (Devesa, 2016).

Alves (2012) emphasises that internal communication should always occupy a prominent place within any organisation, since only companies with a strong internal communication policy can transform crises into new opportunities, for knowing, via communication, "take advantage of corporate intelligence" to find innovative and innovative and effective ways out (Pio, 2017, p. 11).

Objectives

Fundamental to any organisation, good internal communication goes beyond informing employees. When building an internal communication policy, it is essential to think about the strategy to be developed, based on the objectives to be achieved (Pimpão, 2013). For an internal communication policy to be well structured it must achieve a certain group of objectives. Almeida (2013) highlights six objectives:

1. **Providing a General Knowledge of the Organisation:** Ensuring that employees are not only fully aligned with the company's official discourse, but also with the objectives to achieve, both in the short and long term;
2. **To Develop a Sense of Belonging, Pride, and Identification With the Organisation:** Transmitting the organisation's core values to its internal public and leading to greater loyalty, commitment and organisational cohesion and efficiency in day-to-day work;
3. **Favour Employees' Means of Expression:** Making them more influential and integrated;
4. **Clarifying the Needs and Objectives of the Internal Public:** Knowing what the employees want makes it easier to satisfy their needs and contributes to greater happiness and commitment;
5. **Informing Each Employee According to Their Information Needs:** The more information available to employees, the easier it is to carry out their tasks and, consequently, the faster and more effective the goals are achieved;
6. **Fostering Interpersonal Relationships:** Communication is oriented towards the importance of these relationships in the work environment and the promotion of teamwork to achieve more efficiently what was proposed, clearly assuming an integrating function.

The potential benefits of internal communication rely on the ability to deliver relevant messages to employees in appropriate formats and accepted by them (Welsh, 2011). Successful internal communication can promote an employee's sense of belonging and commitment to the organisation, and their identification with the organisation's goals and priorities. Lack of information sharing by employers can create an unpleasant working environment as workers feel they are being 'side-lined' or end up developing feelings of distrust (Floyd, 2013). Workers feel more motivated when they can contribute to the company's decision-making. In this way, open internal communication can promote business, in a world where knowledge and efficient and timely access to information is a critical factor for the success of the organisation (Fishenden, 1997).

To conclude, investing in communication within organisations should be seen as an investment and not as an unnecessary cost. A well-planned and structured internal communication based on a strong communication strategy is essential for any company. As mentioned before, it will be necessary that organisations understand it as a management tool, which provides a healthy relationship between employees and within the company, being success the common goal (Pimpão, 2013).

Forms of Internal Communication

Formal and Informal Communication

The different forms of internal communication should be used considering their suitability to the hierarchical structure, the direction or guidance and the medium used (Alves, 2012). This scholar refers to the hierarchical structure as the establishment of hierarchical channels or communicational levels that differentiate the degree of delegated authority in the communication process. According to Kunsch (2003), the internal communication process flows through two distinct networks: formal and informal, which coexist simultaneously and which the organisation cannot do without. This scholar emphasises that no matter how detailed the formal communication network in the organisation is, it will always have to be complemented by an informal network.

Stacheski (2012) describes formal networks as those which are regulated by the organisation, that is, those that are planned and controlled by the directive bodies, such as meetings, internal notes, internal newspapers, reports, and circulars (Alves, 2012). These formal communication channels are dictated by the structure of the organisation, showing the command line of authority of the company. Therefore, formal communication aims to sustain authority and power relations, facilitating the coordination of activities and tasks developed, in addition, the graphic representation of a structure is known as an organisational chart (Alves, 2012).

On the other hand, informal networks are born from the social relationship in organisations, in other words, they are spontaneous communications, not regulated by the organisation, which are originated not only from the shortcomings of formal communication networks but also, from the natural needs of employees to establish contact with each other (Curvello, 2012). The most common means of informal communication are rumours and gossip which can sometimes have harmful consequences for the organisation (Alves, 2012). Stacheski (2012) explains that this behaviour is real proof that the company is failing in having strong and transparent communication and this is a consequence of the absence or malfunction of an integrated communication system.

In short, communication, whether formal or informal, demonstrates the interactions, relationships, and information exchange processes that occur within the organisation. Although there is the need to use both networks simultaneously, informal networks should never overlap with formal networks, as a result, organisational communication should always be commanded by the formal networks (Oliveira, 2021).

Internal Communication Flows in Organisations

Communication within organisations operates through four flows: downward, upward, horizontal and, with the advent of technologies, also known as the transverse or diagonal flow. These flows indicate the orientation of communication (Devesa, 2016). Also according to this author, downward communication flow is the process of transmitting information, through formal channels of communication, from the management to the employees, known as, top to bottom, and the information shared via this flow corresponds to the objectives, policies, norms, guidelines, and guiding principles necessary for the proper functioning of the organisation.

Curvello (2012) explains that the upward communication flow is characterised by information, usually, suggestions, criticisms and appeals coming from employees and directed to the directive bodies, or, from the bottom up. It is through this communication flow that management can verify if its policies are being well-received by employees (Devesa, 2016). However, this type of communication is not always effective because, many times, the employees are afraid to express their opinions for fear that it will bring negative consequences (Alves, 2012). In this sense, the intensity of the upward flow of information will depend on the philosophy and policy of each organisation (Kunsch, 2003).

Kunsch (2007), outlines horizontal communication flow as the flow of information between departments, sectors, services, or people located at the same hierarchical level of the company. This flow is the one that moves the organisation in its daily life by being responsible for the coordination and combination of the various units. It ends up being part of the informal field that opens doors to the exchange of ideas and opinions essentially linked to innovation, and to the improvement of teamwork and interpersonal relationships (Curvello, 2012).

To Curvello (2012) the cross-communication flow corresponds to the most recent communication flow which was created during the technological revolution that took place in the 20th century. This flow has the power to subvert hierarchies, by allowing the transmission of messages between employees from different sectors, departments, services, or between different hierarchical levels (Curvello, 2012). This communication is found in modern, decentralised, and flexible organisations characterised by participative and integrated management.

In brief, two communication flows enable greater freedom and openness for employees' ideas, the upward flow, and the crossflow (Oliveira, 2021). However, for the development of a good organisational climate, the ideal would be to be able to work with all the above-mentioned communication flows, as suggested by the cross-communication flow (Stacheski, 2012).

Communication Media in Organisations

In organisations, there are several means and channels of communication. It is these channels that ensure the communication process and among the main means of communication are oral, written, audio-visual and, with the technological revolution, the telematic media (Alves, 2012).

Oral media are characterized by spontaneity and physical closeness between collaborators (Pimpão, 2013). The oral media can be divided into direct and indirect oral media. As direct means, we have individual conversations, meetings, and interviews, among others. As indirect means of communication, we have essentially telephone calls (Stacheski, 2012). The main disadvantage associated with these means of communication is their volatility, in the sense that there is a greater likelihood of noise and distortions occurring during the communication process. However, it is an effective, fast, and reciprocal means of transmitting information to employees. On the other hand, they also allow for fostering interpersonal relationships, to the extent that they allow greater interaction since employees can discuss, exchange ideas, and draw conclusions during the exchange of information (Alves, 2012).

For Pimpão (2013), written means of communication are the most used in the organisational context. This is because, unlike oral communication, information that is once written can be consulted by employees whenever needed. The most used means of written communication are reports, internal notes and circulars, the internal newspaper/magazine, the onboarding manual, and opinion surveys, among others (Alves, 2012).

Audio-visual media bring together sound and image, allowing a greater understanding and memorization of information (Pimpão, 2013). As examples of audio-visual media, we have videoconferences, video newspapers, and films about the company, among others (Alves, 2012).

With the Technological Revolution, new means of communication appeared: telematics means. Telematics means correspond to the evolution of the traditional means of communication presented above after the appearance of information technologies. Communication is transmitted through the combined use of computer and telecommunication means. To Stacheski (2012), as telematics media, we have the internet, email, intranet, cell phones, and corporate social networks, among others. The telematics means of communication, came to facilitate the life of organisations, bringing agility, convenience and low cost for companies.

In summary, we again see a great variety and complementarity among internal communication media, and each media can transmit several messages one message can be transmitted by several communication channels and the choice of medium to be used should depend on the message you want to convey, to whom you want to convey it, and the climate and culture of the company (Pimpão, 2013).

Organisational Performance: Concept and Evolution

Organisations play crucial roles in our daily lives. They are considered the engine that drives a nation's economy and its social and political progress. Since companies are constantly changing due to their environment, they and their managers felt it was necessary to be more sensitive about their employees and organisational performance. Consequently, organisational performance has become a major topic for all organisations, for-profit and not-for-profit, which has resulted in a growing interest from managers to find out what factors influence organisational performance (Alrowwad, 2017).

Organisational performance is one of the most important constructs in the management field. The areas of marketing, human resources, strategy, and the operating sector are evaluated based on their contribution to the company's performance. The ability to measure organisational performance is essential to help managers and academics analyse the specific actions of firms and top management, ascertaining where firms stand relative to their competitors and how they develop and perform over time (Richard, 2009). Researchers in the field have sought to determine measures for the concept of performance. However, the literature remains incomplete and in an ongoing debate, regarding theorizing organisational performance (Taouab & Issor, 2019).

In the first decade of the 21st century, the definition of organisational performance focused on the ability and aptitude of a firm to be able to exploit available resources to consistently achieve its goals (Taouab & Issor, 2019). Performance is a measure of a company's success in achieving its goals. This success can be seen through financial, marketing, operations, or human resource performance. Good performance can increase the prosperity of stakeholders (Musthofa, 2017). This construct should be guided by the firm's specific objectives in each business unit. Thus, it should be a multidimensional concept in which it specifies the measures, variables, and measurements, which should have consistency (Barbosa & Cintra, 2012). Consequently, the definition of the construct in question is still under discussion, and there are few studies with consistent definitions and measures (Richard, 2009). Moreover, the definition of the concept may prove to be subjective, since organisational performance can be positive or negative, depending on the objectives of each firm. Thus, each person seems to define performance in general and organisational performance (Alrowwad, 2017).

Regarding organisational performance measurement, academics agree that having a well-defined system is crucial for organisations because it provides information regarding the quality of developed processes, assists in strategy development, and evaluates organisational goals (Alrowwad, 2017). The measurement of organisational performance and an evaluation system are among the most important criteria for analysing the growth of organisations, their actions, and their environments. However, few organisations have a systematic system to measure their performance that reflects their environment and strategies (Felizardo, 2017).

There are several criteria for measuring an organisation's performance, which can be used to define goals to be achieved, considering the various results that an organisation can generate, both in the external and internal environment. Some of the criteria that can be used are profitability, productivity, quality, and customer satisfaction (Brandão, 2012). Additionally, variables such as innovation and efficiency are also accepted by some authors as performance measures (Richard, 2009).

The performance of an organisation depends greatly on the skills that its leaders have when it comes to implementing strategies. The essence of leadership is considered a conditional factor that exists between the manager and leader and their followers, given that organisations always have goals to achieve, and it is important that leaders employ flexible techniques that can accommodate change (Silva, 2014). The performance of an organisation is also dependent on its employees, who are an essential part of the organisation, representing those who work to achieve organisational goals (Almatrooshi, 2016).

Linking Internal Communication and Organisational Performance

To Fiorelli (2009) and Sequesseque (2019) when people are motivated, they become more productive, act with greater satisfaction and tend to produce expected or above-expected results. The creation of a stimulating, satisfying and productive work climate will thus be beneficial both for the organisation and for its members (Perez-Ramos, 1990). In this sense, for an improvement in organisational results, leaders should consider the satisfaction levels of their employees, channelling their efforts towards the achievement of organisational goals and objectives (Meirinhos, 2018).

To Gregory (2011), lack of communication at work is one of the main factors contributing to dissatisfaction, arguing that poor communication makes employees feel disconnected from the organisation and is therefore, detrimental to the well-being of the company because when an employee feels neglected, they tend to underperform, and that employee becomes insecure about his position in the company and questions what his purpose is in the workplace.

Some scholars (e.g., Pool & Pool, 2007; Lok & Crawford, 2004; Shahzadi et al., 2014) argue that there is an inevitable link between motivation and job satisfaction and employee engagement. Therefore, it is not enough for organisations to have teams of talented or competent employees if their informational flow does not work, or if communication processes are not adequate (Almeida, 2013).

To Oliveira (2021) communication is, without a doubt one of the most important tools in an organisation. It is essential to work it in an effective, clear, and enlightening way, having in mind the target audience to which it is intended, thus avoiding the appearance of incorrect or untrue information. Having well-informed employees increases motivation levels, making them feel responsible for the destinies and goals of the company, ready to vibrate with corporate successes and available to defend the company in less favourable times (Ventura, 2012).

For organisations to communicate internally and effectively there must be a strategic rationale because it is on this that the success or failure of the developed actions depends (Cowan, 2014), but, above all, the way internal communication is structured in each organisation should presuppose that it favours team spirit with the involvement of all its members. In this sense, the inputs generated by upward communication are now decisive, because, in addition to providing, for example, the resolution and detection of problems, they also allow to determine suggestions for improvement proposed by employees, giving voice to an effective participatory and inclusive management, that is, that excels in valuing, motivating, and raising the self-esteem of its employees (Brandão & Portugal, 2015).

Internal communication is indispensable for the success of management processes and practices in organisations, namely in the creation and development of a climate of trust, credibility, transparency, and a sense of belonging of its employees with the organisation, helping them to establish a more appropriate and integrated way their functions (Brandão & Portugal, 2015). To this effect, Internal Communication must rely on professionals who plan and implement communication plans that help keep employees informed and motivated and promote the organisation's culture (Broom & Sha, 2013).

Only supported by internal communication, organisations will achieve a real involvement of employees and their inherent organisational performance that passes, above all, by meeting their needs to communicate, by specific information that helps them perform their tasks, by clarity in internal rules, by the vision of the organisation, by information about workplace practices, by the opportunity to be and be involved in the life of the organisation and to have feedback on their performance, to have access to training and to have access to all channels, communication tools in the company (Brandão & Portugal, 2015).

COVID-19 in Organisations

COVID-19 is the name given by the World Health Organisation (WHO), to the disease caused by the new coronavirus SARS-COV-2. This virus was first identified in humans in late 2019 in the Chinese city of Wuhan (SNS24, 2022). On 20 January 2020, the WHO classified the outbreak as a Public Health Emergency of International Concern and on 11 March 2020, as a pandemic (WHO, 2021). The pandemic spread across the world and resulted in significant global social and economic instability, forcing the adaptation and implementation of new social, economic, and political measures (WHO, 2021).

After the World Health Organisation (WHO) characterized the new coronavirus outbreak (SARS-CoV-2 virus) as a pandemic they urged governments to prepare for the first wave of the public health emergency with several drastic measures, including confinement (ILO, 2020). As a result of this confinement, not only have economies stagnated, but ways of living and being have changed, and ways of working and the work experience of employees have been redefined (Workplace, 2021), forcing organisations to rethink their priorities and bringing a series of challenges to be overcome. On the other hand, the confinement instructions issued by governments, it is estimated that four out of ten workers in Europe have entered remote work (Eurofound, 2020, cited in ILO, 2020). Based on the European online survey conducted by Eurofound to study the impact of COVID-19 on the way people in Europe live and work, it is found that in Portugal, around 40% of participants started working from home with the onset of the pandemic (Eurofound, 2020). And, although Eurostat's figures (2018) show that the number of people on remote work has been gradually increasing over the years, the pandemic accelerated the adoption of this work modality, facilitated by the evolution and application of ICT (Eurofound, 2020), a tool adopted by many organisations in this period to cope with the difficult market conditions (Richter & Sinha, 2020).

We are, therefore, facing a new environment of labour communication and remote working is proof of how technology is changing working relationships (CMAveiro, 2020) and is paving the way to transform it and create new ways of working in teams. Change has become the new normal due to a pandemic that has forced organisations to re-evaluate their business models; to adapt their operational methods, now totally different from the past; to be flexible to change to keep up with the pace of the markets, and, to this end, it is essential to establish relationships of greater trust with their employees (Cowan, 2017). The fact that technology is everywhere and facilitates communication brings the challenge to organisations to have an increased effort to get the attention of their employees.

A study conducted by Speak Media and the Public Relations and Communications Association (PRCA) reinforces this idea, having concluded that soon, the focus will need to be much more on the Internal Communication function to help organisations guide employees in a challenging business environment as they adjust to and from new working conditions and inherent uncertainties (Hickman, 2020).

Thus, it is essential to create strategies that combine the best of human interaction and technological facilitation (Cowan, 2017). In a post-pandemic period, internal communication is marked by the need to minimise the amount of content that is shared, due to the multiplication of channels; tailored and personalised messages will become the new norm in the coming years; and the importance of digital has never been clearer when it comes to driving engagement (Gallagher, 2021). One of the trends in internal communication, identified in Gallagher's State of the Sector 2021, also involves giving diverse voices to organisations' communications, allowing employees to speak on behalf of the organisation they represent, fostering their engagement and their work experience (Gallagher, 2021).

METHODOLOGY

Methodological Approach

This is an empirical study that aims to understand how creativity techniques influenced internal communication and consequently organisational performance during the COVID-19 pandemic at Natixis in Portugal. To develop it, the quantitative methodology was adopted according to Bryman and Cramer the research is manipulated by any variable and all data related to selecting the variables will be collected at the same time (Bryman & Cramer, 2012). This is a suitable method (Sousa et al., 2008) once there is the need to question many people and a representative problem exists (Campenhoudt & Quivy, 2008).

This methodology has many advantages, such as (1) the possibility to collect a large quantity of data and since it is standardized, their comparison is easier; and (2) the generalization of the sample results for the population. On the other hand, this method is not free from inconveniences, for example, (a) weight and cost; (b) superficiality of the answers due to the standardization of the questions; (c) individualization leads to loss of social relationships among respondents and (d) difficulty in controlling the response time or who often admits delays in the investigation process (Campenhoudt & Quivy, 2008).

The questionnaire conducted by the employees was done online, through the Microsoft Forms platform. The choice for this method was it was necessary to obtain the opinion of the largest possible number of Natixis employees, spread throughout the country, to better analyse the real impact of internal communication during the confinement of COVID-19.

Data Collection

The first phase of the data collection method was the documentary observation, through consultation of books, magazines, newspapers, scientific reports, news and relevant studies on the theme under analysis, to increase knowledge on the subject under study.

At a later stage, the data collection method used was the questionnaire, which was sent to the employees of Natixis in Portugal. The main objective would be to collect a sample of 10% of the company, i.e. 160 employees.

The questionnaire conducted by the employees was done online, through the Microsoft Forms platform. The choice of this method was because it was necessary to obtain the opinion of at least 10% of the Natixis in Portugal employees, spread throughout the country, to better analyse the real impact of internal communication during the COVID-19 pandemic in the company.

Instrument

The questionnaire conducted was based on the literature analysed and the interests of the Natixis Communication area. From there, the questions to be included in the questionnaire were defined. This questionnaire is thus made up of 21 questions, which include multiple-choice questions and a Likert scale. The prevalence of closed-ended questions was that these facilitate statistical analysis. For example, nominal scales were used in questions seeking to characterise the sample, and a Likert scale was used in questions seeking to assess opinions, beliefs, or value judgements, to record the degree of agreement or disagreement with a given statement (Leavy, 2017; Mukherjee, 2019).

We used a 5-point Likert scale ranging from totally disagree to totally agree. To avoid problems related to the understanding of the questions, at an initial stage the questionnaire was sent to the Marketing Manager, to validate the questionnaire, and only then was it sent to all employees via e-mail by the Communication team on May 14, 2022. The questionnaire was open until 2 June 2022.

The questions for the questionnaire were based on authors used in the literature review, namely Pimpão (2013), about the topic of internal communication, who developed a case study similar to the present study. The linkage between internal communication and organizational performance was based on Pimpão (2013) and Sequesseque (2019). All items are displayed in the Appendix.

Case Study: Natixis

Natixis is a French corporate and investment bank created in November 2006 after the merger of the asset management and investment banking operations of Natexis Banque Populaire (Banque Populaire group) and IXIS (Groupe Caisse d'Epargne). The new brand has been given a lilac hue thanks to the joining of the blue of the former Natexis Banque Populaire and IXIS.

In Portugal, Natixis was set up at the end of 2016 and officially began operating in March 2017. This decision was made because Natixis' new strategic plan placed technological innovation and digitalization as a top priority for the company. Accordingly, Natixis decided to internalize some of its IT services, previously provided by external suppliers or geographically dispersed teams, to internalize technical expertise in core activities, increase the specialized workforce, optimize IT costs and improve operational risk management.

The decision to install the Natixis Centre of Excellence in IT in Portugal, in the city of Porto specifically, resulted from several studies and evaluations in different European countries, based on the following criteria: Education, Innovation and Entrepreneurship, Cultural Adequacy with France and International Mentality/Involvement.

Natixis' mission is to help its customers realise their projects by putting its expertise in asset and wealth management, financing, insurance, and financial services to work so that its customers can turn their ambitions and dreams into reality. Natixis' main objectives are (1) sustainable financial management, and (2) to become an increasingly green and responsible company. Natixis' main values are (a) integrity, (2) strength of spirit, (3) respect for the maxim "the customer always comes first", (c) innovative and entrepreneurial spirit, and (d) "big enough to deliver, small enough to care".

Sample Characterisation

After processing and analyzing the data from the questionnaires the sample consisted of 160 workers from Natixis in Portugal, of which 49% are male, 46% are female, 4% are non-Binary and 1% prefer not to say (Table 2).

Table 2. Gender

		Frequency	Percentage	Valid Percentage	Cumulative Percentage
Valid	Male	79	49%	49%	49%
	Female	74	46%	46%	46%
	Non-Binary	6	4%	4%	4%
	Prefer not to say	1	1%	1%	1%
	Total	160	100%	100%	

Source: Own elaboration.

RESULTS

Natixis in Portugal is a young company, with the highest number of respondents in the 26 to 35 age group, with 34%. Next is the 18 to 25 age group, with 34%, followed by 36- to 45-year-olds with 21%. Finally, the bands 46 to 55 and over 55, are found with 6% and 5%, respectively (Table 3).

Internal Communication

When faced with the question "Does the company give much importance to its internal communication strategy?" 80 employees, which corresponds to 50% of the sample selected the "Totally Agree" option and 70 employees, which corresponds to 44% of the sample, answered Agree. 4% of employees answered, "Neither Disagree or Agree". One employee, who is 1% of the sample, answered Disagree and 3 employees, which 3% of the sample, answered "Totally Disagree" (Table 4).

Table 3. Age

		Frequency	Percentage	Valid Percentage	Cumulative Percentage
Valid	18-25	53	33%	33%	33%
	26-35	55	34%	34%	34%
	36-45	34	21%	21%	21%
	46-55	10	6%	6%	6%
	+55	8	5%	5%	5%
	Total	160	100%	100%	

Source: Own elaboration.

With this, it can be stated that 94% of the sample states that the employees recognise that the company invests and gives great importance to the internal communication strategy. 4% remained neutral and another 4% stated that the company does not give due value to internal communication.

Table 4. Internal communication strategy

Scale	Frequency	Percentage	Valid Percentage	Cumulative Percentage
Totally Agree	80	50%	50%	50%
Agree	70	44%	44%	44%
Neither Disagree nor Agree	6	4%	4%	4%
Disagree	1	1%	1%	1%
Totally Disagree	3	3%	3%	3%
Total	160	100%	100%	

Source: Own elaboration.

This was a question where contributors could choose several answers. In terms of percentages, communications via e-mail, and internal communications, such as internal TV or events, were chosen, by the respondents, as the means of communication which they considered to be the best and the most effective, corresponding to 30% of the sample each.

Next, the means of communication that employees considered the most effective was Yammer, Natixis internal social network, which was considered by 21% of the sample. Finally, internal Newsletters, with 19% of respondents choosing this as the most effective means of communication (Table 5).

When asked whether they felt enthusiastic to use Yammer during the COVID-19 pandemic, 89 contributors, which is 56% of the sample, answered no, while 71 contributors, which is 44% of the sample, showed that they were motivated to use Yammer and interact with the content published on it during the pandemic (Table 6).

Employees who answered no to the previous question were asked, if they wished, to justify the reason for their choice. The answers presented in the following table are some of the most common. A large part of the sample considers Yammer an outdated and useless tool, and it should be replaced by similar but better ones (Table 7).

Table 5. Communication actions

	Frequency	Percentage	Valid Percentage	Cumulative Percentage
Newsletter	74	19%	19%	19%
Internal Communication	120	30%	30%	30%
Yammer	81	21%	21%	21%
E-mail	120	30%	30%	30%
Total	285	100%	100%	

Source: Own elaboration.

Table 6. Motivation to use Yammer

	Frequency	Percentage	Valid Percentage	Cumulative Percentage
Yes	71	44%	44%	44%
No	89	56%	56%	56%
Total	160	100%	100%	

Source: Own elaboration.

Table 7. Yammer comments

Responses
1. Too many apps and not user-friendly.
2. Did not feel like it was useful as an "internal" social network.
3. Most are in French. The company has more than French speakers.
4. I am not used to navigating on Yammer, and do not really know how to take advantage of the tool.
5. I do not care about yammer.
6. I think there are more useful and easier apps that Natixis could use instead of Yammer.
7. So many different channels that I could not focus on what is important.
8. I think it is a useless tool. Natixis should invest in creating a Slack or something that is useful.
9. Yammer is from Jurassic Era. Only Natixis did not get that.
10. I was having panic attacks will all the information.
11. The communication Team should really think about changing to another app. Yammer is just useless.
12. Because I did not like it.

Source: Own elaboration.

Linking Internal Communication and Organisational Performance

In this part of the questionnaire, employees were asked about the main study topic of the thesis, i.e. how internal communication influenced organisational performance during the COVID-19 period. Fifteen questions were asked about the theme of the thesis, which the employees would have to answer, with the help of the Likert scale.

When asked whether they felt that internal communication favoured the means of expression during the pandemic, 40% of the sample, which corresponds to 64 employees responded Agree. The second most chosen option was "Totally Agree", with 37.5%, corresponding to 60 employees, followed by 30 employees who chose the neutral option. This shows that employees identify that the types of communication carried out during the pandemic helped employees to feel more comfortable speaking and expressing themselves to each other. 6 employees chose the "Disagree" and "Totally Disagree" options, 5 and 1 respectively (Table 8).

Table 8. Internal communication strategy favoured the means of expression

Scale	Frequency	Percentage	Valid Percentage	Cumulative Percentage
Totally Agree	60	37.5%	37.5%	37.5%
Agree	64	40%	40%	40%
Neither Disagree nor Agree	30	18.8%	18.8%	18.8%
Disagree	5	3.1%	3.1%	3.1%
Totally disagree	1	0.6%	0.6%	0.6%
Total	160	100%	100%	

Source: Own elaboration.

When asked if the internal communication actions developed by Natixis influenced the feeling of belonging to the company, even at a distance, 134 employees in the study, which represents 83.8% of the sample, show that the internal communication actions had a positive impact on this feeling of belonging. 11.9% of the sample, i.e. 19 employees, responded neutrally and 7 employees, representing 4.4% of the sample, did not feel that the communication actions had any impact on their sense of belonging to the organisation. This shows that the actions were well developed and implemented and that they helped employees to feel part of the company, even from a distance (Table 9).

Table 9. Feeling of belonging

Scale	Frequency	Percentage	Valid Percentage	Cumulative Percentage
Totally Agree	70	43.8%	43.8%	43.8%
Agree	64	40%	40%	40%
Neither Disagree nor Agree	19	11.9%	11.9%	11.9%
Disagree	6	3.8%	3.8%	3.8%
Totally disagree	1	0.6%	0.6%	0.6%
Total	160	100%	100%	

Source: Own elaboration.

This question was asked to understand if the events organised by the team provided moments of connection between employees from teams other than their own. 70 employees answered with "Totally Agree", and 51 employees with "Agree", which is 75.7% of the total sample. 27 employees answered neutrally, and 12 employees answered negatively. This shows a decrease, when compared to the previous question, which shows that, at the level of events, there may have been failures when applying the internal communication strategy (Table 10).

Table 10. Events feedback

Scale	Frequency	Percentage	Valid Percentage	Cumulative Percentage
Totally Agree	70	43.8%	43.8%	43.8%
Agree	51	31.9%	31.9%	31.9%
Neither Disagree nor Agree	27	16.9%	16.9%	16.9%
Disagree	11	6.9%	6.9%	6.9%
Totally disagree	1	0.6%	0.6%	0.6%
Total	160	100%	100%	

Source: Own elaboration.

In terms of feeling important to the company during the pandemic, only 108 respondents, representing 67.5%, chose the "Totally Agree" or "Agree" options. There was a noticeable increase in neutral positions when compared with other questions, with the percentage of neutrals being 26.9%. On the other hand, 9 employees, equivalent to 5.7% of the sample, felt that they did not feel like important people for the company (Table 11).

Table 11. Level of importance

Scale	Frequency	Percentage	Valid Percentage	Cumulative Percentage
Totally Agree	60	37.5%	37.5%	37.5%
Agree	48	30%	30%	30%
Neither Disagree nor Agree	43	26.9%	26.9%	26.9%
Disagree	6	3.8%	3.8%	3.8%
Totally disagree	3	1.9%	1.9%	1.9%
Total	160	100%	100%	

Source: Own elaboration.

About feeling that their work was valued by the company, 116 employees, equivalent to 72.5% of the sample, chose the "Totally Agree" and "Agree" options. 34 employees took a neutral position, equivalent to 21.3% of the sample and 10 employees chose the options "Disagree" or "Totally Disagree", equivalent to 6.3% of the sample. It can be stated that there was a flight from neutral to positive positions when compared to the data from the previous question, i.e. how the company communicated with the employee made them feel that the work they were doing was being valued (Table 12).

Table 12. Value to the company

Scale	Frequency	Percentage	Valid Percentage	Cumulative Percentage
Totally Agree	67	41.9%	41.9%	41.9%
Agree	49	30.6%	30.6%	30.6%
Neither Disagree nor Agree	34	21.3%	21.3%	21.3%
Disagree	7	4.4%	4.4%	4.4%
Totally disagree	3	1.9%	1.9%	1.9%
Total	160	100%	100%	

Source: Own elaboration.

As reviewed earlier, Yammer was not considered by a majority as a useful tool for working or communicating with other co-workers. As can be seen in Table 13, only 63 employees considered Yammer as an essential tool during the pandemic, which corresponds to 39.4%, 10% more than the neutral positions. 31.3% of the sample opted for the "Totally Disagree" and "Disagree" choices, which is 8.1% less of the positive positions. Unlike the other questions in the survey, this one shows the greatest separation of the sample, with no large majority in any of the choices (Table 13).

Table 13. Yammer evaluation

Scale	Frequency	Percentage	Valid Percentage	Cumulative Percentage
Totally Agree	30	18.8%	18.8%	18.8%
Agree	33	20.6%	20.6%	20.6%
Neither Disagree nor Agree	47	29.4%	29.4%	29.4%
Disagree	23	14.4%	14.4%	14.4%
Totally disagree	27	16.9%	16.9%	16.9%
Total	160	100%	100%	

Source: Own elaboration.

As to whether all communications were concise and clear, 109 employees, which equates to 68,2% of the sample chose between the "Totally Agree" and "Agree" options, as shown in Table 14. Thirty-four employees took a neutral position on the statement and 17 employees, equating to 10,6% of the sample, chose the negative options. This shows that there may have been some gaps at the communication level, because although the positive options represent about 68% of the sample, the remaining positions, mainly the neutral ones, show somewhat high values as well (Table 14).

68.2% of the sample, equivalent to 109 employees, recognises that there has been an improvement in the company's communication strategy, thus giving it credit. The numbers of neutral positions remain high, with this question being 26.3% of the sample, and 5.6% corresponding to the negative options of the survey. This shows that there is almost a consensus that the communication strategy during the pandemic has improved when compared to communication strategies before the pandemic (Table 15).

Table 14. Quality of communications

Scale	Frequency	Percentage	Valid Percentage	Cumulative Percentage
Totally Agree	58	36.3%	36.3%	36.3%
Agree	51	31.9%	31.9%	31.9%
Neither Disagree nor Agree	34	21.3%	21.3%	21.3%
Disagree	13	8.1%	8.1%	8.1%
Totally disagree	4	2.5%	2.5%	2.5%
Total	160	100%	100%	

Source: Own elaboration.

Table 15. Improvement of communications

Scale	Frequency	Percentage	Valid Percentage	Cumulative Percentage
Totally Agree	62	38.8%	38.8%	38.8%
Agree	47	29.4%	29.4%	29.4%
Neither Disagree nor Agree	42	26.3%	26.3%	26.3%
Disagree	8	5%	5%	5%
Totally disagree	1	0.6%	0.6%	0.6%
Total	160	100%	100%	g

Source: Own elaboration.

When asked whether they felt Natixis gave much importance to the strategy and communication plan during the pandemic, 127 employees, responded between "Totally Agree" and "Agree", which shows a flight from neutral positions, which had the choice of 28 employees, and from negative positions, which were chosen by 5 employees, to positive positions (Table 16).

Table 16. Importance of communication

Scale	Frequency	Percentage	Valid Percentage	Cumulative Percentage
Totally Agree	64	40%	40%	40%
Agree	63	39.4%	39.4%	39.4%
Neither Disagree nor Agree	28	17.5%	17.5%	17.5%
Disagree	4	2.5%	2.5%	2.5%
Totally disagree	10	0.6%	0.6%	0.6%
Total	160	100%	100%	

Source: Own elaboration.

Concerning the means of communication used, 75.1% of the sample, i.e. 120 employees, state that the means of communication used were sufficient. 18.1% of the sample maintained a neutral position and 6.9% of the sample opted for a negative position. This shows that most employees in this sample felt that the means used to pass on the message were sufficient and did not feel the need to create other means of communication (Table 17).

Table 17. Means of communication

Scale	Frequency	Percentage	Valid Percentage	Cumulative Percentage
Totally Agree	54	41.3%	41.3%	41.3%
Agree	66	38.8%	38.8%	38.8%
Neither Disagree nor Agree	29	18.1%	18.1%	18.1%
Disagree	7	4.4%	4.4%	4.4%
Totally disagree	4	2.5%	2.5%	2.5%
Total	160	100%	100%	

Source: Own elaboration.

When asked about the creativity and originality of all events organised by the company, an overwhelming 81.9% of the sample, corresponding to 131 employees, chose the “Totally Agree” and “Agree” options. The neutral amount of the sample was 14.4%. A small part of the sample, with a weight of 3.8%, opted for the “Disagree” option. A curious fact about this question is that none of the 160 respondents selected the “Totally Disagree” option which shows that the events held by the company were quite creative, original and dynamic, even during the pandemic with the remote working rules in place (Table 18).

Table 18. Creativity in communication

Scale	Frequency	Percentage	Valid Percentage	Cumulative Percentage
Totally Agree	77	48.1%	48.1%	48.1%
Agree	54	33.8%	33.8%	33.8%
Neither Disagree nor Agree	23	14.4%	14.4%	14.4%
Disagree	6	3.8%	3.8%	3.8%
Totally disagree	0	0%	0%	0%
Total	160	100%	100%	

Source: Own elaboration.

This question was asked to reinforce the previous one. Although some employees fled to neutral positions, and “Totally Disagree” reappeared with one employee choosing this option, 76.2% of the sample still state that the events were unique and that the company made an effort not to make repetitive actions, investing in originality and creativity (Table 19).

Table 19. Unique and unrepetitive actions

Scale	Frequency	Percentage	Valid Percentage	Cumulative Percentage
Totally Agree	65	40.6%	40.6%	40.6%
Agree	57	35.6%	35.6%	35.6%
Neither Disagree nor Agree	29	18.1%	18.1%	18.1%
Disagree	8	5%	5%	5%
Totally disagree	1	0.6%	0.6%	0.6%
Total	160	100%	100%	

Source: Own elaboration.

Despite admitting that the internal communication actions carried out by the company were creative and original, only 65% of the sample, which corresponds to 104 employees, felt motivated to participate in these actions. 38 employees decided to opt for the neutral option, which represented 23.8% of the sample and 18 employees did not feel motivated to participate in the actions organised by the company, corresponding to 11.2% of the sample (Table 20).

Table 20. Motivation of employees

Scale	Frequency	Percentage	Valid Percentage	Cumulative Percentage
Totally Agree	60	37.5%	37.5%	37.5%
Agree	44	27.5%	27.5%	27.5%
Neither Disagree nor Agree	38	23.8%	23.8%	23.8%
Disagree	17	10.6%	10.6%	10.6%
Totally disagree	1	0.6%	0.6%	0.6%
Total	160	100%	100%	

Source: Own elaboration.

In December 2020, Natixis decided to offer all its employees, spread out in different parts of the country, a kit with several Christmas gifts. This kit was sent by post which, besides being a way to remind employees that the company cares about them was also a way to generate employment for CTT - Correios de Portugal, during this phase. 78.2% of the sample under study considered this action on the part of the company as unique and distinguished it from its competitors. 14.4% chose the neutral option and 7.5% of the sample did not consider the action to be differentiating from other companies in the market (Table 21).

At the time of the communication of the mandatory quarantine by the Portuguese government in March 2020, companies had to send their employees to remote work with the little information they had, and Natixis was no exception. With this in mind, 73.8% of the employees who were part of this sample considered that Natixis knew how to communicate correctly how things would proceed given the little information that existed from the Portuguese government and WHO. 19.4% of employees decided to choose the neutral option, not considering the communication strategy good or bad and 6.9% of employees considered that the communication strategy and the means of communication used by the company were not the best, choosing the "Totally Disagree" and "Disagree" options (Table 22).

Table 21. Christmas action

Scale	Frequency	Percentage	Valid Percentage	Cumulative Percentage
Totally Agree	86	53.8%	53.8%	53.8%
Agree	39	24.4%	24.4%	24.4%
Neither Disagree nor Agree	23	14.4%	14.4%	14.4%
Disagree	8	5%	5%	5%
Totally disagree	4	2.5%	2.5%	2.5%
Total	160	100%	100%	

Source: Own elaboration.

Table 22. Lockdown communications

Scale	Frequency	Percentage	Valid Percentage	Cumulative Percentage
Totally Agree	71	44.4%	44.4%	44.4%
Agree	47	29.4%	29.4%	29.4%
Neither Disagree nor Agree	31	19.4%	19.4%	19.4%
Disagree	5	3.1%	3.1%	3.1%
Totally disagree	6	3.8%	3.8%	3.8%
Total	160	100%	100%	

Source: Own elaboration.

DISCUSSION AND CONCLUSION

The central theme of this study was the impact of internal communication on organisational performance during the COVID-19 pandemic. To this end, we based ourselves on the particular case of the internal communication of Natixis in Portugal, which developed a specific and differentiating communication strategy during this period. More specifically, the research question that guided the research conducted was: What is the impact of the internal communication strategy of Natixis in Portugal on the organisational performance of its employees during the COVID-19 pandemic?

Based on the literature review together with the analysis of the results collected through the questionnaires conducted among the employees of Natixis in Portugal, we were able to answer the objectives proposed at the beginning of the study. The general objective was to explore and analyse the impact of internal communication on the company's employees during the COVID-19 pandemic. Specifically, in addition to diagnosing the main communication procedures used in the company, we intended to identify and compare the impacts perceived in the internal communication strategy and how these impacted or motivated the employees during this period.

From the results obtained, we can see that Natixis employees recognise the efforts made in the company's internal communication strategy, giving it its due merit, and considering it to be creative, unique, and original. A large part of these employees also recognised the importance that the internal communication strategy implemented by the company had on their organisational performance, feeling, for the most part, more motivated and like part of a whole, even at a distance, corroborating with Fiorelli (2009) and Sequesseque (2019) point of view that says that when people are motivated, they become more productive, act with greater satisfaction and tend to produce expected or above expected results.

The results also show that in some specific situations, there may have been communication failures and that the company should study the possibility of adopting another platform to gradually replace Yammer, which was eventually considered by a large majority of respondents as a not useful platform and to which most employees do not pay attention unless they receive an email or a notification that someone announced the platform, following Pimpão (2013) that states that the chosen platform should rely on the message you want to convey, to whom you want to convey it, and the climate and culture of the company. Therefore, and about the objective of this study, it is possible to have an understanding of the role that internal communication played during the COVID-19 period at Natixis in Portugal.

The results obtained show that around 70% of the employees surveyed consider that the company's internal communication strategy became more effective after the introduction of remote working to make everyone feel integrated and part of a whole. This result is in line with the results of the study by Bussy et. al. (2003) which presented us with the same result. This results from the improvement of all the characteristics essential to internal communication policy, namely: knowledge about the company, feeling of belonging and identification, means of expression, sufficient information, and interpersonal relations.

In any case, there are points where the company can improve. At the level of the means of communication, replacing Yammer with other more informal means of communication already used by other companies and by investing in a communication strategy so that more employees feel like an important part of the company since it was one of the questions that had more negative results.

This study emphasised the importance of companies developing real internal communication plans rather than resorting to isolated communication actions. In this sense, the company's internal communication policy should be part of the overall communication system.

Given that Natixis is a company that is growing more by the day, it was more difficult to target the questionnaire only to employees working in the company before, during and after the first lockdown imposed by the COVID-19 pandemic. Some are no longer in the company; others did not want to answer the questionnaire and others were not in the office on the days when the questionnaire was physically available for those who wanted to answer. Also, the fact that this study was applied to only one organisation makes it limited and cannot be applied to other organisations, even if similar.

It would be interesting, in future research, to compare how the communication strategy has evolved within the company and if creativity and innovation continue to be a constant to keep in mind whenever any internal communication action is developed. It would also be interesting to apply the same type of study to other organisations, both within the banking sector, as is the case of Natixis in Portugal, but also from other sectors, to understand the importance and relevance of internal communication in different sectors.

REFERENCES

Almatrooshi, B., Singh, S. K., & Farouk, S. (2016). Determinants of organizational performance: A proposed framework. *International Journal of Productivity and Performance Management, 65*(6), 844–859. doi:10.1108/IJPPM-02-2016-0038

Almeida, L. A. S. (2013). A importância da comunicação interna para a motivação dos colaboradores. *Exedra, 8*, 91–103.

Alrowwad, A., Obeidat, B., Tarhini, A., & Aqqad, N. (2017). The impact of transformational leadership on organizational performance via the mediating role of corporate social responsibility: A structural equation modeling approach. *International Business Research, 10*(1), 199–221. doi:10.5539/ibr.v10n1p199

Alves, J. C. C. (2012). *A importância da comunicação interna e das atividades de team building*. Lisboa: Instituto Superior de Ciências Sociais e Políticas. Dissertação de Mestrado em Comunicação Social.

Brandão, H. P., Borges-Andrade, J. E., & Guimarães, T. A. (2012). Desempenho organizacional e suas relações com competências gerenciais, suporte organizacional e treinamento. *Revista de Administração (São Paulo), 47*(4), 523–539. doi:10.5700/rausp1056

Brum, A. M. (2010). *Endomarketing de A a Z: como alinhar o pensamento das pessoas à estratégia da empresa, 4ª edição*. Integrate.

Bussy, N. M., Ewing, M. T., & Pitt, L. F. (2003). Stakeholder theory and internal marketing communications: A framework for analysing the influence of new media. *Journal of Marketing Communications, 9*(3), 147–161. doi:10.1080/1352726032000129890

Clemen, P. (2015). *Como implantar uma área de comunicação interna*. Mauad Editora.

Corrêa, E. S. (2005). Comunicação digital: Uma questão de estratégia e de relacionamento com públicos. *Organicom, 2*(3), 94–111. doi:10.11606/issn.2238-2593.organicom.2005.138900

Curvello, J. J. A. (2012). Comunicação interna e cultura organizacional (2ª ed.). Brasília: Casa das Musas.

Devesa, L. M. (2016). *A importância da comunicação organizacional no contexto organizacional*. Instituto Politécnico de Setúbal. Tese de Mestrado em Ciências Empresariais.

Eurofound. (2020). *Living, working and COVID-19*. Luxemburgo: Publications Office of the European Union. Retrieved in May 25th, 2022, from: https://www.eurofound.europa.eu/sites/default/files/ef_publication/field_ef_document/ef20059en.pdf

Fishenden, J. (1997, April). Managing intranets to improve business process. *Aslib Proceedings, 49*(4), 90–96. doi:10.1108/eb051454

Hickman, A. (2020). *Corporate PR requires renewed focus on internal comms post Covid-19*. Retrieved in March 20th, 2022, from: https://www.prweek.com/article/1691759/corporate-pr-requires-renewed-focus-internal-comms-post-covid-19-survey-finds?utm_content=137192127&utm_medium=social&utm_source=linkedin&hss_channel=lcp-29812&fbclid=IwAR1C-HsO3Pk-lMep7gFgIE-0ZZfaNqhWO_sstqJnsQPv3dL

Knowles, J. (2020). *3 tough challenges PR pros are facing amid COVID-19 uncertainty*. Retrieved in March 18th, 2022 from: https://www.prdaily.com/3-tough-challenges-pr-pros-are-face-amid-covid-19-uncertainty/?fbclid=IwAR3JjOOr9B8la7GnfEQ7y58mjr9flKuU53q8SEhvb3PS90fc4hO-EAeWZvQ

Kunsch, M. M. K. (2003). *Planejamento de Relações Públicas na Comunicação Integrada*. Summus Editorial.

Kunsch, M. M. K. (2007). Comunicação organizacional na era digital: Contextos, percursos e possibilidades. *Signo y Pensamiento*, *26*(51), 38–51.

Leavy, P. (2017). *Research design: quantitative, qualitative, mixed methods, arts-based, and community-based participatory research approaches*. The Guilford Press. Retrieved in May 1st, 2022, from: https://r2.vlereader.com/Reader?ean=9781462530038

Lok, P., & Crawford, J. (2004). The effect of organisational culture and leadership style on job satisfaction and organisational commitment: A cross-national comparison. *Journal of Management Development*, *23*(4), 321–338. doi:10.1108/02621710410529785

Mukherjee, S. P. (2019) *A Guide to Research Methodology: An Overview of Research Problems, Tasks and Methods*. Taylor & Francis Group. Retrieved in May 1st, 2022, from: https://ebookcentral.proquest.com/lib/uwestlon/reader.action?docID=5890625

Musthofa, W. S., Farida, N., & Ngatno, N. (2017). Effect of entrepreneurial orientation on business performance. *International Journal of Civil Engineering and Technology*, *8*, 82–90.

Pasquale, P. P., Neto, C. L., & Gomes, C. L. C. C. (2012). *Comunicação Integrada de Marketing: a teoria na prática*. Elsevier.

Pimpão, A. C. P. (2013). A importância da comunicação interna numa empresa – aplicada ao caso Timwe. Lisboa. Business School. Tese de Mestrado em Gestão.

Pio, D. (2017). *A força transformadora da comunicação interna*. Simplissimo Livros.

Pool, S., & Pool, B. (2007). A management development model: Measuring organizational commitment and its impact on job satisfaction among executives in a learning organization. *Journal of Management Development*, *26*(4), 353–369. doi:10.1108/02621710710740101

Richard, P., Devinney, T., Yip, G., & Johnson, G. (2009). Measuring organizational performance: Towards methodological best practice. *Journal of Management*, *35*(3), 718–804. doi:10.1177/0149206308330560

Sequesseque, R. M. A. C. (2019). *Motivação para o desempenho profissional: caso de estudo* (Doctoral dissertation).

Shahzadi, I., Javed, A., Pirzada, S. S., Nasreen, S., & Khanam, F. (2014). Impact of employee motivation on employee performance. *European Journal of Business and Management*, *6*(23), 159–166.

SNS24. (2022). *COVID-19*. Retrieved in April 1st, 2022, from: https://www.sns24.gov.pt/tema/doencas-infecciosas/covid-19/

WHO. (n.d.). *COVID-19*. Retrieved in May 23rd, 2022, from: https://www.who.int/emergencies/diseases/novel-coronavirus-2019/situation-reports

Workplace, Q. (2021). *The Impact of COVID-19 on Employee Engagement*. Retrieved in April 1st, 2022, from: https://www.quantumworkplace.com/impact-of-covid-19-on-employee-engagement

ADDITIONAL READING

Adnjani, M. D., & Prianti, D. D. (2023). Internal Communication Towards Employee Engagement Inside Sultan Agung Islamic University (UNISSULA). *Jurnal Ilmiah Komunikasi Makna*, *1*(1), 1–14. doi:10.30659/jikm.1.1.1-14

Jianga, L., Clark, B. B., & Turbanc, D. B. (2023). Overcoming the challenge of exploration: How decompartmentalization of internal communication enhances the effect of exploration on employee inventive performance. *Technovation*, *119*, 102611. doi:10.1016/j.technovation.2022.102611

Näsi, A. (2023). Visual Discussion as Part of Internal Organization Communication—Functions and Significance. *Journalism and Media*, *4*(1), 60–74. doi:10.3390/journalmedia4010005

Rua, O. L., & Ferreira, A. (2021). Predictive strategic factors in export performance in automotive industry: the mediating effect of innovation. In A. C. Moreira (Ed.), *Cases on Internationalization Challenges for SMEs* (pp. 239–260). IGI Global.

Rua, O. L., França, A., & Fernández, R. O. (2018). Key drivers of SMEs export performance: The mediating effect of competitive advantage. *Journal of Knowledge Management*, *22*(2), 257–270. doi:10.1108/JKM-07-2017-0267

KEY TERMS AND DEFINITIONS

Channels of Communication: Ensure the communication process and the main means of communication are oral, written, audio-visual and, with the technological revolution, the telematic media.

COVID-19: Is the name given by the World Health Organisation, to the disease caused by the new coronavirus SARS-COV-2. This virus was first identified in humans in late 2019 in the Chinese city of Wuhan.

Formal Networks: Are those which are regulated by the organisation, that is, those that are planned and controlled by the directive bodies, such as meetings, internal notes, internal newspapers, reports, and circulars.

Informal Networks: Are born from the social relationship in organisations, in other words, they are spontaneous communications, not regulated by the organisation, which are originated not only from the shortcomings of formal communication networks but also, from the natural needs of employees to establish contact with each other.

Internal Communication: Is a strategic tool for compatibility of the interests of employees and the company, through stimulating dialogue, the exchange of information and experiences and participation at all levels.

Organisational Performance: Is the ability and aptitude of a firm to be able to exploit available resources to consistently achieve its goals.

APPENDIX (QUESTIONNAIRE)

1. Gender:
    1.1. Man
    1.2. Woman
    1.3. Non-binary
    1.4. Prefer not to say
2. Age:
    2.1. 18-25
    2.2. 26-35
    2.3. 36-45
    2.4. 46-55
    2.5. +55
3. Does the company give much importance to its internal communication strategy?
    (1 – Totally disagree; 5 – Totally agree)
4. Which communication actions are being well achieved in the company?
    4.1. Newsletter
    4.2. Internal communications
    4.3. Yammer
    4.4. E-mail
    4.5. +55
5. During the confinement did you feel motivated to use Yammer?
    5.1. Yes
    5.2. No
6. Please rate the following statements regarding the potential of the internal communication strategy during the Covid-19 pandemic according to your degree of agreement or disagreement.
    (1 – Totally disagree; 5 – Totally agree)
    6.1. Do you consider that the company's Internal Communication strategy has favoured the employees' means of expression?
    6.2. Do you think that the company's internal Communication strategy has allowed the development of a feeling of belonging and identification with the company, even at a distance?
    6.3. Do you think that the events held were sufficient to provide moments of connection between the teams and the company?
    6.4. During the pandemic, did you feel like an important part of the company?
    6.5. During the pandemic, did you feel that your work was valued and impacted the company in any way?
    6.6. Do you consider Yammer an essential tool for the Internal Communication Strategy during the pandemic?
    6.7. Do you consider that all communications were clear and concise?
    6.8. Do you consider that the company's internal communication strategy improved in any way its performance during the pandemic?
    6.9. Did you feel Natixis gave much importance to its internal communication strategy during the pandemic?

6.10. Do you consider that the means of communication used were sufficient?

6.11. Do you consider that the internal communication actions carried out by Natixis were original and creative?

6.12. Did you feel that the communications team strived to develop unique and unrepetitive actions?

6.13. Did you feel motivated to participate in the internal communication actions carried out by Natixis?

6.14. Do you consider that sending Christmas presents by post was a differentiating factor from other companies you know?

6.15. Do you consider that Natixis was clear and objective when communicating the lockdown and the telework policies adopted in March 2020, taking into account the information made available by the Portuguese government?

Chapter 3
Reporting and Feeling:
Considerations on the Mental Health of Journalists During the Pandemic

Edson Capoano
Universidade do Minho, Portugal

Renato Essenfelder
Universidade Fernando Pessoa, Portugal

ABSTRACT

This chapter explores the mental health challenges faced by journalists through a review of existing literature and a brief survey of journalists in Brazil. The study suggests that more research is needed on the mental health of journalists and calls for preventive measures such as mental health training in journalism schools and news organizations, as well as identifying and addressing the root causes of mental health issues in the industry. The chapter also highlights various strategies and best practices for journalists to maintain their mental well-being, including techniques for managing stress, establishing boundaries between work and personal life, and seeking support from colleagues. The study emphasizes that addressing the mental health challenges faced by journalists is important for the well-being of individual journalists and the quality of journalism and its role in serving society. The study concludes that, by promoting mental health practices and awareness, the journalism industry can improve the lives of its professionals and better serve the public.

INTRODUCTION

Threats (in an Already Nebulous Horizon)

The theme of mental health has taken advantage of the increasing attention to well-being in contemporary western and urban societies. However, even today, despite the attention given to the subject, investment in mental health care for the population remains insufficient. According to a report by the World Health Organization (2021), the levels of public spending on mental health are low (a global average of 2.1%

DOI: 10.4018/978-1-6684-7353-5.ch003

of government health spending) and particularly scarce in low- and middle-income countries. There is an extreme variation between rich and poor countries (less than two workers per 100,000 inhabitants in low-income countries and more than 60 in high-income countries).

Among the various classes of professionals who report being affected by mental health, journalists are highly susceptible to activities and content that can jeopardize their mental well-being. During the pandemic period of 2020, 61% of journalists surveyed in Brazil reported increased anxiety and stress (FENAJ, as cited in Valadares, 2020). During the same period, the International Center for Journalists (ICFJ, as cited in Posetti, Bell, & Brown, 2020) identified exhausted journalists, with mental health crises, and fearful of losing their jobs.

In 2021, after more than a year of telecommuting, Brazilian journalistic companies began to discuss the return to face-to-face work, albeit gradually - while Covid-19 cases continued to multiply in the country, bringing a new factor of anxiety to the sector. Part of this feeling was captured by support surveys submitted to journalists from two of the largest newsrooms in the country: the newspapers Folha de S. Paulo and O Estado de S. Paulo.

Responses, submitted by 19 journalists, indicate signs of stress. Conducted between the last week of August and the first week of September 2021, the surveys sought to record, as quickly as possible, journalists' feelings in a very specific context. While daily confirmations of Covid-19 cases in the country began to drop from more than 60,000 in July to just under 30,000 by the end of September that year, journalistic companies were discussing the end of remote work, which had become the standard in major Brazilian newsrooms since March 2020.

The possibility of returning to face-to-face work, however, in the midst of an uncertain public health scenario, presumably would generate insecurity among workers. In addition, vaccination against Covid-19 at the time had reached less than 50% of the national population.

As early as July 2021, a survey conducted by the consulting firm Korn Ferry showed that 70% of all professionals working remotely in Brazil believed that remote work was indeed a "new normal" and that returning to the office would be "difficult" and "strange" (Cavallini, 2021), a conclusion corroborated by a study by Essenfelder et al. (2021) specifically with journalists.

To reach the respondents of the brief survey, which contained ten objective questions and an open-ended question, the directors of the two publications were initially contacted. The collaboration of the companies was then requested to distribute the surveys to their journalists, which was done without reservations or pre-conditions in both companies. Participation was spontaneous, not incentivized, and open for a period of ten days.

At the end of a period, which was restrictive precisely because of the intention to capture the temperature of that specific moment in two of the country's most traditional newspapers, we used this survey to stimulate theoretical reflection on the theme of journalists' mental health. The average profile of respondents was men (58%) aged between 31 and 40 years old (47%) with an income between R$ 4,000 and R$ 10,000 (56%), or about 700 to 1700 euros. Regarding the length of time they had been working at their respective companies, 69% indicated that they had been employed for more than five years in the same company - in other words, a typical mid-career profile.

When asked about their evaluation of remote work, the overwhelming majority considered the work model to be positive. Of the possible responses - "excellent," "good," "indifferent," "bad," or "terrible" - almost all respondents (95%) chose "excellent" or "good" as their overall evaluation of the experience. Only 5.3% said that working from home was a bad experience, and no respondent evaluated this production model outside the newsroom as "terrible."

Despite the initial approval of the work-from-home experience, the professionals' evaluations changed when they commented on the support offered by the two companies to perform their functions outside the newsrooms. In questions regarding support for better internet connections at home, the provision of ergonomic chairs and a time-tracking system (electronic clock), as well as the supply of protection masks and hand sanitizer, protective material against Covid-19 for interviews and other activities that required forays outside the home, the percentage of respondents who considered this support terrible was 42.1%. Those who considered the support bad accounted for 21.1%, while 36.8% answered "regular". No one considered it "excellent" or even "good".

The relationship between precarious labor, which in turn affects mental health, and the crisis in the journalism business was already foreshadowed by Salaverría in 2015: "When the media was doing well, the reporters were doing tolerably poorly", he writes. "But when the media is doing very poorly, the situation of journalists could not be worse" (2015, 79).

Mental health issues related to this precariousness also stand out in responses to the surveys conducted in São Paulo in 2021. Among the main problems of the new work-from-home model, journalists cited issues related to increased anxiety, loneliness, depression, a sense of loss of work purpose, and burnout syndrome. Half of the participants reported feeling more anxiety (50%) during remote work, followed by "lack of willingness or energy for work" (33%), and irritability (17%). In addition to affecting the quality of life, mental health problems can also affect professional productivity.

In addition to affecting quality of life, mental health problems can also affect professional productivity. Task fragmentation, labor precariousness, and constant interruptions caused by an excess of communication channels also affect the well-being of professionals. It is estimated that it takes more than 20 minutes for a distracted individual to recompose their attention on an original task (Cabra, 2022). Furthermore, each interruption and restart (context switching) of a task can generate mental fatigue and a work routine with successive fragmented activities can lead to exhaustion. In this context, changing work systems, grouping tasks, and defining specific moments for interruptions can contribute to the well-being of workers.

Considering the complexity of this scenario, this paper presents a debate on the theme – partially illustrated by surveys of journalists – through a literature review of the concept of mental health and its relationship with journalists and journalism, framing the discussion in the pandemic period.

DEVELOPMENT

Reporting and Feeling: Effects of Pandemic Coverage

Among the various definitions of mental health is "emotional, psychological, and social well-being" (Health and Human Services, 2022); "a state of well-being in which individuals realize their own potential, can cope with the normal stresses of life, can work productively and fruitfully, and are able to make a contribution to their community" (WHO, 2022). Dictionaries describe the phenomenon as a synonym for mental hygiene and a state of psychological well-being according to Campbell's Psychiatric Dictionary (Campbell, 2004), or as a state preserved by mental hygiene in the Oxford English Dictionary (Dictionary, 1993).

The concept originated from a conference in 1946 when the World Health Organization (WHO) was established. Before that, the closest term was "mental hygiene," dating back to 1843 (in Mateus Steffens & Rojas Gualdrón, 2009). In the second session of the WHO Mental Health Expert Committee in 1950, the difference between the two terms was established: mental hygiene refers to all activities and techniques that promote and maintain mental health. Mental health is a condition subject to fluctuations due to biological and social factors that allow individuals to achieve a satisfactory synthesis of their own potentially conflicting instincts, form and maintain harmonious relationships with others, and participate in constructive changes in their social and physical environment (2009).

Although mental health problems affect all careers and individuals, a literature review on journalists' mental health published by MacDonald et al. in 2023 concluded that journalists reported higher levels of depression than other professionals. The research identified the main occupational risks leading to an increased incidence of mood disorders: (1) greater exposure to work-related and personal trauma, (2) experience threats to themselves or their family, and (3) reduced levels of family and peer support, social acknowledgment, and education. In 2019, Seely's research indicated that journalists were at a higher risk of experiencing symptoms of anxiety and depression compared to the general population, especially those involved in the coverage of traumatic incidents.

In Brazil, other processes and factors that triggered journalists' mental health loss were identified, such as suffering, stress, depression, mental disorders, occupational health conditions, environment, and management, psychological conflicts, and social and family relationships (Penteado & Gastaldello, 2016). However, the relationship between the exercise of the profession and mental health - and the lack thereof - was usually related to war coverage. However, interest in journalists' mental health has increased since the COVID-19 pandemic (Osmann et al., 2021; Simunjak, 2021).

Class reports such as the Brazilian Journalist Profile (Lima & Mick, 2013) have pointed out that the work environment is more toxic than expected in the country. For example, an analysis of 80 Brazilian reports between 2001 and 2016 found that several practices worsened journalists' mental health, such as invasion of privacy, surveillance, threats, and other violations of journalists' digital rights, beyond physical assaults, deaths, and persecution (Christofoletti & Torres, 2018). Another study, delving into symptoms of 57% of respondents who declare themselves stressed, found that 37% of them were diagnosed with stress, 16% were diagnosed with mental disorder, 24% were diagnosed with RSI (Repetitive Strain Injury) and WRULD (Work-Related Upper Limb Disorder), and 26% regularly use antidepressants (Pontes & Lima, 2019).

During the social isolation and distancing period due to the pandemic (Capoano & Barros, 2021), it was also reported that journalists were prevented from carrying out their activities in full and that there was a lack of barriers between work and personal life (de Souza et al., 2022). During the same period, information recipients reported negative emotions caused by news consumption, including sadness, anger, fear, and shame (Capoano et al., 2021; Capoano & Costa, 2021).

In spontaneous responses to the open-ended question "How does being away from other reporters and editors affect your work?" journalists who responded to the survey we proposed in 2021 reported both more practical issues and others of a psychological nature, such as "Decreased sense of team and creativity," "Lack of dialogue about current issues and agendas," "Feedback and idea exchange processes have been compromised," "Increased prevalence of work in routine," "A certain loneliness. I miss exchanging ideas and experiences with colleagues", "More noise, with people doing the same task, for example".

This problem lies not only in the mental consequences of the pandemic. In the US, a study confirmed that journalists, being the first to respond and eyewitnesses of violent acts, are also among the professionals who carry the most post-traumatic stress disorder and its symptoms (Seely, 2019). By broadening the spectrum of research to English-language journalism, one study identified that journalists who had depressive symptoms had greater exposure to work-related and personal trauma, experienced threats to themselves or their families, and obtained reduced levels of family and peer support, social recognition, and education (MacDonald et al., 2023).

Even in Canada, a country that ranks among the best in the world in terms of quality of life, there are problems, as demonstrated by the Taking Care Report (Lonsdale, 2022): two-thirds of young people aged 20 to 29 and half of professionals aged 50 to 59 emerged from the acute period of the pandemic with difficulty coping with social isolation; two-thirds of those surveyed had problems balancing personal and professional life; two-thirds were negatively affected by covering traumatic events (death, violence, disasters, etc.); in addition to journalists, other professionals declare themselves exposed to traumatic content, such as editors, producers, camera operators, presenters, and librarians; and between 85% and 90% of respondents stated that they received no training to deal with coverage that could affect their mental health (2022).

Globally, Amnesty International recognizes that there is a danger of secondary or vicarious trauma (2019, p.2) in the consumption of images of violence by news workers or social media managers. Signs such as anger, rage, and sadness should be monitored carefully to avoid extreme cases of anxiety, stress, burnout, and post-traumatic disorder. This is due to the brain's ability to experience emotional symptoms similarly if the individual is to experience the same trauma or violence consumed by images in person.

Precarization and Reconfiguration of the Field

The mental health of journalists is also affected by the so-called precarization of work, specifically among journalists (Bulhões & Renault, 2016; Nicoletti & Mick, 2018; Heloani & Silva, 2021), where there is a deregulation of professional practice, an increase in working hours, a breakdown of the boundary between personal and professional life, and a loss of physical environment and relationships with other professionals due to digitized/remote work, among other phenomena. Studies such as those by Roseli Fígaro (2011; et al., 2021) and Roberto Heloani (2005; 2006; & Pinto, 2007) document these and other transformations of journalistic ethos, which can undermine journalists' mental health; however, this field is still underexplored in scientific studies, especially in so-called Global South countries.

In addition to pioneering work scattered across the five continents, several articles have addressed mental health, but as a subject of reporting, relegating the well-being of journalists to a secondary objective of studies. A systematic review carried out in Brazil, for example, identified that national articles on journalists' mental health reached 50% of the collected sample. Of these, 87.5% came from reports carried out by the professionals themselves, while only 12.5% came from the academic community, including journalism students, professors, and Higher Education Institutions (Penteado & Gastaldello, 2016).

Regarding the organizational and business constraints already identified by Max Weber (in Serra & Bergamoba, 2020), which pressure journalists between meeting the demands of the journalistic business and the social function of journalism, it affects not only the credibility of journalism but also the self-esteem and quality of life of journalists. Today, structural changes in the information universe mean that the value of news is spread among niche audiences and customized advertising, which alters the social role of journalism and its professionals' relevance (Fígaro, 2020, 27).

Thus, the transnational interpretative community that Traquina (2002) identified in journalists, based on their reference frames for news production, becomes a group increasingly questioned by other social fields. The distrust with which citizens currently receive information reflects a crisis of journalism's legitimacy and journalists' identity (Fidalgo, 2004). An increasingly competitive and demanding market (2004, 70) accentuates the profession's malaise.

Currently, the journalistic profession and, as a consequence, journalists' routine are in full transformation. The reasons for this were identified by both market professionals and field researchers. Salaverría (2015) highlights at least two simultaneous crises: the economic crisis stemming from the 2007 crisis and the resulting decrease in the purchasing power of information consumers; and the structural crisis resulting from the technological transformation that forces journalistic companies to adapt to a digital ecosystem (2015, 80-81). Neveu (2019) identifies economic (willingness of the public to pay for news), structural (organization of newsrooms and production processes in general), identity (distinction between journalists and other content producers), political (balance of power between sources and journalists), and generational (change in journalists' behavior) dimensions (2019, 198-199).

The crisis of the journalistic business model has also led journalists to seek new forms of work organization, such as virtual newsrooms, independent productive arrangements, and increasingly fragile labor ties with communication companies (Fígaro, 2018; Silva, 2019). Such labor transition is not exclusive to journalists or communicators, but rather the result of the advancement of productive forces and the restructuring of the capitalist system towards the digital, platform, and knowledge economy (2020, 109). In this context, information workers in general are constrained by many limitations, according to Neveu (2021), such as the size and format of their work being defined by computers, without a defined workspace, and where phones and screens replace face-to-face work (2021, 43).

Digital convergence has also caused disruptions in the media business, thanks to the relativization of national borders (content travels globally), commercial barriers (companies compete for the same sectors), editorial cycles (production processes are altered by technology), information monopoly (decreasing the importance of newspapers as public interlocutors), and the business model in general. Moreover, convergence has changed the routine of journalists and their relationship with work, such as the agglomeration of functions, production on numerous platforms, the precariousness of work relationships, and the loss of credibility of the products generated by professionals (Fígaro, 2020, 107).

The digitalization of the profession, an inevitable and welcome process for the performance of professionals, also generates apprehension due to the increasing technicisation of work, lack of time for adaptation, increased speed, and information intermediation tasks (Deuze, 2006, 28). Such changes cause a deterioration in the quality of work life (Heloani, 2005) in a framework where professionals "naturalize" stress and accept constant substitution in their jobs (2003, 77-80).

The latest threats to journalists come from the platformization of information, where users produce data without the need for professionals, and from algorithms and conversation robots, which generate content independent of human action. These and other structural threats generate the hypothesis of journalism without journalists, where the prosumer is the protagonist of the entire information process (Fígaro, 2020, 34), or information workers (Neveu, 2010), "a conglomerate of jobs and activities with the common dimension of offering news and information to audiences" (2010, 33).

The perfect storm over journalists' mental health is complemented by real dangers to the physical integrity of professionals, promoted by extremist groups, coverage of wars, or improper sanitary conditions. The organization Reporters Without Borders (RSF) recorded 1,668 journalists killed in the exercise of their profession over 19 years, with an average of 80 professionals from 2003 to 2022.

The Covid-19 pandemic has already claimed the lives of 2,000 journalists between 2000 and 2022, according to the Press Emblem Campaign - PEC. In addition to the health issue, the pandemic has also forced the adoption of home offices (Capoano & Barros, 2020; Capoano et al., 2021), abruptly altering the work routine of professionals (Sousa et al., 2020), as well as information consumers, generating negative effects on their mental health (Capoano & Costa, 2021; Capoano et al., 2021). This issue is so important to the journalistic field that UNESCO (2020) requested a study on the work of journalists, mental health, and concerns in the early months of the Covid-19 outbreak.

PERSPECTIVES AND REDEFINITIONS

The responses obtained in the support surveys are in line with the literature on the subject and are especially relevant when we consider that journalists are generally more susceptible to mental health issues. Such studies provide evidence that journalists may be very prone to anxiety and other mental health problems due to the nature of their work and the high levels of stress and pressure they may face. In the context of the pandemic, the situation has become especially serious for those who had to do their job in the midst of the coronavirus outbreak, like all other professional categories, but rather about the coronavirus itself, supplying the media industry and society at large with news 24 hours a day.

Therefore, to survive in the new informational ecosystem with mental health, it is necessary to pay attention to the bodily and behavioral signals that each individual emits. However, it also seems necessary to follow the recommendations of researchers in the field, who have identified the causes of the journalistic crisis and therefore have the conditions to identify how to overcome it. All recommendations to follow respond to the demands of the professionals surveyed in our case study, journalists who worked from home during Covid-19.

Neveu (2019) suggests cooperation between journalists and newsrooms to create innovative networks and new partnerships (2019, 200). In fact, the horizontalization of work among different professionals and between them and new information actors (e.g., youtubers and podcasters) can reduce pressure on journalists and make the professional environment healthier. The sociologist also suggests five paths for future communicators to remain more journalists than data bureaucrats - a surprisingly current forecast in times of algorithms and chatbots: obtaining public support and resources for news business sustainability; leveraging new partners in the journalistic chain, such as viewers, prosumers, and amateur journalists; applying techniques from Social Sciences to increase the accuracy of the journalistic product; understanding what the new audiences are and what they want; creativity, innovation, and experimentation to break with exhausted styles and genres (2010, pp. 44-50).

Finally, maintaining the relevance of journalists and journalism for the new configurations of society. Perhaps this is the best recommendation for professionals' mental health, in addition to safeguarding life, employment, and health threats. The perception that the chosen career will not exist, or that it no longer serves to perform it, can generate enormous personal dilemmas. Therefore, it is correct to conclude that renewing oneself professionally protects one's mental health. Salaverría (2015) realized that the modernization of the journalistic business involves the renewal of journalists: "It is about redefining the ways of informing to continue fulfilling a function that society needs. This redefinition also falls to journalists who have their part to do" (2015, p. 82).

The same Salaverría suggests paths for this: technological dexterity, for the renewal of instrumental skills, working on information processing, in addition to filling informational scarcity, which is increasingly rare, moving with ease between media and languages, redefining new routines and workflows, and reorganizing editorial work.

Final Considerations

Therefore, it is important that research in the Global South focus more on this matter, as has already been done by researchers in the Anglo-Saxon and Nordic cultural axes, as well as by professional journalistic entities that publish reports on how journalists can deal with this issue. Our contribution has the limitation of a very small sample, which is still under composition. Nevertheless, it highlights the challenges to journalists' mental health, as identified by reports from the journalistic profession and researchers in the field.

In addition to journalism researchers, sector entities have begun to offer information on how to generate self-care, thus improving the quality of life of these professionals. Among them are manuals, guides, and courses that teach relaxation and stress reduction techniques, focusing on breathing, establishing boundaries between professional and personal life, increasing and improving relationships with other professionals, engaging in physical activity, and practicing techniques for quality sleep (Storm & Crowley, 2022). Regarding practices focused on journalism, there are procedures for dealing with traumatic content, identifying increased stress, and moral and mental harm (Lonsdale, 2022).

Among the recommendations of the Evidence Lab from the Amnesty Internacional Digital Verification team (Amnesty International, 2019) are: turning off automatic playback and download of digital content on social networks or conversation groups; avoiding consumption of photos, audio, or videos in their entirety if they can be identified as traumatic; muting the volume of violent videos, which can attenuate the distress of consumption, limiting the time of contact with explicit images, with periodic breaks, identifying bodily stress reactions during such contact, and talking about possible anxieties with colleagues who understand the experience to which the communication professional may be exposed.

Maintaining well-being through mental health practices can contribute not only to professionals, but also to the outcome of their work and their relationship with the societies they serve. Emotional training and self-awareness practices, for example, can provide relief from psychological problems and cultivate more pro-social behaviors. A study that applied Emotional Balance Cultivation training (Ekman & Ekman, 2013) to teachers, for instance, identified that positive emotional results lasted up to five months, such as the reduction of negative affect traits such as rumination, depression, and anxiety, and an increase in positive affect traits such as mindfulness and compassion – the recognition of emotions in other people.

Considering the picture of journalists' mental health revisited in this article through theoretical review and supportive inquiry, it is necessary to increase research on the phenomenon, both in preventive issues – through courses and training in communication colleges and journalistic companies – and in the causes and effects that generate the loss of well-being and mental health of professionals.

REFERENCES

Amnesty International. (2019, February 20). *Respuesta a las Crisis de Amnistía Internacional. Las víctimas ocultas de la represión: cómo pueden activistas y periodistas protegerse del trauma secundario.* Amnesty International. https://www.amnesty.org/es/latest/news/2019/02/how-activists-and-reporters-can-protect-themselves-from-secondary-trauma/

Bulhões, J., & Renault, D. (2016). A precarização da prática jornalística: uma revisão bibliográfica sobre o impacto das condições de trabalho na saúde e qualidade de vida do jornalista. *Parágrafo, 4*(2), 164-175. https://revistaseletronicas.fiamfaam.br/index.php/recicofi/article/view/414

Cabra, M. (2022, April 10). El fin de la productividad: así pierdes horas sin darte cuenta. *Tecnosaludables.* https://blogs.alimente.elconfidencial.com/bienestar/tecnosaludables/2021-04-10/teletrajo-productividad-reducida-horas-conocimiento-covid_3028024/

Campbell, R. J. (2004). *Campbell's psychiatric dictionary.* Oxford University Press.

Capoano, E. & Barros, V. T. (2020). Jovem, dedicado, confinado e prejudicado: perfis, rotinas e processos jornalísticos durante a pandemia de Covid-19. *Pauta Geral - Estudos em Jornalismo, 7,* 1-15. doi:10.5212/RevistaPautaGeral.v.7.17267.229

Capoano, E., & Costa, P. R. (2021). Emotions, morals and resilience: The consumption of news in Ibero-America during the covid-19 pandemic. In D.M. Berube (Eds.), Pandemic communication and resilience. Risk, systems and decisions (pp. 331-345). Springer. https:// doi:10.1007/978-3-030-77344-1_20

Capoano, E., Costa, P. R., Galhardi, R., & Barros, V. T. (2021). Tristeza, medo, raiva e vergonha: Das emoções ao neuroticismo estimulado pelo consumo de notícias sobre covid-19. In R. C. Oliveira, D. Christino, & E. V. Machado Júnior (Eds.), *Covid-19 e a Comunicação* (pp. 255-277). Cegraf - UFG. https://hdl.handle.net/1822/73640

Capoano, E., Martini, M. R., & de Alencar, V. (2021). Identidades, perfiles y procesos: elementos que componen los periodistas de la Agência Mural Jornalismo das Periferias. In J. M. Valero Pastor (Ed.), *Plataformas, consumo mediático y nuevas realidades digitales. Hacia una perspectiva integradora* (pp. 334–353). Dykinson. https://hdl.handle.net/1822/75482

Cavallini, M. (2021, August 20). Volta ao trabalho presencial será "difícil e estranha para os profissionais", diz pesquisa. *G1.* https://g1.globo.com/economia/concursos-e-emprego/noticia/2021/08/01/volta-ao-trabalho-presencial-sera-dificil-e-estranha-para-os-profissionais-diz-pesquisa.ghtml&gt

Christofoletti, R., & Torres, R. J. (2018). Jornalistas expostos e vulneráveis: Ataques digitais como modalidade de risco profissional. *Famecos, 25*(3), 29210. Advance online publication. doi:10.15448/1980-3729.2018.3.29210

de Sousa, V., Capoano, E. & Paganotti, I. (2022). ¿La Covid-19 ha infectado las noticias? Cómo los periodistas, las audiencias y los procesos de producción son alterados por las pandemias. *Universitas-XXI, 37,* 19-41. doi:10.17163/uni.n37.2022.01

Deuze, M. (2006). O jornalismo e os novos meios de comunicação social. *Comunicação e Sociedade, 9,* 15–37. doi:10.17231/comsoc.9(2006).1152

Dictionary, O. E. (1993). *Oxford English Dictionary.* OUP.

Ekman, E. & Ekman, P. (2013). Cultivating emotional balance: Structure, Research, and implementation. *Compassion: Bridging practice and science,* 398-414.

Essenfelder, R., Sant'Anna, E., & Coca, A. P. (2021, October). *Reconfiguração das Redações brasileiras durante a pandemia de Covid-19* [Paper presentation]. 4º Congresso Internacional Media Ecology and Image Studies-Reflexões sobre o ecossistema midiático pós pandemia. Annual Congress, Brazil.

Figaro, R. (2011). A abordagem ergológica e o mundo do trabalho dos comunicadores. *Trabalho, Educação e Saúde*, *9*(suppl 1), 285–297. doi:10.1590/S1981-77462011000400014

Figaro, R. (2014). Jornalismos e trabalho de jornalistas: desafios para as novas gerações no século XXI. *Parágrafo, 2*(2), 23-37. https://www.eca.usp.br/acervo/producao-academica/002672767.pdf

Figaro, R., Marques, A. F., Camargo, C. A., Rebechi, C. N., de Oliveira, D. F., Kinoshita, J. O., . . . Santana, Y. A. (2021). Os comunicadores no contexto de um ano da pandemia de Covid-19. *Líbero*, (49), 61-89. https://seer.casperlibero.edu.br/index.php/libero/article/view/1621/1310

Figaro, R., & Silva, A. F. M. D. (2020). A comunicação como trabalho no Capitalismo de plataforma: O caso das mudanças no jornalismo. *Contracampo*, *39*(1), 101–115. doi:10.22409/contracampo.v39i1.38566

Health & Human Services. (2022). *Mental Health.* U.S. Department of Health & Human Services. https://www.mentalhealth.gov/

Heloani, J. R. (2005). Mudanças no mundo do trabalho e impactos na qualidade de vida do jornalista. *FGV EAESP – Gvpesquisa,* 1-92. http://hdl.handle.net/10438/3098

Heloani, R. (2006). O trabalho do jornalista: Estresse e qualidade de vida. *Interações*, (22), 171–198. https://www.redalyc.org/articulo.oa?id=35402208

Heloani, R., & Silva, E. P. (2021). Reflexões teóricas e metodológicas sobre pesquisas no campo da saúde mental e trabalho. *Cadernos CERU*, *32*(1), 62–82. doi:10.11606/issn.2595-2536.v32i1p62-82

Lima, S. P., & Mick, J. (2013). Sindicalização e identidade política dos jornalistas brasileiros. *Estudos em Jornalismo e Mídia*, *10*(1), 4–24. doi:10.5007/1984-6924.2013v10n1p4

Lonsdale, C. (Ed.). (2022). Taking Care. A Report on Mental Health, Well-Being & Trauma among Canadian Media Workers. In *Forum on Violence and Trauma.* Canadian Journalism. https://www.journalismforum.ca/taking-care-report

MacDonald, J. B., Hodgins, G., Saliba, A. J., & Metcalf, D. A. (2023). Journalists and depressive symptoms: A systematic literature review. *Trauma, Violence & Abuse*, *24*(1), 86–96. doi:10.1177/15248380211016022 PMID:33998329

MacDonald, J. B., Hodgins, G., Saliba, A. J., & Metcalf, D. A. (2023). Journalists and Depressive Symptoms: A Systematic Literature Review. *Trauma, Violence & Abuse*, *24*(1), 86–96. doi:10.1177/15248380211016022 PMID:33998329

Mateus Steffens, C., & Rojas Gualdrón, D. F. (2009). *Del tratamiento moral de las enfermedades mentales a la salud mental comunitaria. Una aproximación histórico-epistemológica al concepto de salud mental durante el periodo de higiene mental* [Doctoral dissertation]. Universidad Autónoma de Bucaramanga, Colômbia. http://hdl.handle.net/20.500.12749/17629

Neveu, E. (2010). As notícias sem jornalistas: Uma ameaça real ou uma história de terror? *Brazilian Journalism Research, 6*(1), 29–57. doi:10.25200/BJR.v6n1.2010.246

Neveu, E. (2019). O desafio de pensar ecologicamente. *Jornalismo, 20*(1), 198–201. doi:10.1177/1464884918808139

Nicoletti, J., & Mick, J. (2018). Influências da precarização na qualidade jornalística: construção de uma matriz de indicadores. *Passagens, 9*(1), 127-141. http://www.repositorio.ufc.br/handle/riufc/38547

Osmann, J., Selva, M., & Feinstein, A. (2021). How have journalists been affected psychologically by their coverage of the COVID-19 pandemic? A descriptive study of two international organizations. *BMJ Open, 11*(7), e045675. Advance online publication. doi:10.1136/bmjopen-2020-045675 PMID:34253664

Penteado, R. Z., & Gastaldello, L. M. (2016). Saúde e qualidade de vida de jornalistas: Estudo de revisão. *Revista Brasileira em Promoção da Saúde, 29*(2), 295–304. doi:10.5020/18061230.2016.p295

Pinto, E., & Heloani, R. (2007). Aspectos teóricos e metodológicos da pesquisa em saúde mental e trabalho: Reflexões a partir de uma análise comparativa do estresse em jornalistas e guardas municipais. *Cadernos de Psicologia Social do Trabalho, 10*(1), 105–120. doi:10.11606/issn.1981-0490.v10i1p105-120

Pontes, F. S., & Lima, S. P. (2019). Impactos do mercado jornalístico na vida de seus trabalhadores: Um estudo sobre indicadores de saúde dos jornalistas brasileiros. *Famecos, 26*(2), e31729–e31729. doi:10.15448/1980-3729.2019.2.31729

Posetti, J., Bell, E., & Brown, P. (2020). El periodismo y la pandemia: una instantánea global de su impacto. *ICJF/Tow Center for Digital Journalism.* https://www.icfj.org/sites/default/files/2020-11/Journalism%20and%20the%20Pandemic%20Project%20Report%201%202020_Spanish2.pdf

Salaverría, R. (2015). Mídia e Jornalistas, um futuro em comum? *Parágrafo, 3*(1), 79-84. https://revistaseletronicas.fiamfaam.br/index.php/recicofi/article/view/297

Seely, N. (2019). Journalists and mental health: The psychological toll of covering everyday trauma. *Newspaper Research Journal, 40*(2), 239–259. doi:10.1177/0739532919835612

Serra, P., & Bergamoba, A. (2020). Sociologia do Jornalismo: Por uma agenda de pesquisa. *Plural: Revista de Ciências Sociais., 27*(2), 5–21. doi:10.11606/issn.2176-8099.pcso.2020.179833

SousaV.CostaP. R.CapoanoE.PaganottiI. (2020). Riscos, dilemas e oportunidades: atuação jornalística em tempos de Covid-19. *Estudos em Comunicação*, (31), 1-33. https://doi.org/ doi:10.25768/20.04.03.31.01

Storm, H., Crowley, J., Berrie, A., & Mamo, E. (2022, April). Managing our mental health: A guide for journalists and media professionals. In *Headlines/Mind*. Google News Initiative. https://www.mind.org.uk/media/12403/managing-our-mental-health-guide.pdf

Traquina, N. (2002). Uma comunidade interpretativa transnacional: a tribo jornalística. *Media e Jornalismo, 1*(1), 45-64. http://fabricadesites.fcsh.unl.pt/polocicdigital/wp-content/uploads/sites/8/2017/02/mj_1.pdf#page=45

UNESCO. (2020). *The effect of COVID-19 on journalists' mental health*. Reuters Institute for the Study of Journalism e pela University of Toronto. https://www.unesco.org/en/world-media-trends/effect-covid-19-journalists-mental-health

Valadares, G. N. (2020, December 15). Jornalismo compassivo: e se a saúde emocional dos repórteres virar prioridade nas redações em 2021? *Abraji/Farol Jornalismo*. https://medium.com/jornalismo-no-brasil-em-2021/jornalismo-compassivo-e-se-a-sa%C3%BAde-emocional-dos-rep%C3%B3rteres-virar-prioridade-nas-reda%C3%A7%C3%B5es-em-2021-b7dae2698a73

World Health Organization. (2021). *Mental Health Atlas 2020*. World Health Organization. https://www.who.int/publications-detail-redirect/9789240036703

World Health Organization. (2022, June 17). *Mental health: Strengthening our response*. World Health Organization. https://www.who.int/news-room/fact-sheets/mental-health-strengthening-our-response

Chapter 4
The Hype of the Hybrid on Work Culture Compatibility

Mallika Sankar
Christ University, India

Tarannum Malhotra
Christ University, India

ABSTRACT

In the wake of the pandemic, a new working model known as the "hybrid model" has emerged, combining the advantages and disadvantages of both "on-site" and "work from home" cultures to create a balance between the two worlds. This study conducts an in-depth survey of the merits and demerits of diverse working cultures among employees at various hierarchy levels in different industry sectors. Based on the assortment of over 350 white-collar employees working across India in the cultures mentioned earlier, it has been observed that the hype of the hybrid is justified. The study discovered that the majority of the workforce favors the hybrid model, providing the perfect balance between work and personal life. However, this new blend needs to have a better cognizance and acceptance from both the employer and the employee perspectives. The insights would set a benchmark for companies and employees to develop a plan of action.

INTRODUCTION

Covid-19, a significant catastrophe over the past two years, has hampered the socio-economic growth of people all across the globe. Economies have sudden fall, and the governments and the corporate world were struggling to stay afloat. The world has experienced a rather sudden transition from tight labor markets, sustained growth, and scarce talent toward high job instability, growing unemployment, and worrying recessions (Chamorro-Premuzic, 2021). Companies worldwide are in a dilemma to develop a constructive plan of conducive work culture, keeping in mind the safety and interest of the employees without jeopardizing the company's overall growth. Increased job instability, exposure to new modes of working devoid of proper training, domestic compulsions, other financial and non-financial unsteadiness

DOI: 10.4018/978-1-6684-7353-5.ch004

due to the pandemic are fewer difficulties that employees face. Work place culture plays a major role in this context and bring many benefits to both the employees and the organization as a whole. Workplace culture refers to beliefs, attitudes, practices, rules, norms and customs. Ideal workplace culture focuses on activities that generate and demonstrate trust. A strong form of essential values that all employees respect and practice help to build the positivity and effectiveness of a workplace environment. (Beno, 2021). But as of now, as many companies navigate returning to an office in some shape or form, team members are likely contending with vastly different situations. Some have limited or no childcare or are managing their kids' online school; some have health issues that preclude them from returning to in-person work; and some are eager and excited to get out of the house and head back to their cubicles (Knight, 2020). The ever-entangling option of selecting between "On-Site Work Culture" and "Work from Home Culture" has given rise to a new phenomenon called Hybrid Work Culture which amalgamates the pros and cons of both the work cultures to strike a balance between both the Worlds. To make this transition successfully, hybrid work arrangements need to be designed with individual human concerns in mind, not just institutional ones. That requires companies to approach the problem from four different perspectives: (1) jobs and tasks; (2) employee preferences; (3) projects and workflows; and (4) inclusion and fairness (Gratton, 2021). Though a bit successful in foreign lands, this newborn system in India is at a teething stage. It needs to have a better cognizance and acceptance from the perspectives of both - the employer and the employee.

The traditional or the everyday work culture is the 9 am to 5 pm working in a physical space with all the employees of the same company. Once a person enters this stage in their life, it only hustles from thereon. The traditional work environments show higher levels of satisfaction with desk/chair, privacy, storage and general facilities (Appel-Meulenbroek,2015). Where this wasn't enough, the Indian working-class was presented with another much-disliked hurdle, "Change". The role of worker is commonly enacted at a place of work and during specified hours from Monday to Friday, while nonwork roles are typically enacted while one is physically located outside of the office during the evening and weekends (Allen et al., 2014). Earlier. working in the office from 9 to 5 used to be the norm, with companies allowing limited flexibility in where or when employees worked. The pandemic has upended that model, as managers recognize that many employees can work productively anywhere, anytime (Gratton, 2019). A study by the International Workplace Group found that 80% of workers would turn down a job that did not offer a flexible work schedule for one that did, and 76% of workers said they'd consider staying at their current employer if they could work flexible hours (Zucker, 2021).

COVID-19 has intertwined work and nonwork roles in an unprecedented way. Millions of workers have literally brought their work home with them, transforming the home into both home and office (Koetsier, 2020). The year 2019 forcefully entered our lives and ruled over us with an iron throne until the 21st century was struck with a new idea to continue their functionality with a few benefits and charges here and there. Individuals can enact behavioral strategies and create contextual conditions that facilitate their ability to manage boundaries in a way that aligns with their personal preferences (Kossek, 2016; Kossek & Lautsch, 2012; Kreiner, Hollensbe, & Sheep, 2009). The pandemic has reshaped many aspects of our lives, including where and how people want to work. Their experiences working from home, and what they face when they return to the office, have influenced what they want and expect to see in the workplace going forward (Work Better, 2021).

In pure desperation, the companies implemented this ideology one after the other without much questioning. It was like in the time of clinging to the death knell; the businesses were blessed with the face of flexible working hours, reduced expenditure and a possibility of higher prosperity. A report from

Mckinsey conducted among 800 corporate executives indicated that hybrid work pattern will likely be the norm going forward (Stanier et al., 2022). With the fear of uncertainty looming large under the overcast weather of the ongoing Pandemic, the economies have moved southwards, the work cultures have been shattered, and there is unrest and anxiety in the working community. While on the one hand, the Covid 19 crisis has imposed enormous challenges on business organizations, on the other, it necessitated innovations, presenting organizations with opportunities to identify new business models that will allow them to survive through the crisis (Seetharaman, 2020). The lack of a stable, healthy and constructive work environment has led to a downfall in the output and efficiency of the employees, hindering the company's growth and ultimately leading to the economy's collapse. Companies all across the globe are struggling to find a solution to this problem. However, the case of Price Waterhouse Coopers (PwC), a large organization in the consultancy industry, shows that firms can implement hybrid methods without the need to restructure the overall organization. (Magistretti et al., 2019)

While every individual has a different temperament and a defective approach to any situation, it's imperative to analyses this diversity of thoughts minutely and bring everyone on the same ground to work constructively towards one common goal called "Growth". There are good reasons why many companies and employees are excited about this mix of in-person and remote work and equally good reasons why many feel trepidation about the shift (Haas, 2022).

Thus, it is essential to observe the compatibility of the Hybrid model with the traditional Indian Working culture and the various issues faced by employees in the current scenario of working in a Hybrid Model in comparison with their previous traditional work culture. Hence, this research envisions the following objectives, which will further endeavors to assess and provide solutions to mitigate the discrepancies and unsatisfactory performances, to enable a mutually beneficial working environment.

1. To understand the different types of prominent work cultures, their relevance, need, advantages and disadvantages.
2. To understand how well the companies in India have merged their traditional work culture with the pandemic while assessing the justification of the Hype.
3. To compare the pandemic predictions with the current scenario, identify problems and discuss possible solutions.

Globally the various types of work culture are broadly classified into Onsite Work Culture, Work from Home, and Hybrid Work Culture. Understanding these work cultures and their relevance in the current pandemic is essential to comprehend the actual boon derived from the chosen culture. Since the pandemic, companies have adopted the technologies of virtual work remarkably quickly—and employees are seeing the advantages of more flexibility in where and when they work. As leaders recognize what is possible, they are embracing a once-in-a-lifetime opportunity to reset work using a hybrid model (Gratton, 2021). Even so, prior to COVID-19, remote work was an option for only a small percentage of the workforce (Desilver, 2020). Never before has society witnessed a situation in which millions of workers have been forced to transition to remote work across the globe (Merlo, 2020). The agenda of a Hybrid model is only possible through virtual work. Virtual teams allow organizations to leverage high-quality talent from far-flung places and be highly responsive to customer needs (Kirkman, Gibson, & Kim, 2012). When it comes to Hybrid Working, there are two axes to be considered to ensure its successful implementation. Place is the axis that's getting the most attention at the moment. Like Fujitsu's employees, millions of workers around the world this year have made a sudden shift from being place-constrained (working in the office) to being place-unconstrained (Routila, 2021). Perhaps less noticed is the shift many have also made along the time axis, from being time-constrained (working synchronously with others) to being time-unconstrained i.e., working asynchronously whenever they choose (Gratton, 2021). While tackling the new exposure, questions arise like as the leader, how to manage these various circumstances while treating everyone fairly? What protocols can put in place to ensure that the employees in the office are in harmonize with those working from home? How to remain flexible given that plans may change at any moment? And how to help employees manage their stress levels through this transition? (Knight, 2020)

Common boundary management advice to remote workers is to establish a dedicated workspace within the home (e.g., Shockley & Clark, 2020). A home office set up is likely more common for those who plan remote work. However, many who have been thrust into remote work due to the pandemic may lack such a luxury (Merlo, 2020). There's a lot of information that new hires need, from how to work the coffee maker to what the company's strategy is (Klinghoffer et al., 2019). That's why it is empirical that a company should consider assigning the new hire an onboarding "buddy" during their first few months on the job to acquaint the new hire and generate the sense of belonging.

Leaders also need to conceptualize new work arrangements along two axes: place and time. Millions of workers around the world this year have made a sudden shift from being place-constrained (working in the office) to being place-unconstrained (working anywhere). (Merlo, 2020). Many organizations learned in the past year that remote work can be highly effective, with 83% of employers surveyed saying that the shift to remote work has been successful for their company (Zucker, 2021). In addition,54% of workers want to continue working remotely after the pandemic. Now that it's clear where the work is done is not as important as people once thought, the other dimension of flexibility workers crave is the freedom to determine when the work is done (Zucker, 2021).

Onsite Work Culture

Right from the inception of the Employment System, the World has known only this Work Culture. The traditional working culture includes employees assembling in a pre-decided professional and physical place where they collectively perform their respective chores and duties under the supervision of their superiors. Here's how organizational culture might have been handled in the past: The CEO commissions the Human Resources department to produce an effective company culture. HR designs a campaign to tout a mission statement and core values that the CEO and senior management developed (Lee Yohn, 2021). The entire workforce is speculated on time and then leaves for their homes. The central problem is that many of the benefits of working from home are good for the individual, whereas many of the benefits of working from the office are good for the organization and affect the individual more indirectly (Markman, 2021). This work mode has stood strategically relevant, as it prioritizes the behaviors essential to the success of the organization. Such cultures help companies attract and retain great people and contribute to fantastic bottom-line performance (Chatman, 2020). Before the Pandemic struck, the onsite model was all that was acceptable to humanity, as it offered growth and stimulation under the eyes of those with the power to launch your career. The vast increase in remote work caused by the pandemic threatens to weaken even strong corporate cultures (Chatman, 2020). To make sure this doesn't happen, leaders need to make sure their cultures are adaptable and need to practice:

- Hire and promote people who are resilient, adaptable, and show grace in the face of adversity.
- Curate and communicate examples of how the organization is implementing new practices to adhere to its cultural values.
- Exemplify transcendent values.

Saving this culture is rightly so as this model has provided many advantages like:

- It provides a strict working environment for both the employees and the employers to keep track of work, behavior and other essential elements.
- It enables a consistent and disciplined working environment with fewer distractions, letting employees focus on their jobs and work more efficiently. The employees also get a routine life set with no unnecessary obstructions.
- Another on-site bonus is that it is easy for employers to check on the work progress.
- The employees also have ample access to all company resources, which allows them to perform tasks and assignments without any hindrances.
- It also leads to Greater coordination among departments, practical team Work of groups & provides a higher sense of belonging to all recruits.
- Being in an onsite mode, there are decreased chances of insider trading, increased security and data privacy, and the firm is better equipped for cyber-attacks.

But back then, the work profiles included mainly core sector jobs with slight variation. And as time evolved, human needs increased excessively irrespective of income and expenditure. A top-down approach to building company culture no longer works for several reasons. For one, Covid-19 has upended how leaders interact with employees and how coworkers connect with each other (Lee Yohn, 2021). Many new avenues were introduced as job profiles to reduce unemployment and increase job variability. Cities grew more extensive with an ongoing influx of migrants from neighboring places and remote towns to seek better living standards. This had an impact on the Onsite Work Module. It started to lose its sheen because of:

- A marginal increase in the cost of logistics and the never-ending stress levels of commuting from home to work.
- The work evolved so much that it was impossible to only work in a specific time slot. With that, a person's individual and family time was reduced involuntarily.
- There is also more significant intervention from higher authorities and the rigidity of the chain of command.
- Long working hours hamper the employees' creativity and innovation.
- This working model is also vulnerable to numerous disputes and conflicts among the departments or employees.
- It again brings forward a monotonous routine that becomes a liability looming over the team's productivity when combined with other shortcomings.

However, various industry profiles like production, engineering, construction, etc., still require the pre-pandemic conditions where the onsite presence of the employees is imperative. Human Resource being the foremost priority the company's production levels fell marginally due to covid restrictions on employees. The employees' absence led to a downfall of the manufacturing market and a limited product selection for the consumers, with, at times, stock declarations. Since these industry sectors do not have the option of the hybrid working model, they cannot be considered in this study. The sectors chosen for the study are all white-collar employees, where different working models are applicable.

Impact of the Pandemic on Onsite Work Model

If it weren't for the pandemic, a shift to work from home or Hybrid mode wouldn't have been introduced this early to all professions. According to society, the traditional method in India used to be the only viable working option; the stereotype is that only a white-collar implies a high salary and a non-lazy employee. Since westernization happened in our traditional lands, these Ideologies have been getting more rigid and disapproving of new standards and requirements. This concept, however, could not be applied when the pandemic struck.

The pandemic has hastened a rise in remote working for knowledge-based organizations. This has notable benefits: Companies can save on real estate costs, hire and utilize talent globally, mitigate immigration issues, and experience productivity gains, while workers can enjoy geographic flexibility (Choudhury, 2020).

Covid 19 emerged as a pandemic posing a threat worldwide and the governments all across the globe brought in significant work restrictions wherein the employees were asked to work from their homes or some remote locations, and in industries where this type of work was not possible, they were asked to close down. The Onsite Work model suffered a significant setback with the onset of pandemic barring a few necessary industries like healthcare, food and medicine. Apart from this, all other Onsite Work Stations were forced to shut down or work at lesser capacity and even alternately. At the same time, concerns include how to communicate across time zones, share knowledge that isn't yet codified, socialize virtually and prevent professional isolation, protect client data, and avoid slacking (Choudhury, 2020). According to research by Steelcase, people want to get back to the office because they want connection to company purpose, a sense of community and support for their productivity. But the study also finds 87% of business leaders expect to offer more flexibility. In addition, while 23% expect the office to be the primary venue for work, 72% expect a hybrid model of working. (Brower, 2021).

Here are a few questions the survey takers working in an Onsite Mode were asked, with their cumulative answers and analysis. Yes, No, Maybe were the options presented and the percentages represent the no. of employees that selected that option.

In the traditional model, an issue was raised for monotonous and rigid routine posing a threat to creativity and innovation, to which a majority of 41% denied however more were certain and uncertain about the same. Around 46.2% agreed that the professional environment, disciplined working and access to all company resources outweigh the stress of daily commuting whereas a mere 25% said a professional environment is better. However, a majority stood on the fact that Hybrid Mode leads to no demarcation between work space and that it does indeed have a negative impact of the focus and productivity of an employee. Yet a majority says that they would prefer the Hybrid Mode even after the pandemic which presumably is due to comfort levels and a habit to personal environment.

Table 1. Employee perspective: onsite model

S.No.	Statements	In Favor	Against	Neutral
1.	The monotonous and rigid routine of On-Site Mode poses a threat to creativity and innovation	30.8%	41%	28.2%
2.	The professional environment, disciplined working and access to all company resources outweighs the stress of daily commuting.	46.2%	25.6%	28.2%
3.	Hybrid Mode leads to no demarcation between work space; both office and home become working spaces having a negative impact.	46.1%	28.2%	25.6%
4.	Hybrid Mode is overrated	20.5%	56.4%	23.1%
5.	Hybrid mode is the best for structure, sociability, independence and flexibility.	53.8%	15.4%	30.8%
6.	Hybrid Mode helps achieve personal goals better than on-site.	59%	28.2%	12.8%

Work From Home Model

Although the pandemic has intensified the discussion around the pros and cons of working from home, and what working without an office means, it is safe to conclude that the best alternative is not to opt between one or the other, but to give employees the option (Chamorro-premuzic, 2021). Here the employees working in specific sectors were provided with an option to work remotely from any location, provided they complete the given task. Virtual work has been defined in many different ways, but common to these definitions are geographic dispersion and dependence on technology in work-related interactions between employees (Gibson & Gibbs, 2006; Kirkman & Mathieu, 2005; Nilles, 1994; O'Leary & Cummings, 2007; Walther & Bunz, 2005).

Earlier research studies estimated 20% of the employees worked from home before the pandemic. However, the pandemic strike did not leave the other sectors with this option. Spring's abrupt closure of offices and workstations forced the companies to move their operations to an online platform. This indulged the sharp surge in the information technology department as many companies had to set impenetrable digital accounts to keep track of all employees and maintain a progress report. The category of work that can be shifted to home depends not only upon the nature of the work but also on cross-country heterogeneity. Occupations related to hospitality and tourism have a more difficult time shifting into a WFH mode, while software development, banking, and financial services are the occupations that appear to be the easiest to adapt to a WFH situation (Jean-Victor et al., 2020).

The Onsite Work Model was losing popularity even before the pandemic, with its demerits overweighing its merits. With ever-evolving human needs, a new spectrum of work profiles had come into the picture, which did not require the employees to be physically present at the worksite. It was noticed that their working from remote locations away from the disciplined and professional office space did not hamper their progress. With the evolution and advancements in technologies like performance appraisal software, online financial analysis terminals, data sharing through cloud computing and monitoring software, this model commenced with flying colors. It overcame many obstacles of onsite working like,

- There is no stressful commuting back and forth between home and office in remote working. The employees are to stay at their homes or any place they wish to, provided it does not hamper their work life. Almost 70% of the survey takers agree with this advantage.

- The above reason also deducts the opportunity cost of the employee of all travelling expenses of extensive distances.
- Work from home is also the perfect model for more family time, a sense of happiness, and security.
- The flexibility of working hours is another bounty point for all employees. Specific deadlines are set, but the timeframe is flexible, increasing creativity and leading to better judgment.
- Staying in their comfort zones, employees' performance and output levels are boosted, and job satisfaction heightens.

While it is undeniable that a remote work model would lead to the success and growth of many, but cannot ignore the fact that it does not suit for all types of organizations. The service sector especially might face many difficulties if shifted online wholly. Some studies suggest that a WFH arrangement provides freedom and flexibility to the employees to plan when, where, and how they work (Putnam & Mumby, 2016), resulting in less commuting time and more family time. Blurred lines between work and home (Giruge & Vanessa, 2020), increased care giving duties due to the closure of schools, and less than optimal time to set up communication infrastructures at home (Hoffman et al., 2020). Earlier studies describe WFH as an inter-role conflict between work and private life, in which pressures from both work and private life are incompatible (Chawla et al., 2020; Greenhaus & Beutell, 1985). There are other reasons companies opt for a work-from-home model; for instance, content writers do not necessarily require a fixed professional space for their work. The responses of survey takers who have worked remotely have been asking for the grounds on which their respective companies have opted for WFH mode and not a Hybrid or Onsite.

- "The Client-Service provider interfaces are cumbersome online and create misunderstandings."
- "Work from home model is adding more profits to the company due to savings on procurement cost, electricity and rental expenses,"
- "Planning and implementing new changes are not easy. Currently, WFH is more effective and successful."

The challenges of this model since many believe that the opportunity cost of forgoing overhead office expenditure is nothing compared to the loss of efficiency and productivity of employees. Some studies suggest the downside of WFH include the loss of a sense of workplace belongingness leading to a reduction in productivity (Bertschek & Niebel, 2016). The limitations would be:

- More than 50% of the survey takers say that the first and foremost bane is that the companies overburden their employees with work due to flexible hours.
- The same survey takers believe that another significant hindrance is making effective collaboration with coworkers. This also results in stagnant growth as peers have no competitive environment or motivation.
- The employees are prone to laziness, and extensive isolation from social contact can cause mental issues.
- There exists a more considerable dilemma in keeping track of employees' work progress online and the ordeal of creating a sense of belonging for the employees without any strong work relations.

- Others have threatened repeated interruption from family members and time management, while a few believe that none of the above issues is problematic.

Impact of the Pandemic on Remote Work Model

As we have established, the COVID-19 has brought about a major change in the world's workings, especially in the business context. Before the pandemic, only 6% of the employed worked primarily from home. Whereas as soon as the pandemic hit the shore, all companies, irrespective of the nature of their business, shut down operations temporarily. Pressured companies took their obligations home and created a network for their employees to work from a distance. About 100% of the White-collar employees were coerced into continuing their corporate activities from the comfort of their own homes. Due to the prolonged period where manufacturing companies could not continue their business, in 2019-20 fiscal, about 3,380 companies had wound up their operations. As per Ministry of Corporate Affairs (MCA) data, the highest number of companies dissolved in Haryana was 436 compared with Punjab (315) and Himachal Pradesh (192). Below is a cumulative table of questions and responses from the survey takers working in a work from home mode.

Table 2. Employee perspective: WFH model

S.No.	Statements	In Favor	Against	Neutral
1.	Employees are facing problems while accessing training and development to stay up to date with the evolving working styles.	15.5%	65.2%	19.3%
2.	Work From Home helps better achieve personal goals than Hybrid	40.9%	40.9%	18.2%
3.	Less cost of operations and access to distant and diversified talent outweighs the danger of data theft and Insider trading	23.8%	38.1%	38.1%
4.	Hybrid Mode is overrated in the industry	11.6%	69.1%	19.3%
5.	Hybrid mode is the best for structure, sociability, independence and flexibility	61.3%	12.2%	26.5%

The issue was raised about employees facing problems accessing training and development to stay up to date with the evolving working styles. A majority of white-collar employees answered that they faced no issue at all. However, a significant group of employees posed that they were unsure and faced issues in the technical department. A few of the remote working employees have opined that their organization would place better in the market if they were to shift their working style to a onsite model. We can also notice from the above-collected data that a majority of (62%) of the remote workers have established that the Hybrid model indeed provides the benefit of balancing between structure, sociability, independence and flexibility. Hence, again, the majority consider it a practical approach to working systems, whereas a mere 12% of employees consider it overrated. If we were to take a stand on which mode helps achieve personal goals better, the employees do not see much change due to either mode.

Hybrid Mode

Hybrid working is the combination of working both from an office and from home wherever the roles will allow and wherever they work best, Greater control on working styles and flexibility at work are the core reasons to choose hybrid working model in organizations. (Ateeq, n.d.). Pandemic forced employers to adapt a new way of working that keeps employees' safety in check and does not marginally hamper productivity and efficiency. The new model consists of a mixture of the above two models discussed. Here the employer's half combined remote and on-site work to solve their problem. The past decades have been marked by a rapid increase in the availability of technological tools that have changed where we work and the way by which work is done (Olson-Buchanan, Boswell, & Morgan, 2016). This has incredibly helped in setting a strong base for the successful implementation of Hybrid culture.

The employers and the employees are perplexed about developing a working environment that suits the entire working class. Whereas a 100% Onsite workforce ensures high efficiency and productivity, it puts the employees at greater risk of infection due to proximity and physical touch. On the other hand, a work from home routine offers safe and flexible working hours to the employees, negates professional communication, and checks on the workings of the employee and the overall work efficiency. The upper management was compelled to think of a solution that combines the plus points of both the working models and tries to upstroke as many limitations as possible. Hence, the Hybrid model was born. In India, many companies, discarded the mandatory five-day work-from-office norm in favor of flexible work model for certain segments of the workforce such as hybrid working, permanent remote working, and work-from-home (WFH) with fixed hours. This model is relatively apparent and the frequent visits to the office ensure decorum, performance tracking providing effective control. Advantages that the survey takers have responded to are:

- The freedom to work anytime, anywhere and lesser stressful commuting
- Helps break the monotonous routine and consistent restricted environment
- Fewer distractions from colleagues combined with heightened creativity and innovation leading to increased employee productivity
- Increased employee engagement as they get the perfect mix of family, home comfort and work life.
- Spending more time with family has also marginally increased, which has led to boost job satisfaction for all the above reasons.

Like every coin has two sides, so does the perfect Hybrid Mode. In the era of Covid-19, the hybrid workplace one in which some employees are co-located in an office and others are doing their jobs remotely presents a number of challenges for managers (Knight, 2020). Our respondents have gone ahead and picked a few drawbacks that they have experienced while practicing the same:

- Overworked or even burnt-out employees as there are no time limits in a day
- There is a lack of belongingness and motivation that an employee usually gets from working alongside friends and colleagues.
- No competitive and restricted environment has led the employees to be prone to laziness and procrastination.
- Difficulty in keeping track of work progress and in maintaining working relationships

- Extensive social isolation can hamper employee mental health alongside the constant interruption from family members
- Lastly, there exists a greater vulnerability to cyber-attacks.

The management needs to create practices that ensure employees in the office are in line with those working from home, and also build fairness and flexibility into the workflow (Knight, 2021). According to a study by the Society for Human Resource Management, two-thirds of employers are struggling to maintain employee morale, and more than one-third are facing challenges maintaining company culture (Brower, 2021). Many companies have designed a buddy program where an old employee is partnered with a new hire to enable a smooth organizational transition. However, one can never overcome all the drawbacks of a working model.

The way Hybrid Mode Cuts off the challenges of the other two Modes:

- It helps establish the perfect balance between work and family.
- Stimulates a balance between a lazy and professional environment.
- Breaks the monotonous routine
- Helps equally focus on organizational and personal goals
- Tones down the level of interference from the upper management while ensuring a better product flow.
- It also helps even out the impact of a competitive work environment.

Below is a cumulative table of questions and responses from the survey takers working in a Hybrid Mode. Yes, No, Maybe were the options presented and the percentages represent the no. of employees that selected that option.

Table 3. Employee perspective: Hybrid model

S.No.	Statements	In Favor	Against	Neutral
1.	Hybrid Mode has increased the need for Cyber Security	78.5%	11.5%	10%
2.	Hybrid Mode is preferred by many even after the pandemic ends	70%	8%	22%
3.	Hybrid Mode makes no distinction between workspace; office and home become working spaces and may have a negative impact	40%	28.5%	31.5%
4.	Hybrid Mode is overrated	8.6%	73.2%	18.2%
5.	Hybrid mode is the best for structure, sociability, independence and flexibility	53.3%	13.2%	35.5%

The most prominent cyber-attacks in hybrid mode observed are malware attacks, insider trading, information hacks, security breach and phishing attacks. The biggest threats to cyber security in hybrid mode that companies face is negligent employees, weak cyber security policies, non-tech savvy employees, weak passwords, and vulnerable communication platforms.

CONCLUSION

At present, the economy is facing a sudden splurge due to the downside of the previous years and is back to yet another predicted recession. With due attention, the corporate world has yet again warmed up and adopted the Hybrid work arrangements, combining in-person and remote work. Though this has marginally helped organizations in saving costs and better utilization of resources, the problem arisen as the virtual world does not treat roles and tasks equally. While hybrid work model has many potential benefits, such as increased flexibility and reduced commuting time, it can also have drawbacks, particularly in terms of workplace culture compatibility. Finally, the hype around hybrid work models has brought to light the importance of workplace culture compatibility in ensuring the success of such models. Organizations that embrace hybrid work must carefully take steps to ensure that the remote workers are included in company culture and that they feel connected to their in-person colleagues. This can be achieved through regular communication, team-building activities, and a focus on inclusivity. Employers must ensure that their culture and values are aligned with the needs and preferences of their hybrid workforce to foster collaboration, productivity, and employee satisfaction. Moreover, companies must acknowledge that hybrid work is not suitable for every role or every employee. Some positions require in-person collaboration and interaction, while others can be done entirely remotely. Employers must assess each job individually and determine whether hybrid work is appropriate or not. It is also essential to provide employees with the necessary tools and resources to work effectively in a hybrid environment. By doing so, companies can leverage the benefits of hybrid work models, such as increased flexibility and access to talent, while maintaining a positive and inclusive workplace culture. Ultimately, the success of the hybrid work model depends on a careful balance between technology, communication, and culture.

REFERENCES

Allen, M. S., Walter, E. E., McDermott, M. S., Kaur, J., & Rosenbaum, D. A. (2014). The effects of mindfulness meditation training on multitasking in a high-stress information environment. *Proceedings of the Human Factors and Ergonomics Society Annual Meeting*, *58*(1), 2296–2300. doi:10.1177/1541931214581445

Appel-Meulenbroek, R. (2015). The physical environment and user behaviour. In P. Forsyth & D. Huguenin (Eds.), *The Routledge Handbook of Transport Economics* (pp. 191–203). Routledge.

Ateeq, K. (n.d.). *Hybrid Working Method: An Integrative Review. Hybrid Working Method: An Integrative Review.* Retrieved July 24, 2022, from https://ieeexplore.ieee.org/abstract/document/9759041

Beno, M. (2021, September 5). On-Site and Hybrid Workplace Culture of Positivity and Effectiveness: Case Study from Austria. *Academic Journal of Interdisciplinary Studies*. Retrieved from https://www.richtmann.org/journal/index.php/ajis/article/view/12658

Bertschek, I., & Niebel, T. (2016). *The impact of broadband internet on the economy: Final report for the European Commission*. ZEW-Centre for European Economic Research.

Brower, A. M. (2021). *The challenges of creating and maintaining company culture during the pandemic.* Society for Human Resource Management. https://www.shrm.org/resourcesandtools/hr-topics/employee-relations/pages/the-challenges-of-creating-and-maintaining-company-culture-during-the-pandemic.aspx

Chamorro-Premuzic, T. (2021). Why hybrid work is the future of work. *Harvard Business Review*, *99*(1), 18–20.

Chatman, J. A. (2020, December 9). Building corporate culture in a remote-work world. *Harvard Business Review*. https://hbr.org/2020/12/building-corporate-culture-in-a-remote-work-world

Chawla, N., Sarkar, S., & Sharma, I. (2020). Work from Home and Inter-role Conflict: A Study of Indian Working Women. *Journal of Work and Organizational Psychology*, *36*(2), 135–143.

Choudhury, S. R. (2020). Remote work is here to stay. Benefits and challenges. *Financial Times*. https://www.ft.com/content/4b0fe724-67d9-11ea-a3c9-1fe6fedcca75

Desilver, D. (2020, April 24). *Unemployment rose higher in three months of COVID-19 than it did in two years of the Great Recession*. Pew Research Center. https://www.pewresearch.org/fact-tank/2020/04/24/unemployment-rose-higher-in-three-months-of-covid-19-than-it-did-in-two-years-of-the-great-recession/

Gibson, C. B., & Gibbs, J. L. (2006). Unpacking the concept of virtuality: The effects of geographic dispersion, electronic dependence, dynamic structure, and national diversity on team innovation. *Administrative Science Quarterly*, *51*(3), 451–495. doi:10.2189/asqu.51.3.451

Giruge, F. V., & Vanessa, S. (2020). *How Working from Home during COVID-19 Affects Parental Stress*. Social Science Research Network.

Gratton, L. (2019). Agile working: How to do it. *Strategic HR Review*, *18*(3), 151–156. doi:10.1108/SHR-02-2019-0025

Greenhaus, J. H., & Beutell, N. J. (1985). Sources of conflict between work and family roles. *Academy of Management Review*, *10*(1), 76–88. doi:10.2307/258214

Griffis, H. (2022, June 2). *What Is a Hybrid Work Model, and How Do We Make It Work?* Built In. https://builtin.com/remote-work/hybrid-work-model

Hoffman, M., Litzky, B. E., & Jain, A. (2020). *Workforce Reduction and Remote Work: Implications for Job Quality and Income Inequality*. Social Science Research Network.

Jean-Victor, A., Bendavid, Y., Fouksman, O., & Milgrom, E. (2020). The cross-country shift to home-based work and its implications for the future of work. *Journal of Public Economics*, *189*, 104270. doi:10.1016/j.jpubeco.2020.104270

Kirkman, B. L., Gibson, C. B., & Kim, K. (2012). Across borders and technologies: Advancements in virtual teams research. *Advances in Global Leadership*, *7*, 251–288. doi:10.1093/oxfordhb/9780199928286.013.0025

Kirkman, B. L., & Mathieu, J. E. (2005). The dimensions and antecedents of team virtuality. *Journal of Management*, *31*(5), 700–718. doi:10.1177/0149206305279113

Knight, R. (2021). *Hybrid workforces are the future. Here's how to make them successful*. World Economic Forum. https://www.weforum.org/agenda/2021/03/hybrid-workforces-are-the-future-heres-how-to-make-them-successful/

Koetsier, J. (2020, April 6). 4 ways remote work is changing tech salaries. *Forbes*. Retrieved from https://www.forbes.com/sites/johnkoetsier/2020/04/06/4-ways-remote-work-is-changing-tech-salaries/?sh=4c4d46261f0f

Kossek, E. E., & Lautsch, B. A. (2012). Work–life flexibility for whom? Occupational status and work–life inequality in upper, middle, and lower level jobs. *The Sociological Quarterly*, *53*(3), 282–314. doi:10.1111/j.1533-8525.2012.01248.x

Kreiner, G. E., Hollensbe, E. C., & Sheep, M. L. (2009). Balancing borders and bridges: Negotiating the work-home interface via boundary work tactics. *Academy of Management Journal*, *52*(4), 704–730. doi:10.5465/amj.2009.43669916

Lee Yohn. (2021). Culture is not a campaign. *Forbes*. https://www.forbes.com/sites/leeyohn/2021/03/30/culture-is-not-a-campaign/?sh=1f6469a37481

Magistretti, S., Trabucchi, D., Dell'Era, C., & Buganza, T. (2019). A new path toward a hybrid model: Insights from PwC's Italian experience Centre. *Research Technology Management*, *62*(5), 30–37. doi: 10.1080/08956308.2019.1638223

Markman, A. (2021, January 27). How to weigh the benefits and drawbacks of working from home. *Harvard Business Review*. https://hbr.org/2021/01/how-to-weigh-the-benefits-and-drawbacks-of-working-from-home

McKinsey & Company. (2022, May 27). *COVID-19: Implications for business*. https://www.mckinsey.com/business-functions/risk-and-resilience/our-insights/covid-19-implications-for-business

Nilles, J. M. (1994). The geography of telecommuting. In J. Fulk & C. Steinfield (Eds.), *Organizations and communication technology* (pp. 243–264). Sage.

O'Leary, M. B., & Cummings, J. N. (2007). The spatial, temporal, and configurational characteristics of geographic dispersion in work teams. *Management Information Systems Quarterly*, *31*(3), 433–452. doi:10.2307/25148802

Olson-Buchanan, J., Boswell, W. R., & Morgan, B. B. (2016). The future of work: The role of technology in reshaping the nature of work. In P. L. Perrewé, J. R. B. Halbesleben, & C. C. Rosen (Eds.), *The role of technology in workplace stress, health, and well-being* (pp. 9–36). Emerald Group Publishing Limited.

Putnam, L. L., & Mumby, D. K. (2016). *Organizations and Organizing: Rational, Natural and Open Systems Perspectives*. Routledge.

Seetharaman, P. (2020). Business models shifts: Impact of Covid-19. *International Journal of Information Management*, *54*, 102173. doi:10.1016/j.ijinfomgt.2020.102173 PMID:32834338

Shockley, K. M., & Clark, M. A. (2020). Psychological safety in remote teams: The role of task complexity. *Journal of Business and Psychology*, *35*(6), 761–774. doi:10.100710869-019-09647-z

Stanier, J., Li, M., & Anderson, J. (2022, March 16). What Great Hybrid Cultures Do Differently. *Harvard Business Review*. https://hbr.org/2022/03/what-great-hybrid-cultures-do-differently

Walther, J. B., & Bunz, U. (2005). The rules of virtual groups: Trust, liking, and performance in computer-mediated communication. *Journal of Communication*, *55*(4), 828–846. doi:10.1111/j.1460-2466.2005.tb03025.x

Work Better. (2021, January 11). *Steelcase*. www.steelcase.com. https://www.steelcase.com/research/articles/work-better/?utm_source=forbes&utm_medium=tb-article&utm_campaign=work-better&utm_term=work-better-article

Zucker, J. (2021, March 2). The next big thing in employee benefits: Flexibility. *Forbes*. Retrieved from: https://www.forbes.com/sites/forbeshumanresourcescouncil/2021/03/02/the-next-big-thing-in-employee-benefits-flexibility/?sh=31c5588e2105

Chapter 5
The Luxury Stores of the Future:
The Impact of Technology on the Relationship Between Consumers and the Brand's Staff

Leonor Diogo
Universidade Católica Portuguesa, Portugal

ABSTRACT

The growing investment and interest of leading brands in the applicability of digital transformation strategies seeks to respond to the high expectations of a consumer profile that is progressively more informed and consequently more detailed. Consumers, as we know them today, demand effective monitoring in their relationship with brands, adapted to each profile, increasingly based on a digital universe. The level of connectivity registered by customers demonstrates the adoption of an always-on behavior in line with the lifestyle and pace of life of the majority. This chapter intends to explore the impact and influence of technology on the consumer experience in physical stores of brands in the luxury sector, as well as identify technological and digital trends that contribute to a more interesting and successful relationship between consumers and the staff that accompanies them.

INTRODUCTION

The changing environment surrounding the luxury sector was accentuated with the most recent phenomena that we have witnessed. The Covid-19 pandemic tested the resistance of retail and physical spaces, causing strong economic and social consequences. This new reality forced brands to adapt and sharply accelerated the growth of their online channels in view of its characteristics, making this option essential for consumption. In this way, the chapter "The luxury stores of the future: the impact of technology on the relationship between consumers and sales advisors" intends to understand the effects of digital transformation in a physical store environment in luxury retail, having as main objectives: to analyze and understand how digital transformation can affect and influence the consumer experience

DOI: 10.4018/978-1-6684-7353-5.ch005

in physical stores of brands in the luxury sector, as well as identify technological and digital trends that contribute to a more appealing and attractive experience in store giving the staff tools that enrich the clients experiences.

From this study, it is intended to project possible trends in the digital aspect within the scope of its implementation in the channel that is assumed to be irreplaceable in the luxury area: the physical channel. The collection and analysis of data seek to support an objective and clear reflection on the path that is being followed by brands in Portugal and in which directions they tend to evolve.

Digital transformation is seen by the consumers as necessary and as a symbol of modernity, but its importance during their physical store experiences varies. Its benefits are not unanimous, but the value that consumers attribute to the efficiency and agility that technology can bring to the service that brands provide is clear. Hyperpersonalization is also highlighted as a differentiating factor for the applicability of technological and digital elements in luxury physical stores, enabling the fulfillment of consumers' desires.

Observing the luxury sector and its particularities with regard to the progressive digitization of communication and interaction with consumers, it is possible to verify that the data collected through automated digital mechanisms serve as the basis for the exclusive service and as they provide. Keeping the human factor of the staff in physical stores, luxury brands intend to use different technological innovations to improve the consumer experience, always reinforcing a deep and intimate connection with their preferences. In the case of the luxury sector, it reinforces the importance of providing the staff of these brands with as much information as possible, articulated with the objectives of the brand and with a strategic direction outlined which must have the consumer and their satisfaction as a central point.

BACKGROUND

Firstly, it's relevant to address the impact of digital transformation within the scope of the relationship between brands in the luxury sector and their consumers. The commitment of businesses to a digital adaptation that synchronizes with consumer behavior provides, as a consequence, an improvement in sales, an optimized presence and a reinforcement of differentiation as current brands. In this perspective, digital transformation enhances the relationship between brands and consumers and allows for more effective acquisition and retention (Kapferer et al., 2017).

The knowledge acquired by the brands about their customers was, until very recently, retained by the ambassadors and employees of these brands. The natural expansion of the businesses had an impact on the increase and diversification of the teams that had direct access to consumers, and it became essential to centralize and capture all the information that they collected to date in a safe and more evolved universe.

The digital transformation thus represents an added value for brands, as it allows the capture of real-time data about their customers and their behavior. In this way, the brands have valuable information about the different customer profiles that follow and visit them, managing through this knowledge to provide impactful and lasting memories and emotions for each one of them (Chamorro-Premuzic, 2021).

There are, therefore, improvements which greatly impact not only the business itself of any brand, but fundamentally the consumer's perception of these same brands. The improvement in customer response, in terms of time and content, is notorious and quite significant (Reinartz et al., 2018).

In this way, the relationship between brands and consumers has been stimulated through different dimensions in the context of digital transformation. Standing out in the universe of consumer experience are the optimized and transparent customer support processes across different channels, as well as the permanent availability offered by the brands.

Complementarily, personalized service is also extremely important for a successful consumer experience and has been the subject of significant improvements from digital techniques based on the data collected (Sahu, Deng & Mollah, 2018).

In the case of the luxury sector, it reinforces the importance of providing the staff of these brands with as much information as possible, articulated with the objectives of the brand and with a strategic direction that must have the consumer and their satisfaction as a central point. The personalization and curation of products and services provided within this sector characterize its essence and underlying approach towards its consumers (Clarke, 2021).

The underlying advantages of digital transformation are appealing when it comes to the luxury sector. From a more practical and utilitarian point of view, emphasis should be placed on the convenience that new technologies represent for brand staff, allowing a more qualified service through quicker stock checks or access to the product catalog and even greater knowledge of the background and consumer profile. In addition, these new digital technologies have an impact on the interaction with customers of luxury brands, adding value to a purchase process that is already differentiating, as the sector demands (Holmqvist, Wirtz & Fritze, 2020).

The service provided by staff in physical stores is seen as fundamental in the consumer experience, especially in a physical store that is distinguished precisely by the human factor, "The behavior of the staff influences customers' experiences in a variety of ways; for instance their willingness to help and their professional knowledge and skills, as well as their attitude and ways of treating in-store customers" (Backstrom and Johansson, 2017, p. 250).

The entry of brands in the luxury sector into the digital age has been managed gradually and cautiously. Even so, consumer expectations are increasingly high, imposing an adapted purchasing process on brands, in synergy with the online channel, which has stood out in recent years as essential (Klaus, 2020). These new ambitions of the consumers can also be seen as a post COVID-19 consequence, as customers have become familiar with the online channel and its amenities and now return to the physical store more aware of the technological features that facilitate a purchase. Observing the current context of retail and the in-store experience of luxury brands, it is increasingly noticeable the implementation of various digital elements and it's future is still very open and full of possibilities.

MAIN FOCUS OF THE CHAPTER

The aim of this investigation is to understand the effects of digital transformation in a physical store environment in luxury retail, identifying as main objectives: to analyze and understand how digital transformation can affect and influence the consumer experience in physical stores of brands in the luxury sector, as well as identifying the technological and digital trends that contribute to a more complex and interesting relationship between both parties involved: consumers and staff. These responses must be obtained following the methodological strategy selected, thus making it possible to present the current scenario regarding digitization in luxury physical spaces, as well as project the future considering the perspectives of the sample included in this investigation.

METHODOLOGICAL APPROACH

The approach followed to collect and interpret data related with the subject in question is a qualitative research design contemplating a process of reflection about the results obtained (Maxwell, 2005).

Regarding the objectives of this article, an attempt was made to identify and verify the implications of the phenomenon of digital transformation in the consumer experience in physical stores, starting from two essential dimensions for the present study: luxury brands and their consumers. It is also important to expose the current state of retail after the pandemic in order to establish new behaviors, necessities and approaches.

In this context, one major research question arise that surround this issue:

- How can the digital transformation affect and influence the consumer experience in the physical stores of brands in the luxury sector?

Initially, the methodological study was enumerated and faced with this question, a qualitative approach was chosen for data collection through interviews. This technique allowed an overview of the perspectives within the two dimensions under analysis: brands and luxury consumers. Starting from a unique context, the portuguese reality, it was intended to understand and interpret the perception of the phenomenon of digital transformation and how it influences the relationship between brands and their consumers.

The sample used includes the perspective of 10 luxury consumers and, simultaneously, that of 5 luxury brands. The luxury consumers selected for this investigation meet two requirements defined for the implementation of the interviews carried out, being that they are, in their entirety, resident in Portugal, and have a consumption history that includes at least 3 of the brands interviewed within the scope of this theme. On the other hand, the luxury brands addressed in this investigation form a heterogeneous group within the luxury sector, with different business areas also contributing to a comprehensive view of reality with the specifics of each company. The following portuguese luxury brands were interviewed: Vista Alegre, Castelbel, Dara Jewels, Quartier Latin and Mariano Shoes.

The Vista Alegre brand, founded in 1824, is recognized nationally and internationally for its creations in porcelain and crystal, elevating the luxury sector in terms of creativity and rigor combined with quality and tradition. It is awarded consecutively for the design of its releases and represents Portuguese know-how in different markets, globally, through porcelain and crystal lines that include classic traits, but increasingly combined with innovative and contemporary lines. The Portuguese brand highlights sophistication, rigor and versatility as key values, uniting history and modernity in its production. Evolution is notorious and the brand has already expanded across borders with different collaborations with impactful names in international design, thus granting even more exclusivity and differentiation to its offer. In addition, the brand also offers a personalization service upon request and has its collectors' club in operation, which brings together the most loyal and special customers of the brand. In order to understand how this century-old brand approaches the technology and its impact on the business we interviewed the current Chief Digital Officer of Vista Alegre, Carla Graça.

Secondly Castelbel, the brand that produces and sells perfumed soaps, fragrances and body care products, with over twenty years of production. It is recognized for the quality of its completely unique aromas in the market, being created in detail and tailored to the brand and its values. Castelbel seeks to convey traditional elements in its products by spreading its handcrafted production. The offer is characterized by collections with different elements related to Portuguese culture such as filigree, sardines or tiles. The brand already has a presence in more than fifty countries and a surprising turnover that exceeds 10 million euros annually. The interview with the brand was granted by the current head of Marketing and Communication for the brand, André Castro.

Then, the Dara Jewels brand was included, which opened its first physical store in 1980, starting at that time its journey in Portuguese luxury jewelry. This family-owned business values the customization of the jewels it makes available, accompanying customers in an adapted and molded way to each need. They are characterized by the variety of jewelry services they offer and promote the exclusivity of their products. The interview included in this dissertation was conducted with the brand's current Marketing manager, David Gomes.

The Mariano Shoes brand is historic in the area of national shoemaking, having started its activity in 1945. Its business is recognized for its craftsmanship, with all shoes produced following strict quality verification steps, contributing to an excellent result. Mariano Shoes also stands out for its concern with the materials it uses, choosing ecological solutions with a reduced environmental impact. The current executive director of the brand, Fátima Oliveira, was interviewed.

Finally, the sample of Portuguese luxury brands includes Quartier Latin, a second-hand luxury fashion business. The brand opened its first physical store in Porto in 2010 with a vast collection of renowned national and international brands. The commercialized parts are carefully selected and present quality maintenance conditions. The interview was conducted with the founder of the brand, Isadora Fevereiro.

All these interviews happened during the months of May and June of 2022 gathering the current state of the brand's strategy at this precise moment. Based on the responses collected from consumers and luxury brands, it was possible to understand and trace the current context of both parties regarding the digital transformation and its implementation in physical stores.

Consumers register different experiences regarding the impact of technology but consider the physical channel as irreplaceable for now, especially when talking about the luxury sector, and it is essential to maintain this point as a differentiator for the relationship with the clients. The human factor persists as an essential element regardless of technological evolution, consumers valuing the personalized support provided by the brand's employees.

RESULTS

Focusing on the prime question of this subject that intends to explore how can the digital transformation affect and influence the consumer experience in the physical stores of brands in the luxury sector there were four central themes that monopolized the interpretation and development of the results: the impact of the integration of digital technologies in stores with the subtopics advantages and disadvantages; the existence of human staff; entertainment in physical stores and the physicality of retail.

THE IMPACT OF THE INTEGRATION OF DIGITAL TECHNOLOGIES IN STORES: ADVANTAGES AND DISADVANTAGES

Consumers, when asked about the possible impact that technologies and digital elements could have on their experiences in physical stores, point out some advantages in the face of these elements. In one case, digital elements are praised because they facilitate the process in store and navigation in space. It is also attributed to these elements the ability to generate confidence and security among the final consumers.

On the other hand, the integration of digital technologies in stores also simultaneously symbolizes some disadvantages for consumers, even registering a feeling of duality when facing their presence because they feel overwhelmed by the sensation of digitization in the spaces they visit.

THE EXISTENCE OF HUMAN STAFF

The second theme follows, which is directly related to the existence of human staff in physical stores. During the interviews, this was a point highlighted by some of the interviewees, with several stating the importance of its presence, especially in the luxury sector.

Consumers reinforce that they expect personalized service in the luxury sector to mark their experience. The staff thus plays a fundamental role in the consumer's journey, reinforcing the interviewees that the human character is still, in their view, irreplaceable.

Comparing the existence of human staff with digital elements, consumers point out that there are barriers that have not been overcome, praising the follow-up that the store teams provide as incomparable.

Nevertheless, the existence of a team formed and knowledgeable of the brand it represents was praised, demonstrating confidence and know-how when selling. Consumers also pointed out that technology can be an important ally for the staff in the luxury sector giving teams more information and knowledge on the spot and making possible to answer and attend to consumers in more active and complete way.

Even so, it should be noted that one of the consumers mentioned that the insistence on the part of the members of these teams can sometimes act as an obstacle to a good consumer experience, becoming intrusive and having the opposite effect.

ENTERTAINMENT IN PHYSICAL STORES

During the content analysis of the interviews applied to luxury consumers, a third theme of the implementation of digital elements in physical stores that function as entertainment providers in the environment of physical stores was identified. In a product promotion logic, it can be considered an impactful approach according to one of the consumers interviewed during the methodological application.

However, and from the perspective of one of the interviewees, entertainment techniques can be interpreted as something little aligned with the luxury sector since consumers associate the sector with sober and restricted environments.

Additionally, another consumer shares that this type of content is, in his opinion, more present in brands from sectors other than luxury, having observed digital elements applied in mass market stores.

PHYSICALITY OF RETAIL

Finally, the last topic concerns the physicality of luxury retail and its importance. According to the collected content, several consumers emphasize the value that the existence of a physical space has for a relevant positioning in the luxury sector. For these consumers, the experience involves sensations and emotions that cannot be replicated in exclusively digital environments. Purchases in this sector are therefore preferably carried out in the physical space of the brand, with luxury goods themselves being perceived as different compared to the rest.

The experience lived in a physical store in the luxury sector is relevant for consumers, reinforcing that despite the recognition of the importance of a physical space, interconnection with the digital space is also possible.

Observing the first research question, we can conclude that consumers can benefit from digital transformation. Starting from the collected content, the exaltation of technology as a complement is notorious and its utilitarian and functional character is reinforced.

In the future, technology seems to represent an added value for consumers in terms of optimizing and improving operating procedures in physical stores. These emphasize characteristics such as agility, quickness and interactivity, these tools being used by the staff as assets for a better service (Clarke, 2021).

In general, consumers do not praise the digital transformation as a determining factor for completing a purchase, but rather because of modernity and even as an effort by brands to keep up with trends.

The in-store experience continues to be associated with emotions and sensations, as consumers value the essence of luxury brands and seek to experience something unique and different in the physical spaces of this sector (Atwal & Williams, 2009).

DISCUSSION

The knowledge obtained through the methodological strategy developed gave an overview of the perception of consumers and luxury brands in the portuguese context in the face of digitalization.

Even so, and considering the research carried out, it is possible to identify, in addition to the foreseeable limitations of a qualitative methodology, an obstacle that is related to the time factor of the work. The research presents the current and current view of the phenomenon explored and with the galloping evolution of digitization and society itself, there are perspectives and scenarios that can change.

The future, considering the portuguese context, is still uncertain in terms of digital transformation, and the adoption of technological elements by brands is not uniform. It is also visible the disagreement between luxury consumers regarding technology and its impact on their experiences. However, the importance and relevance of the physical channel in luxury is a point of consensus for both dimensions studied, brands and consumers, reinforcing these that digital, despite the different advantages it brings, still cannot combat the experience in store. The human presence remains indisputable and necessary from the perspective of consumers. These clients still value the relationship between them and the staff as well the sense of security that they bring, enhancing their existence and refusing, for the time being, their replacement by digital elements in the brands' physical environments. From the feedback collected from the interviewed consumers, the set of technological tools already created that promise to mimic human behavior and, therefore, make the presence of people unnecessary proposed by Kotler, Kartajaya and

Setiawan (2021) seems to be still a long way off. Still, consumers find advantages in technological tools that seem to bring different insights, innovation and modernity to physical stores and their experiences.

Online consumption currently represents a convenience and satisfies needs, but even so, and for purchases in the luxury sector, the existence of a physical store continues to be required and is often associated with a symbol of safety for consumers when they are shopping of high values.

Finally, it may be relevant, starting from the research base presented, to deepen the impact of the digital transformation phenomenon including a direct comparison with a global and broader sample. The digital transformation is felt worldwide, and it is important to understand the pace of its applicability in different cultures. In terms of technological evolution, it would also be advantageous to include the perspective of the staff of the brands of the sector to gather both sides of the theme. The teams that work directly with consumers instore would be able to pass on their vision on the entry of technological elements and the impact that these have on their performance and on the relationship, they have with their customers.

CONCLUSION

The luxury consumers interviewed reinforce the importance of the physical space, which is still considered irreplaceable for different reasons, since there are still barriers that digital does not overcome, especially in terms of experience. However, it is consolidated that technology can represent added value in terms of the operation of the brands themselves, thus providing a more complete and effective service. Thus, technology is referred to as a valuable complement to a lasting and fruitful relationship between brands and luxury consumers.

The physical store experience is essential, and consumers are looking for experiences that are unique and memorable. Brands, especially those that are part of a sector as differentiated as luxury, have the great challenge of providing iconic sensations and emotions in their spaces, contributing to greater customer loyalty.

As a result, technology can improve customer service and provide customers an easier and more efficient experience with brands. Multiple testimonies evoke the efficiency of the gadgets and digital tools that some stores already have providing the sense that these complement and help their purchases.

Hyperpersonalization is also highlighted as a differentiating factor for the applicability of technological and digital elements in physical luxury stores, enabling the realization of consumer desires.

Different scenarios stand out among luxury brands, and some of them still do not have technological and digital elements applied in their physical spaces. This reality is justified by the impossibility of applying the necessary investment for these tools, but simultaneously by the barrier between highly manual and classic businesses and technology. The importance of digitization is valued and accompanied by brands, but it is still premature for them to include some type of digital element in their spaces that accompanies and fully adapts to their consumers. Even so, there are luxury brands that have already started to introduce technology into their spaces through digital devices or integrated systems, wanting to evolve and follow trends in this field.

The ability of digital tools to shape the content presented according to the profile of each consumer has given space to brands to develop and to deepen the relationship with their customers, as they began to feel truly heard and interpreted. Consumers' desires are more aligned with the suggestions and offers of each brand and the products, without losing their intrinsic exclusivity, become more accessible.

The new wave of consumers has introduced trends that unify channels and strategies. We are witnessing a forcibly interconnected relationship between e-commerce and physical stores.

The ability to interpret and subsequently present cohesive content, products and experiences is crucial for retaining current consumers. The modern brand communication model must be governed by a hybrid system that operates in both the digital and physical dimensions, awakening and strengthening its relationships with consumers.

The rapid and constant evolution of society and what surrounds us prevents a closed forecast of the future, but the undeniable convenience that channels, tools and digital platforms have brought to consumers' reality, making this preferential route for the following years. Additionally, atypical and never before seen situations, such as the COVID-19 pandemic, add even more unpredictability to the brand's strategy, since the consequences of these phenomena tend to outweigh economic and social damage and completely change consumer behavior and needs. Its critical and much necessary the creation and consolidation of a community that is loyal and devoted to luxury brands, as there will be an ever-increasing correspondence between what they provide and expectations of customers. In this way, the digital transformation is declared to be a valuable process for brands, particularly in the luxury sector, perpetuating and reinforcing their identity and presence with consumers.

REFERENCES

Atwal, G., & Williams, A. (2009). Luxury brand marketing: The experience is everything! *Journal of Brand Management, 16*(5-6), 16. doi:10.1057/bm.2008.48

Backstrom, K., & Johansson, U. (2017). An exploration of consumers' experiences in physical stores: Comparing consumers' and retailers' perspectives in past and present time. *International Review of Retail, Distribution and Consumer Research, 27*(3), 241–259. doi:10.1080/09593969.2017.1314865

Chamorro-Premuzic, T. (2021). The Essential Components of Digital Transformation. *Access on*, 20.

Clarke, S. (2021). *How Luxury Brands Create Exclusive Digital Experiences*. https://www.publicissapient.com/insights/how-luxury-brands-create-exclusive-digital-experiences

Fevereiro. (2022). https://hbr.org/2021/11/the-essential-components-of-digital-transformation

Holmqvist, J., Wirtz, J., & Fritze, M. (2020). Luxury in the digital age: A multi-actor service encounter perspective. *Journal of Business Research, 121*, 747–756. doi:10.1016/j.jbusres.2020.05.038

Kapferer. J.N., Kemstock, J., Brexendorf. T., & Powell, S. (2017). Advances in Luxury Brand Management. *Journal of Brand Management.*

Klaus, P. (2020). The End of The World as We Know It? The Influence of Online Channels on the Luxury Customer Experience. *Journal of Retailing and Consumer Services, 57*, 102248. doi:10.1016/j.jretconser.2020.102248

Kotler, P., Kartajaya, H., & Setiawan, I. (2021). *Marketing 5.0: Tecnology for Humanity* (1st ed.). Wiley.

Maxwell, J. (2005). *Qualitative Research Design: An Interactive Approach. Social Science.*

McCarthy, J. (1998). What Is Artificial Intelligence? Stanford University.

Reinartz, W., Wiegand, N., & Imschloss, M. (2018). The impact of digital transformation on the retailing value chain. *International Journal of Research in Marketing*.

Sahu, N., Deng, H., & Mollah, A. (2018). Investigating The Critical Success Factors Of Digital Transformation For Improving Customer Experience. *International Conference on Information Resources Management*.

Chapter 6
Is Internal Communication a "Bet on the Right Horse" on the Path for Promoting Employees' Eco-Friendly Behavior?
The Mediator Role of Organizational Green Culture

Alexandra Leandro
https://orcid.org/0000-0002-9166-1925
School of Education, Polytechnic University of Coimbra, Portugal

Neuza Ribeiro
https://orcid.org/0000-0002-1228-2522
CARME, School of Technology and Management, Polytechnic Univeristy of Leiria, Portugal

Daniel Gomes
School of Education, Polytechnic University of Coimbra, Portugal & ICNOVA, Portugal

Eduardo Ortega
Ceber, FEUC- Faculty of Economics, University of Coimbra, Portugal

Gabriela Pedro Gomes
https://orcid.org/0000-0003-4143-4705
Ceber, FEUC- Faculty of Economics, University of Coimbra, Portugal

ABSTRACT

Sustainable Development Goals' (SDGs) orientations consist of a key developmental area for contemporary organizations. The commitment towards the development of internal organizational policies with SDGs' alignment clearly invites the adoption of environmentally friendly actions guided for the workers, in which the role of internal communication (IC) policies and practices should be discussed. The main objective of this study is to evaluate the impact of IC on employees' adoption of eco-friendly behaviors (EFB), and specifically, to understand the mediating effect of organizational green culture (OGC) over

DOI: 10.4018/978-1-6684-7353-5.ch006

this relation. A quantitative study was developed through a questionnaire with 237 valid participants. Main results show that IC is significantly and positively correlated with OGC and with employees' EFB, and that there is also a total mediation effect of OGC in the relationship between IC and employees' EFB. Results seem to support the idea that IC practices may influence the shaping and stimulation of organizational culture's contents guided towards the building of an OGC.

INTRODUCTION

Sustainable Development Goals' (SDGs) orientations consist of a key developmental area for modern organizations with different kinds of perspectives and aims. Indeed, current worldwide economic scenarios are heavily pressured by a post-covid and high inflation rates period, bringing renewed stresses for organizational development under the sustainability compromise. Such a setting pushes managers to find new approaches and apply effective practices aiming at the enhancement of sustainability in organizations, in regard to energy consumption, ecological protection, digital internal procedures for supporting paper-free management systems, and sustainable internal policies for human resources at large.

The commitment towards the development of internal organizational policies with the SDGs alignment, thus, clearly invites the adoption of environmentally friendly actions guided towards the workers, in which the role of Internal Communication (IC) policies and practices should be discussed. Specifically, IC may have a very critical role in regard to how people are well aligned with internal policies aiming at the adoption of sustainable management practices. IC has the ability of strategically manage relationships and interactions within an organization with strong alignment with organization's goals and objectives through a systematic process of information management (Verghese, 2017), by stimulating the organization's members to work together, cooperate and interpret the organization's ever-changing needs and activities (Kreps, 1995). The area can bring actions aiming to inform the internal publics of the organization by creating flows of communication and information exchange in different directions to facilitate the production, circulation, and the management of information (Almeida, 2003), and consequently, supporting internal cohesion, shared knowledge and interaction within the organization. Thus, the functions of IC may very well assume a strategic role, by serving as a key reference source of values and cultural factors for employees, and by acting as a decisive element of organizations regarding integration, organizational change management or internal cohesion.

The impacts of IC are widely recognized both by researchers and by practitioners in what concerns people management and alignment with organization's goals and aims (Ruck & Welch, 2012; Ishtiaque & Habib, 2016; Men & Bowen, 2017; Dermol & Širca, 2018). Given the sense of urgency recently given to SDGs orientations, it seems relevant to develop a research attempt to establish the impact of IC on workers' adherence to behaviors aligned with SDGs, such as eco-friendly behavior. This specific kind of behavior improves the organization's environmental performance (Daily, Bishop & Govindarajulu, 2009), and therefore, seems quite relevant to follow the purpose of enhancing a firm's ecological compromise. In addition, eco-friendly behavior should be seen as the result of a set of well-established strategically foreseen practices and can be defined as a voluntary and conscious protective behavior of the environment made by a person (Kim, Kim, Choi & Phetvaroon, 2019). In entrepreneurial contexts, this behavior should be interpreted in alignment with the global organizational orientations over this matter and resulting from a sense of knowledge shared by the workers.

Given that both IC and eco-friendly behavior seem to have a nature of association with the sense of shared knowledge, it seems pertinent to discuss the role of organizational culture over these issues, and specifically Organizational Green Culture (OGC). Indeed, organizational culture is rooted on cognitive structures that help explain how workers behave (Pettigrew, 1979), and can also be approached as a framework of common values (Robbins & Sanghi, 2007) that can have a direct influence over the individuals that are associated with the organization (Stewart, 2010). OGC shares the notion of an internalization of knowledge throughout the organization, leading "employees to accept green innovation as a fundamental value of the organization and to feel more involved in environmental issues" (Chao-Hung, 2019). Given the content attributed to OGC, it seems to expect an existing positive and significant relation with both IC and employee's eco-friendly behavior, thus, it seems relevant to evaluate the nature of these relations. Accordingly, the main objective of this study is to evaluate the impact of IC on employee's adoption of eco-friendly behaviors, and specifically, to understand the mediating effect of OGC over this relation.

To achieve the aforementioned objectives, a cross-sectional quantitative study was developed, whose data was obtained through a structured questionnaire containing the measures of the study variables. In accordance with the results obtained, sample characteristics are as follows: 237 individuals from all districts of Portugal and the Islands have participated in the study. Genders were 66.2% female and 33,8% male, with ages ranging from 21 years to over 61 years, 58,6% having a graduation and 17,3% a Msc graduation level.

Regarding data treatment procedure, we have applied the Harman test and bootstrapping method previously to the results' assessment. The mediation study hypothesis was evaluated using Baron and Kenny's (1986) linear regression method, and subsequently complemented using Sobel Test (Sobel, 1982). The main results obtained show that IC is significantly and positively correlated with OGC and with employee's eco-friendly behavior, and that there is also a total mediation effect of OGC in the relationship between IC and employee's eco-friendly behavior, thus confirming the main study hypotheses.

These results seem to support the idea that internal communication practices may influence the shaping and stimulation of organizational culture's contents guided towards the building of an Organizational Green Culture. IC also seems to be a quite relevant indicator for managers to help promote the adoption of behaviors that encourage the environment's protection, resulting from the stimulation of eco-friendly behaviors. Lastly, results also point that IC can activate a viable process of stimulation of workers eco-friendly behavior through the effect of the shaping and stimulation of organizational green culture.

THEORETICAL REASONING

Sustainable Development Goals' Scenario

Sustainability is hardly a new subject in management literature (e.g.: Aras & Crowther, 2009). It has become a target of dedicated research for at least two decades and gained renewed urgency in the last few years along with the wide calls for actions facing global climate changes. With effect, the new millennium agenda has brought the common purpose of promoting sustainable development worldwide, and the Sustainable Development Goals (SDGs) approved by the UN's General Assembly on 25th September 2015 have launched the common grounds for a model of governance shaped by the compromise towards the end of poverty and fostering economic prosperity as well as environmental protection.

Sustainable Development Goals' (SDGs) orientations seem critical on current worldwide economic scenarios heavily pressured by a post-covid and high inflation rates period, and bring renewed pressures for organizational development under the sustainability compromise. In such a scenario, managers are being strongly pressured in finding and applying practices aiming at enhancing sustainability of organizations in energy consumption, ecological protection, digital internal procedures for supporting paper-free management procedures, and effective sustainable internal policies for human resources. Thus, Human Resources Managers have become one of the management areas interested in understanding in what way can this be an area that promotes sustainability in organizations and the achievement of businesses or performance (eg.: Wikhamn, 2019).

Globally, the areas focused on finding solutions for the human side of the organizations are human resources management and internal communication, and both areas seem to be gathering positive influence by this sustainability agenda. Effectively, HRM literature has been shifting its research agenda's orientation towards the examination of the association between hrm and sustainability (eg.: De Prins, Van Beirendonck, De Vos & Segers, 2014; Diaz-Carrion, Lopez-Fernandez & Romero-Fernandez, 2018). Main results seem to support the investment in sustainable human resources management as a valid path for the promotion of business success, bonds between worker and organization, and also, productivity (eg.: Zhang, et. al., 2019; Ari et. al., 2021).

Internal Communication and Eco-Friendly Behavior

Internal Communication

IC produces a very critical role in what regards how people are well aligned with internal policies aiming at the adoption of management practices. Brandão (2018) shares some very interesting thoughts over IC in organizations, by defining IC as a complex interaction system allowing to share organizational values and meanings between employees, and thus, permitting the assimilation of organization's values. The same author also states that IC in organizations allows to share cultural references amongst employees, and thus is an important agent of organizational change and internal cohesion. Similar line of reasoning is followed by Gomes, Asseiro and Ribeiro (2014), stating that IC strategy should be highly committed to a wide plethora of visible contributions to the organization, such as the ones related to productive and job coordination activities, socialization, and innovation.

IC is both strategic and instrumental for organizations and managers, as on the one hand, the way how information is made available for internal publics forms strategic construction for long term organizational compromises, but on the other hand, IC is built on a day-to-day basis nurtured by the availability of instruments and actions that help the worker to feel connected to an organizational reality. Thus, IC has the ability of strategically manage relationships and interactions within an organization with strong alignment with organization's goals and objectives through a systematic process of information management (Verghese, 2017), by stimulating the organization's members to work together, cooperate and interpret the organization's ever-changing needs and activities (Kreps, 1995).

IC produces actions aiming to inform the internal publics of the organization by creating flows of communication and information exchange in different directions to facilitate the production, circulation and the management of information (Almeida, 2009), and consequently, supporting internal cohesion, shared knowledge and interaction within the organization. Therefore, the functions of IC should assume a strategic role, by serving as a key reference source of values and cultural factors for employees, and by acting as a decisive element of organizations regarding integration, organizational change management or internal cohesion. This area consists of a specific side of organizational communication dealing with the quality, type and the direction of information towards the internal publics of an organization based on the strategic "communication processes through which an organization creates, manages and develops itself" (Almeida, 2003, p.24).

According to Brault (1992), IC delivers seven exclusive functions offering precious inputs for organizations, such as informative, behavioral, organizational change promoter, image management, signaling, integrative and retroactive. Myers and Myers (1982) also propose that IC has an exclusive space in organizations promoting competitiveness and internal efficiency by delivering three main functions: innovation support, production activities, and socialization of new-hired workers. In accordance with all of these indications, these IC functions imply that IC effectively contributes for a wide range of organizational activities shaping internal functioning, and with strong strategic impact of the organization as a whole.

Eco-Friendly Behavior

The aforementioned SDGs' scenario is a perfect platform to put IC to work towards a more pro-environmental setting within organizations. IC can propel green knowledge, create pro-environmental opportunities for employees, and reinforce the eco-guidelines that the company chose to follow to keep up with sustainability demands. Such a framework will most certainly help organizations to promote eco-friendly behavior (EFB) in their workforce. Enhancing EFB is a strategy followed by organizations to improve their environmental performance and achieve sustainability goals is to develop employees' eco-friendly behaviors (Aboramadan et al., 2021; DuBois and Dubois, 2012). Eco-friendly, green or pro-environmental behavior can be defined as the intentional actions or behaviors of employees that have a favorable effect on the environment, reducing the impact of human actions on the environment and bringing about positive changes for environmental sustainability (Juárez-Nájera et al., 2010; Unsworth et al., 2013). According to Kollmuss and Agyeman (2002), eco-friendly behavior can be defined as only an individual action for reducing one's harmful influence on the environment.

Eco-friendly behavior focuses on specific behaviors related to, for instance, energy usage, water conservation, waste reduction, recycling and efficient use of resources. These behaviors are critical to an organization's environmental management success since they increase the organization's environmental performance (Daily et al., 2009).

Relating Internal Communication and Eco-Friendly Behaviors

Given the aforementioned scenario of SDGs, Internal Communication (IC) and its commitment towards the development of policies that are aligned with the Sustainability paradigm, it clearly invites the adoption of environmentally friendly actions guided towards the workers, in which the role of IC policies and practices should be discussed. Furthermore, amongst the array of factors that explain effectiveness and efficiency of organizations, IC should be seen as one of the most important assets of modern organizations (Men & Stacks, 2014), working as a critical management area dealing with the way how strategic information is managed within an organization, helping to build bonds and relationships between workers and organization, and shaping organizational culture and internal climate (Men, 2014).

Important to say, at this point, that IC has to be properly managed in order to accomplish all the contributions that are attributed to it. According to Gomes (2011), one of the core concerns that every organization must have when managing IC is that the area should be aligned with a two-way strategic reference pillar: the organizational communication policy – dealing with the communication global orientations that are developed by the organization; and the organizational global development policy – strategic aims for organizational development.

An insightful and compelling way of seeing how IC can deliver its aspects, contributions and virtues deals with developing symmetrical plans of actions. With effect, Grunig (1992) has proposed the Symmetrical Communication Model, postulating that whenever IC is developed according with symmetrical orientations, the higher will be the possibility of having stimulation of openness and workers' reciprocity regarding organizational values and culture in a basis of mutual understanding and acceptance (Yue, Men & Fergusson, 2020).

Symmetrical Internal Communication is based on the notion that the circulation of information in both top-down and bottom-up circuits are critical for the maximization of IC strategy for the organization. As such, symmetrical internal communication is well based on the notion that both the interests of the organization as well as of the workers should be considered in a similar manner (Men & Stacks, 2014). Consequently, the promotion of internal ideas, workers' participation in strategy development and the fostering of mutual respect should be critical aspects to achieve with this type of orientation regarding IC principle of action based on top-down and bottom-up circuits of information.

Prior research has revealed that practices of green human resources management (e.g., providing green training and recognizing and rewarding green behavior) can promote eco-friendly behaviors (Ribeiro et al., 2022; Gill et al., 2021; Kim et al., 2019; Pham et al., 2019). That is, the adoption of green human resources management practices in organizations to stimulate the development of environmental values among employees can contribute to better business performance and determine a competitive advantage for organizations (Kim et al., 2019).

This leads us to hypothesize that IC has a positive impact on employee's adoption of eco-friendly behavior (H1).

Organizational Green Culture

As aforementioned, internal communication (IC) and eco-friendly behavior (EFB) seem to be associated with shared knowledge, which leads to convoke organizational culture and its role in these issues. It has been established that organizational culture is rooted on cognitive structures that help explain how workers behave (Pettigrew, 1979), and can also be approached as a framework of common values (Robbins & Sanghi, 2007) that can have a direct influence over the individuals that are associated with the organization (Stewart, 2010).

On the path to full-on sustainability, especially echoing the global environmental urgency, companies and scholars have been called upon to accomplish best practices that will help business and their workers to pitch in. One of the first concerns to be expressed in academia about this topic was how "organizations might be 'greened'", as Harris and Crane stated (2002, p. 214). Either top-down or emerging from individuals and permeating all others, organizational cultural change towards an eco-friendly behavior has been an inevitable link. How does a company change its ways without changing its more rooted thoughts, beliefs, and soul? Seemingly doesn't. As Gurlek and Tuna (2018) mention, culture pressures the individuals to comply with cultural values, as they also indicate that the actual implementation of eco-friendly practices requires a culture based on the ecological values. And now, it is becoming a well-established reasoning, much due to the efforts of researchers. With the dawn of the "Brundtland Report", in 1987, sustainability was born as a movement, as a new-paradigm, an agenda for all organizations, with the strong appeal to meet the needs of today without damaging the future generations' possibilities. Decades passed, sustainability has specific global goals to be achieved and is also viewed as part of the contemporary corporate culture: "sustainable culture is defined as a culture in which shared assumptions and beliefs are held by organizational members about importance of balancing environmental accountability, economic efficiency and social equity" (Tahir et al., 2019, p. 25). Production, consumption and all its circumstances, have a very heavy impact on nature, which can be protected, as Liu and Lin (2020) suggest, by a green culture in action within organizations.

Crane (1995) had concluded that mere legal norms and managers' policies to prompt environmental actions do not suffice to lead organizations to face the green innovations demands. Tahir et al. (2019) explain that those pressures on companies have amounted from several sources. Corporate scandals and greenwashing exposures have led the media and public opinion to zoom in business practices. Moreover, on the back of globalization, there is evidence of how beneficial it has been for companies to incorporate green practices in their strategies (Liu & Lin, 2020). Even the increased environmental consciousness of individuals, have turned consumers into a more demanding stakeholder and workers into a force to be reckoned with when it comes to unfiltered messages about shallow eco-branding. Furthermore, "with the detrimental effects the environment is facing today, the production team, dealers, and consumers have become increasingly sensitive to developing and consuming green services and products (Liu & Lin, 2020, p. 3). Al-Swidi (2021) added that given that extra attention paid to workers' role in environmental issues, companies were adapting their initiatives to include employees in the eco-friendly path. And indeed, it seems it has to be holistic to work: "the sustainability program must be recognized as a company-wide goal that includes all aspects of business activity." (Shah et al., 2021, p. 7).

The conceptualization does not seem to be as hard as the fixation of a terminology, though. As Tahir et al. (2019, pp. 24, 25) developed a literature review of 'Green Organizational Culture', they clarify that terms like "environment friendly culture, eco-friendly culture, pro-environmental culture, green consciousness, sustainability culture, Triple Bottom Line (TBL), sustainability culture and broadly corporate social responsibility [CSR] is also used to refer it.". Similarly to CSR itself, OGC appears to suffer from a wordy academic life. Wang et al. (2022) take their turn defining OCG as the organizational culture where environmental protection is viewed as crucial. Shah et al. (2021, p. 7) conceptualize OGC as "a collection of principles, icons, assumptions, and organizations, representing the commitment or willingness to be an environmentally sustainable organization". Moreover, it should be featured in the company's mission statement, inducing everyone to be accountable for its accomplishment (Wang et al., 2022, apud Abbas & Dogan, 2022).

As far as definitions of OGC are concerned, Harris and Crane (2002) propound that it is a set of values, symbols, assumptions, and organizational artifacts - aligned with Schein's (1992) solid theory on organizational culture - but with the specific intent of reflecting the obligation or desire of trying to be an eco-friendly company. Still having Schein's work in mind (1992), Liu and Lin (2020, p. 3) give notice that OGC can be defined as having three levels, "including values, assumptions, and artifacts, which reflects companies' requirements and desires concerning their environmentally sustainable operations. And, as Tahir et al. state (2019, p. 25, apud Marshall et al., 2015), OGC "is the pattern of shared basic assumptions about environmental issues and environmental management.". Gurlek and Tuna (2018) agree and add that OGC encompasses symbols and social stereotypes towards environmental consciousness, which will lead to a symbolic scenario that enables the standardization of employees' behaviors (*apud* Chen, 2011a, Chang, 2015). As Abbas and Dogan refer (2022, p. 60026, *apud* Abbas, 2020b), "taking corporate culture to a green context and realizing ecological equilibrium are the foundations of this environment-friendly and sustainability-oriented culture". They (*ibidem*) also elaborate on the *liaison* between CSR and OGC, believing that they are both leading business towards sustainability. They state that OGC is the internal side of such endeavor, molding beliefs and behaviors, and CSR is the external side, referring to the set of practices that accommodate stakeholders' needs. Both have a crucial role to build a sustainable organization (Abbas & Dogan, 2022): "under CSR, companies that bear a green culture thrive in the sustainability business while making strides in protecting the environment and attracting the most talented employees in the process", as Liu and Lin (2020, p.3) put it.

Liu and Lin (2020) share that companies must make an effort to align their principles with their strategies and actions to a green purpose. Mainly, the key element here is that consistency between values, intentions and behaviors and, as such, focusing on the latter, Pan et al. (2022) state that green organizations are, for example, more active on searching for technologies that will minimize the harming of nature (*apud* Qu et al., 2021). However, measures taken upon physical resources only don't seem to suffice. By prompting a green culture, organizations instill green behaviors among employees that will, afterwards, feel compelled to have individual green behaviors, such as energy saving actions, avoid paper waste, recycle as much as possible (Pan et al., 2022). As Abbas and Dogan (2022, p. 60026, *apud* Parletta, 2019) put it, OGC "provides a healthier workplace with better efficiency and incentives". Most authors that studied OGC do agree that employees are a key element of the organization, and culture is the paradigm for their attitudes and behaviors towards environmental protection: "employees are deliberately indoctrinated into the presumptions of the organization's culture." (Abbas & Dogan, 2022, p. 60026). Fernandez et al. (2003), on their turn, state that managers should use incentives for workers to take part in the eco-programmes, as simultaneously keeping them educated about green goals. It appears to be consensual that "companies can't achieve sustainability goals unless they go green with their employees." (Abbas & Dogan, 2022, p. 60026). Utilizing training tools and courses, employees should be duly informed of what it means to be environmentally responsible (Abbas & Dogan, 2022, *apud* Mendis & Welmilla, 2021). It is not linear to create a green culture, so it does imply a deepened and widened knowledge of what it means to be eco-friendly within the organization (Abbas & Dogan, 2022). Also, Pan et al. (2022) found that because of being in an eco-friendly workplace, people tend to look more positively to life at large. Fundamentally, "employees exposed to green practices become more socially conscious within their organizations and society", as Abbas and Dogan (2022, p. 60026) confirm.

Focusing on the communication of OGC, besides the aforementioned suggestion of including green commitments in the mission statements, Al-Swidi et al (2021) add that workers should have a way to give feedback on their eco-friendly behavior, as well as suggest new ideas that can contribute to a more environmentally conscious workplace. Fernandez et al. (2003) refer to some pre-requirements for a green culture, and they also reinforce the role of a healthy IC, as employees should be free to put forward their ideas on how to become greener, company should educate them on the environmental context, and reward those who are committed to such purposes, thus thickening the green culture by acting positively on it. Chandra et al. (2021) summarized the managerial implications of their research on OGC having a positive impact on green competitive advantage and organizational performance as such: firstly, companies must implement a green strategy that covers organizational economic, operational and environmental aspects; secondly, to keep an eco-friendly competitive advantage, those companies must promote a green organizational culture, among other reasons, because it is very hard to imitate the cultural DNA of companies; and finally, those companies must try to partner with stakeholders (community, educational institutions) that will work with them towards a greener performance.

Al-Swidi et al. (2021) stress that it is not enough for managers to go green just to cope with social pressures, and neither is the employees' tendency to just meet the employers' expectations. If the bet is on cultural greening, then there will be more awareness of environmental impacts of their actions. For all that has been mentioned, indeed, as Al-Swidi et al. (2021) enhance, human resources management should encourage green culture that permeates both people and products in organizations. In summary, as Wang et al. (2022, *apud* Lee et al., 2022) state, OGC will develop employees' environmental concerns and that will end up having a positive effect on their overall performance at work. On the other hand, to grow a green culture, top management needs to be clear about their commitment to environmental protection (Wang et al., 2022, *apud* Azhar & Yang, 2021).

Some positive associations have been found in research done so far in this topic. Tahir et al. (2019) have highlighted Chen's (2011, cited in Tahir et al., 2019) conclusions that green competitive advantage is preceded by green leadership and OGC, especially in large companies. Also Fry and Slocum (cited in Tahir et al., 2019) found that spiritual leadership has a positive effect in the TBL, namely the well-being of the workforce, organizational commitment and CSR. Also, entrepreneurial orientation has been identified as a moderator of the relationship of a sustainability culture and practices along the supply chain (Marshall et al, 2015, cited in Tahir et al., 2019). Strong evidence in several studies indicate the positive link between HR practices and the successful implementation of green practices (Sroufe et al., 2010, cited in Tahir et al., 2019). Designing a proper HR framework, allows employees to further understand which behaviors and postures will contribute to their role as a 'planet-keeper'. Pham et al. (2018) reinforce this thought, claiming that training for workers to learn about environmental protection, will push forward their initiative in doing just that. If the company creates opportunities for the workers to get involved in eco-tasks, even better. They cite the empirical works of Dumont et al. (2017, cited in Pham et al., 2018) to highlight that green human resources management will have more effect in the pro-environmental practices of employees if the firm bets on having an eco-climate in the organization. Al-Swidi et al. (2021) confirmed that OGC has a positive relationship with both eco-friendly behavior of employees and organizational green performance. Moreover, the authors stress that OGC mediates the relationship between environmental concern, green human resource management, green leadership behavior and employees' eco-friendly behavior (Al-Swidi et al., 2021). Al-Swidi et al. (2021) refer to the studies of Kim et al. (2019, cited in Al-Swidi et al., 2021) and Muisyo and Qin (2021, *ibidem*) that concluded that green human resources management does positively affect the workforce's eco-friendly commitment and molds eco-friendly behavior. The same authors also found the works of Rehman et al. (2021) to confirm that eco-centric HR management enhances eco-innovation in employees. As mentioned before, OGC shares the notion of an internalization of knowledge throughout the organization, leading workers to embrace green innovation as a crucial value of the organization and enhancing their involvement in environmental issues (Chao-Hung, 2019). Al-Swidi et al. (2021, *apud* Anwar et al., 2020; Levy & Marans, 2012; Mittal & Dhar, 2016) propose that OGC is analyzed as a mediator in variables that impact eco-friendly behavior.

Social identity theory helps explain the relationship between an organization and its employees (Ashforth & Mael, 1989). The employees who integrate their organization's green values tend to exhibit more eco-friendly behaviors. Drawing from the social identity theory, the authors expect that OGC will lead to a high level of eco-friendly behavior. In other words, OGC promotes a better understand the importance of organizations' environmental policies and consequently make employees more aware, in turn, they feel a greater identification with their organization because OGC should create a positive image/reputation of the organization and, as the social identity theory suggests, employees may identify themselves with such organizations (Shen, Dumont and Deng, 2018). Therefore, having a greater body of people that have shared social meaning attribution to an implicit or explicit green code, will also better the workplace environment: a cleaner, a more conscious workplace, that is the result of everybody's EFB.

Given the present review of OGC, it seems to expect an existing positive and significant relation with both IC and employee's eco-friendly behavior, thus, it seems relevant to evaluate the nature of these relations. Therefore, it is hypothesized that IC is positively and meaningfully associated with OGC (H2); OGC is also associated in a positive and significant way with EFB (H3); and that OGC has a mediator effect on the relation of IC and EFB (H4).

METHOD

Sample and Procedure

On what concerns the data treatment regarding the testing of the study hypotheses, the authors developed a quantitative methodology, following in a *cross-sectional study* design. The data collection procedure was based upon a questionnaire using the *Google Forms platform* and made it available on the Social Network *Facebook,* thus allowing diversified admission of study participants.

Regarding the construction of the instrument, the following items were considered to measure the study variables, using a *Likert scale* from 1 (totally disagree) to 5 (totally agree) in relation to the statements presented:

Internal Communication: Scale of 6 items based on Dozier et al. (1995). Sample item includes: *most communication between management and employees can be said to be two-way communication.* Internal consistency level (α–,90).

Eco-Friendly Behavior: Assessed using 7 items adapted from Kim, et al. (2019). Sample item includes: "*I sort and recycle garbage in the workplace*". Internal consistency level (α=.91).

Organizational green Culture: Scale of 6 items adapted from Jabbour et al. (2010) and Masri and Jaaron (2017). Sample item includes: *"This organization's vision/mission statements include environmental improvement"*. Internal consistency level (α=0,87).

The study sample is an occasional non-probabilistic convenience sample and is composed of 237 participants that have voluntarily agreed to participate in the study. Regarding qualifications, the sample includes participants from various levels of qualifications (16% having high school graduation, 58,6% having a graduation and 17,3% a Msc graduation level), and it was possible to see that 66,7% of respondents to the questionnaire were female. On what concerns their ages, the highest percentage falls in the age group of 39 to 54 years (45,6%) and also 22 to 38 years old (44,7%). Regarding seniority in the organization, it was possible to see that the higher values of seniority were between 1 and 5 years (37,6%) and between 6 and 10 years (25,3%) representing the answers with the highest percentages. The lower percentages were of 11 to 15 year seniority (5,1%).

SPSS version 23 was used for data treatment. Regarding data treatment procedure, we have applied the Harman test to assure that results don't account for a significant amount of common method bias and as a cautionary procedure to assure data robustness. We have also performed our results' assessment using Bootstrapping method at 1000 units, as a way of enhancing the qualities of our study sample.

RESULTS

The analysis of the data presented in the correlation matrix (Table 1) shows that the study variables are significantly associated with each other. It was found that IC is positively and significantly correlated with OGC (*r.*=,688; *sig.* ≤.05) and with EFB (*r.*=,350; *sig.* ≤.05). Moreover, OGC and EFB are also positively and significantly correlated with each other (*r.*=,376; *sig.* ≤.05).

Table 1. Correlation matrix

	Mean	S.D	1	2	3
1. Internal Communication	3,87	1,03	1		
2. Organizational Green Culture	3,51	1,10	,688**	1	
3. Employee's Eco-friendly Behavior	4,55	0,52	,350**	,376**	1

In addition to the testing of the correlations between variables, and the hypotheses' testing validations, the following regression weights were performed in order to assess the relation between IC and OGC (β=,668; sig. ≤, 05) (H2), between OGC and EFB (β=,374; sig. ≤, 05) (H3), and lastly, between IC and EFB (β=,350; sig. ≤, 05) (H1), in which all effects showed to be significant and positive. Facing these results, it seems verified that the first three study hypotheses are verified, thus confirming the first indications analyzed in the correlation matrix. In accordance with these positive and significant results, it seems that IC of organizations is related to the way how OGC is perceived and with the way how EFB are valued, in a sense that the more the investment on IC, the higher the influence on OGC and on EFB. In the same sense, it also seems verified that the investment on OGC of an organization, seems to stimulate EFB.

To investigate the mediation effect predicted in H4, predicting the existence of a mediation effect of the OGC in the relationship between IC and EFB, the methodological procedure proposed by Baron and Kenny (1986) was used. According to the authors, for the mediation effect to be assessed, the following regression equations should be estimated: (1) perform a regression of the mediator variable with the predictor variable; (2) perform a regression of the criterion variable on the predictor variable; (3) perform a regression of the criterion variable on the predictor variable, controlling the mediator variable. Still according to the authors, for the existence of a mediation effect, the following circumstances must occur: (1) the predictor variable must affect the mediating variable in the first regression equation; (2) the predictor variable must be affected by the criterion variable in the second equation; (3) the mediating variable must affect the criterion variable in the third equation.

Regarding the first steps, it was possible to see that the relation between IC and EFB is significant (β=,350; sig. ≤, 05) (1st step), and that the relation between IC and OGC is also significant (β=,668; sig. ≤, 05) (2nd step). Regarding the following steps, in accordance with Table 2, IC has a significant association with EFB.

Table 2. Regression results

Model		Non stand. coeff B	Error	Stand. Coeff. Beta	t	Sig.
1	(Constant)	4.077	.242		16.867	.000
	Gender	.006	.071	.005	.081	.935
	Age	.152	.052	.191	2.948	.004
	Qualifications	.016	.033	.031	.477	.634
2	(Constant)	3.500	.250		13.992	.000
	Gender	-.016	.067	-.014	-.237	.813
	Age	.132	.049	.166	2.709	.007
	Qualifications	.015	.031	.030	.495	.621
	Internal Communication	.171	.031	.338	5.555	**.000**
3	(Constant)	3.322	.250		13.282	.000
	Gender	-.043	.066	-.039	-.655	.513
	Age	.138	.048	.173	2.889	.004
	Qualifications	.037	.031	.073	1.197	.233
	Internal Communication	.072	.042	.143	1.727	**.086**
	Green Organizational Culture	.136	.040	.286	3.402	**.001**

a. Dependant variable: Employees' eco-friendly behavior

When controlling for the effect of OGC over the relation between IC and EFB, the relation stops being significant (β=,072; *n.s.*), showing the existence of total mediation effect. Thus, H4 is also confirmed (Model: $R^{2adjust.}$ =, 172; sig. ≤, 05).

As an option for adding the mediation hypothesis confirmation more robustness and security, we have conducted the Sobel Test as it addresses the indirect effect in a more direct way. Sobel Test results have confirmed the mediation hypothesis of the indirect effect of OGC over the relation between IC and EFB (Sobel test: Z=3,31409402; sig. ≤, 05).

DISCUSSION AND CONCLUSIONS

Discussion

Business models' alignment with the SDGs worldwide have clearly invited organizations to search for renewed opportunities to enhance organizational development through alternative ways of making business. With effect, the way how organizations act towards the environment, internal publics, customers, or stakeholders has changed in a more positive, informed and directed way. This framework also presents itself as another opportunity to enhance shared values, common behaviors, that ultimately will result in a more cohesive, happier, balanced, organizational climate.

The commitment towards the development of internal organizational policies with the SDGs alignment, has also invited the adoption of environmentally friendly actions aimed towards the workers. Under this remit, IC development policies and practices have gained renewed interest and importance regarding valid ways of adopting internal sustainable management policies. As IC has the strategic ability of managing relationships and interactions within an organization with strong alignment with organization's goals, it was discussed if these properties could support internal cohesion and shared knowledge amongst the workers directed towards environmental concerns. We have also discussed that IC may assume a strategic orientation regarding the building of internal significance regarding the shaping of organizational green culture stimulating workers' behavior in accordance with environmental concerns, notably, eco-friendly behavior.

Eco-friendly behavior is a specific kind of behavior improving an organization's environmental performance and enhances a firm's ecological compromise (Daily, Bishop & Govindarajulu, 2009). As such, this specific behavior should be seen as a consequence of well-established strategically foreseen practices, and provoques alignment with SDGs' orientations, especially, if resulting from a sense of knowledge shared by the workers. Following this reasoning, it seemed important to understand in what way OGC has contribution for the relation between IC and eco-friendly behavior. With effect, OGC shares the notion of an internalization of knowledge throughout the organization, leading "employees to accept green innovation as a fundamental value of the organization and to feel more involved in environmental issues" (Chao-Hung, 2019). As such, the main objective of this study is to evaluate the impact of IC on employee's adoption of eco-friendly behaviors, and specifically, to understand the mediating effect of OGC over this relation.

The main results of our study showed that IC is significantly and positively correlated with OGC and also with employee's eco-friendly behavior. Our results have also tested for a mediation effect of OGC over the relation between IC and eco-friendly behavior and found that there is in fact a total mediation effect of OGC over this relation. This implies that IC can activate a viable process of stimulation of workers eco-friendly behavior through the effect of the shaping and stimulation of organizational green culture. Thus, these results support the idea that IC practices influence the shaping and stimulation of organizational culture's contents guided towards the building of an Organizational Green Culture. IC also seems to be a relevant indicator for managers to promote the adoption of behaviors that encourage the environment's protection, resulting from the stimulation of eco-friendly behaviors.

Conclusion

Our results also raise some additional theoretical, empirical and practical questions. Firstly, this research enriches the body of knowledge on the relevance of internal communication and its importance to create common grounds, shared meanings, and pave the paths for all organization's members to walk on. Such a way is built either top-down as bottom-up, and sideways: a symmetrical internal communication will stress the equally important role played by every individual towards a collective well-being. Our study also invites reasoning over the way to conceive sustainable internal communication theoretical models, as our results clearly invites reasoning over this matter, notably to the positive effects IC can produce over the development of green culture and the behavioral stimulation of workers actions towards environmental protection. Secondly, promoting a pro-environmental culture, an OGC, will create the right tone for every individual to feel their green behavior can be appreciated, that is, having a greater body of people that have shared social meaning attribution to an implicit or explicit green code, will also better the workplace environment: a cleaner, a more conscious workplace, that is the result of everybody's EFB. Thirdly, still on what concerns the theoretical questions that can arise from this study, to promote an EFB, it will certainly be easier if an OGC is in use, and IC is actively contributing to make that culture a reality.

Our empirical model has had the virtue of researching over internal aspects of organizational activity, that is usually assessed through human resources management, thus bringing the added value of having a different line up over these matters. Our results also stimulate debate over additional factors that may very well contribute for future development of empirical models aimed at completing the important findings we were able to address. For instance, it would be interesting to see the role of leadership as an additional variable of our empirical model, notably, over the examination of the compared predictive effects with IC over workers' eco-friendly behavior.

Regarding practical implications, our study clearly invites practitioners to use the responsibility of developing internal communication planning towards the development of organizations under the SDG's and the sustainability compromises remits. These orientations may very well guide IC practices regarding renewed ways of committing workers with sustainability values. In addition, given that we have verified that IC has positive impact over workers' eco-friendly behaviors, IC practitioners should plan internal communication with the sense of contributing towards sustainability accomplishment issues.

This study's results should be read with some conditionings. Firstly, the sample of the study is of convenience, which brings generalizations limitations. Secondly, despite all efforts pursued to control for the impact of common method variance, the data gathering procedure was not totally immune to these kinds of variance. Thirdly, our model of analysis is theoretically rooted. Alternative models are possible to conceive having similar interest to existing knowledge, that at this point were not possible to estimate.

REFERENCES

Abbas, J., & Dogan, E. (2022). The impacts of organizational green culture and corporate social responsibility on employees' responsible behaviour towards the society. *Environmental Science and Pollution Research International*, *29*(40), 60024–60034. doi:10.100711356-022-20072-w PMID:35414156

Aboramadan, M., Kundi, Y., & Farao, C. (2021). Examining the effects of environmentally specific servant leadership on green work outcomes among hotel employees: The mediating role of climate for green creativity. *Journal of Hospitality Marketing & Management*, *30*(8), 929–956. Advance online publication. doi:10.1080/19368623.2021.1912681

Al-Swidi, A. K., Gelaidan, H. M., & Redhwan, M. S. (2021). The joint impact of green human resource management, leadership and organizational culture on employees' green behaviour and organisational environmental performance. *Journal of Cleaner Production*, *316*, 1–19. doi:10.1016/j.jclepro.2021.128112

Almeida, V. (2003). *A Comunicação Interna na Empresa*. Áreas Editora.

Baron, R. M., & Kenny, D. A. (1986). The moderator–mediator variable distinction in social psychological research: Conceptual, strategic, and statistical considerations. *Journal of Personality and Social Psychology*, *51*(6), 1173–1182. doi:10.1037/0022-3514.51.6.1173 PMID:3806354

Chandra, K., Arafah, W., & Basri, Y. Z. (2021). Analysis of the Effect of Green Organizational Culture on Organizational Performance and Competitive Advantages of Green through Green Innovation in Manufacturing Industries. *Hunan Daxue Xuebao. Shehui Kexue Ban*, *48*(6), 112–121.

Chao-Hung, W. (2019). How organizational green culture influences green performance and competitive advantage: The mediating role of green innovation. *Journal of Manufacturing Technology Management*, *30*(4), 666–683. doi:10.1108/JMTM-09-2018-0314

Crane, A. (1995). Rhetoric and Reality in the Greening of Organisational Culture. *Greener Management International*, *12*, 49–62.

Daily, B., Bishop, J., & Govindarajulu, N. (2009). A conceptual model for organizational citizenship behavior directed toward the environment. *Business & Society*, *48*(2), 243–256. doi:10.1177/0007650308315439

Dermol, V., & Širca, N. (2018). Communication, Company Mission, Organizational Values, and Company Performance. *Procedia - Social and Behavioral Sciences, 238*, 542-551. doi:10.1016/j.sbspro.2018.04.034

Fernández, E., Junquera, B., & Ordiz, M. (2003). Organizational culture and human resources in the environmental issue: A review of the literature. *International Journal of Human Resource Management*, *14*(4), 634–656. doi:10.1080/0958519032000057628

Gill, A., Ahmad, B., & Kazmi, S. (2021). The effect of green human resource management on environmental performance: The mediating role of employee eco-friendly behavior. *Management Science Letters*, *11*, 1725–1736. doi:10.5267/j.msl.2021.2.010

Harris, L. C., & Crane, A. (2002). The greening of organizational culture - management views in the depth, degree and diffusion of change. *Journal of Organizational Change Management*, *15*(3), 214–234. doi:10.1108/09534810210429273

Ishtiaque, F. & Habib, L. (2016). Impact of Internal Communication on Organizational Development. *International Journal of Trend in Research and Development, 3*, 242-247.

Kim, Y., Kim, W., Choi, H., & Phetvaroon, K. (2019). The effect of green human resources management on hotel employees' eco-friendly behavior and environmental performance. *International Journal of Hospitality Management*, *76*, 83–93. doi:10.1016/j.ijhm.2018.04.007

Kreps, G. L. (1995). *La comunicación en las organizaciones*. Addison-Wesley Iberoamericana.

Liu, X., & Lin, K.-L. (2020). Green Organizational Culture, Corporate Social Responsibility Implementation, and Food Safety. *Frontiers in Psychology*, *11*, 1–7. doi:10.3389/fpsyg.2020.585435 PMID:33240175

Men, R., & Bowen, S. (2017). *Excellence in internal communication management*. Business Expert Press.

Pan, C., Abbas, J., Álvarez-Otero, S., Khan, H., & Cheng, C. (2022). Interplay between corporate social responsibility and organizational green culture and their role in employees' responsible behavior towards the environment and society. *Journal of Cleaner Production*, *366*, 1–8. doi:10.1016/j.jclepro.2022.132878

Pettigrew, A. (1979). Studying organizational culture. *Administrative Science Quarterly*, *24*(4), 570–581. doi:10.2307/2392363

Robbins, S. P., & Sanghi, S. (2007). *Organizational Behavior*. Pearson Education.

Ruck, K., & Welch, M. (2012). Valuing internal communication; management and employee perspectives. *Public Relations Review, 38*(2), 294-302. doi:10.1016/j.pubrev.2011.12.016

Schein, E. H. (1992). Organizational culture and leadership (2ª ed.). São Francisco: Jossey-Bass Publishers.

Shah, S. M. A., Jiang, Y., Wu, H., Ahmed, Z., Ullah, I., & Adebayo, T. S. (2021). Linking Green Human Resource Practices and Environmental Economics Performance: The Role of Green Economic Organizational Culture and Green Psychological Climate. *International Journal of Environmental Research and Public Health*, *18*(20), 1–17. doi:10.3390/ijerph182010953 PMID:34682698

Sobel, M. E. (1982). Asymptotic Confidence Intervals for Indirect Effects in Structural Equation Models. *Sociological Methodology*, *13*, 290–321. doi:10.2307/270723

Stewart, D. (2010). *Growing the Corporate Culture.* https://www.wachovia.com/foundation/v/index.jsp?vgnextoid

Tahir, R., Athar, M. R., Faisal, F., Shahani, N., & Solangi, B. (2019). Green organizational culture: A review of literature and future research agenda. *Annals of Contemporary Developments in Management & HR*, *1*(1), 23–38. doi:10.33166/ACDMHR.2019.01.004

Verghese, A. K. (2017). Internal communication: practices and implications. *SCMS Journal of Indian Management*,103-113.

Wang, S., Abbas, J., Sial, M. S., Álvarez-Otero, S., & Cioca, L. (2022). Achieving green innovation and sustainable development goals through green knowledge management: Moderating role of organizational green culture. *Journal of Innovation & Knowledge*, *7*(4), 1–9. doi:10.1016/j.jik.2022.100272

Chapter 7
Spillover Stress From "The Great Resignation" in the United States:
Broken Cross-Departmental Dependencies

Michael C. Zalot
https://orcid.org/0000-0001-6117-8740
Cedar Crest College, USA

ABSTRACT

This chapter examines spillover stress in the wake of the so-called "Great Resignation" in the United States after the COVID-19 pandemic. Increased turnover led to a shifting of work to those remaining in organizations. This additional workload impacted not only the departments where the turnover was occurring, but also those to whom they provided services. The chapter uses the case of a faltering marketing department in a four-year college in the Northeast United States missing deliverables, and the resultant stress on the requestor, who was relying on their services. Employment dates by title and role transitions by quarter are aligned to the deliverable challenges. Spillover stress from broken cross-departmental dependencies is indicated as a source of individual stress, and in particular, leadership transitions—both structural and within role—are identified as a particularly important source of missed outcomes. Potential monitoring and intervention strategies are suggested for departments in turnover crisis to attempt to prevent broken dependencies and spillover stress.

INTRODUCTION: "THE GREAT RESIGNATION" AFTER COVID-19

In the United States and elsewhere, the aftermath of the COVID-19 pandemic was a disruption of the labour market known as "The Great Resignation". As businesses shut down in-person activities, many office-based positions, such as administrative and professional roles, began to operate remotely. Telecommuting platforms were adopted as an alternative to in-person work, and many roles were able to shift to virtual from physical presence (Endresen, 2020). This ultimately made plain the notion that remote

DOI: 10.4018/978-1-6684-7353-5.ch007

office work had been possible for quite some time, due to advancements in virtual meeting software. The stress of shifting work environments was combined with the personal stress of pandemic health risks for workers and their families, and shortages of household items such as toilet paper, disinfectant wipes, and hand sanitizer. Some workers, of course, had no virtual options, such as those in the physical trades. Government unemployment benefits were increased, proving some minor cushioning for those unable to work or going through a job transition.

In short, workers reassessed their relationships with their current employers, particularly with regard to compensation, advancement, and a sense of respect (Parker and Horowitz, 2022). Those workers who needed physical presence or enjoyed the social aspects of the workplace environment were dissatisfied with remote work requirements. Those workers who felt unsafe from the contagion working in a building with those whose vaccination status could not be known found themselves dissatisfied with requests to come back to the office. Workers with long commuting times and high commuting costs found relief from the commute and wanted to prolong working from home (Price Waterhouse Coopers, 2021). These conditions led to massive resignations from existing positions, or for those keeping a role but performing the bare minimum necessary to sustain it, a "quiet quitting" (Hare, 2022). Many organizations found themselves struggling to retain essential employees as prospects elsewhere brightened into job offers with higher salaries, better benefits, or more preferable working conditions. Labour became a seller's market, advantaging job seekers.

Meanwhile, organizations that relied on revenue from customers faced challenges from both broken supply chains, and redirection of consumer discretionary dollars. Many reduced their target headcount to attempt to rebalance expanded salary and bonus expenditures with declining income. In some cases, open positions were simply not filled. In other cases, the work was too important to necessary operations, and companies began competing more intensely for available qualified candidates. This ultimately meant fewer workers in some organizations trying to produce the same amount of work. Employees who remained felt pressure to expand either the scope or output of their existing roles, resulting in longer hours (Beheshti, 2021). Persistent employees paid the price of additional workload stress in challenging social and psychological pandemic conditions, while their peers moved on to often better-paying, and perhaps more-flexible employment elsewhere. In the face of increasing work, these retained employees may have had less wherewithal to perform or overextend, particularly a decline in executive functioning (Farahat, *et. al.*, 2021) as they faced personal and family health threats and organizational uncertainty.

This chapter documents this turnover and captures what The Great Resignation looks like for a single department, including both line-level and leadership positions. It is important to take a moment to clarify the use of the terms management and leadership here. Some of the roles identified herein contain the term "manager", but this does not refer to the direction of labour within the department. These roles are process managers, without any supervisory responsibility for personnel. They are managerial in the sense that they are responsible for certain kinds of work and have a high degree of autonomy, but no direct reports. This distinction can be used as the basis for salary (annual) pay structure, as opposed to wage (hourly) type pay structure (Eggcellentwork.com, 2022). To avoid confusion, only the term "leadership" is used herein to indicate those who direct and control the work of others. The relevant job titles in this chapter are Director, Assistant Director, and Vice President. This separation is done for the clarity of the reader, who may otherwise assume that any position containing the term "manager" must be supervisory.

This chapter captures also what turnover stress looks like, not for the department in question, but for those who depend on its work product. In other words, does turnover (including leadership turnover) affect the output of a department that provides services to others in the same organization? Throughout, a case study is used: that of a college Marketing and Communications department struggling with turnover and leadership transitions, and the fallout levied on someone requesting work from that department as part of their own work process. Seen from the requestor's view, this chapter looks at the additional workplace stress placed on those attempting to collect work product from a service-providing department in crisis. While the formal research questions and hypotheses will be presented in a later section, the starting assumption that drove the research was that the departmental turnover would create stress outside of that department, as work-product deliverables are not met in a timely fashion. While the college name and individual employee names have been anonymized, the job titles, deliverables, and dates of hire and transition are actual data.

Context of the Study: Job Change, Turnover, and Workplace Stress

Employees generally dislike and feel threatened by any workplace change, at least in the United States, where most employment is "at will". This is why the majority of the body of literature on change management focuses on careful, systematic change in an organization. Organizational change is seen as necessary to support fit between the organization and its environment (Burke, 2017), but if not approached carefully, can send workers scrambling for their resumes in the wake of the uncertainty that it creates. Change can create resistance, negative attachment, and a sense of betrayal of psychological employer/ employee contract (Chowdhury, 2009, p. 34), including agreed-upon role duties as spelled out in the job description (Jackson, *et. al.*, 2012, p. 157). It can create stress and anxiety that spill over into family life, particularly for mid-career workers (Matteson and Ivancevich, 2014, p. 145). How workers handle their own individual change is based at least in part on what coping mechanisms they have, including not only their personality strengths, but also the degree to which their available resources meet the demands of the transition (Rudisill, *et. al.*, 2010, p. 118). Challenges surrounding COVID represent additional strain on psychological wherewithal and thus, resilience.

Where workers are not replaced, additional stress is created on the remaining employees who have to split up the workload (Erat, *et. al.*, 2017, p. 228). Unfilled positions represent uncompleted work, and even when new employees are hired, they do not perform efficiently at first (Aamodt, 2013, p. 387). Spillover work represents a shift in the work/life balance, can create time management issues, and ultimately, can be seen as a net reduction in pay vs. work performed. This can create resentment on the part of the employees remaining, as any change to a job represents additional stress and added uncertainty (Workforce Hub, n.d.). Turnover can reduce output, and increase mistakes from inexperience (Jackson, *et. al.*, 2012, p. 189). Each departing employee represents a loss of process knowledge, and a loss of business contacts for the organization (Jackson, *et. al.*, *op. cit.*, p. 190). A survey of literature suggests that losing a worker is most impactful when monthly turnover is low, but has a diminishing effect on departmental performance when turnover is high (Aamodt, 2013, p. 387).

Duties re-allocated from other workers can even create resentment when the missing worker is out on family leave (Jacobs and Gerson, 2005). Cognitive and emotional burnout from overwork can create the risk of additional employee resignations (Maslach and Jackson, 1984), perpetuating the situation. However, employee turnover usually is not instant—it is a process of disengagement that can take weeks or months (Aamodt, 2013, p. 388). Similarly, ramping up a new hire to adequate performance levels takes time, and represents an investment risk to the hiring organization (Lussier and Hendon, 2016, p. 150). Even before the COVID pandemic, worker shortages were predicted due to demographic shifts in the US, and there was difficulty filling open positions. The notion of "talent wars" in recruiting already suggested a seller's market for labour before shutdowns, and employers were increasingly turning to contingent workers to fill the gap (Lussier and Hendon, 2016, p. 183). Importantly, this demand was not level across the board, and fields like higher education, where staff trends were heading downward, did not present as many opportunities. Of course, European models of recruitment and retention are generally less open than in the United States due to the constraints placed on organizations by the state and unions, and the contract of employment is considered to be far less contingent (Mayrhofer and Brewster, 2007, p. 243).

Case Study: The Requestor and Delayed Work From Marketing

At a four-year, private college in the Northeastern United States, an academic program director, hereafter known as the "Requestor", was asking for standard marketing and communications work from the internal Marketing and Communications department. This consisted of two projects, both of which were specifically designed to increase enrolments in the coming Fall 2022 semester. Project 1 was a simple press release to indicate the availability of new undergraduate academic programs. This would be added to the college's website as well as sent to social and local media. Project 2 was a set of textual website updates that would help explain important student-facing changes to an existing graduate program. These were textual edits to existing content, and not a structural change for the site overall.

However, the work was not delivered in a timely fashion, and the desired potential student candidate pools were not reached quickly enough to satisfy the Requestor. Project 1, the press release, was requested in March 2022, and not delivered for several months. While this timeline would have been too tight to affect incoming traditional students, the college also has significant numbers of transfer students from local community colleges as well as some returning adult undergraduates, for whom a timely notification of new program availability in March 2022 might have made a decision difference for a Fall 2022 start. The Requestor ultimately ended up providing a draft of the document to help speed the process along, out of frustration, before trying to involve the Provost. This material was ultimately largely unused in the final copy except for one quote. Project 2, the website update, took more than a month. This was a month going into the normal recruiting window for Fall of 2022. The graduate program in question had faster turnarounds, so there was a sense that any time missed resulted in missed contact opportunities for students who might have been interested in the new program focus. The Requestor, familiar with web coding, had even offered to draft the HTML code changes to update the website; however, they ultimately did not do so and opted to intervene through other personnel instead.

The Requestor indicated that these "missed" deliverables (note: there was no promised made by the Marketing and Communication department about timelines, only the previous speed of delivery from the department) affected their work and well-being. They were aware of the personnel changes happening in the department, and began to question their own role is assuring that the work was completed. The Requestor began sending follow-up emails asking for status updates, and even asking other employees to help intervene. It was only through one such intervention that Project 2 was completed. An associate from Admissions walked over to the physical desk of the Webmaster and Electronic Marketing Specialist, and asked personally for expedited progress.

The Requestor felt that their scope of control had expanded to include monitoring employees in the service-providing department, and that this required a personal favour to accomplish, expanding personal social capital in the effort. Moreover, this was in addition to managing classes, curriculum, student issues, research, and their own pandemic-related stresses. Adequate control over work is essential in assuring output through coordination and direction (Flamholtz, 1996, p. 5). Ultimately, while the work was completed, the timeframe was not acceptable, and the Requestor felt that the two projects, initiatives to boost falling enrolments in the Fall 2022, were ineffective. This generated emotional stress in addition to the cognitive load required in attempting to exert control over the situation. It is important to note that the college in question is largely tuition driven, and while efforts had been made throughout the pandemic to prevent layoffs by eliminating open positions, there was a real sense for the Requestor that staffing level changes (viz, the vulnerability of their own position) could be prevented through stabilizing and increasing enrolments.

PROBLEM STATEMENT

A Marketing and Communications department for a four-year, private college in the United States experiences significant turnover in the wake of the "Great Resignation". Its internal clients suffer from delayed action on their requests, and this generates emotional and psychological stress on those requesting the work. It generates an unfulfilled need for requestors to extend their own scope of control into the service-providing department, which represents a role expansion. The Marketing and Communications department is going through personnel transitions, including leadership transitions, but that does not affect their clients' needs to have work completed as part of their own workflows. To what extent is personnel transition an issue contributing to the stress felt by those requesting the services and needing to try to "oversee" processes normally functioning effectively and opaquely?

METHODOLOGY

The author became aware of the situation from the Requestor through personal contact. The Requestor was interviewed using a key informant methodology, where the goal is not to identify statistical patterns through representative samples, but rather to discover and capture perspectives for those who have actually been through a particular experience (Akhter, 2022, p. 390). Such a methodology is particularly helpful where the experience is novel, but may generate valuable insight into a particular phenomenon. The Requestor had two projects fail to meet perceived deliverables, and suspected that turnover in the Marketing and Communication department may have been a contributing factor to the issue. The particular experience of the Requestor's frustration may have been a unique and situational reaction. However, the notion that turnover in a service-providing department affects its clients has more widespread applicability, and can be studied more quantitatively once established.

The Requestor researched the history of department transitions, initially in email messaging about personnel sent on the college's behalf. They then provided the names of key employees in the Marketing and Communications department, as well as their dates of tenure in their roles from information available on LinkedIn. The Requestor also connected the author with a representative from the Human Resources department at the college in question, to verify employment data and account for any potential missing information, such as unaccounted for transitions or additional personnel. Two Half-Time employees were identified who had previously not been accounted for. The question of supervision of student workers was raised. The departmental reporting structure was verified, and one key role identified that had never been filled—Assistant Director of Marketing.

Table 1. Role tenure and transitions, marketing and communications, 2016 to 2022

	2016				2017				2018				2019				2020				2021				2022			
	1	2	3	4	1	2	3	4	1	2	3	4	1	2	3	4	1	2	3	4	1	2	3	4	1	2	3	4
VP Enrollment Management and Marketing (P1)																		*	X	X	X	X	X	X	X	*		
Director of Marketing and Communications (P2)		*	X	X	X	X	X	X	X	X	X	X	X	X	X	X	X	X	*									
Director of Marketing and Communications (P3)																										*	X	X
Assistant Director of Marketing & Communications (Vacant)																			-	-	-	-	-	-	-			
Communications and Content Manager (P4)					*	X	X	X	X	X	X	X	X	*														
Communications and Content Manger (P5)															*	X	X	X	X	*								
Communications and Content Manager (P6)																			*	X	X	X	X	X	X	X	X	X
Marketing Manager (P5, Title Change)																					*	X	*					
Digital Content Specialist (Half-Time, P7)											*	X	X	X	X	*												
Social Media Manager (P8)																							*	X	X	X	X	*
Graphic Designer (P9)					*	X	X	X	X	X	X	X	X	X	X	X	X	X	X	X	X	X	X	X	X	*		
Graphic Designer (P10)																											*	X

continues on following page

Table 1. Continued

	2016				2017				2018				2019				2020				2021				2022			
	1	2	3	4	1	2	3	4	1	2	3	4	1	2	3	4	1	2	3	4	1	2	3	4	1	2	3	4
Webmaster and Electronic Marketing Specialist (P11)	X	X	X	X	X	X	X	X	X	X	X	X	X	X	X	X	X	X	X	X	X	X	X	X	X	X	X	X
Administrative Assistant (Half-Time, P12)			*	X	X	X	X	X	X	X	X	X	X	X	X	X	*											
Role Transitions Captured		1	1		2						1			1	1	1	1		2	1	1		2			3	1	1
Project 1: Press Release (Undergraduate)																										R	D	
Project 2: Website Updates (Graduate)																										R/D		

A chart was constructed reconstructing the timelines of all employees in the department by role. This chart is Table 1. Per Marr (2018, p. 97), simple charts, combined with explanatory narrative, can be helpful in assessing employee churn. It is worth noting that the college in question used both an Academic (August-July) and a Fiscal year (July-June) calendar, but the dates here are represented using standard Calendar quarters, for ease of use of the reader. This also represents the way that the data itself was captured from its source on LinkedIn. Thus, there is no risk of mistake in conversion of the data to a different calendar basis. Quarter 1 is January, February, and March. Quarter 2 is April, May, and June. Quarter 3 is July, August, and September, and Quarter 4 is October, November, and December. While the monthly service dates are available in Table 2, calendar months were not chosen as a basis for analysis. Rather, standard calendar quarters were used as they more closely reflect the reality that transitions into and out of a role take time, focus, and emotional effort (cf., Aamodt, 2013, pp. 387-388). The challenge with the assumption is that an employee transitioning at the end of a quarter is treated the same as an employee transitioning at the beginning of the quarter, but it does represent the larger ramp-up (or ramp-off) transition period better than individual months would. Employee time-in-role is indicated by an "X" in Table 1, and transitional quarters are marked with an asterisk "*". Each individual employee is given a sequential "P" (Person) number in both Table 1 and Table 2 to show different incumbents in the same role, as well as the title change for Person 5 (P5).

RESEARCH QUESTIONS AND HYPOTHESES

This section lists and discusses the research questions and lists the hypotheses.

RQ1. What does employee turnover look like for a department affected by the "Great Resignation"? Addressing this question alone provides substantial value to the reader from the data collected here for the chapter. What is captured here is a timeline of personnel transitions in a department that was affected by the post-COVID job transitions that were rampant in administrative and professional work in the United States. Again, these are indicated by standard calendar quarter in Table 1, and by standard calendar month in Table 2. Thus, a true picture of a department in transition is shown, and the specific context is in the increased turnover following the pandemic. This data may be of use for future research. It follows that other external or internal factors may contribute to future turnover in other organizations and other departments, which may generate similar organizational challenges.

H1. Employee turnover will be more significant in the years following the pandemic.

RQ2. To what extent did employee turnover correlate with missed deliverables? While additional factors leading to the missed deliverables may be indeed by identified—experience is discussed in the results section—the disruption of personnel turnover is seen as primary in this analysis. As mentioned above, while the context of this particular set of events is the COVID pandemic's impact on the stability of US organizations, the results can be extrapolated to other situations, and in particular, where a service department is failing to provide requested services to its clients in a timely manner. The psychological and emotional stress on the Requestor, and need to attempt to expand control on an external department's processes, in particular can be seen indicative of what happens when a service-providing department fails. Additionally, the specific roles of personnel involved beg the question to what degree leadership in the department failed, as opposed to only the production personnel.

H2a. Employee turnover will correlate with missed deliverables.
H2b. Leadership turnover will correlate with missed deliverables.

RESULTS OF ANALYSIS

Table 1 shows the transitions in the department, thus answering Research Question #1. 2016 and 2017 each only have two role transitions, and 2018 has but a single role transition. 2019 shows increasing role transitions; there are 3. 2020 has 4, and 2021 has 3. Clearly, there was an increase in role transitions around 2019, peaking at 5 transitions in 2022, post-pandemic and highly correlated with the "Great Resignation". Hypothesis #1 is thus asserted to have been proven true from the data shown. The average number of role transitions in 2016-2019 is 2 per year. The average number of role transitions in 2020-2022 is 4—double that of the changes before the COVID pandemic. This doubling of role transitions documents, in fact, the Great Resignation pattern using actual employee data for a single existing department. Please see Table 3 for a summary, including overall employee turnover, and separated data for leadership and non-leadership roles.

It is also clear from Table 1 that the requested and missed deliverables happened in the Quarter (2Q 2022) where transitions were the highest recorded—three. "R" indicates requested work, and "D" indicates delivered work. There can be no doubt that these role transitions represented instability in the service-providing department just when the Requestor was relying most heavily on their services. Thus, Research Question #2 is answered by the notion that employee turnover was most highly correlated with the Requestor's missing deliverables. While other factors cannot be eliminated, such as having a particularly inexperienced Communications and Content Manager, turnover is strongly indicated as the motivating factor. Hypothesis #2a is thus asserted to have been proven by the data shown in Table 1.

Table 2. Role titles and incumbent tenure (February 2023)

Role	Start	End	Months in Role
VP Enrollment Management and Marketing (P1)	May 2020	June 2022	26
Director of Marketing and Communications (P2)	June 2016	September 2020	52
Director of Marketing and Communications (P3)	June 2022	Current	9
Communications and Content Manager (P4)	January 2017	May 2019	29
Communications and Content Manger (P5)	July 2019	December 2020	9
Communications and Content Manager (P6)	September 2020	Current	30
Marketing Manager (P5, Title Change)	January 2021	September 2021	18
Digital Content Specialist (Half-Time, P7)	August 2018	December 2019	17
Social Media Manager (P8)	October 2021	November 2022	14
Graphic Designer (P9)	January 2017	June 2022	66
Graphic Designer (P10)	September 2022	Current	6
Webmaster and Electronic Marketing Specialist (P11)	September 2003	Current	234

For Hypothesis 2b, the data also show that there was indeed a leadership transition taking place. Moreover, it was a structural change as well. As per Figure 1, normally only the Director role had supervisory oversight over the departmental processes and workers.

Figure 1. Reporting structure: Q2 2017 vs. Q2 2021

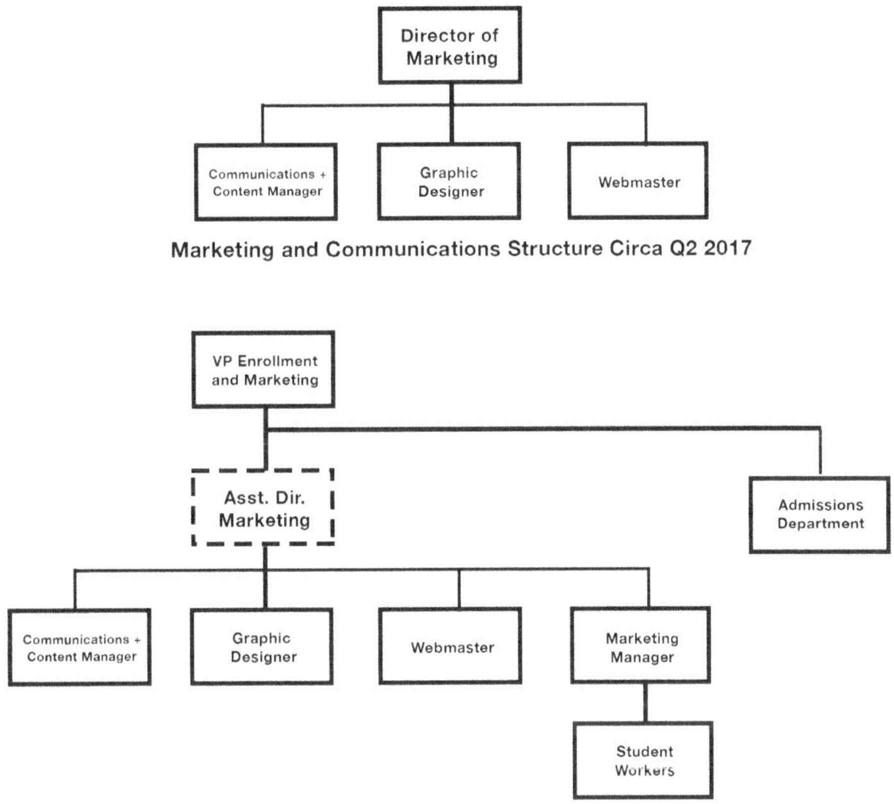

When the Vice President of Enrollment Management and Marketing (VPEMM) was overseeing the department work processes, there was an unfilled Assistant Director of Marketing position that would have been in charge of day-to-day operations and workflows. It can be argued that because the VPEMM had oversight of two separate departments (Marketing and Communication, and the Admissions department, which had approximately the same number of workers), that such a level of supervision was insufficient to ensure results. Indeed, that supposition is argued by the existence and advertisement of a position to do specifically that supervisory work—a position that was never filled. The short-tenured Marketing Manager position was developed to supervise student workers, whose positions rotated on a semester basis. There were three available student positions, but sometimes only 2 were filled. This transient pool of part-time workers was not considered in the formal analysis, because the student employment data was not available on LinkedIn or from Human Resources. However, it should be noted that the Marketing Manager lasted less than a year, and was not continued when the incumbent moved on from the organization.

Table 3. Marketing and communications department turnover

Pre-"Great Resignation"	All Employee Turnover	Non-Leadership Turnover	Leadership Turnover
2016	2	1	1
2017	2	2	0
2018	1	1	0
2019	3	3	0
Average	***2***	***1.75***	***0.25***
"Great Resignation"	**All Employee Turnover**	**Non-Leadership Turnover**	**Leadership Turnover**
2020	4	2	2
2021	3	3	0
2022	5	3	2
Average	***4***	***2.67***	***1.33***

What finalizes the case for proof of Hypothesis 2B, however, is that the work requested—a press release and a set of website updates—could have been completed by those still employed through the leadership change. That is, Project 1, the press release for new undergraduate programs, should have been completed by the Communications and Content Manager, as it ultimately was after the delay. Project 2, the website updates for an existing graduate program, should have been completed by the Webmaster and Electronic Marketing Specialist, as it ultimately was. Neither of these employees transitioned into or out of their roles during the time of the delayed requests. While the Communications and Content Manager was fairly new to the role, and had limited prior experience, the Webmaster had been in their role since 2003. Both were subjected to continuing requests for work while experiencing leadership change in both personnel and overall reporting structure. Thus, while employee transitions can indeed be seen as a cause of missed deliverables, it is most specifically the leadership transitions in the department here that should be seen as responsible for the perceived failure to deliver, and thus generating the stress on the Requestor.

LIMITATIONS

A key limitation to the study is the lack of control data for successful marketing projects that were perceived to have been delivered in a timely fashion. Anecdotal commentary from the Requestor indicates that there had not been previous problems with requests to the Marketing and Communications department. Perception of timeliness may in fact by context-driven, or in this case, results driven as specific deliverable windows were needed to generate interest in new and revitalized programs before the Fall 2022 semester start. That is to say, true comparable controls may not have even been possible given the weight of the situation under study. Nevertheless, Project 1 and Project 2 are the only times that the Requestor feels that the Marketing and Communications department did not successfully deliver needed results.

Another limitation is that the employees and former employees of the Marketing and Communications department were not interviewed for the study. This was done in part to preserve the anonymity of the Requestor and to gain the cooperation of Human Resources in verifying the employment data, which the author felt was more central to the aims of the study. In addition, it would not be seen as positive on the part of the author or Requestor to reach out to co-workers and former co-workers to ask them why they had failed. Such requests would be seen as hostile and blame-placing in a worse case scenario, and at best, simply in poor taste. Further, they would have the potential to exacerbate the stress of the situation for the Requestor, and even for the former employees who had undergone potentially stressful job transitions during labour disruptions and workplace upheaval following a global pandemic.

DISCUSSION OF RESULTS: STRESS IN HIGHER EDUCATION

The impact of the psychological spillover stress generated for the Requestor must be understood in the context of United States higher education during the pandemic emergency. In the US, many colleges and universities often depend on tuition to sustain operations (Stabile, 2007, p. 9). In effect, they compete for potential students by offering a compelling experience, attractive programs and facilities, and acceptable job placement results. This is also in part due to reduced state funding. Of course, larger state schools or those with nationally recognized brands have no shortage of applicants, but smaller regional schools face extinction if their applicant pool diminishes to nothing (Gardner, 2023). The funds generated by tuition revenue represent an existential necessity for colleges, who despite sufficient "nest-egg" endowments (which may be in fact partially earmarked for specific purposes), may be in effect living from "paycheck to paycheck" to keep programs running. Increasingly, these programs have critical mass problems, in that it is not cost effective to run a class for only a few students, and yet a strong diversity of academic program offerings run against a diminishing pool of available students can split students into groups too small to progress. Some colleges even publish minimum class sizes to help better manage student expectations for course completion (e.g., Minot State, 2009). Inability to sustain sufficient class sizes as "normal" operations can lead to situations where alternate compensation models need to be considered for both full-time and adjunct faculty. Any change to job roles or compensation induces uncertainty and represents stress, as described above. Faculty compensation in particular is closely tied to faculty morale in United States higher education (Schuster and Finkelstein, 2008, p. 234). Martinez-Ramon and colleagues (2021) note that educators are prone to burnout from stress, particularly where they suffer from lack of agency.

To this notion must be added the so-called "Enrollment Cliff" model. The US Financial Crisis of 2007-2008 led to decreased birth rates, and 18 years later, it follows that there would be a smaller entering freshman class in 2025 or 2026 (Adams, 2020). The reduction in expected income had already been on the horizon before the pandemic, and colleges were already undertaking austerity measures in advance of a 10-15% expected reduction in revenue. COVID realized those reductions early as many schools switched to online instruction. Community colleges realized an approximate 20% reduction in entering freshmen (Nadwarny, 2021). Incoming students took a "gap year" in some cases as the value of higher education online was called into question, or parents' ability to pay (Koenig, 2021). Other factors included rising tuition year over year, increasing availability of alternatives for job training, and decreasing requirements in industry for bachelor's degrees in entry-level jobs (Schroeder, 2021). Student mental health issues, lack of motivation, and desire for extended options and additional flexibility represent increased stress for professors (Supiano, 2023).

Changes in American Higher Education have led to decreasing opportunities for tenure-track faculty. The increase in accessibility and acceptance of doctoral programs has led to market saturation of faculty candidates, and in parallel, colleges have increased use of adjunct and non-tenure track faculty (Bowen and Tobin, 2017, p. 154). This in part reflects a distillation of operational efficiency measures learned from for-profit industries, as graduate students, adjuncts, and retirees from industries can run courses (Bousquet and Nelson, 2008, p. 9). Full-time faculty positions are tightly-networked by academic discipline (Flood and Leap, 2018, p. 30), and thus insider bias represents an additional challenge to finding a new position within academia above the already rigorous tenure process. Tenure in most US Higher Education Institutions, when offered, is typically a six-year "up or out" model, where the tenure-track candidate must earn tenure at the end of years, or find employment outside of that role, which can induce anxiety (Whicker, *et. al.,* 1993, p. 39). Against the notion of lifetime employment once offered, colleges increasingly are able to separate even tenured faculty positions due to "financial exigency" (e.g., Kaplin and Lee, 2006, p. 582). Thus, should the programs fail for the Requestor, that person's career trajectory could ultimately be threatened, despite increasing opportunities for those in the service-providing department. They were not bound to higher education and could find employment in multiple industries that require marketing and communication services. Thus, the notion that the marketing department had delayed requested project work had created a sense of personal failure and resentment on the part of the Requestor, whose felt that their career path was disproportionately challenged by their failure to deliver timely work product.

What could have been effective in reducing the chance for failure and thus reducing the stress generated for the Requestor? The Requestor was aware that there were issues in the Marketing and Communications department related to turnover, including leadership change. Yet they did not attempt to engage with their own supervisor (a department Chair). They ultimately did reach out to the Provost (the second-tier supervisor) for help in getting the press release completed, and this was because the Provost had been instrumental in helping to put together the new programs launch in the first place. The Requestor did not attempt to engage with Human Resources regarding the issue, as they felt that they did not want to get the employees into trouble, given the problems already existing in the department. Further, the Requestor feared that reporting the failure of deliverables to Human Resources might have caused backlash from the remaining Marketing and Communications staff and delayed the required work product even longer.

While planned organizational change can be positive if it allows organizations to meet the competitive needs of the market (Picot, *et. al.,* 2008), any change is disruptive. Change, even with the best of intentions, upends functional processes and creates short-term inefficiencies. Continual or unplanned change results in longer-term inefficiencies. It creates fear and may generate toxic workplaces; it may decrease information sharing and contribute to job protectionism. Leadership change, including leadership structural change, may be particularly devastating as it strips away departmental control. As has been shown, the stress generated by leadership and personnel change in a service-providing department can spread outward like a contagion to others who had depended on their services.

In this case, the short-term merger of the responsibilities under the Vice President of Enrollment and Marketing is likely central to the problem. This decision was not made at the departmental level, but rather at the higher strategic management level, as was the decision to walk back the merger when the results proved ineffective. The two functions seem, on the surface, related, as the effectiveness of public-facing material created to attract students can, in fact, be measured by how many students are so attracted, at least into the start of the admissions funnel. Whether they go on to deposit and then register for classes would be influenced by the efficiency of the admissions staff.

Organizations can prevent work slippage through the implementation of automatic control systems, of the kind that can be seen in IT helpdesk software. This kind of software tracks work assignments, work completion, and work in process, and can generate productivity metrics for individual employees (Hartmann, *et. al.,* 2020, p. 223). Advanced versions of these platforms can show work in progress, what is uncompleted, who is assigned, and what is needed to move the projects forward (e.g., Kissflow, 2020), and this can aid with cross-departmental collaboration. Where general cross-departmental coupling is low, standard operating procedures are the most influential control system, as opposed to budget or statistical reporting (Macintosh and Daft, 1987). This would be the standard "black box" model of request and timely completion. The person requesting the services does not need to know how they are accomplished, if the work product is delivered on time and to acceptable standards. Statistical reporting and discussions of operating budget both increase effectiveness of cross-departmental collaboration when interdependency is moderate (Macintosh and Daft, *op. cit.*), such as would be represented by stronger work control and allocation of any additional resources needed to sustain operations in personnel crisis.

Work control software could not be implemented in the middle of a turnover crisis such as the Great Resignation, but would have been helpful had it already been in place. The transparency created by this kind of program may create resentment on the part of employees using it, as it seems to reflect a lack of trust in their ability to work independently. Yet, it can help alleviate blurred accountabilities, unclear processes, and job protectionism. It can help with "quiet quitting" as the results of an employee's contributions to the organization would be visible outside of the department—vital when leadership fails to motivate performance, yet the organization itself depends on the work product.

Employees in a failing department have no motivation to disclose weakness in job performance, such as the inability to complete requested work. Such disclosures may generate fear of negative performance reviews, despite the undue work shifted on to them from employee and leadership turnover. This fear needs to be mitigated through transparency, as surviving department members cannot be expected to accomplish leadership tasks if they have no training, are ill-suited, and have no formal responsibility for them. Yet these very department members may shoulder the weight and expectations of department performance until replacement workers and leaders can be hired, on-boarded, and trained. Clear communication with an organization's upper management is necessary when team members and departmental leaders leave their roles. It is important to balance expectations and workload for a department suffering excessive transitions, and this clear communication can result in the allocation of additional resources, such as consultants, outsourced production, or outsourced project managers.

Proactive intervention requires cooperation from other departments, including Human Resources and likely Finance as well, if expenditures are required to assure deliverables. Should organizations choose not to intervene and mitigate in times of excess employee turnover, this must be a calculated decision, looking at the opportunity cost associated with doing nothing. It is not merely a temporary decrease in departmental salary requirements, and assuming that those who persist will "step up" to complete any work required in the meantime. The company needs to realistically assess the strategic impact of missed deadlines, decreased production output, and increased risk of cognitive and emotional burnout leading to additional departures from poor job satisfaction (see Maslach and Jackson, 1984). Particularly in cases where the departmental leader is missing or not engaged, the need to perform this kind of risk assessment may not be recognized until it is too late. Human Resources will be aware of departmental departures, and the degree to which employee churn is evident will already be a part of their workflow. Data from exit interviews should serve as input into the decision to become involved in setting expectations for a department in crisis. The key to successful intervention will be knowing when and how to engage a faltering department without assigning blame to those who persist.

This can be accomplished through intervention after a set turnover metric (Holliday, 2021). Such an intervention could take the form of an assessment of work to be completed, and progress, as well as the contributions expected from those remaining. It will realistically look at the need for additional resources from outside the department (c.f., Macintosh and Daft, 1987), and be open to contractors, management consultants, and outsourcing. It is only in this way that the added burden of perceived need to control can be contained from spreading to other departments, along with its accompanying risk of contagious burnout, or burn-through of repeated failed hires. The process may be stressful, but the context would already indicate stress on the organization. Intervention represents the best possible outcome for the organization as a whole, even if it requires unexpected allocation of resources towards task accomplishment.

CONCLUSION AND RECOMMENDATIONS FOR FURTHER STUDY

It has been demonstrated that the Great Resignation model can be used to explain increasing employee turnover for a Marketing and Communications department at the 4-year, private Northeastern US college under study. This study has also demonstrated that such turnover, specifically including leadership transitions, affected deliverables for at least one internal client (the Requestor). In addition to challenging employment trends, the failed deliverables were a source of emotional and cognitive "spillover" stress for the Requestor. This was in addition to pandemic stress, industry stress, and any personal stress already present.

What remains to expand upon are similar scenarios at other institutions where disruption of services may have similarly been experienced with resulting added stresses. A collection of similar analyses could be made in the form of a meta-analysis of how departmental turnover affects workers in the same organization, but outside of the churning department. Time will tell what the Great Resignation has done to productivity across departments, but the present chapter presents a significant start to compiling future research.

REFERENCES

Aamodt, M. (2013). *Industrial/organizational psychology, 7e*. Wadsworth.

Adams, M. (2020). *The demographic cliff is already here—And it's about to get worse*. Education Advisory Board (EAB). Retrieved from: https://eab.com/insights/expert-insight/enrollment/the-demographic-cliff-is-already-here-and-its-about-to-get-worse/

Akhter, S. (2022). Key informants' interviews. In M. Islam, N. Khan, & R. Baikady (Eds.), *Principles of social research methodology* (pp. 389–404). Springer Nature. doi:10.1007/978-981-19-5441-2_27

Beheshti, N. (2021). We worked longer hours during the pandemic: Research says we need to work smarter, not harder. *Forbes*. Retrieved from: https://www.forbes.com/sites/nazbeheshti/2021/08/18/we-worked-longer-hours-during-the-pandemic-research-says-we-need-to-work-smarter-not-harder/?sh=627804bb1805

Bousquet, M., & Nelson, C. (2008). *How the university works: Higher education and the low-wage nation*. New York University Press.

Bowen, W., & Tobin, E. (2017). *Locus of authority: The evolution of faculty roles in higher education*. Princeton University Press.

Burke, W. (2017). Organization change: Theory and practice (5th ed.). New York, NY: SAGE.

Chowdhury, D. (2009). *Structured approach to improve passive aggressive organizational behavior of ABC Technologies: An empirical research* [Dissertation]. Lulu.com. Retrieved from: https://www.google.com/books/edition/Structured_Approach_to_Improve_Passive_A/L28h-OPPl1sC?hl=en&gbpv=0

Eggcellentwork.com. (2022). *Manager title without direct reports—Is it good or bad?* Retrieved from: https://eggcellentwork.com/manager-title-without-direct-reports/

Endresen, J. (2020). *COVID-19's impact of work, workers, and the workplace of the future*. Cornell Business. Retrieved from: https://business.cornell.edu/hub/2020/09/25/covid-19s-impact-work-workers-workplace-future/

Erat, S., Kitapci, H., & Comez, P. (2017). The effect of organizational loads on work stress, emotional commitment, and turnover intention. International Journal of Organizational Leadership, 6, 221-231. doi:10.19236/IJOL.2017.02.07

Farahat, S., Amin, O., Hamdy, H., & Fouad, M. (2021). The impact of work-related stress of the cognition domain of executive functioning of health care workers during the COVID-19 pandemic. *International Archives of Occupational and Environmental Health*. Advance online publication. doi:10.100700420-021-01814-8 PMID:34734341

Flamholtz, E. (1996). *Effective managerial control: Theory and practice*. Kluwer Academic Publishers. doi:10.1007/978-1-4613-1359-5

Flood, J., & Leap, T. (2018). *Managing risk in high-stakes faculty employment decisions*. ILR Press. doi:10.7591/cornell/9781501728952.001.0001

Gardner, L. (2023). Flagships prosper, while regionals suffer: Competition is fierce and the gap is widening. *Chronicle of Higher Education*. Retrieved from: https://www.chronicle.com/article/flagships-prosper-while-regionals-suffer

Hare, N. (2022). What is quiet quitting and how should leaders respond? *Forbes*. Retrieved from: https://www.forbes.com/sites/allbusiness/2022/09/01/what-is-quiet-quitting-and-how-should-leaders-respond/?sh=20f6b7ae6de0

Hartmann, F., Kraus, K., Nilsson, G., Anthony, R., & Govindarajan, V. (2020). Management control systems (2nd ed.). Boston, MA: McGraw-Hill.

Holliday, M. (2021). *10 causes of employee turnover & how to prevent/reduce them*. Oracle NetSuite. Retrieved from: https://www.netsuite.com/portal/resource/articles/human-resources/employee-turnover-causes.shtml

Jackson, S., Schuler, R., & Werner, S. (n.d.). Managing human resources (11th ed.). Mason, OH: South-Western.

Jacobs, J., & Gerson, K. (2005). *The time divide: Work, family, and gender inequity*. Harvard University Press.

Kaplin, W., & Lee, B. (2006). *The law of higher education: A comprehensive guide to legal implications of administrative decision-making*. Jossey-Bass.

Kissflow. (2020). 4 cross-departmental collaboration challenges and how to overcome them. *Kissflow*. Retrieved from: https://kissflow.com/digital-workplace/collaboration/challenges-in-cross-departmental-collaboration/

Koenig, K. (2021). Did students really take pandemic gap years? *EdSurge*. Retrieved from: https://www.edsurge.com/news/2021-11-08-did-students-really-take-pandemic-gap-years

Lussier, R., & Hendon, J. (2016). Human resource management: Functions, application, and skill development (2nd ed.). Thousand Oaks, CA: Sage.

Macintosh, N., & Daft, R. (1987). Management control systems and department interdependencies: An empirical study. *Accounting, Organizations and Society*, *12*(1), 49–61. doi:10.1016/0361-3682(87)90015-8

Marr, B. (2018). *Data-driven HR: How to use analytics and metrics to drive performance*. Kogan Page.

Martinez-Ramon, J., Morales-Rodriguez, F., & Perez-Lopez, S. (2021). Burnout, resilience, and COVID-19 among teachers: Predictive capacity of an artificial neural network. *Applied Sciences, 11*, 8206. doi:10.3390/app11178206

Maslach, C., & Jackson, S. (1984). Burnout in organizational settings. *Applied Social Psychology Annual*, *5*, 133–153.

Matteson, M., & Ivancevich, J. (2014). Merger and acquisition stress: fear and uncertainty at mid-career. In R. Hess (Ed.), *Career stress in changing times*. Routledge.

Mayrhofer, W., & Brewster, C. (2007). European human resource management: Researching developments over time. In R. Schuler & S. Jackson (Eds.), Strategic human resource management (2nd ed.). Malden, MA: Blackwell.

Minot State. (2009). *Registrar's office: Minimum class size policy*. Minot State University. Retrieved from: https://www.minotstateu.edu/records/pages/policy-minimum-class-size.shtml

Nadwarny, E. (2021). College enrollment plummeted during the pandemic. This fall, it's even worse. *NPR Morning Edition*. Retrieved from: https://www.npr.org/2021/10/26/1048955023/college-enrollment-down-pandemic-economy

Parker, K., & Horowitz, J. (2022). Majority of workers who quit a job in 2021 cite low pay, no opportunities for advancement, feeling disrespected. *Pew Research Center*. Retrieved from: https://www.pewresearch.org/fact-tank/2022/03/09/majority-of-workers-who-quit-a-job-in-2021-cite-low-pay-no-opportunities-for-advancement-feeling-disrespected/

Price Waterhouse Coopers. (2021). *It's time to reimagine how and where work will get done: PwC's US remote work survey*. PwC. Retrieved from: https://www.pwc.com/us/en/services/consulting/business-transformation/library/covid-19-us-remote-work-survey.html

Rudisill, J., Edwards, J., Hershberger, P., Jadwin, J., & McKee, J. (2010). Coping with job transitions over the work life. In T. Miller (Ed.), *Handbook of stressful transitions across the lifespan* (pp. 111–132). Springer. doi:10.1007/978-1-4419-0748-6_6

Schroeder, R. (2021). A second demographic cliff adds urgency for change. *Inside Higher Education*. Retrieved from: https://www.insidehighered.com/digital-learning/blogs/online-trending-now/second-demographic-cliff-adds-urgency-change

Schuster, J., & Finkelstein, M. (2008). *The American faculty: The restructuring of academic work and careers*. The Johns Hopkins University Press.

Stabile, D. (2007). *Economics, competition, and academia: An intellectual history of sophism versus virtue*. Edward Elgar Publishing. doi:10.4337/9781847207166

Supiano, B. (2023). Course correction: Students expect total flexibility in the pandemic-era classroom. But is that what they really need? *Chronicle of Higher Education*. Retrieved from: https://www.chronicle.com/article/course-correction

Whicker, M., Kronenfeld, J., & Stricker, R. (1993). *Getting tenure (Survival skills for scholars)*. Sage.

Workforce Hub. (n.d.). Churn rate. *Workforce Hub*. Retrieved from: https://www.workforcehub.com/glossary/churn-rate/

KEY TERMS AND DEFINITIONS

Control: Ability of a manager or organization to assure successful completion of a process and produce desired outcomes.

Cross-Departmental Dependencies: Processes that require collaboration between two or more departments to function.

Great Resignation: Changes to the workforce, particularly in the United States, as a result of the COVID-19 pandemic.

Leader: Within this chapter, an employee who is given supervisory responsibilities, including controlling the work process of others.

Manager: Within this chapter, an employee given responsibility for controlling a particular process, who may not have direct reports.

Requestor: Within this chapter, an employee requesting work product from an external department.

Spillover Stress: Stress generated from within an organization, but outside of one's home department.

Chapter 8
Inside Out-Radio Being Radio Outside the Studio:
Renascença's Communication During the First Wave of COVID-19

Rita Curvelo
Universidade Católica Portuguesa, Portugal

ABSTRACT

With the pandemic crisis, radio had to rethink its strategies and resort to new digital technologies and devices to continue its broadcasting. This new "at home" reality caused by COVID-19 forced radio to map new communication practices, and to draw new production processes and contents to meet the new demands and needs of its audiences. The purpose of this chapter is to explore employees' routines and work strategies in the Radio Renascença during the Corona Virus pandemic. In this context, there are identified internal communication antecedents and technological processes which enabled the station's teleworking. To carry out this research, semi-structured interviews were conducted with several radio presenters and producers, the channel's director and deputy director, and the sound engineer chief. Further information followed the participant observation method since it came from the author's personal experience, since she worked for 16 years.

INTRODUCTION

In times of crisis, wars or natural disasters, radio has always proved to be a present medium, managing to fulfil its news and entertainment function, "narrating the events, mobilizing empathy and solidarity" (Lopez, Kischinhevsky and Benzecry, 2020: 8), conveying useful, clear and objective information (when it was not at leaders or political factions service in the case of wars), and being permanently updated, at the same time that it distracts and accompanies the listeners who listen to it throughout the day.

DOI: 10.4018/978-1-6684-7353-5.ch008

In the 2020 health crisis, radio remained relevant, even achieving, in certain periods, an increase in listening habits on analogue, and an authentic digital audience's success (Cardoso et al.: 2020). However, "the COVID-19 crisis dramatically changed the environment in which organizations and their customers operate" (Ebersberger and Kuckertz, 2020: 127) and many companies "had to find new ways of leading, organizing and communicating when employees were told to adopt social distancing at work or work from home" (Ruck and Men, 2021).

The first case of the SARS-Cov-2 virus was reported in Portugal on March 2, 2020, with the Portuguese Presidency declaring "a state of emergency, due to (…) a public calamity situation"[1] and a necessary strict confinement, between March 18 and May 2. In the case of the media, imposed social distancing forced most of its professionals to work from home, making it necessary, for this reason, to change production practices and routines in order to guarantee the continuity of programming (in the case of radio and television) and printing (in the case of newspapers).

Radio was forced to rethink its strategies and resort to new technologies and digital devices in order not only to comply with the rules of social distancing, but also to continue broadcasting, ensuring permanent news updates on the evolution of the pandemic, on the different health measures, and sharing the restrictions that were being implemented by different governments.

Indeed, the digital sphere has enlarged its presence in the Portuguese media usage (Cardoso et al., 2020, pp. 24-25), visible in the listening growth patterns, in the news and web content viewing and reading escalade, in the streaming platforms subscriptions and applications downloads increase, and in the exponential resource of videoconferencing services (Ibidem: 25), such as Zoom or Microsoft Teams, and video applications such as Facetime or Skype and WhatsApp video calls. In other words, the outbreak underlined "the extreme degree to which the world is interconnected" (Budhwar and Cumming, 2020, p. 441). Isolated, but connected, is how we all began to live from March 2020 onwards. Radio *Renascença's* collaborators were no exception.

Renascença: History and Identity

To better understand the transformations and adjustments carried out by *Renascença*, with the arrival of COVID-19 in Portugal, to maintain its programming and presence in its listeners and followers' lives, albeit from a distance, a channel description and characterization will be presented, as well as its identity, objectives, and main targets.

Rádio *Renascença* is a nearly 85-year-old Portuguese Catholic broadcast. It was founded two years after the first radio station in Portugal - the Public *Emissora Nacional* - and just six years after the first radio station in the Vatican implementation, assuming itself from the very beginning as a "station at the Catholics service"[2].

The first broadcasts, still in AM and only for the Lisbon region, began on January 1, 1937. It was only in the 60s that they began to be listened to throughout the country on FM.

Monsignor Lopes da Cruz, its founder, who died in 1969, was succeeded by Monsignor Sezinando Rosa. In this regard, it should be mentioned that, even today, the *Renascença* Board of Directors has always been assured by a Church member establishing, in this way, a link of continuity at the top of the hierarchy, consistent with its Catholic identity.

In the 70s, *Renascença* already broadcasted 24 hours a day, inaugurating its news service in 1972, as well as its advertising commercialization, through a protocol established with the newly created independent company – Intervoz.

In 1979, the channel asserted itself as the Portugal audience front-runner, a leadership that would last, largely due to its morning show – *Despertar* (Awakening) – until the first years of the new millennium.

Renascença was conceived to address a predominantly Catholic audience, essentially urban, belonging mainly to the middle class, aged between 35 and 54 years old. Considering this target audience, the station offers a playlist where music from the 80s predominates, that is, a list of the songs most listened to by the target audience in their youth and not the latest musical hits, while also providing comprehensive information and leisure content.

Alongside the channel consolidation, the first regional studios were created in 1985 and, two years later, the company´s second major station - *RFM* - would emerge, assuming itself as a music radio, aimed at an urban younger audience (25-45). Independent of the *Renascença* channel, it also broadcasted in modulated frequency, to the whole country. This was followed by *Mega FM*, a music station made by young presenters for young people (from 15 to 18 years old), on air since 1998 in Lisbon and Porto (and later Sintra, Coimbra and Aveiro). This year also saw *Renascença* channel's website launch, which was followed by the other two stations web pages take-off. Through the internet, it had the ability to transmit its broadcasts to the whole world in a direct signal.

Throughout the last years of the 20th century, the group was an essential vector in helping to create broadcasters across borders, and in training technicians and Catholic broadcasters from various countries such as Guinea, Cape Verde, São Tomé and Príncipe, Angola, Mozambique, and Timor.

The first decade of the 21st century was marked by strong expansion and a diversification business desire: the group acquired the *Intervoz* entire share capital, which, in 2002, took over the advertising spaces of the three channels commercialization. By 2007, the radio's first digital newspaper was created – *Página* Um (Page one) – a free online newspaper from the News Department, which is common to the three radio stations. A year later, the company decided to go outside its core business with the creation of *Génios Y Meios*, dedicated to the events promotion and training proposals. During the same year, three uninterrupted web radios were launched by *RFM - 80's RFM, RFM Clubbing* and *Oceano Pacífico*. In 2008, a new AM channel was created - *Rádio Sim* - aimed at a senior audience, over 65 years old – which was discontinued in 2020, "for reasons of economic sustainability"[3], according to a Board of Directors statement.

The company has, however, expanded its degree of market penetration while continuing its growth with the launch of two Web TVs – *RFM's Vi* and *Renascença V+*. By 2010 it presented a new institutional image, changing its name to Grupo r/com – *Renascença*, Comunicação e Multimédia, a change motivated, according to one of its top managers, José Luís Ramos Pinheiro, by the need to "reorganize the structure that went through the reduction of its staff through an invitation to resign made to around 320 employees of the holding", and which obeyed the objective of "mirroring in the new designation the various areas of activity and companies of the group that are no longer focused on FM radio and medium wave"[4] .

The new image had as a strategic plan to communicate its scope, diversity, and dynamics: "The R/com Group – *Renascença* Comunicação Multimédia, is a Portuguese media group with radio brands in FM and Medium Wave (RR; RFM, MEGA HITS, Rádio SIM), web radios, an online newspaper, websites, web TVs, commercialization, marketing, events, entertainment and training (Genius y Meios)"[5] .

Being a Catholic mass media group, all its stations should pursue the aim of answering the information, educational, religious, and social needs of the Portuguese population. However, *Renascença* and *Rádio Sim* are the ones that most closely follow the originally defined evangelization mission since they broadcast to an older and more Catholic audience. For that reason, they are more attentive and interested in religious nature programs, with a broadcasting that continues to ensure the Rosary transmission, the Sunday Mass and the Fatima Ceremonies, and other Catholic vocation programs, although, nowadays, the broadcast bulk is concentrated on varied programming, with a music high rotation and a strong news commitment. It is an option which makes sense, insofar as the current listeners needs are not the same as the ones when the channel was created, a period when there were no church radios or television channels that broadcasted ceremonies or religious programmes.

In addition to pursuing its expansion by raising the number of transmitters across the country, the company, being a private Group, also aims to ensure leadership and share, to guarantee a good slice of advertisers in order to continue prospering in the audio-visual field.

Renascença: Property, Structure and Offer

For more than 70 years based on Rua Ivens (Chiado), in the heart of Lisbon's historic area, the *Renascença* building underwent successive renovations, following the number of channels enlargement and the new services multiplication, namely the growing digital media team.

Now headquartered at Quinta do Bom Pastor, on the capital's outskirts, the new facilities, built from scratch, are larger, have more studios with better technical conditions and digital equipment, which streamlines whether for dial or digital recording and editing schedules. According to the former President, Canon João Aguiar, "the new headquarters were designed to enhance synergies between areas and services"[6].

Therefore, the different channels studios are all currently placed on the same floor (contrary to what happened in Chiado), a proximity which allows for greater communication between the different channel's presenters and technicians as well as between them and the journalists. In *Renascença's* specific case, the two main departments (news and programming) previously physically apart are now gathered in the same open space and, as its current Director, Pedro Leal, recalls that: "in the new facilities there are no longer any offices. I don't have an office because I believe that we should all talk to each other. Although each area – news and programming – has its specificities and responsibilities, these must converge (…) if we do not carry out a conjugation exercise, the antenna is divided"[7].

The multimedia group nowadays has around 250 full-time employees, whose average seniority is around 10/15 years, with a greater concentration of collaborators in the News Department (common to the three channels), next is *Renascença's* Programming Department, and then the RFM team. The commercial and marketing departments, the HR department, the financial, planning, and documentation departments are, like the newsroom, common to the three radio stations, as are the operating and broadcasting sectors and studio maintenance office.

Recently renamed *Renascença Multimédia Group,* the organization remains private and, for this reason, independent of State bodies, being jointly owned by the Patriarchate of Lisbon (60%) and by the Portuguese Episcopal Conference (40%).

The top management Board is currently chaired by D. Américo Aguiar, Lisbon Auxiliary Bishop and other two members: José Luís Ramos Pinheiro (programming area) and Ana Braga (financial department). Father Américo Aguiar is also Chairman of the Board of Directors of *Intervoz*.

The older stations (*Renascença* and *RFM*) have a director and deputy director. The younger station now named *Mega Hits*, on the other hand, being smaller only has a director, the same happening in the Group departments.

As a media company, *Renascença Multimédia Group* is a service company (news and entertainment), thus not offering a tangible product, which implies a transfer of ownership. It should also be noted that there is a clear difference in the way in which the radio contents are "consumed" compared to goods or services. According to Lovelock and Wirtz, regarding services delivered by the media, they provide "access to a variety of value-creating elements rather than transfer of ownership" (Lovelock and Wirtz, 2011: 37). A media group is also different from other companies due to the social value that its services assume: "media constitute a powerful instrument of education whose nature and diversity considerably shape the collective values of society" (Anderson and Gabszewicz, 2005: 4). In the case of a radio station, there are several gratifications one can find when listening: pure entertainment, news, or companionship, for example.

Bearing in mind a means of social communication such as radio, there is another variable to consider: *Renascença* (and other commercial stations) operates in a bilateral market or "two-sided market", in the sense of Simon R. Anderson and Jean J. Gabszewicz (2005), which means that it directs its services to two preferential targets: listeners and advertisers: "Media firms need advertisers to make the production of media content worthwhile, while advertisers need media firms to make their products known to potential consumers. Consequently, the media industry sells a joint product to two different categories of buyers: the medium itself to advertisers, and the medium content to media consumers (readers, TV-watchers, web-surfers, etc.)" (Anderson e Gabszewicz, 2005:4).

In this sense, it isn´t the audience that (directly) guarantees the Group's sustainability, but the clients/companies who invest in it. However, to generate a good revenue, radio stations need a significant number of listeners to make the advertising investment attractive, something that has been achieved by *Renascença´s* group over the years.

To better define the channel and *Renascença's* brand, it also makes sense in this study to briefly analyse its recent path. After successive direction leaderships, different seasons, and board reshuffles in the last 8-10 years, the channel has been trying to conquer the 35-54 years old segment, especially the middle and senior management class, an objective that has faced many obstacles since it is still seen today (by both non-listeners and several advertisers) as a popular radio station, for the elderly and practicing Catholics. This incorrect perception does not help *Renascença's* reputation considering the current radio listeners panorama. Its repositioning attempt had the core idea that an audience with greater purchasing power could bring more advertising investment. However, this posture did not invalidate the fact that the channel continued presenting a programming punctuated by various religious contents and with a proximity communication with its audience.

In a media group, a service provider such as *Renascença Multimédia*, most employees' voices represent the service and the company where they work. In the case of radio presenters and journalists, they are the personification of the respective channels, the representatives of their brands. As Carole Fleming emphasizes "people see presenters not only as massive stars but also as a kind of their friend (...) The audience needs to feel that presenters have got life experience, that they're warm and they care" (Fleming, 2010, p.95). Elwyn Evans has the same thought, stating that "the listener needs to feel that he is being spoken to personally, to a particular individual" (Evans, 1977, p. 20). One of the goals of *Renascença*, given its identity and objectives is to strengthen ties with its audience and has been a positioning adopted by the station's entertainers. The relationship with the listener is established not only on air, but also through the internet or social networks. In fact, the emergence of new digital platforms has created more demands on the broadcaster/entertainer, since these are assumed as another extension or means of contact with listeners, which must be permanently nourished to maintain.

Renascença: Main Internal Communication Channels and Technological Devices

Many studies have already emphasised that well-informed employees feel a sense of commitment and trust in their organization (Adamu and Mohamad, 2019; Ecklebe and Löffler, 2021; Rowlings, 2008). In this sense, it can be stated that it is necessary to constantly share information with employees so that they feel up to date about what is happening within their organisation, thus promoting a greater sense of belonging and motivation.

With this in mind, in the present research we will analyse the Group's main internal communication channels to understand how *Renascença*, in particular, kept its employees informed about the tasks to be performed during the first wave of COVID-19 in Portugal.

The *Renascença Multimedia Group* does not have any internal communication department, only a Human Resources Director responsible for salary management, training, and performance evaluation of employees (when they exist), contractual regimes and collaborators records, career management, and facilities maintenance. The Marketing Department is responsible for managing information on the various channel's different initiatives, both on the intranet and on the internal Facebook page, communication tools that will be studied below[8].

Regarding interpersonal communication actions, there are currently few general and interdepartmental meetings and contacts between management and employees. There is, however, a weekly top management meeting with the current Directors of the three channels in which the content to be developed on air the following week are presented and discussed, as well as meetings with elements of the marketing and commercial departments, aimed at aligning specific promotions. On the Group's anniversary, a meeting is held in the Auditorium to honour employees who complete 25 years of service with the company, in the presence of the Chairman of the Management Board[9].

Within each directorate there are weekly meetings (news and programming departments) where the contents and actions to be developed in the short term are planned. In the case of the *Renascença* Programme Directorate, there is a weekly meeting with only the station's animators, the Director, and the Deputy Director. There are also recurring meetings with the employees directly involved in specific initiatives. Occasionally, small briefings are given to the whole team during specifically scheduled meetings, regarding future actions of the channel, such as, for example, the Open Day, in which the three radio stations open their doors to listeners who want to visit the studios. Otherwise, every week, the *Renascença* team receives by email the promotional contents to be aired in each programme, such as concerts or other cultural events sponsor, station's special broadcasts highlights, football matches reports or weekly programmes highpoints.

In the News Department the panorama is not very different. Every week there is an editor's meeting with Director and/or Deputy Director and the editor-in-chief. This meeting is not attended by most journalists from all the channels, their technicians, and assistants.

Regarding work meetings that simultaneously bring together programming and newsroom elements, there is only one, every two months, organised by the strategic marketing department, with the purpose of reporting on the latest audience figures. However, it should be noted that the two main channel department employees who were previously physically separated on different floors of the old building, are now gathered in an open space, facilitating interpersonal communication between everyone.

The company has an intranet where the Broadcaster timeline can be found, the departments description, collaborator's interviews, applications (such as access to the traffic service), the units and directorates composition, the employees contacts, internal documents, and a news archive. This page has a banner whose objective is to stress the most important or recent action launched by one of the Group's channels. The organization also has an internal Facebook page. Communicated on its wall are the external actions of the three radio stations of the group, either in the form of press releases that highlight not only audiences' data, but also the various initiatives the channels sponsor, or in the form of photographs or promotional videos"[10].

In technological terms, remote radio programming is not an entirely new challenge. In recent years, in parallel with the extension of radio to online, we have also witnessed a greater computerization of the medium, with the introduction of "automation programs that organize the selection and combine musical sequences" (Cordeiro, 2010, p. 155) known as the Radio Computing Service, or RCS. This is a provider of programming and broadcasting software for radio stations, and one of its major features is the Selector. This music programming software creates and fine-tunes daily music schedules to ensure that there are no long sequences of musical themes with the same beat/energy or mood, as well as maintaining a music library and constructing the line-ups for the various broadcasting hours, according to the defined format criteria. These alignments, or clocks, are very useful to visualise the content's distribution throughout each hour of broadcasting.

RCS also provides a scheduling system for non-musical elements (such as entertainer markers, advertising spots and station self-promotions, jingles, and medleys) called Linker, a digital automation system for PC broadcasting called Master Control, and a commercial traffic system known as Airwaves.

The scheduling, or production of the station's musical line-up, thus speeds up the programming process and avoids unnecessary errors or repetitions. In addition to incorporating and sequencing songs, this content scheduling procedure may also establish the order of callsigns, jingles or station medleys, advertising blocks, promotions, thus balancing word time with music time.

Like most radio stations, the *Renascença* channel has also unreservedly accepted and integrated the various versions of the automation programs and the digital advances since the appearance of the Internet and the social networks. With the pandemic, a greater investment in online production and in the respective distribution in different digital formats has been reinforced.

Renascença: Internal and External Response to the Pandemic Challenges

With the COVID-19 arrival, many radio stations already had the technology to operate at a distance, although its potential was not being fully exploited because the pre-pandemic context did not justify it. With the crisis caused by the Corona virus, its greater use was felt since telework became the reality for almost all its professionals.

According to Cardoso, the pandemic affected the traditional Portuguese media sector, particularly the media which had invested less in digital and were, therefore, less prepared to work remotely, as was the case of the written press. The same researcher also stated that there was a "change in the consumption mindset, from out-of-home to in-home" and the players who had adjusted better and incorporated the technological and digital advances were less affected[11].

In the case of radio stations in general, the crisis caused by the Corona virus accelerated the process of taking advantage of the digital potentialities that radio already had, but rarely used. As José Loureiro, *Renascença's Multimédia Group* sound engineer, recalls: "at the organization's radio stations first we had to guarantee the connectivity of the employees to the company structure (...) we already had a history of VPN connections, that is, secure connections through the internet outside the company that were already used with some regularity, by a restricted number of people. As of March 11, 2020, with the pandemic and the necessary social distancing, this number multiplied because almost all people went home to work".

Also contributing to the radio to remain remotely operational was the aforementioned automation and content management system that the group´s radio stations adopted in 2015 - the RCS Zetta - which, over the past few years, had given the group´s radio events that are done live or outdoors, had been developing remote access tools. In other words, this software already had many designed features for outside use on computers that did not have to be connected via a web page: "Every time a new update came out (...) I found in the programme many more features for outdoors use than inside the studio: Zetta2GO for example, which gave us control of the Zetta Automation/Playout system from any web browser, Zetta on the move (…) with the pandemic we found that we already had the material to ensure continuous radio broadcasts"[12].

Dina Isabel, the station's Deputy Director, recalled however that overseeing the Group´s three radio stations meant that some choices had to be made since there wasn´t enough equipment for all the hosts. Without enough laptops, the obvious answer would be to simply buy more, however, the issue was that there were no computers available in the market given the growth in demand, restrictions placed on European carriers, and a lack of material in continents such as Asia: "There could even be technical solutions to ensure the broadcast from all of the presenter's homes, but it was no longer possible to buy anything else"[13].

Even so, as José Loureiro remembered: "I got microphone cables from the studios, I dismantled hard microphones from the booth so that the animators could work from home, I bought and borrowed from some suppliers mixing desks and interfaces to connect to the computers... I collected everything I could. The next step was to go to each host's house to set up the available equipment and explain how it should be used: there were those who did the radio inside the wardrobe or under a duvet to muffle the echo"[14].

Even with limited means, Dina Isabel recalled that *Renascença* was able to keep the morning show team and three other radio hosts presenting their shows from home, while the remaining animators started producing content[15].

In the case of the programme "As três da manhã" ("Morning three"), presented by three announcers - Ana Galvão, Joana Marques and Carla Rocha, later replaced by Filipa Galrão - between 7 a.m. and 10 a.m., the show "continued to be centralised in the *Renascença*'s studios, with the animators broadcasting remotely. Nevertheless, the newscasts were broadcasted from the headquarters, with technician support, so that the three hosts could receive the signal at home"[16].

Away from the broadcasting studios, the production routines took place via team meetings in a remote environment – Zoom or Teams[17] – and through WhatsApp working group messages. These tools ended up assuming an important role in this context as a means of contact between colleagues.

Even remotely connected, however, the pandemic showed that social distancing is hard to handle for humans since "man is a social animal and social relations and the social interactions are integral to human civilization" (Singh and Singh, 2020, p. 169). In this regard, Pedro Leal recalled that "it was difficult to manage information at a distance" because his job is to "talk face to face with the collaborators"[18].

In operational terms, the morning show producer, Sandra Torres, stated that "the first month of the pandemic was not very easy, because we have a team with many elements and many contributions, which is difficult to manage from a distance. There are many people with whom we must cross-check information…the technicians were tireless in this phase, they were our beacon, they were the few who didn't go home and were in the cabin allowing everything to happen"[19]. Regarding specific working hours, João Duarte, assistant producer of the same programme mentioned "the difficulty of having a concrete schedule to work. There were (non-informative) contents that we only closed at midnight, because when the programme ended at 10am, each one had a different routine"[20].

Figure 1. Morning show hosts in a teleworking environment

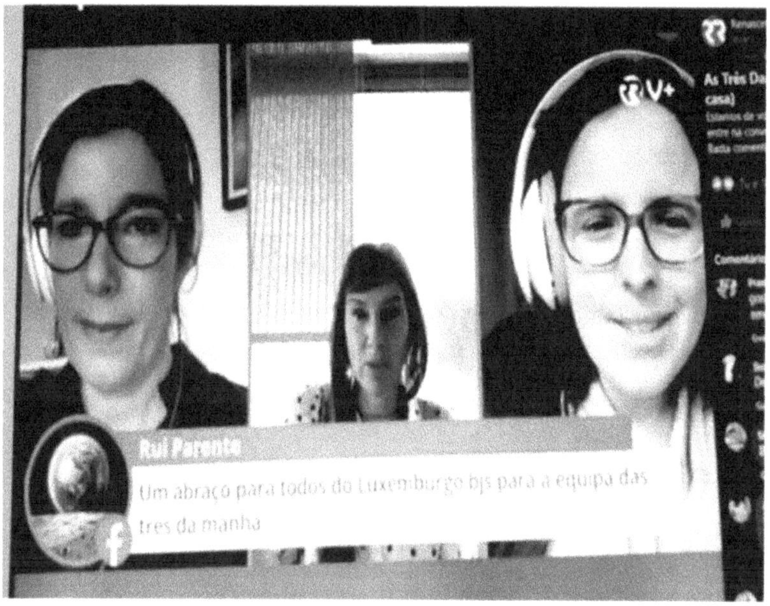

Figure 2.

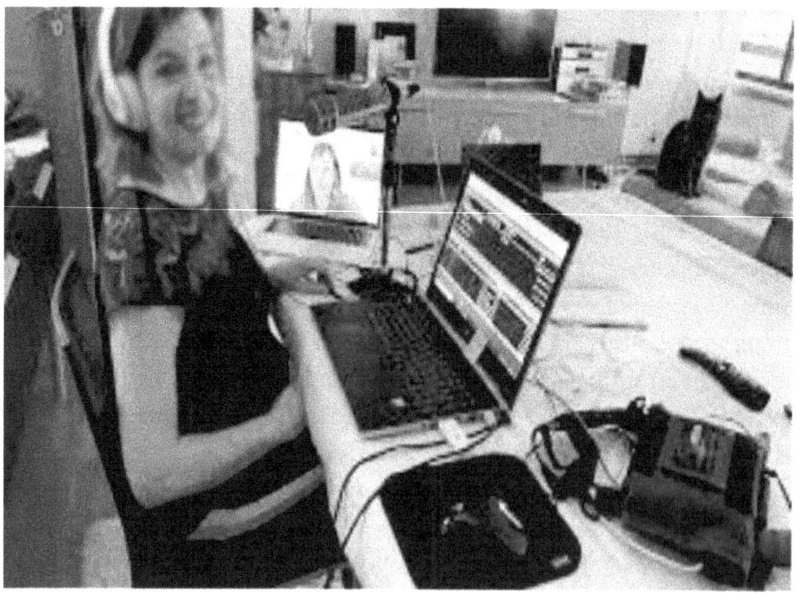

With regard to the dialogue between the news and programming directorates, except for the Director's emails, already mentioned in the specific morning show case, the communication was ensured by its producer via email, telephone or WhatsApp: "I ended up making the bridge between everyone because we were no longer in the same room. As there are many of us, there was a need for someone to centralise the information that would go on the air"[21].

On air, the social distance teleworking had some constraints. Ana Galvão, one of the morning show's three hosts recalled that "at home, separated, without big issues to talk about (...) we would see each other by Facetime but the sound was horrible. The programme lives a lot from our conversations and, when you are not looking at who you are talking to, or looking at them with some delay, it creates some moments of silence because you don't know if any of them are going to move on to talk and you don't want to interrupt". Another problem, the host pointed out, was to "understand what people's new schedule was: who wakes up at 7 in the morning if they are at home?"[22] and having to understand what contents would make sense for those who continued to wake up early. Indeed, with lockdown, listening patterns also changed.

As referred to in the Obercom study of April 2020[23], there was a decrease in the number of listeners "in commuter car migrations". There was no longer a concentration between 7 and 10 a.m. on the car radio. Instead, it was becoming more dispersed, from home, registering a significant increase in share (one listens for longer periods of time) and number of listeners outside of prime time, during the day, and especially in digital, through listening on the computer or on mobile devices[24].

The new at home reality brought about by COVID-19, also made people spend less time in the car (reducing the need for traffic information), and forced the cancellation of sporting events and shows, which, at first, contributed to a decrease in entertainment content that used to regularly punctuate Renaissance's programmes.

Bearing this new normal reality in mind, Sandra Torres stressed that "we could not stop talking about the pandemic and, therefore, naturally, the news block was bigger because more info was demanded. People wanted to listen to what health specialists had to say... we felt that we could not stop informing people, but at a certain point, we also had to remind them that there was life beyond Covid, even though the days all seemed the same"[25].

Being deprived from collecting in loco testimonies, the newsroom and its journalists started "recording via zoom or clean feed and edited interviews at home"[26], and very few people were working in person in the newsroom: "we had access to our operating system through computers that went to the collaborator's homes, together with a microphone in the case of the radio programme presenters". Since this was a radio station, however, "it was necessary to keep some professionals working at the headquarters, in shifts, since their work could not be done from home, as was the case of some journalists, studio maintenance staff and sound technicians"[27].

COVID-19 was, indeed, the trigger for the experimentation and execution of remote programmes daily, from the animators' homes, either via radio, but also on the respective websites through streaming, and social networks such as Facebook or Instagram.

The rapid adaptation to new contexts by big national coverage radios was, however, not a total novelty. Living in a new multimedia and hypermedia environment, the medium was developing and calibrating its websites to the potentialities that the technological world was offering, creating its channels also online, providing podcasts of its own items, performing streams on its websites or social networks, that is, being present on "multiple platforms, showing its ability and agility of adaptation to expand the distribution of produced content" (Lima et al, 2021: 63). In other words: radio had already gone through a long path of adaptation towards a "hybrid system of multimedia content distribution, following a "multiplatform and convergent model in both production and diffusion" (ibid). *Renascença* followed the trends that were being observed across borders.

It is curious to mention that in December 2019, without suspecting the impact of a pandemic, *Renascença's* program *As Três da Manhã* (*Three in the Morning*), held a special Christmas broadcast, from the homes of its presenters, welcoming several guests, simultaneously on the radio and on social networks. This three-hour long broadcast, from a distance, would end up being the proof that the station was prepared to guarantee its programming outside of the studios.

Despite being a generalist channel, *Renascença* ended up, in first phase (March/April 2020), filling its grid with more news content than entertainment to meet the new needs of its audience: constant information updates on the increase of new cases, on the procedures of the General Directorate of Health (DGS), and interviews with medicine and virology specialists (Table 1).

The arrival of an external threat such as the Corona Virus also caused a retraction in advertising investment. According to the ERC (Communication Regulator Entity) report of 2021, *Renascença* had to face a decrease in sales and services rendered that fell "33.6%, to 14 million 783 thousand euros", reflecting "the restrictions imposed by the pandemic and its effects on advertising revenues and the holding of events". In this sense and reliant on data from the same report, the Catholic station was forced to resort to "the moratorium on bank loans as part of the measures to mitigate the effects of the pandemic crisis"[28].

Working in adversity, at a distance and with financial constraints, "many of its professionals worked more... with less, given that advertising revenues fell significantly" (Cardoso et al, 2021). But the radio did not forget its companion dimension to the many who, due to the Corona virus, were deprived of the conviviality with family and friends.

It was therefore necessary, as Pedro Leal, Programming Director, stated "to be up to date with people's lives" and to strengthen even more the proximity with the audience. In the case of *Renascença*, at the beginning of the pandemic, special programs were carried out (Table 1) with the listener's participation, such as "A hora da Júlia" ("Julia's Hour"), with the famous TV presenter Júlia Pinheiro who had been away from the radio microphones for a long time and offered herself to talk at night, live, with the listeners; the programme "Quarto do Fundo" (Back room), with the entertainer Carla Rocha and a psychologist; on social networks, with "Prisão Domiciliária" ("House Arrest"), a humorous video content starring comedians Joana Marques and Daniel Leitão; and "No Ar com Ana Galvão" ("On air with Ana Galvão"), a daily half-hour Instagram live (at 9pm) on in which she spoke with various music, theatre, music, humour artists TV personalities, and other public figures: "I started doing a live on Instagram every day between 9h and 9h30 with public figures...I think I'll never be able to do something similar again because it was during the confinement and the interviewees were always available…there was a spirit of mutual help and a need to comfort each other…I started receiving messages from people who were available to talk to me in that half hour, precisely because they were in isolation at home, like me"[29].

Radio was being done inside out, in a "decentralized" way, from a new office or improvised studio: the living room, the balcony or the bedroom, to the listeners homes. Everyone was going through the same thing, but it was up to the radio to be the unifying link, accompanying and helping all of those who were confined.

Off air there was also the idea of holding Friday zoom meetings (Table 1), after the morning show, between the hosts and some listeners who signed up, so that they could have another moment to share their stories and experiences, say what they were doing and confess what worried them the most: "they told their stories, how they were living the pandemic, what they were doing, where they were listening to us. We used some stories for content and the listeners also suggested topics and we would research and talk about them later"[30].

Deep down, social isolation ended up, ironically, being an opportunity to strengthen bonds with the audience, perhaps more fragile because of the isolation: in the case of *Renascença*, there was even a WhatsApp messages increase during the first two waves of the Corona virus, a boost which was also due to the "hosts greater appeal to the listeners participation…we could not receive guests in studio and we felt the need to know how people were living that time"[31].

Throughout this process, the team, however, began to feel "the need to talk about other topics, although the days seemed all the same" recalled the producer of the morning, Sandra Torres. In this regard, Ana Galvão reinforced that "at a certain point, we only talked about animals, children, domestic environment realities…I, taught Joana how to iron, for example", while the comedian Joana Marques mentioned that "we talked about what we had done the day before, which was not very different, and we tried not to talk only about Covid". However, since there were no outdoor events, outside the news, the content was more about what people were doing at home: "from gymnastics to cooking bread, going to the supermarket and to the pharmacy and plant treatment".

Table 1.

Audience New Needs	Radio Response
Detailed information	Adjustments in the programme's alignment concerning the pandemics impact: more and extended news bulletins on air. Experts interviews on air with doctors, epidemiologists, and virologists.
Useful information	Constant info updating regarding mandatory confinement rules and authorized travel, respiratory etiquette, open services; reopening of stores and restaurants and their constraints; clarifications on the different stages of vaccination; suggestions about shows that people could watch online, without leaving home.
Company, proximity	Special daily night show programmes with listeners' phone calls. Psychologists' participation in a weekend show. Friday zoom meetings with listeners and the morning show hosts.
More online contents	Humorous video contents on the station's social media and internet. Daily lives on Instagram with several music, theatre or humour personalities and other public figures. Daily host's stories about their daily life at home.

In other moments, it was therefore necessary to offer other types of content, not related to the pandemic, to mitigate the excess of information (the so-called "info fatigue") on the pandemic crisis: "there was a need to go out there and focus more on other issues and entertainment"[32]. In this sense, as soon as it was allowed, Ana Galvão went to the street to report twice a week and interview people who were out working.

José Loureiro recalled that during this period, "both the mask and the plastic visor were very detrimental to the quality of speech, although this was a minor evil. Even so, we never plasticised the microphones, opting instead to disinfect the microphone wind blowers after each use, and to take more than one microphone outdoors to ensure that reporter and interviewee complied with the distance rules imposed by the Government"[33].

In the second wave of the Pandemic, the team moved to the radio station's headquarters, but in separate studios, "with a plexiglass screen separating us from the few guests we could receive at the time". Little by little, the programme's usual content was resumed, and the news sections and routines imposed by the outbreak were reduced. Sandra Torres gave as an example of a new section created during this period: "on Fridays we started giving suggestions about shows that people could watch online, without leaving home. We tried to maintain a certain contact with the artists, and the presenters' shared stories about what was happening to them"[34].

In May 2020, according to *NetAudience* studies published by the company, the *Renascença* Multimedia Group had quadrupled its audience, leading radio in digital. This online leadership would be confirmed in the following year, when the Group was once again in 1st place in the Radio digital medium "with three times the 'reach' of the competition"[35].

With more digital traffic, radio "managed to resist in a considerably positive way to the disruptive effects of the coronavirus and the confinement period", something that is due to Internet radio listening that, in Portugal reached "2 million and 844 thousand Portuguese (...) 33.2% of the universe under analysis (Cardoso et al., 2021).

In almost 85 years of existence, *Renascença* has already been "25 years in digital and 15 years in the production of video contents", factors that, with the pandemic, could assure the continuity of its presence on air and online[36].

Despite all the setbacks in a lockdown context, some of the interviewees mentioned positive aspects of telework. João Duarte, for example, stated that "work has improved considerably among all of us. I usually waste a lot of time on the radio because I am constantly interrupted, and I get distracted. An hour at home was more profitable than three hours on the radio…I also woke up later, I slept more"[37].

In turn, radio presenter Filipa Galrão highlighted the (more) time she spent with her children: "this more present parenthood was important although I recognize that, for some people, it was hard"[38].

The station's Deputy Director, Dina Isabel, pointed out that it was a time in which there was a lot of mutual help: in that period nobody questioned anything. Everyone asked what help was necessary for those who were on air. There was a great solidarity and a great capacity of adaptation by everyone to make radio from home…some announcers set up real studios at home, with equipment bought by themselves…There were no schedules, but there were rules, the work had to be delivered on time"[39].

Regarding less positive aspects, Sandra Torres confessed that she worked more at home, although she felt that she produced less: "when the programme ended, after many phone calls and e-mails, we went to team meetings much more tired because, during the show, we had no moments of pause"[40].

The sound engineer, José Loureiro, noted, in turn, that "the adaptation to remote work was easier for the younger ones, from *Mega Hits* station: they live well in combining an entire programme through WhatsApp messages. The older ones, from *Renascença* and *RFM* missed more the studio, the mixing desk. There's a lot happening in radio walls that arises from spontaneous interactions, from exchanging ideas in the moment. Although we have the technology at our disposal, we lose ideas, we lose that immediate conversation". As for the need for more social contact, he underlined that "face-to-face interaction was most felt by *Mega's* animators, since they are younger and closer, given that their team is smaller"[41].

CONCLUSION

COVID-19 evidenced that traditional media's value, namely radio, is still a critical source of information and entertainment during a state of emergency. The pandemic crisis was even a trigger for the experimentation and execution of distance programmes on a daily basis, from the animators' homes, either via radio, but also through streaming on its websites and on social media, such as Facebook or Instagram. The Outbreak also activated resilience, experimentation of new formats and the emergence of more listener's information and companionship.

This study identified several precedent dissemination information strategies and company's goals, namely, providing serious and credible information, companion, and entertainment, following its Catholic mission, which were crucial for the station to continue its broadcasting. *Renascença* was able to respond to the different challenges that the Corona virus imposed in the first months of social distancing. Internally, accurate information circulated vertically from the Director and the deputy director to their team, and horizontally, between colleagues. The research also demonstrated that a good working environment promotes a great spirit of solidarity and mutual help among colleagues in times of crisis.

There was also a fast adaptation to the teleworking context facilitated by the technological updates that *Renascença* had been embracing before the Pandemics, namely their VPN connections and their remote automation programmes. Therefore, this investigation is a clear example that companies which invested in new digital technologies before the Pandemics were the ones that best coped with the communication challenges of the social distancing.

Externally, there was an accurate and objective spread of information, with more extended news and specialists on air when the crisis begun. The station also presented new contents having in mind the new listening habits: no longer centred on prime-time (7am-10am) and more spread throughout the day – not in the car but at home.

During the COVID-19 first waves, *Renascença* registered an on air and, especially an online listening growth, which allowed the station to resist in a largely positive way to the Corona virus confinement more disturbing outcomes.

REFERENCES

Adamu, A., & Mohamad, B. (2019). A reliable and valid measurement scale for assessing internal crisis communication. *Journal of Communication Management (London)*, *23*(2), 90–108. doi:10.1108/JCOM-07-2018-0068

Anderson, S. P., & Gabszewicz, J. J. (2005). The media and advertising: a tale of two-sided markets. In *Handbook of Cultural Economics*. Elsevier Science.

Budhwar, P., & Cumming, D. (2020). New Directions in Management Research and Communication: Lessons from the COVID-19 Pandemic. *British Journal of Management*, *31*(3). doi:10.1111/1467-8551.12426

Cardoso, G., Baldi, V., Paisana, M., & Quintanilha, T. L. (2020). *Pandemia e consumos mediáticos*. OberCom - Observatório da Comunicação.

Cordeiro, P. (2010). *A Rádio e as Indústrias culturais. Estratégias de Programação na transição para o digital*. Livros Horizonte.

Ebersberger, B., & Kuckertz, A. (2021). Hop to it! The impact of organization type on innovation response time to the COVID-19 crisis. *Journal of Business Research*, *124*, 126–135. doi:10.1016/j.jbusres.2020.11.051 PMID:36540106

Ecklebe, S., & Löffler, N. (2021). A question of quality: Perceptions of internal communication during the COVID-19 pandemic in Germany. *Journal of Communication Management (London)*, *25*(3), 214–232. doi:10.1108/JCOM-09-2020-0101

Evans, E. (1977). *Radio. A Guide to Broadcasting Techniques*. Barrie & Jenkins.

Fleming, C. (2010). *The Radio Handbook*. Routledge.

Lima, C. A. R., Fechine, Veloso, A., Melo, P. R., & Dantas, I. H. (2021). O rádio expandido no enfrentamento à pandemia de COVID-19: A experiência da Rádio Universitária Paulo Freire. *Radiofonias – Revista de Estudos em Mídia Sonora, Mariana-MG, 12*(1), 58-90.

Lopes, F., Santos, C. A., Peixinho, A. T., Magalhães, O. E., & Araújo, R. (2021). COVID-19: Uma pandemia que reconfigura o jornalismo? *Media & Jornalismo*, *21*(39), 57–75. doi:10.14195/2183-5462_39_3

Lovelock, C., & Wirtz, J. (2011). *Services Marketing: People, Technology*. Pearson.

Rawlins, B. L. (2008). Give the emperor a mirror: Toward developing a stakeholder measurement of organizational transparency. *Journal of Public Relations Research*, *21*(1), 71–99. doi:10.1080/10627260802153421

Ruck, K., & Men, L. R. (2021). Guest editorial: Internal communication during the COVID-19 pandemic. *Journal of Communication Management (London)*, *25*(3), 185–195. doi:10.1108/JCOM-08-2021-163

Singh, J., & Singh, J. (2020). *COVID-19 and its impact on society. Electronic Research Journal of Social Sciences and Humanities*, 2.

ENDNOTES

1. https://dre.pt/dre/detalhe/decreto-presidente-republica/14-a-2020-130399862, accessed on February 10th, 2023.
2. Jorge Silva, in QSP – Revista de Rádio e Comunicações, accessed on October 23, 2021
3. https://expresso.pt/economia/2020-01-03-Grupo-Renascenca-anuncia-fim-da-Radio-Sim, accessed on November 12, 2022.
4. https://www.meiosepublicidade.pt/2010/02/grupo-renascenca-e-agora-rcom/, accessed on April 7, 2022.
5. https://gruporcom.wordpress.com/about/, accessed on April 7, 2022.
6. https://rr.sapo.pt/noticia/pais/2016/05/11/grupo-renascenca-multimedia-tem-novas-instala-coes/53860/, accessed on April 7, 2022.
7. Pedro Leal - interview July 13, 2021.

8 Data obtained by the author through participation observation while working at the channel, between 1998 and 2015.
9 Data obtained by the author through participation observation.
10 Data obtained by the author through participation observation.
11 https://obercom.pt/wp-content/uploads/2020/06/DNR_PT_2020_16jun.pdf, accessed on November 12, 2022.
12 José Loureiro - interview 31 August 2021.
13 Dina Isabel - interview 29 July 2021.
14 José Loureiro - interview 31 August 2021
15 Dina Isabel - interview 29 July 2021.
16 José Loureiro - interview 31 August 2021.
17 Zoom Video conferencing is a communication's platform which connects users through video, audio, or cell phone. Microsoft Teams is a collaboration app also created to maintain the connection between its users in a hybrid working scenario.
18 Pedro Leal - interview July 13, 2021.
19 Sandra Torres - interview July 12, 2021.
20 João Duarte - interview July 20, 2021
21 Sandra Torres - interview July 12, 2021.
22 Ana Galvão - interview August 30, 2021.
23 https://obercom.pt/wp-content/uploads/2020/06/DNR_PT_2020_16jun.pdf, accessed on November 12, 2022.
24 https://marketeer.sapo.pt/ha-cada-vez-mais-portugueses-a-ouvir-radio-pela-internet/, accessed on November 12, 2022.
25 Sandra Torres interview
26 Dina Isabel interview.
27 José Loureiro interview.
28 https://portaltransparencia.erc.pt/media/1071/an%C3%A1lise-econ%C3%B3mico-financeira-do-setor-de-media-em-2020.pdf, accessed on November 13, 2022.
29 Ana Galvão - interview August 30, 2021.
30 Filipa Galrão - interview July 13, 2021.
31 Sandra Torres interview
32 Sandra Torres interview.
33 José Loureiro interview.
34 Sandra Torres interview.
35 https://gruporenascencamultimedia.com/2020/05/13/grupo-renascenca-lidera-radio-no-digital-renascenca-quadruplica-audiencia/, accessed on Abril 8, 2022.
36 https://rr.sapo.pt/fotogaleria/vida/2022/04/08/renascenca-faz-85-anos-conheca-a-historia-desta-radio-que-ainda-esta-ai-para-as-curvas/279246/, accessed on April 8, 2022.
37 João Duarte interview.
38 Filipa Galrão interview.
39 Dina Isabel interview.
40 Sandra Torres interview.
41 José Loureiro interview.

Chapter 9
The Post-COVID-19 Communicator:
What Makes the Professional's Head in New Times?

Margareth Boarini
Pontifícia Universidade Católica de São Paulo, Brazil

ABSTRACT

The chapter aims to highlight how the theme of mental health has become a relevant agenda for Brazilian professionals in organizational communication and public relations, and who work in agencies, since the pandemic caused by COVID-19. After successive disruptions in areas of digital technology, microbiology has also shown itself capable of revolutionizing habits and ways of working in society. Time management, priority management, and hybrid work are now considered fundamental among communicators. Through a qualitative exploratory methodology, the chatper includes in-depth interviews, a multiple-question questionnaire, and an interview with the Brazilian Association of Communication Agencies. The research is also supported by a multidisciplinary bibliographic and documental base.

INTRODUCTION

There are many events that somehow mark the existence of humanity. From experience or from information, we know how life in society was punctuated during and after World War II, because of the economic crisis of 1929 or the effects of the one known as the subprime crisis (2008), the daily life before and after the arrival of the computer, the internet, social networks, and the smartphone. More recently, the pandemic enacted by Covid-19 has become responsible for demarcating history between before and after March 2020.

The disruption caused by the spread of the coronavirus shook important structures responsible for the functioning of a society, such as the triad people, work, and social life. It forced the decree of a pandemic state by the World Health Organization and brought support to Schwab's (2016, p. 16-17) thesis that the

DOI: 10.4018/978-1-6684-7353-5.ch009

Fourth Industrial Revolution is configured as a period impacted by disruptions not exclusively caused in the universe of intelligent and connected machines, but also by those resulting from innovations in genetics, nanotechnology, quantum computing, among others. The Fourth Industrial Revolution is a period marked by the joint governance of several sectors, the fusion of technologies in several areas and their interaction with physical, digital and biological domains (Schwab, 2016).

In Morin's (2021) reflection, the unprecedented crisis caused by Covid-19 showed that everything that seemed to be separate is, in fact, inseparable due to the combination of the most varied situations and crises, such as political, climatic, economic, and social, with a process of mutual sustaining components, interactions, and indeterminations. Emerged under such a context, the pandemic expressed the meaning of complexus, that which is woven together, constituted by several different elements (Morin, 2021).

Until March 2020, the word disruption permeated our minds most strongly under the aegis of digital technology. It referred to big data, artificial intelligence, blockchain, internet of things, quantum computing, technological nomenclatures added to life in digital social networks and the rise of digital influencers as strong opinion makers. Finally, in the last decades, the word disruption has remained closely linked to the technological issue, until microbiology reminded everyone that it can also bring impactful changes, capable of reconfiguring life in society.

A virus has shown itself to be equally capable of revolutionizing patterns and having extreme impacts on society. It is worth noting that a virus is not considered a living being, since it is not made up of cells. A parasite, it needs a host to survive and reproduce, and we all become potential hosts.

The coronavirus then, in 2020, imploded geographical barriers between work and private life, confined people around the world in their homes, generated economic and health crises. As Morin (2021) emphasized, the belief that man would be the great lord of nature dissipated before a virus, whose size is measured in micron (thousandth of a millimeter), such is its smallness to human eyes.

Like all areas, communication has suffered the effects of all these events. Kunsch (2016) has always reinforced the need for organizational communication to be attentive to the world around us and to contemporary socioeconomic contexts, in order to create adequate approaches. Supported by Castells, the author (2016) echoes the risk of stagnation of business practice if it does not assimilate the impacts of world events, going through specific movements of social contexts, of institutions and of companies, among many others.

Saad (2021) also alerts to the imperativeness of exercising a vision of the world beyond corporate borders as a way to highlight communication as a "connector medium" of the intense process of digital transformation, which, among other effects, has altered forms of sociability and social relations.

The pandemic context, object of this work, has brought about an unusual situation. Professionals traditionally trained and dedicated to working generally under pressure and to managing special situations, managing risks and crises, were forced to experience a double and exhausting journey.

While maintaining their work obligations within the context of a health crisis, meeting the demands of others and creating communication campaigns appropriate to the scenario, they themselves faced the challenges as ordinary citizens, vulnerable to Covid-19 and all its impacts. This group included many types of professionals, such as those in the health and basic services fields, as well as those in organizational communication and public relations.

In a first moment, the digitalization of society monopolized attention. Communicators (professionals and companies), who had already been training themselves to take advantage of the opportunities of technological innovations, had no problem in joining digitalization in a massive way in their daily lives. However, as the pandemic period proved to be tense, intense, threatening, and with marked particularities, the mental health theme surfaced with great force in a general way. The "pandemic anxiety proved our inability to deal with uncertainty," said the Portuguese psychiatrist Vítor Cotovio, in an interview to the magazine Prevenir (Augusto, 2022).

The communicators, accustomed and trained to manage risk and crisis situations of client organizations, were faced, as citizens, with the need to manage a special situation involving themselves in the field of mental health. From one hour to another they needed to work remotely, managing family and work. In addition, the exercise of the profession demanded creative actions to the lived context. Working under pressure took on a different tone due to the fact that professionals and citizens had to overcome the same challenges simultaneously. Customer service and crisis management within a new situation, with the aggravating factor of new and lethal coexistence, suffered from the intensity of the pressure. The context had become more complex and more tense.

Supported in this unprecedented moment for the communicator, the proposal of the article was to highlight the concern of the Brazilian professional of organizational communication and public relations with the theme of mental health from the pandemic by Covid-19, which occurred within a context of ruptures in various areas, characteristic of this period of the Fourth Industrial Revolution. The tripod technology, human being, ruptures gives the keynote of what has been experienced in these last years.

METHODOLOGY

The research focused on the communicator who works in corporate communication agencies, since the agency is a type of company that is an important link between organizations (clients) and audiences of all kinds.

The Brazilian market for communication agencies is robust, with a turnover for 2021 of around R$3.7 billion, according to the Anuário da Comunicação Corporativa 2022, published by Mega Brasil. According to data from the Brazilian Association of Communication Agencies (Abracom), Brazil has about 800 corporate communication agencies. We consider it relevant to note that the term "corporate communication" is the term widely used in the Brazilian market to generally designate communication agencies by the associations that represent the category and, for this reason, the article also cites this nomenclature.

The methodology employed was based on a qualitative exploratory nature, based on bibliographic and documental research, in-depth semi-structured interviews, by quotas, within a non-probabilistic sampling, and by a brief survey with closed questions. For Malhotra et al. (2008, p. 120), sampling by quotas helps to present a minimum representative of the group that one intends to study. In turn, the in-depth interview has the advantage of discussing the elements that enable an understanding about a situation or complex problems (Duarte, 2015).

The bibliographic and documentary research presents the multidisciplinary character, with authors from organizational communication and public relations, digital technology, mental health.

The in-depth interviews were conducted with five professionals in the sector with more than five years of experience in communication agencies and with a representative of the Brazilian Association of Communication Agencies (Abracom).

The brief survey (questionnaire) was conducted through the Google Forms platform and had seven multiple choice questions and one short answer, directed to corporate communication professionals in agencies, with no distinction of minimum time of experience. In total, 57 professionals answered the questionnaire.

As the sector is very competitive, we chose to keep anonymous the names of all the professionals (interviewed and who participated in the short survey) and all the respective agencies where they work, in order to encourage more natural and trustworthy answers. All the interviews (in-depth) and the questionnaire (Google Forms platform) took place between December 12 and 14, 2022, and were conducted by phone, email, WhatsApp messenger and Google Forms, according to the availability of the participant's schedule.

The questions in the questionnaire cover the period from the beginning of the pandemic (March, 2020) until December, 2022, a period in which the World Health Organization had not yet decreed its end. One of the questions refers specifically to 2021, while the others leave the period open, since mental health care does not demand a set time to be realized.

One of the questions asks the respondent about his or her professional qualification regarding technological innovations before the outbreak of the pandemic, and was created precisely for the purpose of highlighting the communicator's concern in adapting to the demands of digital transformation and of a communication process practically disintermediated. We consider such questioning relevant, because the pandemic happened in the middle of a strong digital transformation of contemporary society, and also because it was the technological advances in the most diverse areas that enabled the maintenance of business activities, entertainment, record development of vaccines, among other things.

The pandemic emerged within a period in which a second disruptive wave of communication was already forcing communicators to increasingly incorporate pervasive technologies in their daily lives, such as data capture and analysis and use of artificial intelligence and phenomena such as misinformation, fake news and digital influencers (Boarini, 2022).

In the case of influencers, Karhawi (2021) warns of the need for discussion between points of closeness and conflict between them and organizational communication. In the case of fake news, what Ferrari (2020) calls the parasite of the 21st century, the professional's work goes beyond the identification of a possible crisis and requires constant monitoring.

The transformative context impacted the way brands and organizations began to undertake their communication strategy. Disintermediation has caused new ways of presenting products, services, and relationships, forcing organizational communication and public relations to be perceived and recognized as a useful tool for users-consumers-citizens, as Terra (2021) reflects.

THE LETHAL CRISIS IN EVERYDAY LIFE

The professional experience in the area of corporate communication shows us that the day to day of those who work with public relations and organizational communication has never been smooth. The element of surprise has always been part of the agenda, as well as the pressure in the search for information, for training an executive, during the management of a crisis situation.

If we can observe an advantage of the communication professional to face the challenges of a troubled moment over several other areas, it is precisely his preparation to face risk and crisis situations and to know how to work under pressure. The communicator learns in university and in his job to work under pressure (of time, the client, the emergencies that arise during the course of a job), to manage the most diverse situations, to manage the expectations of clients or audiences, to quickly find an adequate response to the eventual crises that come up in front of him.

Crisis is a situation that goes beyond control, a significant rupture with normality, which requires prompt action (Forni, 2021). In today's times, the scenario is more challenging when promoting, according to Machado (2021), the media hypervisibility, housing the digital multiplatforms, being impacted by a participating user, present, creator of its own content and owner of a powerful network of audiences. All this added to the phenomena of fake news and influence.

Life-threatening crises are, by consensus, the most dramatic. In the case of the Covid-19 pandemic, the lives of all the inhabitants of the planet, both in their role as professionals and as citizens, are now at risk.

Communication professionals are faced with the need to manage not only their work-related crises, but also their own and those of their families. They have faced the risk of unemployment, job restructuring, pressure for results, an excess of communication channels to manage, a possible contractual revision between their employer and clients, the management of private life in a context turbo charged with the excessive consumption of communication. Not to mention the lack of a geographical barrier between family and work.

Childcare and household chores took place in the same physical environment where work was performed between screens and computers.

At the professional level, Claudia Rondon, then president of Abracom's Board of Directors and founding partner of RPMA Comunicação (2020, p. 8) recalls that the crisis brought by the pandemic launched, in its beginning, questions such as how to maintain communication in the midst of a crisis of these dimensions, what to communicate, how to communicate, how to involve strategic audiences so that brands and their key messages remain present in the imagination of each stakeholder? The moment showed that citizens, consumers, the general public, in short, did not want to see brands with disclosure focused only on products and services, but collectively engaged to bring relevant content, positive messages and show public utility actions (Rondon, 2020).

In the 2022 edition of the Brazilian publication Anuário de Comunicação Corporativa (Mega Brazil), the portrait of the sector showed an intense contraction in 2020, the first year of the pandemic, and uncertainties about the direction of the business in 2021, sometimes indicating a recovery, sometimes instability. Among the negative points of the pandemic highlighted in the publication are the cancellation of in-person corporate events, fiercer market competition, difficulties in managing the current work model and in the relationship with the press.

We consider it relevant to emphasize that such negative points impacted not only the communication business itself, but affects all of its agents, whether C-level executives or agency owners or employees at all levels of the hierarchy.

Among the positive points listed in the publication, the growth of the importance of corporate communication in companies, the deepening of digital communication, media, and online services, the breaking of the cultural barrier with respect to home office, and the expansion of prospecting with a larger scope of work to be performed and offered by agencies were highlighted.

Throughout 2021, reduction in contract values reached 47.8% of clients, followed by contract suspension (24.6%), contract cancellation (22.0%). Employee layoffs reached 9.1%, followed by provisional suspension of employee contracts (6.9%), reduction in employee compensation (6.0%) (Corporate Communication Yearbook 2022).

On a personal level, the communicator felt the effects of the pandemic like an ordinary citizen, feeling fear and unpreparedness to deal with the uncertain and the lethality of the disease. The crisis brought on by Covid-19 took place in all spheres.

Forni (2021) states that there is no crisis like any other and that there is no ready-made recipe to manage crises. However, the scholar lists some actions that can mitigate the effects and contribute to a better management of this challenging moment. Some of them are: immediate communication, not trying to stifle the situation, not being overwhelmed despite the high level of stress, not panicking, keeping control of actions and communication.

In the specific case of the pandemic, in its initial moment, when everything was surrounded by great ignorance about contagion and treatment, with no effective medication identified and sometimes no vaccine available to everyone, two of these actions, however, got out of control even of those who were trained to face crises. How can one not panic and be overwhelmed in the face of a potentially lethal scenario?

Cotovio states that when experiencing a crisis we are subject to a combination of fear, anxiety, and anguish: Fear occurs as an emotional or physiological response to a real threat; anxiety is the anticipation of a future threat; anguish would be the threat that results from emptiness and loss of meaning. The doctor warns that the ideal would be for leaders and organizations to take this into account to create protective measures to ensure good mental health within their environments (Augusto, 2022).

REMOTE WORK AS A ROUTINE

The experimentation of remote work and, later, of the hybrid format (face-to-face and remote) proved to be productive and overturned the thesis that it is necessary to be physically available at the workplace during the entire working day. The digital technology ecosystem allows this service configuration and what we observed was that, within the universe of corporate communication agencies, this adaptation happened smoothly and quickly.

"On the seventh day of the restrictive measures, 97% of the agencies associated with Abracom had already migrated 100% of their teams to remote work," Rondon told Mega Brasil's Anuário da Comunicação Corporativa 2020.

The 2022 Yearbook showed that the adoption of home office, continuously or sporadically, has become a reality. Many agencies have reduced the physical space of their offices permanently. Over 2021, 91% of agency employees spent 2021 in permanent home office, 81% had the hybrid working model, and only 18% worked face-to-face, according to the publication's survey. For the future, the yearbook poll points out that 77.2% intend to keep the hybrid model, while 21.1% consider exclusively home office as a work option.

The research "Remote work and social isolation", carried out in 2020 by 4CO, consulting and communication agency specialized in employee relations, and by Banco Original, shows the effects of this work model among people, in general. From the findings, it is possible to observe the movement that started with the initial euphoria of being at home, working informally, with no commuting costs, and that culminated with the exhaustion of merging personal and professional life until realizing the state of burnout. 57% of the respondents stated that they felt more tired in the home office, although the routine was much less hectic.

Carramenha (2020), one of the research coordinators, says he has no doubts that the home office is already consolidated as a work model, regardless of the end of the pandemic, but reinforces the need for professionals to seek a balance between personal life and work. The adoption of home office inaugurated the fusion between personal and work at home, but people must create a differentiation between these two areas.

The study on remote work focused on formal workers and was divided into two waves. The first wave was surveyed in March and April 2020. The second wave covered the month of May 2020. In the study that covered the period of the first wave, 73% of people said that they needed to adapt how they organized their activities several times and 59% said that they spent more hours working in the home office than when they were in the office in person. The results showed the need to adapt to this new work model.

In Carramenha's (2020) evaluation, not being able to balance the home office with personal activities can generate emotional disturbances, such as burnout syndrome. Hence the importance of establishing initiatives that favor good mental health. A fact that called attention is that 57% of the respondents stated that the home office has become very tiring within a scenario of social isolation. At this point, we can gauge the emotional weight caused by a pandemic scenario, which forced social isolation and even brought the fear of contagion from a potentially lethal disease, in addition to the excessive use of screens.

After the one-month period, the study, in its second wave, signaled an adaptation to the home office, and showed that 84% of people already felt they were living in a more adequate routine. However, we observed that the fear of the pandemic persisted strong when 80% of the respondents stated that remote work would be a better experience if it did not exist and if it was not included within a context with a pandemic and with isolation.

Overall, the discrepancy between the expectation of remote work and the perception when participating in it has been accentuated because of the pandemic effect by Covid-19. The home office gained adherence from communicators, as we will see in the interview responses (more on this later), but throughout 2020 and 2021, years in which the pandemic required strict social isolation to save lives, the fear of getting sick outweighed the advantages of this work model.

Internal communication has proven to be more relevant and imperative than ever. The communication agencies, which have always recommended this resource to their clients, had to reinforce the area internally. Ruão (1999) also alerts to the relevance and the obligation of alignment in the intramural communication of an organization because of the complexity and variety of communication networks present at the most diverse levels, channels and purposes, among other factors.

The unity of the message disseminated among all audiences (external and internal) results from a deep work of communicational alignment, responsible for creating and managing the good reputation of any type of organization (Riel, 2013).

Below, we will present the results of the in-depth interviews with the communicators, the brief questionnaire and the interview with the Abracom representative.

FROM THE HOME SCREEN TO THE WORLD

The in-depth Interviews: Pressure, Time, and Fear

The objective of this stage of the research was to gauge more directly how the communicator lived the most critical period of the pandemic (2020/2021), how he felt his mental health was affected, and how he evaluates the best work option for the present moment and for the coming years.

Five Brazilian communicators with more than five years of experience in corporate communication and working in agencies were interviewed. The answers were given by different means, respecting the schedule of each one of the respondents: telephone contact, email, or through the WhatsApp messaging platform.

The questions asked were:

- Did you have covid-19? If yes, when?
- After the most difficult period of the pandemic, did you need to go back to face-to-face work or did you keep home office?
- Was the mandatory hybrid work a good experience? Did anything about this new context change your mood at the time? What was it?
- Was your mental health impacted? In what way?
- Did mental health become a more relevant issue for you after this experience in the pandemic? What have you been doing to take care of it?
- Which competency did you need to develop or feel you explored the most during the initial pandemic time?
- After the impact of the technological disruptions of the last few years and the disruption caused by pandemic life, what do you prioritize today as a professional (answer taking into account your personal and professional life?

Table 1. The respondents

	Time of Experience	Did You Have COVID-19?
Respondent 1	16 years	Yes – Jan 2022
Respondent 2	20 years	No
Respondent 3	21 years	No
Respondent 4	30 years	Yes – Jun 2022
Respondent 5	14 years	Yes – Jun 2022

To make the analysis of the situation more fluid, the presentation of the answers follows the order of the questions.

After the most difficult period of the pandemic, did you have to go back to face-to-face work or did you maintain home office?

Of the five communicators interviewed, two of them said they would still (December 2022) work remotely on a daily basis, with face-to-face meetings only sporadically. The rest have been working within the hybrid model and are satisfied with this determination of the companies. The main reasons are the possibility of flexible scheduling that this system offers and the possibility of mixing virtual and face-to-face meetings. In most cases, professionals have dedicated two full days to the home office, two days in a face-to-face scheme, and one day divided between working from home and in the office. The agenda can be shaped according to the demand of the client being served.

Was the mandatory hybrid job a good experience in the end? Did anything about this new context change your mood at the time? What was it?

The hybrid work model, which combines remote and face-to-face work, is recognized as the best option among the respondents, because it allows both the physical meeting with colleagues and mitigates the difficulties and costs with commuting between home and work in big cities. Even those who live in small towns also said they prefer this model because they can schedule domestic activities that used to be impossible to do.

Right at the beginning of the pandemic period, the home office was not considered a good option by everyone. There were respondents who felt relieved because of "the deadly threat of the disease", but there were also those who said they were wary of the possibility of being productive without being in the office. As time went by, however, the perception that it would be possible to conciliate work and virtual meetings with more time dedicated to the children, made the home office be considered a good option.

The consequent partial return of physical presence in the office, since the softening of the pandemic, was well accepted by most of the communicators heard. Among the reasons for this are the informal conversations, the interaction and exchange of ideas that take place in the physical environment and that are more difficult to happen on screens, and the difficulty in maintaining focus on work when one is exclusively at home.

One of the interviewees even stated that he felt a jolt in his mental health and worsening mood from not being able to manage time indoors and losing the quality in relationships with colleagues in the office with screen-only interaction. "That's really missed."

Has your mental health been impacted? In what ways?

There were several triggers to shake the mental health of communicators during the most dramatic phases of the pandemic. Below, we list some of the accounts:

"Fear of losing clients and being online all the time."

"The lethality of the disease, the inoperativeness of the federal government in the face of the pandemic, the stories of families losing people, friends becoming infected. A former co-worker lost his father and mother in a short interval."

"The fear of contracting the disease made me seek online therapy. I could no longer produce briefings, reports and so many other materials."

"To circumvent negative thoughts, I forced myself to practice leisure activities, such as watching more series and movies daily."

Has mental health become a more relevant issue for you after this experience in the pandemic? What have you done to take care of it?

What we observed was that mental health became a constant topic of concern among the interviewees. All five communicators said that fear of illness, apathy, mood loss, and weight gain had turned on a yellow light. There were those who began to practice physical activity, such as walking and yoga, and there were those who created regular meetings with friends through the screens to talk about amenities, among other topics.

Which competency did you need to develop or felt you explored the most during the initial pandemic time?

What we can observe is that experiencing the pandemic through Covid-19 and all that it brought along awakened in communicators the need to develop specific competencies. We list below some of the statements that illustrate the interviewees' quests in this regard:

"I needed to develop resilience, patience, tolerance, and the ability to resignify scenarios."

"I sought to learn to manage time and priorities not in order of arrival, but in order of importance, in order to reduce stress."

"I had to develop the ability to be patient in order to manage the large volume of messages coming in through many different channels and platforms. The excess of audio messages on WhatsApp was also very annoying and time consuming. This made me create a management technique to listen to all the messages."

"I looked for new ways to connect with people to replace the physical meeting."

After the impact of the technological disruptions of the last years and the disruption caused by pandemic life, what do you prioritize today as a professional (answer taking into account your personal and professional life?

Although in December 2022, when the research was undertaken, the World Health Organization, had not yet decreed the suspension of the pandemic status by Covid-19, the resumption of social life was shown to be designed with new elements of conviviality at work and in private life. Balance and appreciation of personal and family life were the key words, as we show below:

"Maintaining balance between personal and professional life."

"Self and family well-being."

"Professional improvement based on technological innovations to have better performance at work."

"Priority on keeping flexible working hours and the possibility of home office."

"Change mindset and engage in humanitarian causes, taking focus away from products and services."

"Stay informed at all times."

The Questionnaire: Mental Health as a Concern

Eight questions (seven multiple choice and one short answer) guided the questionnaire answered by 57 Brazilian communicators from corporate communication agencies, between December 12 and 14, 2022.

Of the total respondents, 80.7% have more than ten years of work in the area. The length of time working in the sector is considered important by us, since it indicates the experience and the experience in adverse situations in the corporate communication market. The vast majority of the respondents said they had already contracted Covid-19 (75.4%).

Home Office (Figure 1): In relation to the home office, the questionnaire presented the alternatives: worked for a year, worked for more than a year, returned to work in person continuously, kept the home office continuously, currently works in a hybrid way. What we can observe is that the home office is the work model that is most employed by Brazilian communication agencies today. This is because the continuous home office reaches 59.6%, while work in the hybrid model reached 29.8%. The answers indicating exclusive face-to-face work added up to only 1.18%.

Figure 1. Home office

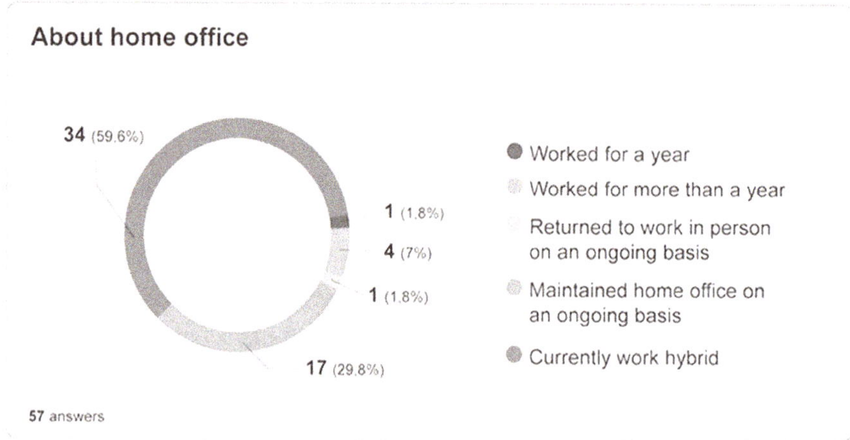

Mental Health (Figure 2): Mental health has been impacted, in the communicators' view, as shown in the figure below. Between the positive perception and the uncertainty of whether or not it has been impacted, the questionnaire revealed more than 50%, which allows us to see that the theme deserves permanent attention.

Figure 2. Mental health

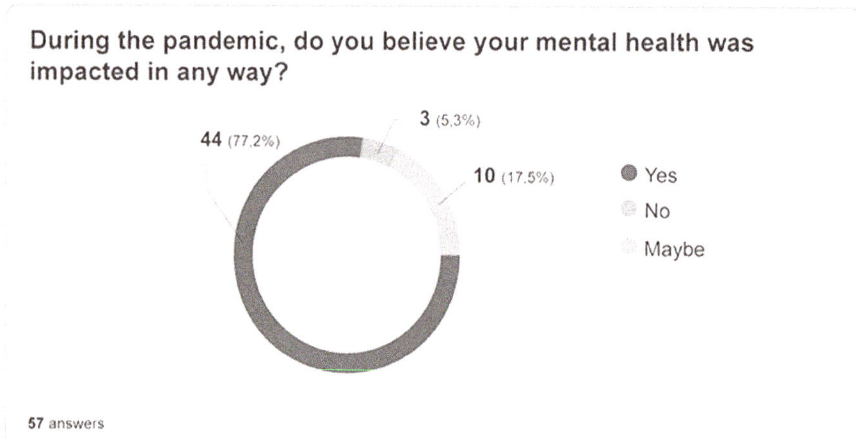

Emotional Support (Figure 3): Asked if the company provided technical and emotional support during the pandemic, the communicators, 54.4% responded positively, while 26.3% said they received only technical support and 19.3% said they received neither technical nor emotional support from their employers. Although more than half of the answers indicate this concern, we note that this is a topic that deserves to be followed up in order to observe if communication agencies, in fact, are concerned in creating initiatives that help communicators to have this kind of welfare.

Figure 3. Emotional support

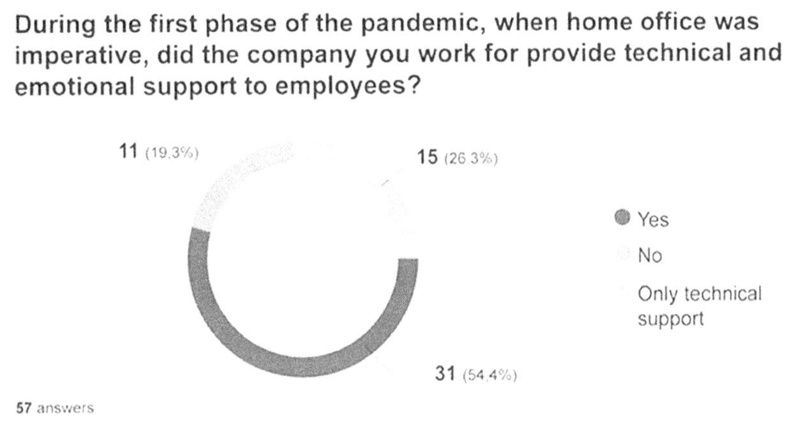

New Habits (Figure 4): Communicators sought ways to relieve the pressure during the most worrying period of the pandemic, a fact that signals that the search for balance between personal and professional life can remain active for the coming years.

Figure 4. New habits

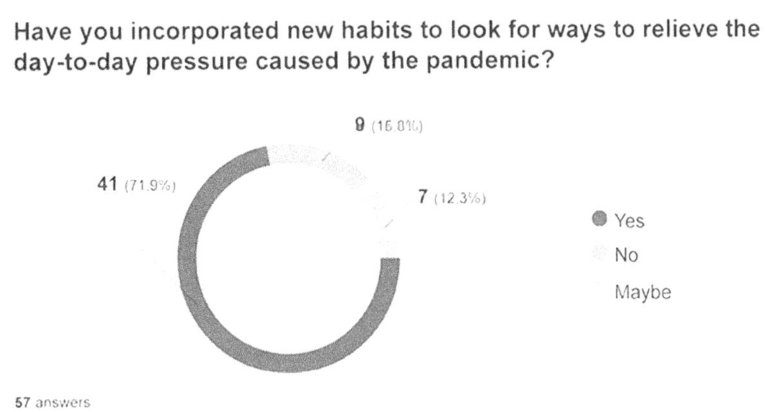

December 2022 (Figure 5): By presenting a question about which work model the communicator prioritizes post-critical period of the pandemic, the questionnaire shows us the concern about maintaining a balance between personal life and work and keeping mental well-being on the radar.

Professional Qualification: Regarding professional improvement linked to new technologies, the areas sought to improve knowledge were digital communication, inbound marketing, SEO, training given by the agency itself, and post-graduate studies in data analysis. There was even one communicator who sought another area to expand his knowledge, such as public policy, and another who took an online

Figure 5. After critical periods

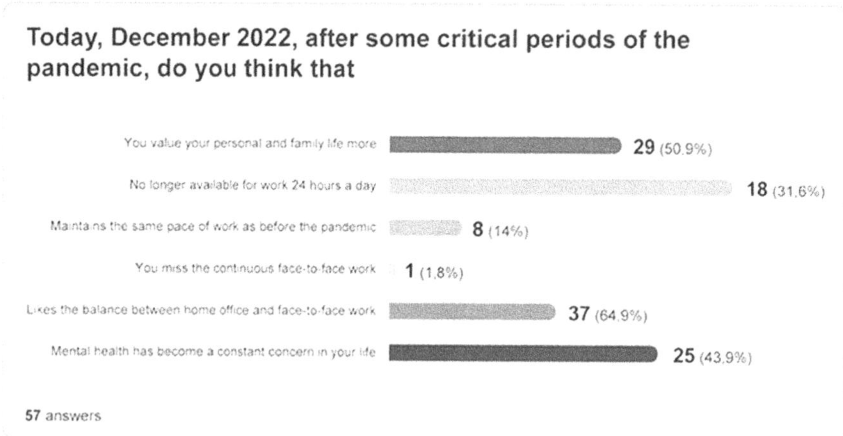

course at a renowned North American institution. Participation in congresses and online events were also mentioned. Of all the respondents, 28.1% said they had not taken any courses in this area.

Demands of the New Times: ABRACOM

Working remotely caused not only changes in the way of working, but also evidenced the need to develop competencies related to maintaining focus, relationships with colleagues, leaders, clients, managing time and the volume of messages, and improving the strategic vision for the business within the hybrid working model.

The vice-president of the Brazilian Association of Communication Agencies (Abracom), executive José Luiz Schiavoni, states that because of the change in the work model from an exclusively face-to-face model to a hybrid format, the market now demands a professional profile with a greater capacity for organization, strategic vision, and resilience. The executive reinforces that the topic of mental health has gained relevance and should remain on the agenda from now on. "Most agencies have paid attention to it and many companies have created specific initiatives to support their employees in this regard because of the pressure and all the particularities of the pandemic," says Schiavoni.

Technical knowledge remains fundamental, but in the face of changing paradigms one must recognize the fact that other points have also become non-negotiable. "No one wants to sit in traffic every day and spend a lot of money for lunch away from home anymore. People want more time with their families," says the executive. For him, the relations between the parties, company and professional, must take this into consideration. Schiavoni points out that, despite the benefits, remote work makes it possible to extend working hours at home, and for this reason the professional must pay attention to time organization.

Remote work also requires that the professional knows how to relate, work, and interact through screens. It is necessary not only to know how to participate in an online meeting, using the technology in the most appropriate way, but also to interact with colleagues and clients.

In Schiavoni's evaluation, professional improvement is imperative and must remain constant. There is a lack of professionals specialized in data analysis and capable of undertaking a digital transformation process within agencies. The metaverse and Web3 are also good business and professional growth opportunities, and the communicator must be aware of all this.

CONCLUSION

There is no doubt that the pandemic was an overwhelming event, both in the period of its enactment by the World Health Organization (March, 2020), and in its most critical period (2020 and 2021).

There is also no doubt that professionals of specific categories felt twice the pressure of the moment and the dual roles in facing the situation, exercising simultaneously their role as professionals qualified to manage risks and crises with the role of an ordinary citizen being threatened by a lethal disease.

The organizational communication and public relations professional faced his worst crisis since the pandemic. Nothing spared the communicator from the feeling of helplessness, anguish, and the fear of losing loved ones. It was an unprecedented experience for someone who was always trained to work under pressure, to be multitasking, to mediate relationships with the most diverse internal and external audiences, to be able to use all kinds of technology in their favor.

One of the interviewees stated that work, before being a source of income, is passion, but the pandemic taught him to value life with his family, because death interrupts the good moments.

The professional who is used to using rationality to do his job, was surprised by his emotions and succumbed. The lethality of Covid-19 brought the warning of the fragility of the human being. Mental health has become a present concern among communication professionals.

The research undertaken to prepare this article reflects the search for balance between personal and family life and work, with the incorporation of habits that contribute to physical and emotional well-being.

The technical competencies remain relevant, and new technologies and knowledge in diverse areas guide the communicators' plans, but the picture taken from the last three years (2020, 2021, and 2022) reveals the concern with mental health, with family relationships, with the preservation of life.

A number of challenges are posed in the organizational communication and public relations market from then on.

For universities, the challenge is to prepare professionals for a disruptive environment, presenting technological innovations and their applicability in the day-to-day work while presenting reflections on how to reconcile the profession with private life.

Studying risk and crisis management should contain, from then on, a deep reflection on how the pandemic impacted professionals in the exercise of their work and on their human side. It should also bring discussions on how to face situations of the magnitude and extent as the pandemic by Covid-19. Organizational communication and public relations showed creativity, adequacy of channels and narratives, actions with a focus on citizenship.

For employers, specifically corporate communication agencies, studied here, the challenges lie in improving the view of the human, to always have relevant communication among their internal publics, and to keep the mental health of professionals as a permanent agenda.

For professionals, the challenge is to learn to manage time and priorities, maintain the search for balance, and not let mental health concerns dissipate as the pandemic slows down and the lethality of the disease decreases.

In crisis management, there is a very valuable lesson: the creation of a crisis diary at its end. The purpose of the diary is to record all actions taken, initiatives adopted, so that its future reading can help us to be aware of mistakes and successes made and to be better prepared for the next special situations.

May the pandemic have its crisis diary among all professionals involved in organizational communication and public relations, universities, corporate communication agencies, and professionals in organizational communication and public relations.

This article does not exhaust the proposed theme. We consider it relevant to conduct further, more robust and comprehensive research, with more interviewees, to assess the effects of this event on professionals, and to portray how the communication aimed at employees was structured after this experience in which a virus that is imperceptible to the naked eye revolutionized contemporary society.

REFERENCES

Anuário da Comunicação Corporativa. (2020). *Mega Brasi*l. Retrieved September, 16, 2022 from, https://portal.megabrasil.com.br/anuario

Anuário da Comunicação Corporativa. (2021). *Mega Brasil*. Retrieved September, 16, 2022 from, https://portal.megabrasil.com.br/anuario

Anuário da Comunicação Corporativa. (2022). *Mega Brasil*. Retrieved September, 16, 2022 from, https://portal.megabrasil.com.br/anuario

Aprigio, M. (2020). *Pesquisa revela que trabalhadores estão mais cansados por causa do home office*. UOL. Retrieved November, 02, 2022 from https://jc.ne10.uol.com.br/economia/2020/05/5609492-pesquisa-revela-que-trabalhadores-estao-mais-cansados-por-causa-de-home-office.html

Augusto, C. E. (2022). *Vítor Cotovio: a ansiedade pandémica provou a nossa incapacidade para lidar com a incerteza*. Revista Prevenir. Retrieved from. https://www.prevenir.pt/literacia-em-saude/entrevista/vitor-cotovio-a-ansiedade-pandemica-provou-a-nossa-incapacidade-de-lidar-com-a-incerteza/#

Boarini, M. (2022). Disruptive communication: Challenges and opportunities of the 21st century. In J. G. Andrade (Ed.), *Navigating digital communication and challenges for organizations* (pp. 39–57). IGI Global. doi:10.4018/978-1-7998-9790-3.ch003

Cappellano, T., Carramenha, B. (2020). *Trabalho remoto e isolamento social – Segunda onda*. Banco Original. 4CO. Retrieved November, 02, 2022 from file:///D:/Users/OneDrive/%C3%81rea%20de%20Trabalho/ACADEMIA/ARTIGOS%20E%20EVENTOS/REVISTAS%20ARTIGOS/IGI%20GLOBAL%20Z%C3%89%20GABRIEL/2022-2023/MATERIAL%20DE%20APOIO/PESQUISA%204CO%20%20%20TRABALHO%20REMOTO%202a%20ONDA.pdf

Cappellano, T., & Carramenha, B. (2020). *Trabalho remoto e isolamento social – Primeira onda*. Banco Original. 4CO. Retrieved November, 02, 2022 from https://4co.com.br/wp-content/uploads/2022/01/Trabalho_remoto_v2.2.pdf

Duarte, J. (2015). Entrevista em profundidade. In J. Duarte (Ed.), *Métodos e técnicas de pesquisa em comunicação* (2nd ed., pp. 62–83). Ed. Atlas.

Ferrari, P. (2020). *Como sair das bolhas*. Educ.

Forni, J. J. (2021). *Gestão de Crises e Comunicação*. Atlas. Edição do Kindle.

Karhawi, I. (2021). Comunicação organizacional e influenciadores digitais: aproximações e conflitos. In *Comunicação organizacional: práticas, desafios e perspectivas digitais* (pp. 141–153). Summus Editorial.

Kunsch, M. M. K. (2016). A comunicação nas organizações: dos fluxos lineares às dimensões humana e estratégica. In M. M. K. Kunsch (Ed.), *Comunicação organizacional estratégica: aportes conceituais e aplicados* (pp. 37–58). Summus Editorial.

Malhotra, N. K., Rocha, I., Laudisio, M. C., Altheman, É., Borges, F. M., & Taylor, R. B. (2005). *Introdução à pesquisa de marketing*. Academic Press.

Medeiros, T. (2016). Retrieved November, 02, 2022 from https://drauziovarella.uol.com.br/infectologia/virus/

Morin, E. (2021). *É hora de mudarmos de via: As lições do coronavírus*. Bertrand Brasil. Edição do Kindle.

Riel, C. B. M. v. (2013). *Reputação*. Campus.

Rondon, C. (2020). *A hora da retomada*. Anuário da Comunicação Corporativa 2020. Mega Purilub. Tamanho de um vírus. Retrieved November, 02, 2022 from https://www.purilub.com.br/blog/tamanho-de-um-virus/65

Ruão, T. (1999). A Comunicação Organizacional e a gestão de Recursos Humanos: Evolução e actualidade. Comunicação e Sociedade 1. *Cadernos do Noroeste, 12*(1-2), 179-194. Retrieved February, 18, 2023 from https://repositorium.sdum.uminho.pt/bitstream/1822/60017/1/1999_Ruao_Comunicacao-organizacional.pdf

Saad, E. (2021). Comunicação organizacional e transformação digital: novos cenários, novos olhares. In Comunicação organizacional. São Paulo: Summus Editorial.

Schwab, K. (2016). *A Quarta Revolução Industrial*. Edipro.

Terra, C.F. (2021). *Marcas influenciadoras digitais*. São Caetano do Sul: Difusão Editora.

Chapter 10
Hybrid Work Organisation and Well-Being Strategies in Advertising Agencies During the COVID-19 Pandemic

Mădălina Moraru
https://orcid.org/0000-0001-5976-7968
University of Bucharest, Romania

Romina Surugiu
https://orcid.org/0000-0003-2731-2058
University of Bucharest, Romania

ABSTRACT

The chapter focuses on how advertising agencies organised hybrid work and developed well-being strategies for employees during the pandemic timespan (2020-2022) in Romania. It starts with an overview of academic perspective on hybrid work organization in companies. Then it unfolds the issue of well-being and the features of work in advertising agencies (flexibility, creativity, innovation). The chapter also presents several transformations brought by the COVID-19 pandemic to work organization in Romania. The second part analyzes the findings of 14 semi-structured interviews with advertising professionals from Romania. The findings show that some companies started the process of adaptation to hybrid work before the pandemic, while others implemented strategies for remote work during the lockdown. Online and hybrid work generated work-life imbalance because of the blurring lines between personal and professional space and time. Companies' management focused on rapid solutions for improving internal communication and for increasing adaptation to online/hybrid work.

DOI: 10.4018/978-1-6684-7353-5.ch010

INTRODUCTION

The pandemic essentially changed both work style and attitude towards work itself, by challenging people to rethink the balance between the professional and personal life. In this respect, the employees from the cultural and creative industries were forced to re-assess priorities and work frames in order to adapt to the ever-changing circumstances. This health crisis affected the conditions of work worldwide, yet the adaptation to them differed from one country to another.

The chapter's aim is to analyse how advertising agencies organised hybrid work and implemented well-being strategies for employees during 2020 and 2022 - the pandemic period - in Romania. The first section of the chapter presents an overview of academic perspectives on hybrid work organization in companies before and during the pandemic. It also unfolds the issue of well-being at the workplace which is of high importance for both employers and employees and has relevance at societal level. Then it contextualizes the features of work in advertising agencies, taking into consideration the flexibility, the creativity, the dynamics, the innovative and the tech-driven aspects of jobs in the communication industry. To clarify the challenges brought by the COVID-19 pandemic in Romania, several information is provided regarding the lockdown/state of alert time spans and related work changes.

The second section of the chapter analyzes the findings of the semi-structured interviews with advertising professionals, selected from representative agencies located in Romania.

The research questions are:

Q1: How was online and hybrid work organised during the COVID-19 pandemic in Romanian advertising agencies?

Q2: Which were the perceptions of advertising professionals on the online and hybrid work organisation in the pandemic context?

Q3: How did the employees perceive the work transformations in the professional activity and personal life in relation to their well-being while performing online and hybrid work?

Q4: How did the management of the agencies conceive strategies for ensuring the well-being of their employees during the pandemic?

HYBRID WORK

The hybrid organisation of work could be understood as both "relocation of work into domestic space" and "dislocation of work into cyberspace" (Halford, 2005, p. 19). Implemented globally in the 2000s, hybrid work brought important challenges for companies, especially in the white-collar sector (as argued by Halford, 2005).

At the beginning of 2000s, it was expected that the mixture of cyberspace with office, domestic and other public spaces (coffee shops for example) would produce "new practices, relationships and managerial challenges" (Halford, 2005, p. 30). The pandemic accelerated the transition to hybrid work by first imposing the online work procedures (during the lockdown), and then encouraged the mixture between online and offline office activities, taking into the consideration the specificity of each job. Hybrid work is associated with new technologies and the transformation they brought into industry and society.

According to a systematic analysis of journal articles on digital transformation done by Vial (2019), new technologies fuel disruptions related to consumer behaviour, competition etc. and trigger strategic responses from the part of organisations. Digital transformations lead to structural changes (organisational structure and culture, leadership roles and employees' skills) and are affected by organisational barriers (inertia and resistance to change) (Vial, 2019).

Technology is framed concerning reorganisation of work in terms of efficiency, productivity and employees' autonomy. The digital transformation requires the reorganisation of work and leads to changes in the way employees achieve their tasks (Anderson-Connolly et al., 2002 in Nagel, 2020, p. 862). Among the disruptive technologies, with a high impact on work organisation and companies' management and society, there are: "computing, artificial intelligence, the Internet of Things, cloud technology, advanced robotics, and 3-D printing" (Scully-Russ&Torraco, 2020, p. 75-76).

At the same time, technological challenges may affect the well-being of employees and can generate new dynamics in organisations.

WELL-BEING OF EMPLOYEES

In the context of digital transformation related to work, the issue of well-being is of high importance for both employers and employees and has relevance at societal level, too. "Employees expect their employers to value, support, and respect their efforts towards attainment of organisational objectives and as such are looking to employers to help them to achieve this, since a large proportion of their lives are spent at work", explains Cvenkel (2020, p. 29).

The definition of well-being at the workplace relates, as states Cvenkel (2020), to employee welfare obtained through positive work experiences and job satisfaction in a functioning organisation. The academic approach on well-being in organizations argues that a multidimensional perspective would be appropriate to understand this emerging domain (Baptise, 2008 in Cvenkel, 2020, pp.13-14). The multidimensional perspective takes into consideration various aspects of well-being: "psychological, physical, intellectual, mental health, material/rewards, career, spiritual, and financial and work/family well-being" (Cvenkel, 2020, p. 31), but also organisational side, i.e. policies, programmes and management intervention.

"Wellness, particularly a more holistic well-being platform, can help to build a thriving, vibrant workplace that boosts morale, fosters engagement, enhances human performance, and attracts and retains top talent. An increasing number of workers, especially millennials, now expect potential employers to care about them—and this includes offering workplace wellness", argues Putnam (2015, p.18).

The role of management in well-being is considered to be relevant. According to Wood (2008, p. 163), who statistically investigated a sample of 22,451 employees in the UK, job characteristics together with supportive, informative and consultative management are associated with well-being.

Structural changes may result in high levels of anxiety on the part of employees and managers altogether. Therefore, reengineering the workplace could also become a factor of well-being. Connolly *et al.* (2002, p. 409) argue that the employees have the possibility to get involved in the transformation of the workplace, contributing to its reengineering for their own well-being.

Well-being also depends on the work-life balance which increases job satisfaction and the level of attainment of employees. The work-life balance depends on individual factors, but, more importantly on organizational policies and strategies (Cvenkel, 2020, p. 244). The management of the company should be aware of the challenges in the employees' life in order to offer support in specific circumstances: "It is essential for organisational leaders to have greater insight into the life challenges that individuals experience in their personal lives that are interconnected to their ability to perform and be creative and innovate at work" (Cvenkel, 2020, p. 258).

In the advertising industry, well-being is contemporarily considered as an imperative for agencies due to structural and technological changes. The managers state that the wellness dimension should be "holistic", and "embedded" in companies' culture, based on top-down and bottom-up initiatives (Kemp, 2018). One in two employees in the advertising industry expresses the need for a clear focus on well-being at the company level (Kemp, 2018).

FEATURES OF WORK IN ADVERTISING

Work in advertising agencies displays several characteristics, such as: flexibility, creativity, dynamics and an innovative side. These features are usually present in jobs associated with the communication industry (Finkel et. al. 2017, Bridges, 2018 *inter al.*).

Flexibility refers to specific elements connected to the work framework of creative jobs: autonomy, compressed work schedule, job sharing, flexible working time (flexitime), flexible working arrangements, part-time/project-based employment. According to Stich (2021, p. 359), flexibility includes the possibility of employees to work outside of their workplace/offices and beyond the fixed working hours as well ("9 to 5"). This organization of work may bring a high level of job satisfaction and may increase well-being (Deery et al., 2017 in Stich, 2021, p. 359).

Besides flexibility, creative industries promise to encourage employees' creativity that can be applied in product design, task solving or project implementation. Rosengren *et al.* (2020, p. 52) explain that the most known dimension of creativity is originality, but it should also be linked with the appropriateness of consumer's needs and efficiency in brand promotion.

The dynamics of advertising work relies on several dimensions: the relationship with the clients, the ever-changing consumers, the economic competition among agencies and the adaptation to technological trends (Davis and Prince, 2005, p. 3 in Shah et al., 2020, p. 3).

Innovation is mostly seen as connected to technology use, and there are many challenges associated with this relationship. Shah *et al.* (2020, p.19) argue that Artificial Intelligence and Machine Learning present "practical and conceptual challenges" in the advertising industry, among them being: "high error susceptibility" and "interpretability". Nevertheless, major brands have started to implement platforms using machine learning and Artificial Intelligence, and this process is nowadays influencing advertising agencies across the globe (Shah et al., 2020, p. 20).

The above-mentioned characteristics also display an ideological side that has been assessed by literature. Bridges underlines that the discourse on individual freedom and creativity is often associated with the "freedom for capital to skim the surplus value of that labour, and freedom for the state to deregulate markets to allow this exchange to happen freely'' (Bridges, 2018, p. 1304). In this sense, the analysis of work organization should also include the perceptions and opinions of employees, not only the managers' side.

WORK DURING PANDEMIC IN ROMANIA

The pandemic had two main stages in Romania: the lockdown lasted from March 16 to May 15, 2020 and the state of alert from May 16, 2020 to March 8, 2022. These stages were characterised by particular features of work depending on the health crisis situation.

During the lockdown, the Romanian state authorities imposed work from home and restrictions of movement with the exception of employees and companies considered as vital such as hospitals, army, police, fire, emergency services, retail and production of FMCG (fast-moving consumer goods).

In teleworking, the work-life imbalance affected numerous families because they experienced challenging conditions since children had to attend distance-education courses in the same space, sometimes using the same technological resources: computers, wi-fi/mobile Internet connection (Ionescu et al. 2022, p.2).

The Government Emergency Ordinance No 132/2020 adopted specific measures to strengthen the labour market and prevent unemployment at the national level. Companies supported employees whose jobs were cut-off by offering financial compensations, whereas others reduced working hours to compensate for poor conditions of remote work. According to the above-mentioned ordinance, employers were asked to decrease the working time by a maximum of 50% of the initial schedule of the individual employment contract except for the vital jobs (Government Emergency Ordinance no. 132/2020, 2020).

These regulations were meant to reduce the negative social effect generated by the health crisis. It is relevant to mention that remote work or teleworking had been firstly implemented in Romania two years before the pandemic, by the Law no. 81 released on March 30, 2018. The first article of the law specified the possibility of working from home. In the second article, teleworking was defined as a form of work organization through which the employee, regularly and voluntarily, fulfils his/her duties specific to his/her position, occupation and job in another place than the one organized by the employer, using technology of information and communication (Lege nr. 81, 2018).

Therefore, it had been offered the opportunity of teleworking one day per week even before the pandemic, a situation that may explain the rapid adaptation of some companies and employees to the circumstances brought by the lockdown. The Law 296/2020 mentioned the possibility of employers to pay employees' bills (for electricity) within the limit of 400 lei (approximately 80 Euros) per month (Law 296/2020, 2020).

During the state of alert, the Government kept supporting employers and employees financially and socially by extending the measures adopted during the lockdown. The Government Emergency Ordinance 36/2021 published on May 5, made telecommuting easier by introducing the electronic signature and offering a high level of flexibility when it comes to the working hours.

After the state of alert, the Government Emergency Ordinance No 73/ 2022 voted on May 30 adopted measures to reduce unemployment, inflation, social, economic crisis and also the effects of humanitarian and military crisis generated by the conflict between Russia and Ukraine, by applying the above similar mentioned measures to Ordinance No 132/ 2020.

METHODOLOGY

The present research displays a certain degree of novelty in regard to the topic of the analysis (work organization during pandemic) and the unit of analysis (advertising companies). The pandemic has brought about many challenges to work organization in different fields and economic sectors (Eurofound,

2020), and their research is only at the beginning. Therefore, an inductive qualitative research approach was chosen. To produce consistent findings on the selected topic, that could serve as basis for future research projects, there were applied semi-structured interviews which could bring valuable insights for the research of organisations (King, 2004). Given that the interviews were supposed to bring insights on the work organization in companies, a realistic epistemological approach was preferred, with a focus on the accuracy and comparability of accounts, as King (2004, p.12) recommends.

The interviews were conducted face-to-face (N=14) and had four categories of questions designed to provide answers to the research questions. Based on the research notes related to pandemic labour transformation in Romania combined with the characteristics of advertising work (flexibility, creativity, dynamics and innovation), the first seven questions explored the features of work organisation during 2020-2022. Then, the second group of questions was aimed at underlining the specific digital challenges of work during the pandemic. Furthermore, the third set unveiled the communication practices and challenges during the same timespan. Drawing from the literature review on the relevance of well-being at work, the last four questions were designed to highlight the strategies adopted by advertising agencies.

The interviewees are advertising professionals, selected from representative agencies based in Bucharest, the capital city of Romania. The respondents were chosen from a larger pool of possible participants in order to meet the criterion of having a variety of job positions, professional experiences, types of agency, and age. Also, it was intended to have an equal distribution of gender. The age of the interviewed professionals varies between 25 and 48 years old. The selected professionals perform various types of jobs (account executive, media planner, account director, copywriter etc.) and managerial positions (head of department, chief growth officer, managing partner, CEO).

The respondents' selection displays a variety and balance of seniority to facilitate a better understanding of work challenges in advertising during the pandemic: juniors, 1-9 years of experience (N=5); mid-career, 10-20 years of experience (N=4); seniors, +20 years of experience in the field (N=5). The respondents work for different types of agencies: local advertising agencies (Arsenoaiei & Matasel Consulting SRL, CAP COMPAS SRL, Friends/TBWA, Next Advertising, Screen Native, Sonica Works), and branches of global multinational advertising companies (Dentsu Romania, McCann Worldwide Romania, MRM, Universal Media McCann).

The research approach of the interviews relied on the design suggestions formulated by King (2004), and K. Charmaz (2014). The participants were informed on the objectives of the interviews and on their right to withdraw from the study.

The interviews – that lasted between 26 and 49 minutes – were conducted in the Romanian language, between August, 5 and September, 5, 2022 by authors. The interviews were recorded and transcribed verbatim in Romanian. One key informant reviewed the draft of the findings and formulated remarks. The fragments selected for the present chapter were translated into English and were quoted as follows: I.1 for Informant 1, I.2 for Informant 2 etc. (see the annex of the chapter). In this way, the anonymity of respondents was preserved.

The findings were interpreted through thematic analysis (Clarke and Braun, 2017, Nowell *et al*, 2017), which enabled the identification of the key themes and sub-themes, in the context of rich data yielded from the semi-structured interviews. From the major key themes identified in the analysis, three were selected for the chapter: practices of hybrid work, life-work balance/imbalance, well-being strategies.

PRACTICES OF HYBRIDISATION IN ADVERTISING COMPANIES

The interviewees explained that every company differently understood hybridity and implemented various types of work arrangements in order to complete the projects and obtain efficiency during the pandemic. There were three situations that were included by the interviewees under the umbrella of the concept of hybrid work: (1) the mixture between online and offline work; (2) a blend of workspaces: office, home, and other locations; (3) a combination of flexible working hours with fixed office schedule. There were also interviewees that mentioned the possibility to alternate the online work at the office with the offline work in other locations different from the office.

One interviewed manager asserted: "Hybrid work is very cool, as long as you manage to teach them [employees] to do it right, hybrid is the best of all. I encouraged people [to do it]. You want to stay two weeks in the countryside or at the mountains or wherever, do it! Perfect! Cool! Live it! (...) But you need a routine in this kind of work. (...) If you manage to plan right, then you can be more efficient than in the normal way, but it is important to be organised and fair to yourself" (I. 5).

The interviewees did not yield a homogenous definition of hybridity as a concept, although many interviewees mentioned several practices associated with it. One interviewee explained that hybrid work should be perceived as a combination between face-to-face teamwork (mostly at the office) and individual activity (at home) (I. 2). In this case, the mixture between different spaces is of utmost importance for work organisation. Another respondent underlined the relevance of online work for the hybridity concept, emphasising the unlimited possibilities of virtual activity. "I think that everything could be done online, practically everything, apart from the interaction with other people, which is so important. It is 99% versus 1%, but that 1% is similar to 99%. That's it. Human interaction - or at least staying face-to-face in the same office -, this cannot be transferred to an online [environment]." (I. 13)

In the same line of argument, one of the interviewees (I. 5) explained that the face-to-face work should be applied to brainstorming, project design and development, and complex story writing. The direct, unmediated interaction with the fellow workers is connected to keeping internal cohesion: "Interaction with your group is important to keep the culture of the [advertising] agency" (I. 5).

The common feature drawn from the interviews is that the clients and the partner companies had a major influence on how hybrid work was organised and also on the communication practices in advertising agencies.

One account director from a local agency explained that the clients pushed for a rapid adaptation to online communication. "Our corporate clients already had knowledge [of online communication practices], and we 'stole' the tools of the trade from them. Many had previous experience with [Microsoft] Teams and knew how to handle it..." (I. 11). Another respondent from a client service department also stressed out that the corporate clients were better organised from the online communication perspective, and managed to influence the work flow in the advertising agencies (I. 6). One of the benefits of that online communication was the lasting improvement of the relationship between the clients and the client service departments in agencies (I. 6).

As previously mentioned, there were many differences in organising the hybrid work in advertising agencies in Romania. As one interviewee pointed out: "so many agencies, so many customs" (I. 11). The differences related to the actual time of implementing the online communication (some companies started using it before the pandemic, others rushed to apply it in the first days of the emergency state), to the rhythm of implementation (different from one company to another) and the type of hybrid work procedures as well as workspaces.

Some companies had already implemented the hybrid work before the pandemic, especially the local branches of global advertising companies (for example McCann Worldwide Romania, Universal Media McCann, Tribal Worldwide Romania). In one example, the respondent explained that he firstly had seen a hybrid organisation more than a decade before the pandemic, while visiting the UK office of a global communications company. On returning to Bucharest, the respondent implemented the same work organisation in his local company, by reducing office space and allowing the employees to work from home or other locations: "This business should not be deployed inside four walls, I truly think that in 2022 people should work remotely" (I. 1).

Other agencies were in the situation to move for a sudden adaptation to online work, in March 2020, on the first days of the lockdown. "We did not have any tools for online work before the lockdown" (I. 6). The rhythm of adaptation to online was influenced both by the clients, and the motivation and knowledge of the employees.

The interviews also yielded the negative aspects of hybrid work: a decrease in work quality; poor time management (failure to meet deadlines); lack of efficiency; sudden changes of communication practices among employees (with many redundant online meetings or online calls); difficulty of adaptation to technical/digital tools; superficial relationships among team workers; difficult on-boarding of employees; feedback delay even in the case of small tasks.

"I feel that because of this hybrid work, I am much less effective" (I. 6).

"We worked much more but productivity was lower" (I. 3).

"The socialising part of small talk, let me say, (...) has somehow been lost, and so have the relationships between colleagues: we are less friends than before or we are more colleagues now when working remotely. Relationships [at workplace] decline, they no longer rely on this side of friendship with people (I. 12).

DISRUPTION OF PERSONAL AND WORK LIFE

The relation between work arrangements and private life was a major concern for the interviewees. Online working during the lockdown - that lasted for two months in Romania - was embraced without major criticism on the part of advertising professionals, and the interviewees underlined that the behaviour of fellow colleagues was considered to be supportive, nice and caring.

The respondents stated that they displayed empathy towards the personal life of their colleagues: "At first, everyone tried to be empathetic and tried to take into consideration the possible mitigating circumstances. . . . It seemed to me that there was much more understanding on a human level as well. All companies tried to provide incentives to make people get over the unpleasant period more easily" (I. 3).

Many interviewees admitted that after the lockdown the level of tolerance (towards colleagues, other people's personal problems etc.) started to decrease progressively. Some respondents explained that people stopped being nice to their colleagues and became self-oriented. There was a general expectation that hybrid work would make things easier, but the reality was different.

During the 22-month state of alert, when online fatigue had already been installed, it became very difficult for advertising professionals to manage the balance of work-life, especially for those who kept working from home. They felt there were no limits between personal and professional worlds, as the space of working and living was the same: "you didn't go anywhere anymore, you stayed at home and it was very easy to fall into this trap because you wore pyjamas, you were still on TV, you were still using the laptop and that was very dangerous. When these worlds emerged, it was most exhausting, and it was also very difficult to concentrate... It was chaos…" (I. 5).

The family life was affected, and several interviewees complained that they did not find time to stay with their beloved although they shared the same domestic space. The professional life was also negatively influenced because some employees had to take over the work of others (who did not manage to adapt or were less efficient) in order to fulfil clients' demands in due time. Several respondents felt that their colleagues differently prioritised their life, paying less attention to work: "One of the challenges was when we couldn't find each other over the phone. When somebody didn't answer the phone, you felt that you were left alone in a project. It seemed that no one could hear you, your voice could no longer be heard, you had the feeling that you were working alone. Basically, in online work, you can't rely on a prompt answer from the others, especially when you need it. Failure to meet deadlines was also a problem. It was harder to assume the responsibility, the priorities [of other people] seemed to be different [than mine] and somehow the deadlines became blurred [than they used to be]. (I. 6).

The respondents felt that during the pandemic the efficiency of work declined, but the workload remained unchanged. Therefore, people had to spend more hours working to meet the deadlines, and that situation clearly affected the personal life of everybody. All the mixed work arrangements, be it face-to-face&hybrid, hybrid&online, face-to-face&online, did not manage to organize the activity efficiently, but this could be caused also by the context of the general health crisis.

Time management of many employees and managers was negatively influenced by the pervasive online communication (i.e. online meetings, online calls, online presentations) that was considered to be extremely exhausting and did not leave any time for the execution of tasks, implementation/supervision of projects or pitching new businesses. The working time was prolonged and there was no room left for lunch break or personal life. Several interviewees tried to impose limits or separate personal life from work, but this was an individual option (not a general rule) and it was not very easy to achieve. "Personally, I am trying to set very clear limits [between work and personal life], and unless there are absolutely exceptional situations, I try to respect the lunch break, the work program, because during the pandemic, the lack of limits affected me" (I. 11).

Some respondents admitted that coming back to the office was the best solution to regain their personal life, and to return to pre-pandemic activities without giving up their work responsibilities: "That's why I preferred to go to the office whenever it was possible. This organized me and helped me organize to keep my personal time separated from work time" (I. 3).

The employees got tired of the hybrid work organisation especially when they felt that companies did not use management practices to deal with crisis, to make arrangements regarding the time and space for work. Many interviewees displayed the "Zoom fatigue", due to several factors: too many online meetings, lack of organisational coherence, lack of internal communication, lack of informal meetings (that used to take place before 2020 at the cafeteria or during the break, the lunch or on other informal occasions).

Several respondents explained that their departments had to organise by themselves very quickly and did not have tools or appropriate procedures and had to rely on trial-error practice (learning by doing). The work pace was described as too fast and not fair for all employees. Some of them experienced burnout while others managed to work less than their colleagues. "Generally speaking people tried to be kind to each other (...) but they put up with this pandemic period more easily or with more difficulty. I don't know for sure… maybe not necessarily because of the pandemic, or because of unfortunate personal events overlapping, but there were people who went into a kind of depression or burnout and then they stopped working properly." (I. 3)

MANAGEMENT INTERVENTIONS

Even if the advertising professionals are prone to innovation and are tech-driven, there were employees and departments that displayed resistance to change in terms of hybridization of work.

Some refused to use digital tools to fulfil their tasks and openly insisted on traditional work practices. "We had team members that did not embrace this [online technology], but not because they were unable to do it, but simply because they did not want to open themselves up, and value this. There were departments, such as the creative one, that managed to work using tools like pencil and notebook and did not display a high interest in accessing advanced planning tools…e-mail management [apps], Notes [app], and so on. They used the 'basic' package, and used to say: 'I need a laptop with a functional camera, a software for video calls, and further I will manage with what is at hand." (I. 11)

The context of the reluctance to use online tools or technology could be explained by the professionals' focus on individual work projects and on their team or department activities, especially as a consequence of the pandemic restrictions.

During the lockdown, all major companies in Romania, excepting the vital ones (i.e., hospitals, police, pharmacies, firefighters, retails a.s.o.), deployed remote work. Public authorities transmitted the message to stay home and restrict at the minimum the social contacts, even with the relatives. Also, in the state of alert, people were strongly advised to follow the social distancing measures. Freedom of movement was restricted in the case of unvaccinated persons, especially in the fall of 2021.

The advertising companies also followed the rules, and, as a result, many employees had to work from home or in hybrid arrangements to observe social distancing. Some of them felt alienated from their colleagues and from the companies, encountering difficulties when working. Others felt overwhelmed by the workload and, consequently, tried to find solutions to avoid burnout or a possible depression. There were also cases of people who took advantage of the situation, working less and putting the blame on technology.

Moreover, the interviewees explained they had colleagues who showed resistance to open their cameras during video meetings or video calls.

"Yes, we had colleagues that I seldom see with open cameras [during online meetings]. I found myself in one unpleasant situation in which I was supposed to introduce a new member of our team to our client and, as a result, we had an online meeting, but, the young colleague did not open the camera." (I. 3)

By not opening the cameras during the online meetings, the employees tried to protect their personal life (intimacy), but, at the same time, they limited the interactions with their teams and clients. That context created tensions among departments and generated internal conflicts.

Several respondents underlined that, when the restrictions started to be lifted (2021), there were team members who refused to participate in offline meetings either with clients, or with their colleagues. The advertising professionals interviewed during this research recognised that the most successful pitches and presentations for clients are those who take place face-to-face with the entire team. The online meetings should be kept as a back-up, because: "They were a useful tool during the pandemic and it could be further used, but not as a main practice, but as a back-up solution. It is good to have it, but I think we should always opt for a physical presence [for meetings with clients]. . . . In the online [environment], the quality of a presentation decreases" (I. 6)

Confronted with the above-mentioned issues, companies tried to ease the situation of employees by making use of strategies to enforce their well-being. At first, social distancing and medical advice to prevent COVID-19 infection were included in the internal communication of companies. Also, social distancing motivated companies to organize offline work in shifts (by departments) and to modify the space in order to respect the rules imposed by the authorities.

Work was organised by objective factors (related to the prevention of COVID-19) combined with specific factors (related to the characteristics of advertising creative side, production and project implementation). "At the space level, firstly we tried to respect the social distancing rules, but not in a mechanical way, so we tried to have 'our view'. We designed a project and we sent it to our designers [with the message]: 'Let's re-design all of these related to distancing'. We had several imposed aspects and we kept them, but we told them to implement them in our way. That became a project. First of all, we tried to make them be friendly. . . . Not something like: 'Masks again?'. We tried to integrate such rules [related to social distancing and mask wearing] in our [organizational] culture". (I. 5)

Secondly, the managers tried to motivate people to make the initial transition from face-to-face work to online, and then from online to hybrid work.

"It was hard at first because no one was used to working from home for more than a day if it was a one-time situation, and then you find yourself between four walls with no people and everything (...) is mediated by the screen of a smartphone or laptop. So, this changed everything. At the level of communication and internal organization, we had to move completely to digital and use all the tools we had". (I. 13)

Space was considered vital for the new ways of work and was redesigned considering the employees' needs to communicate and cooperate in different projects.

"We changed the concept of working space from the very beginning [of the pandemic] (...) half of the spaces are now for meetings and collaborations, and basically our aim is to encourage people to come to the office with a specific purpose: to teamwork, to exchange ideas, to give feedback, to prepare things, to collaborate". (I. 2)

In terms of work organization, there were two important stages during the pandemic period: lockdown and state of alert - that prompted different managerial approaches.

The management of work during lockdown took into consideration the cohesion of the team and the human factor. At that moment, the managers encouraged employees to use the office equipment at their home desks (people took home the office computers, PC monitors, office chairs and desks, and other necessary material to organise the domestic space as a workspace). Internal cohesion was obtained by online staff meetings, organised, in most cases, on a daily basis.

After the lockdown, in the state of alert, the management teams tried to maintain the community spirit by gathering people in one-day training, for short Fridays, for special anniversaries and even inviting employees to come to work to informal spaces. One major challenge was to keep the employees' loyalty. The departments that were mainly offline-oriented (such as the Events Division and Production Division) were reorganised in order to keep the jobs.

Another major challenge was to overcome the fear that some employees experienced. Fear was caused by rapid digitization, workload, societal changes, deadlines, and clients' pressures.

Crisis management was also a point of concern for managers, as the online work environment raised many obstacles and employees could not communicate properly among them and with the management. Many employees displayed frustration and lack of confidence in themselves, and felt the need to be encouraged and positively assessed: "There were emails sent to all, that functioned as 'energy pills', sent on a regular basis and providing an overview [on the company]: from who did what on a personal level (...), who made a successful presentation [for clients], which team managed to impress the client, until various resources meant to help people to get over that period. There were also different articles containing pieces of advice regarding what to read, how to do sports… there were also work related, but also on the topic of well-being." (I. 11)

"There were many crises…but they were solved by micro-group discussion, even one-to-one, by investing a lot of time in direct communication, even if it was online. And managers engaged in one-to-one discussion, or small teams' discussion - groups of three - to make sure that all voices were heard. Micro-management. In real life [offline], meetings can accommodate many participants, but in online the voice of non-vocal people can easily be lost." (I. 6)

The management intervention during the pandemic focused on specific organisation of work that could foster the well-being of employees. The main aspects relevant for the present research refer to: a flexible space management (with different hybrid work arrangements, and special places for teamwork), respecting social distancing rules (with a creative approach), downplaying the negative effects of online work by strengthening interpersonal communication and internal cohesion, using direct informal communication by phone, and by social media platforms (mainly WhatsApp), and even one-to-one video call (in case of crises in communication among crew members).

DISCUSSION

The present chapter unveils the strategies used by advertising agencies to adapt to hybrid work and develop well-being tactics for employees during the pandemic period in Romania. The literature review showed that pandemic accelerated the transition to hybrid work and encouraged a blend of online and offline office activities. Hybrid work relies on new technologies adoption in society and at the workplace. The research questions aimed at elucidating the features of online and hybrid work organised during the COVID-19 pandemic in Romanian advertising agencies (Q1), the perceptions of advertising professionals (Q2), the work transformations and their influence on personal life and well-being (Q3), and management strategies to ensure the well-being of their employees during the pandemic (Q4).

In Romanian advertising agencies, the hybrid work organization was imposed as a solution by the pandemic context in advertising agencies, as well as in other companies.

Before the pandemic, there were cases of agencies that implemented several tools for hybrid work, mainly referring to client-agency relationships, when it comes to cross-border (global) contracts. In addition, there were agencies that offered employees the possibility to work from home in specific, time-limited, creative projects.

The lockdown brought a sudden change for all companies. The state of emergency imposed by the authorities meant that all work should have been done from home, excepting vital jobs (medical staff, police officers etc.). Advertising professionals worked from home for the period March 16-May 15, 2020, and implemented hybrid work arrangements in the next two years (up to March 2022). In specific cases, the labour contracts were re-drawn, several remote work conditions being included.

The interviews conducted during the present research yielded that there was not a single perspective on hybrid work across the communication sector, and that there were advantages and disadvantages for advertising professionals. One important idea is that hybrid work should be kept further, but under specific circumstances: to be done according to a routine, under the supervision of the management, and by respecting and monitoring the same time schedule for the entire team. Among the negative aspects associated with hybrid work, there were mentioned: decrease in work quality, poor time management, lack of efficiency, time-consuming online meetings, gaps in communication among team workers, difficult on-boarding of employees, and feedback delay even in the case of small tasks.

The perceptions of advertising professionals on the online and hybrid work organisation in the pandemic context varied from resistance to change to quick adaptation, and on the nature of work in different departments. There was a general expectation that rapid adoption of technology would simplify tasks, but the reality was perceived as being different. Many interviewees underlined that online fatigue installed after the first 2-5 months, and brought challenges in terms of work efficiency and management of the work-life balance. The respondents felt there were blurring limits between personal and professional worlds.

The management of the companies tried to ease the situation of employees by implementing strategies to enforce the well-being. Social distancing and medical advice were included in the internal communication of companies. The managers motivated people to support the transition from face-to-face to online work, and then from online to hybrid work. The management also was concerned about keeping the team cohesion by online staff meetings, organised daily. The community spirit was reinforced by formal arrangements (one-day trainings, reducing the working hours), and informal events (special anniversaries, parties, charity events etc.).

The management intervention aimed at fostering the well-being of employees by offering a flexible space and time organization, respecting social distancing and reducing the negative effects of online work by strengthening internal communication.

CONCLUSION

During the pandemic, the hybrid work brought technological challenges but, also, raised problems related to the well-being of the employees. The advertising agencies had to deal with the online fatigue of the former, different internal communication crises, and interpersonal conflicts. Their objectives were to keep their employees at work and strengthen the community spirit within organisations.

Online and hybrid work generated the work-life imbalance. The disruption of personal life negatively affected the employees, in limited cases leading to burnout or depression. Employees displayed frustration and lack of confidence in themselves and felt the need to be encouraged and positively assessed.

During the first part of the lockdown, the management intervention was improvised, as it focused on rapid solutions for improving internal communication and sudden adaptation to online work. After the lockdown, there were conceived strategies for smooth communication and improvement of employees' well-being: a flexible approach on workspace and work time, internal cohesion projects, a better organisation of online meetings, thus enhancing the culture of responsible teamwork and community spirit.

The current research is limited to advertising professionals who are fully employed by Bucharest-based advertising agencies during the pandemic. The number of respondents could be extended and also compared with interviewees working in advertising in other countries. To better understand the transformation of work in the communication industry it would also be recommended to extend the research on part-time employees and freelancers. Also, a gender perspective on the consequences of pandemic hybrid work over life-work balance and well-being would be of interest for future research in the advertising field.

REFERENCES

Anderson-Connoly, R., Grunberg, L., Greenberg, S. E., & Moore, S. (2002). Is lean mean? Workplace transformation and employee well-being. *Work, Employment and Society*, *16*(3), 389–423. doi:10.1177/095001702762217407

Bridges, L. E. (2018). Flexible as freedom? The dynamics of creative industry work and a case study of the editor in publishing. *New Media & Society*, *4*(4), 1303–1319. doi:10.1177/1461444816688920

Charmaz, K. (2014). *Constructing grounded theory* (2nd ed.). Sage.

Clarke, V., & Braun, V. (2017). Thematic analysis. *The Journal of Positive Psychology*, *12*(3), 297–298. doi:10.1080/17439760.2016.1262613

Cvenkel, N. (2020). *Well-Being in the Workplace: Governance and Sustainability Insights to Promote Workplace Health*. Springer.

Davis, M., & Prince, M. (2005). Dynamics of trust between clients and their advertising agencies: Advanced in performanced theory. *Academy of Marketing Review*, *11*, 1–32.

Deery, S., Walsh, J., Zatzick, C. D., & Hayes, A. F. (2017). Exploring the relationship between compressed work hours satisfaction and absenteeism in front-line service work. *European Journal of Work and Organizational Psychology*, *26*(1), 42–52. doi:10.1080/1359432X.2016.1197907

Eurofound. (2020). *Living, working and COVID-19*. Publications Office of the European Union.

Finkel, R., Jones, D., Sang, K., & Russel, D. S. (2017). Diversifying the creative: Creative work, creative industries, creative identities. *Organization*, *24*(3), 281–288. doi:10.1177/1350508417690167

Government Emergency Ordinance no. 132/2020, on support measures for employees and employers in the context of SARS-COV2-pandemic, as well as for stimulating employment growth in force since August 2020, https://www.pwc.ro/en/tax-legal/alerts/law-no--153-2020-entering-into-force-on-24-july-2020--amending-a1.html

Halford, S. (2005). Hybrid workspace: Re-spatialisation of work, organisation and management. *New Technology, Work and Employment*, *20*(1), 19–33. doi:10.1111/j.1468-005X.2005.00141.x

Kemp, N. (2018). *Is the advertising industry doing enough to protect and promote the mental wellbeing of employees?* https://www.campaignlive.co.uk/article/advertising-industry-doing-enough-protect-promote-mental-wellbeing-employees/1495437

King, N. (2004). Using interviews in qualitative research. In C. Cassell & G. Symon (Eds.), *Essential Guide to Qualitative Methods in Organizational Research* (pp. 11–22). Sage. https://legislatie.just.ro/Public/DetaliiDocument/199418

Law no. 296/2020 amending and completing the fiscal code, https://www.pwc.ro/en/tax-legal/alerts/law-no--296-2020-amending-and-completing-the-fiscal-code-.html

Nagel, L. (2020). The influence of the COVID-19 pandemic on the digital transformation of work. *The International Journal of Sociology and Social Policy*, *40*(9/10), 861–875. doi:10.1108/IJSSP-07-2020-0323

Nowell, L. S., Norris, J. M., White, D. E., & Moules, N. J. (2017). Thematic Analysis: Striving to Meet the Trustworthiness Criteria. *International Journal of Qualitative Methods, 16*(1), 1–13. doi:10.1177/1609406917733847

Ordonanța de urgență nr. 36 din 5 mai 2021, privind utilizarea semnăturii electronice avansate sau semnăturii electronice calificate, însoțite de marca temporală electronică sau marca temporală electronică calificată și sigiliul electronic calificat al angajatorului în domeniul relațiilor de muncă, și pentru modificarea și completarea unor acte normative [Government Emergency Ordinance No.36/ 5 May 2021 regarding the use of the advanced or qualified electronic signature accompanied by the electronic temporary marc or by qualified electronic temporary mark and the qualified electronic seal of the employer in the field of work relationships, and for modifying and filling of some normative acts]. https://legislatie.just.ro/Public/DetaliiDocumentAfis/242068

Ordonanța de Urgență nr. 72 din 30 mai 2022 pentru modificarea și completarea Ordonanței de urgență a Guvernului nr. 63/2022 privind unele măsuri temporare pentru acordarea de sprijin material categoriilor de persoane aflate în situații de risc de deprivare materială și/sau risc de sărăcie extremă, suportate parțial din fonduri externe nerambursabile, precum și unele măsuri de distribuire a acestuia [Government Emergency Ordinance No. 72/ 30 May 2022 regarding the modification and completion of the Government Emergency Ordinance No. 63/2020 regarding some temporary measures for the grant of material support to categories of citizens under risks of material deprivation and/or in risk of extreme poverty, supported partially from external non-refundable funds, as well as some measures of fund this distribution]. https://legislatie.just.ro/Public/DetaliiDocumentAfis/255838

Putnam, L. (2015). *Workplace wellness that works: 10 steps to infuse well-being and vitality into your organisation*. Wiley. doi:10.1002/9781119154839

Renard, K., Cornu, F., Emery, Y., & Giauque, D. (2021). The Impact of New Ways of Working on Organizations and Employees: A Systematic Review of Literature. *Administrative Sciences, 11*(2), 38. doi:10.3390/admsci11020038

Rosengren, S., Eisend, M., Koslow, S., & Dahlen, M. (2020). A Meta-analysis of when and how advertising creativity works. *Journal of Marketing, 84*(6), 39–56. doi:10.1177/0022242920929288

Scully-Russ, E., & Torraco, R. (2020). The changing nature and organization of work: An integrative review of the literature. *Human Resource Development Review, 19*(1), 66–93.

Shah, N., Engineer, S. Bhagat, N., Chauhan, H. & Shah, M. (2020). Research trends on the usage of machine learning and Artificial Intelligence. *Advertising Augmented Human Research, 5*(19), 1–15.

Stich, J.-F. (2021). Flexible working and applicant-attraction: A person-job fit approach. *Personnel Review, 50*(1), 358–378. doi:10.1108/PR-12-2019-0672

Wood, S. (2008). Job characteristics, employee voice and wellbeing in Britain. *Industrial Relations Journal, 39*(2), 153–168. doi:10.1111/j.1468-2338.2007.00482.x

APPENDIX

Table 1.

No	Present Job Position of Interviewee	Type of Agency of Interviewee	Experience in the Field of the Interviewee	Gender of Interviewee	Date of Interview
Informant 1	Head of strategy and Partner (director)	Independent, local, specialized, strategy	24	M	12.08.2022
Informant 2	CEO, media	Global, media	23	M	5.09.2022
Informant 3	Media planner	Global, full service	22	F	22.08.2022
Informant 4	Managing Partner-creative planner	Independent, local, digital agency	21	M	30.08.2022
Informant 5	CO-CEO Chief Creative Officer	Global, full service	20	M	29.08.2022
Informant 6	Account Director-CS	Independent, local, creative boutique	18	F	5.08.2022
Informant 7	Chief Growth Officer-CS	Global, full service	17	F	25.08.2022
Informant 8	Group Account Director	Global, full service	16	F	29.08.2022
Informant 9	Executive Creative Director	Global, full services	13	F	11.08.2022
Informant 10	Copywriter	Independent local, creative boutique	8	M	2.09.2022
Informant 11	Account Director	Independent local, full service	7	F	23.08.2022
Informant 12	Social media strategy	Independent local agency	7	M	1.09.2022
Informant 13	Senior Account Manage	Independent local, full service	5	F	2.09.2022
Informant 14	Junior art director	Global, full service	2	M	1.09.2022

Chapter 11
Reimagining Communication in the Pharmaceutical Industry in the Next Normal

Amílcar Barreto
Universidade Catolica Portuguesa, Portugal

ABSTRACT

The crisis of COVID-19 has resulted in pharmaceutical organizations moving towards new communication strategies with some launching new business models to survive and reach their target audience that in turn were layered onto, and dramatically accelerated, long-standing trends such as digitization and sustainability. In many ways, the changes in healthcare professionals and patient behavior are an acceleration of digital trends that were in motion before the pandemic hit. Pharma companies are experiencing a wave of innovations in the way they engage with their target audiences from new treatment modalities (home based) to smart machines, advanced analytics, and digital connectivity. The latest technologies and digital can make communication better, faster, more agile, more reliable, more compliant, and more efficient. Pharma companies can transform the way they communicate to deliver more efficient and efficacious communication in a cost-efficient way. The strategy is changing from a tell-and-sell model to a partner-and-solve model.

REMOTE WORK AND HYBRID WORK ORGANIZATIONS

The importance of work from a broader organisational and socio-economic perspective is the central theme of many studies addressing some economic, political, environmental, and social challenges. Thus, Kastelan Mrak and Sokolic, (2017) define organizations based on four dimensions, organizations are characterized and described by physical and material spaces built and, experiencing social processes. They are also classified as sources of new ideas, innovation, and creativity (innovation dimension), are inserted in a cultural, economic, social, and political context as a human dimension and are defined as hierarchical places of power and control (hierarchical dimension) (Kastelan Mrak and Sokolic, 2017).

DOI: 10.4018/978-1-6684-7353-5.ch011

It should be noted that technological development has enabled and continues to allow the introduction of new forms of work, leading to a need to rethink the meaning of some dimensions and elements of the organization. In this sense, the development of information and communication technologies (ICT), accompanied by digitization, allowed a physical distance work practice from the company's site, which is referred to as telework (Delbridge and Sallaz, 2015). This phenomenon includes remote work.

As all dimensions of the organization are interrelated, changes in a certain dimension lead to the change of other dimensions, although telework has been practiced in some organizations since the beginning of the 21st century, initially only as an occasional alternative form of work beyond the standard workplace. With the development of information and ICT, it became more present in the organizational context.

Progress in the field of information technology and the wide availability of devices as well as communications links have affected many areas of life including education. Many studies have been devoted to technological solutions and the possibilities of their application, as well as changes in teaching methods, didactics, organization, or the evolution of the role of information sources in the modern world (Laurillard, 2013; Venkatesh et al., 2016).

Consumer culture represents a process offered to the world, imposed by technological, economic, political, and cultural oppressions, lifestyles and geographies. Consumer culture is a cultural process that is mirrored through the mass media today, whether on radio, television, and the internet, such as advertisements and social networks that hypnotize people to consume their effects related to the subconscious. In this sense, the process is global and popular in constant change, transformation, and innovation (McDonald, 2015).

In this respect, Adam Smith referred that "consumption is the sole end and purpose of all production and the welfare of the producer to be attended to, only so far as is necessary to promote that of the consumer" (Smith, 1930, p. 625). Consumer sovereignty assumes that all economic production is driven by consumer preferences, and the shift in demand has been stimulated by marketing efforts.

Considering the importance of rapid transaction development, digital marketing as a concept highlights a set of profiles and processes that span all digital channels to promote a product or service or to build a digital brand.

From economic practice, digital, marketing originally developed around the Web demonstrates a robustness of redirected traffic to the advertising industry, bidding. According to Mark Sceats, digital marketing is feasible over the internet as a work and display environment (Kalyanam & MacIntyre, 2002).

The constant and uncontrollable changes in business in the contemporary environment require permanent adaptations and adjustments in products and production and management procedures, and those who seek to adapt to new environmental conditions will face difficulties to grow and survive (Lamb, Hair & McDaniel, 2008).

According to Evans (2012: 35), we can describe social media as "a collaborative process through which information is created, shared, changed and destroyed". It can also be described as the use of mobile and web technologies to create platforms on which users can interact with each other, sharing content created by themselves. One of the most used tools in social media is social networks.

There are three levels of digital integration that relate to each other, scanning, typing and digital transformation. At its most basic level, there is typing, that is, analog data is converted into a digital format product, at the mid level, there is digitization that is supported by the innovation of computer-aided information processing and explores digital opportunities. At the higher level, digital transformation emerges as a restructuring at the system level through digital diffusion that stimulates knowledge (George et al., 2018).

The old notion of the importance of the material environment in the construction and model of power relations, meanings and practices was left aside without analyzing the main long-term consequences of human and organizational well-being (Savage and Warde, 1993). Due to technology and social and economic changes, spatial distance and partial elimination of the traditional workplace, the way of work began to change, leading to a recomposition of organizations and the relationships between their elements (Dingel and Neiman, 2020).

Nevertheless, the pandemic has significantly transformed the way we work. According to the International Labour Organization (ILO, 2021), in the second half of 2020, about 17.4% of the global workforce already worked from home, however, not all work or sector is suitable for working from home. Developing countries and economies with lower growth and many jobs requiring low-skilled workers have less access to remote work models (OECD, 2021).

When the pandemic began telework in the form of remote work it became the fastest alternative to the standard workplace, an attempt to avoid major interruptions that led to the failure of organizations and consequently to economies (Choudhury et al., 2021). This allowed operations to continue as usual while maintaining a pandemic-proof environment, although it raised other questions about the impact of remote work control and telework on further organisational development on economic, social and psychological contexts.

The organization's environment is volatile and managers must be open to changes, and increased performance and job satisfaction from a workers' perspective can be reported positively or negatively. However, the relationship between remote work and performance is scarce in literature studies.

Remote work includes different benefits such as saving time and other expenses, integrating the work of specialized employees and expanding cooperation. There are studies that determine the benefits and limitations of remote work (Kowalski et al., 2022), namely, the most common benefits are work flexibility, creativity and motivation. And as disadvantages, it boils down to the lack of work-related contacts.

Several assumptions are associated with remote work due to the flexibility and autonomy given to employees when they work remotely. First, it is assumed that remote work can decrease employee stress and burnout and reduce job fatigue and work-home conflict, thereby increasing engagement and job satisfaction and performance (Allen et al., 2015). On the other hand, there are other assumptions about the possible disadvantages of remote work at individual and organizational levels, for example, employees working from home may face problems associated with poor ergonomic facilities, leading to muscle injuries, or even working longer hours than at work. office (Stankevičiūtė and Kunskaja, 2022). In addition, work isolation can compromise feelings of belonging to the organization, compromise the receipt of social benefits, support from colleagues, and increase anxiety (Moglia et al., 2021).

Work needs are physical, social or organizational that require physical or mental effort, consume energy, resources and are associated with physiological and psychological costs such as health complaints and exhaustion. In this sense, job resources are aspects of work that fulfill basic psychological needs and can be used to alleviate work needs. To improve workers' ability to meet the needs of their work, it is necessary to incorporate the notion of personal needs, the individual standards that people set for their own performance, behavior, and personal resources (Bakker & Demerouti, 2017).

According to Perry et al. (2018) despite differences in work performance among workers with various personality characteristics, few studies have discussed the role of personality and behavior in determining the well-being of teleworkers. In this regard, two field studies determined that workers who had high emotional stability and high autonomy experienced lower levels of psychological strain. There was a negative relationship between the extent of telework and the fatigue of these workers, which the authors attributed to the need for relationships through remote work (Abel et al., 2021; Petrou & Bakker, 2016).

The use of digital devices and the introduction of online social networks have transformed many aspects of clinical practice. Both patients and doctors are increasingly using the internet and social media platforms to provide, obtain, share, and comment on health information (Lavorgna et al., 2018).

In social media, users create and share content and participate in social media projects. Each of these activities can be used by physicians or patients to communicate, retrieve, or transmit information about health problems, illnesses (Moorhead et al., 2013).

Likewise, the amount of information available on the internet and the increase in its use in the health area have led to a flow of specialization in their own fields. Neurologists can benefit from the advantages of electronic communication, the powerful mechanism for accessing information and, above all, the strengthening of professional collaboration. More specifically, physicians and the pharmaceutical industry share a convergence of interests in providing safe and effective medicines to patients, but they differ in their practices and ethical standards. Their interactions are desirable and inevitable and may generate conflicts of interest for physicians.

On the other hand, pharmaceutical companies are increasingly involved in neurology education, due to rapid advances in the pharmacotherapy of neurological diseases, and in part because of economic trends affecting medicine and academic medical centers. Thus, the growing role of the pharmaceutical industry in education has both positive results and negative consequences. Neurologists need to be informed about the drugs and clinical trials they provide and evidence from their practice. It is in this sense that it sets as its objective – "Understanding how neurologists interact with the information they receive online from the pharmaceutical industry and how they use this information in their clinical practice".

While there is a wealth of health information available, there is often no guarantee of its quality. The average information source is the main criterion for its credibility and quality. The problems associated with distinguishing less credible information relate to the problem of assessing source accuracy. This aspect led us to the objective "Understanding the criteria used to assess the credibility of information".

Despite the significant increase in interest and investments at the scientific level, this area has shown some profile gaps in recent decades, essentially demonstrated by beliefs supported by interest groups that are highly effective in promoting communication.

For many years, efforts have been made to increase and improve scientific communication, more evident in times of the global COVID-19 pandemic, when scientists and epidemiologists themselves were called upon to communicate science publicly. So, in my opinion, the way in which this communication is effective, clear, and reliable affects people all over the world. in this sense, the volume of scientific dissemination has grown over time, and despite its growing production, the issue of ensuring quality in scientific communication remains critical. Barriers and lack of incentives in scientific communication need to be identified as a starting point for developing stimuli to promote scientific communication and for wider audiences.

In my opinion, the main factors that affect the quality of scientific information start with the scientists themselves, and the issues that affect their way of communicating and their challenges in different areas of communication such as journalism, social media need to be improved.

STRATEGIC COMMUNICATION IN THE DIGITAL AGE

Despite integrating several theories from many disciplines in order to broaden their knowledge base, strategic communication can be alternatively called corporate communication, or communication management. Initially, Ruler, Vercic and Sriramesh (2007) defined strategic communication as the "objective of the use of communication by an organization to fulfill its mission" (p. 3).

Subsequently, Holtzhausen and Zerfass (2013) expanded this concept to include a set of contexts where to set goals, government, and management control. However, the dominant strategic communication literature has been criticized for three interrelated deficiencies. First, his management discourse and focus on the organization perpetuate elite interest as the top priority and control as a problematic issue (Murphy, 2011, p. 3).

Second, organizational interest itself is reinforced by a predominant research focus on the organizational site, and especially in large companies with little attention to broader audiences, communities and societies (Smith, 2010). Finally, thirdly, disability results from the lack of informal explanatory power and, sometimes discursive, role of the communication strategy. The constantly changing digital technologies and proliferation of social media, ranging from big data, crowdsourcing, mobile apps and social networks and relationship sites (SNS), which have transformed the environment where communication strategies are practiced, and also require a re-imagination of theories.

In this sense, Gawer (2009) focused on the historical perspective with the modern economy, distinguishing between internal platforms and the supply chain and industry. And, he added a fourth category of multifaceted platforms described as "several companies that trade with others by intermedious to a double-sided market" (p.45).

There is growing interest in technology platforms where value creation is based on interaction between different actors, such as content providers and users. Examples include the growth of its use in companies, but as a way of doing business (McIntyre and Srinivasan, 2017).

As mentioned above, there are several definitions of digital platforms that adopt technical, socio-technical or ecosystem perspectives (Reuver et al., 2018). The studies that adopt a platform, integrate several modules that extend the functionality of the software (Tiwana and Konsynski 2010). From a socio-technical perspective, digital platforms are conceived as bilateral and multilateral markets with different socio-economic conditions.

An overview of recent academic studies reveals four patterns that place strategic communication in the digital age at a crossroads, each with a different view of future development. One of the most prevalent themes is cyber optimism that portrays an image of strategic communication advanced by various digital technologies that provide immediacy, openness and interactivity. It is believed that the characteristics contribute to the construction of the public sphere and the democratization of societies (van Osch & Coursaris, 2014).

Another popular view is the determinism of technology that positions digital and social media as cost-benefit and as driving factors for organizational success and social progress. Those who own and master the latest technologies thrive in the competitive and globalized world (Harkaway, 2012).

The other notable trend is called formenti as digital capitalism and reflects the tendency of strategic communication to explore and colonize digital and social platforms for commercial purposes (cited in Valentini, 2015). In an attempt to identify the main indicators of strategic communication, the various authors re-examined theories, communication practices in various contexts, at multiple levels and from different perspectives (Kennedy & Sommerfeldt, 2015).

Digital Communication in Health

Digital health has been used in Europe and Portugal especially through a set and successful experiences, when the solution's own planning teams are part of end-users (Shared Services of the Ministry of Health [SPMS], 2019). The increasing use of this type of services has a strong basis in the evolution of information and communication technologies (ICT), which in association with human resources and processes represent fundamental vectors for the success of their implementation.

It should be noted that health systems continually face challenges that jeopardise their sustainability. The demographic transition that is linked to the increased prevalence of chronic and degenerative diseases, and to the increasing increase in morbidity, which alone require continuous contact with the health system and overload the health system that is already in a fragile way due to its limitation of human resources (OECD, 2019).

In this sense, the implementation of digital technologies in the health sector provides a series of substantial improvements in the efficiency of health systems, because they enable an increase in capacity, facilitate accessibility and at the same time promote patient-centered care that will lead to a higher quality of services (WHO, 2021). As the most striking and current example, during the COVID-19 pandemic, decreed by the World Health Organization in March 2020, many of the digital health tools were considered great opportunities for an immediate need to ensure health care and information sharing (WHO, 2021).

In most of the literature on the subject, several factors have been mentioned that may limit the implementation of digital health. Most of the barriers in the implementation of digital health in pathatic son lie essentially in the difficulties in facilitating broader changes at the individual, organizational and system levels. According to Ross et al. (2018) interoperability, cost, adaptation and pre-existing systems, dislocations in interactions between healthcare professionals and users and the lack of implementation planning also represent barriers in the implementation of digital health.

Digital health has evolved as a broad term that includes electronically captured data, in association with technical information and communications infrastructure and applications in the health and care ecosystem. Remarkable advances in digital health are transforming health, medicine and biomedical science and redefining it by taking advantage of the tools needed to create a healthier future (Mboera et al., 2021).

Developments such as cloud computing, artificial intelligence, digital learning, blockchain, digitally mediated diagnosis and treatment, television health and consumer-facing mobile health applications are currently used in self-management of healthcare and biomedical science. However, these developments drive early diagnosis and interventions, improve outcomes and support the most involved patients (Kottke et al., 2016; McGovern et al., 2014).

Despite significant gains over the past two decades, providers of electronic health records, with targeted progress towards interoperable systems and advanced technology for disease management and care coordination, the promise of digital health remains unillusioned. The ability to use interoperable digital technology to improve the effectiveness, efficiency, equity and continuity of health management remains conceptual (Lee, 2022). As an example, in digital interfaces in hospitals care systems are often clumsy, health data volumes are isolated , inaccessible, and difficult to aggregate significantly, partly due to the continuing need for evolving data standards.

In this sense, the notion of digital tools can be applied in a generalized way to coordinate health organizations and public health efforts to identify and involve specific risks of social, public and environmental behavior (Buttorff et al., 2017). Researchers and drug manufacturers are also leveraging various digital forms for virtual involvement between physicians and their patients, and also in the search for up-to-date medical information (Lamberti et al., 2019).

Most treatment decisions can be increased by clinical decision support systems and enriched with advanced features. In this context, an editorial *in the New England Journal of Medicine* assumed that the complexity of medicine now exceeds the capacity of the human mind (Eddy, 1982). Although artificial intelligence-based systems are not yet able to discern the face, notice a sweat or hear a tremor in the patient. These digital systems can provide the opportunity to increase clinical performance, create order, and transform large amounts of data into clinically actionable information to support real care. This area, although still incipient, is evolving rapidly (Goh et al., 2021).

Similarly, studies have documented the potential for health information exchange and interoperability to improve care coordination and cost reduction. An example of the use of the exchange of health information to support the coordination of care is the real-time provision of technical and scientific information to physicians and other professionals about a given drug (Biel et al., 2019).

By successfully applying digital tools used in other industries, such as personalized recommendations and communications, the healthcare system can be positioned to develop a more robust partnership between individuals, families and professionals. Digital health data and tools serve as a linking agent in the shared understanding of the customer's health status (Shrank et al., 2019).

To achieve the full potential of digital health, the health sector, industry and government leaders must collaborate, cooperate and develop shared governance to create a unified community in the architecture of the digital health system, from building blocks of infrastructure with independent operation. Since the main priorities must be identified and pursued in both environmental and technical contexts to achieve the full potential of digital health, these priorities include customer focus, equity integration and transparency as first principles and nurturing an ethos of the learning health system.

Digital Communication in the Pharmaceutical Industry

Pharmaceutical companies are currently facing major competitive, regulatory and community pressures, and for decades have tried to use different types of communications to reach doctors and customers. Andcompared to other industries, the pharmaceutical industry has been relatively slow to adopt the internet. The main reasons are that the reticence is multiple, including the imperative to be cautious or conservative in such an important area as the health and absence of many drivers who have contributed to the growth of e-business.

The internet as a communication channel with customers, whether these patients, their families, consumers or professionals allows pharmaceutical companies to interact more consciously and on a virtual basis. There is a wealth of opportunities for health, well-being and diseases on the internet, such as management programs to build sustainable and trust-based relationships, and in the case of providing medical and scientific information is increasingly accentuated (Pereira and Puggina, 2017).

Traditionally, the pharmaceutical industry has been focused on physicians and providing real-time information. The commercialization of prescription drugs, strongly focused on the sales representative, remains the cornerstone of the activities of pharmaceutical companies although we have seen some advances in areas such as more accessible professional information systems (Grossman, 2014).

The theme of credibility and reliability is central to scientific dissemination and public understanding of science. Although, some topics deserve more attention in this context. We live in a communication environment radically different from the past and, paradoxically, we continue to invoke traditional forms of certification of information reliability (Bucchi, 2022).

In the age of scientific communication 1.0 the reputation of sources or brands was sufficient to ensure the credibility of the content. The quality of information has a cost, in scientific dissemination as in other areas, is to report information in a credible way. (Schneider, 2017).

The rationalities, objectives and strategies of scientific communication are widely researched by science communicators (Grand et al., 2015), although perhaps very little of these are filtered by scientists. It is felt that the strategies and concepts of the field of scientific and academic communication are not sufficiently well communicated with specialized audiences. In this respect, Burns et al. (2003) defined scientific communication as the "use of appropriate skills, media, activities and dialogue to produce one or more of the following personal responses to Consciousness, Pleasure, Interest, Formation of Opinion and Understanding" (p. 183).

In recent decades, the different barriers that hinder quality in scientific dissemination have begun to be identified. First, focusing on scientists it has been demonstrated that they are interested and recognize the value of communicating outside the academy to the public, but feel that this time-consuming activity is not sufficiently recognized in career progression (Olson, 2018).

Secondly, the media is also vulnerable to challenges that affect the quality of scientific communication. Most of the literature reveals some of the major changes in practice and consumption in recent nanos, with the advent of digital production, social media, web 2.0 and 3.0 (Auriga, 2016).

In this respect, Davies et al. (2011) highlighted issues that include the decreasing influence of traditional inherited media, in association with the well-developed public wishes for themes posted in social media about science that are sometimes unintentionally misleading or deliberately manipulated to spread false news and pseudoscience. Still, the role of professionals and scientists in today's society and their importance to democracy are probably more critical than ever (Pfisterer, Paschke and Pasotti, 2019).

And thirdly the internet is becoming a primary source of information on scientific issues. In this sense, social media in particular quickly became the main sources of information for many of its users, and the amount of information that competes for their attention is high (Shearer and Grieco, 2019).

Confrontation with opposing views is almost non-existent, and scientists and communicators are often guilty of hiding in their metaphorical. In such a polarized context, the need to make scientific communication effective, avoiding the risk of collective preaching, is a fundamental challenge (Schmidt, Zollo, Del Vicario et al., 2017; Schmidt, Zollo, Scala et al., 2018).

MAKING DIGITAL COMMUNICATION IN THE PHARMACEUTICAL INDUSTRY MORE PREDICTIVE

The pharmaceutical industry has resisted digitization, mainly due to the complexity of the development and manufacturing processes involved, however, there is a clear need to digitize, because the need for traditional and new drugs is constantly growing (Reinhardt et al., 2021). Contract Development Manufacturing Organizations have a specific digitization challenge, which should be related to key aspects of good practice and succeed in digitizing processes. Close collaboration with constantly changing stakeholders is another important factor that should be a focus on digitization in the pharmaceutical industry.

It should be noted that the pharmaceutical industry's 4.0 industry can contribute to the future of intelligent automation technology and can support increased manufacturing, such as a customized drug, additive manufacturing, localized 3D printing of treatments and information available to physicians (Hariry et al., 2021).

It was precisely at the time of the COVID-19 pandemic that digitised technology played a key role in enabling companies in all sectors to improve performance through better manufacturing productivity, stronger competitive skills, more accurate planning and forecasting, and financial sustainability (Faraj et al., 2021). In this context, the old product-driven business model is being challenged by patent expirations, increased customer demand, increased competition and increased price pressure.

Industries are currently being shaped by digital transformation, as digital services beyond the product are being integrated into the pool of offerings, and it is in this scenario that the health face is changing due to digitisation, health connected with the potential to benefit all stakeholders based on the objective, provide a better care experience, increase health outcomes and reduce per capita costs (Iglehart, 2014).

In the pharmaceutical industry, digitization and data analysis can help reduce the large amounts of downtime pharmaceutical factories tend to experience, and machine-to-machine communication and artificial learning intelligence enable continuous procedures, automatic corrective actions, and predictive maintenance through the Internet of Things (Ngamvichaikit, 2021).

Because the pharmaceutical manufacturing environment is tightly controlled and highly sensitive, the smallest errors can have life-altering consequences for patients, and may also be a commercial, legal and reputational impact for the manufacturer (Sehlstedt et al., 2016). In this sense, one of the most striking examples is the fact that a global pharmaceutical manufacturer had to choose almost half a million tablets a few years ago due to irregularities in packaging and human monitoring at the production plant.

Digitization and automation are currently ensuring that companies can reduce similar errors in the future, reducing financial and reputational damage (Kitson et al., 2018). Likewise, to avoid +data transfer problems between digital units and robotics pharmaceutical companies have invested in high availability computing technology, resulting in a fully automated production line that makes it easier to maintain cleanroom procedures, capture and manage electronic batch logs and process performance analysis to identify and implement significant changes (Anthony Jnr and Abbas Petersen, 2021).

Despite supply and demand management it is also improved as a result of integrating digital information up and down the supply chain (Zhou, 2013). And with pharmaceutical companies undergoing major transformations, pharmaceutical companies are still in the experimental phase when it comes to offering digital services beyond traditional products (Parida et al., 2019). Thus, digitisation can be very beneficial for small and large enterprises, because by using digitisation for the development of counterfeit-proof pharmaceuticals with traceable serial numbers throughout the supply chain it must ensure quality while meeting future serial regulations (Anderson, 2018; Rosenbaum et al., 2017).

Pharmaceutical companies can also adopt digitization to meet the anticipated increase in the need for global markets, and can use it to comply with regulations, identify manufacturing efficiencies to reduce costs and interact with suppliers and distributors more quickly, using cloud-based information exchanges (van Velthoven et al., 2019). In addition, automation, intelligent sensors and social media and health applications can be used to track drug compliance and predict the need in all regions, thus enabling real-time manufacturing

Unlike other businesses, the health sector is also struggling to make digital tools available to end users, and when it comes to digital transformation, it is identified that it has also transformed business models in various health sectors (Lakshmi and Patel, 2020). Although, the pharmaceutical industry has a history of reluctance to adapt to new technologies and adopt digital solutions, and it is for this reason that the acceptance of digital services in the pharmaceutical industry has progressed slowly (Lee et al., 2019).

Is it pertinent, given data and digital, to question how they can help the pharmaceutical industry bring better drugs to patients more quickly and efficiently? To this aspect to prove safety and efficacy, most professionals design clinical studies and perform them in medical centers around the world.

The pharmaceutical industry continues to improve the practices and processes used in drug development to develop new products, however historically the industry has not been at the forefront of the data and digital revolution. The drug development process involves time-consuming tasks that can take weeks to complete.

According to Mijuk (2018) the pharmaceutical industry is primarily a data-driven business along the value chain, research and market, and to prove its safety and efficacy, and to inform healthcare professionals about how to use them in the treatment of patients to improve, involve their molecules with data. However, when it comes to operational data, the pharmaceutical industry has had to open new paths in many areas and rethink how to integrate, analyze and use this data to support decisions (Ghangurde, 2020).

THE DIGITAL DIALOGUE OF ORGANIZATIONS

At the historical level, the use of mass communication channels in public relations practice has reflected the diffusion of new technologies. Public relations efforts in the early 20th century relied heavily on newspapers and magazines as channels to promote clients and causes. Radio and television became basic tools for public relations after the introduction and mass dissemination by society. In general, these technologies were considered one-way communication tools for the transmission of information to the public, and most of the time, content should be passed first by the investigation of social media advocates

However, with the introduction and wide penetration of the Internet, communication professionals were able to communicate directly with their audience on an unprecedented scale. Through Web 1.0 platforms, such as old websites and blogs, professionals could create their own digital content and directly reach their audiences (Wirtz & Zimbres, 2018).

The dialogue was essentially centered on the attitudes of each party in interaction. In this respect, Botan (1997) stated that the dialogue "elevates audiences to the status of communication equal to the organization" (p. 196). And, Kent & Taylor (1998) accepted the challenge of translating this deeply interpersonal theory into web-mediated communicative relationships, and the goal of their work was to provide theory-based strategies to improve relationships between organizations and the public, making the Web more personal.

These strategies based on the assumptions of dialogue have taken the form of five principles of communication via the web (Figure 1).

By building these strategies on websites, Kent & Taylor noted that organizations could work to fulfill the "dialogical promise" of digital media, and successfully integrate a form of interpersonal dialogue into Web-based communication. And since this moment, the principles have been adapted to several studies and measures have been developed with the aim of demonstrating the degree to which each principle manifests itself on website platforms (Yang & Taylor, 2010).

Figure 1. Five principles of web communication

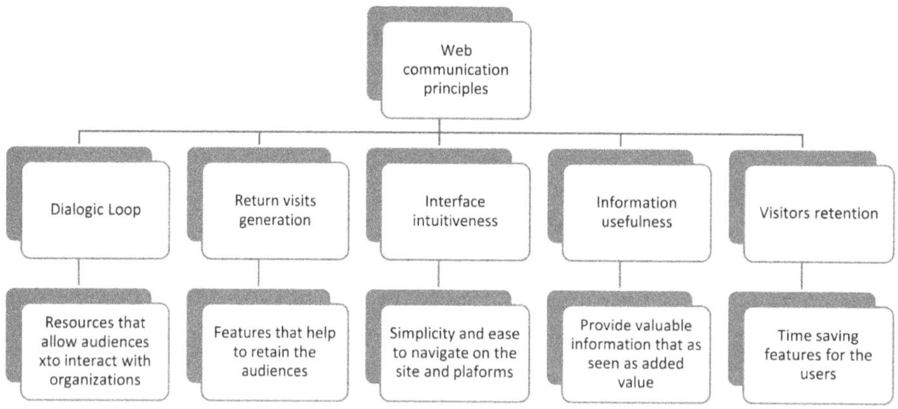

These tools allowed researchers to assess the extent to which organizations' websites are dialogical and analyze the connection between the use of dialogical principles and the real responsiveness and accessibility (Callison & Seltzer, 2010). These tools have been widely applied in the analysis of communication in the social media of organizations, using the approach to build the public-organization relationship. Most of these studies have identified that while social media such as platforms demonstrates dialogical potential more than websites, many organizations still cannot fully utilize the potential of social media to be dialogical (Sommerfeldt & Yang, 2018).

According to Kent & Lane (2017, p.571), one of the most prominent criticisms in the literature of dialogical communication is the frequent confusion of dialogue with symmetrical communication, where researchers perform dialogue as a set of procedures. This confusion is generally manifested in studies in which researchers treat the presence of any interactive resources or functions on the websites of organizations and social media accounts as evidence of a dialogical approach

On the other hand, the principles of dialogical communication were also challenged by professionals who cannot observe the value of the dialogical approach in daily practice, or are constrained by their positions of problems and organizational resources for the implementation of dialogical communication (Sommerfeldt, Kent, & Taylor, 2012). However, other authors criticized the theory for not taking into account the imbalances of power between organizations and their audiences and the influence of factors such as social, political and economic contexts in dialogical communication (Ihlen & Levenshus, 2017).

Actors in the Digital Communicative Process: Senders and Receivers

Cognitively, new social media requires a nonlinear nature and the creation of expectations for content, which directly influences how people use the media. Socially, the most manifested impact of new social media is the effect of demassification and it represents that traditional design for a homogeneous audience is disappearing and is being replaced by a specific and individual appeal, allowing the public to access and create messages they wish to produce (Olason & Pollard, 2004).

Visually, the new social media bring a new vision of digital aesthetics, which refers to the interactivity, manipulation, prepurpose and reuse of media content, in the creation of a content experience in the media, deliberately in the creation of the virtual experience and sampling as a means of generating new content (Chen, 2007, p. 95).

New social media is also a force that accelerates the trend of globalisation in human society. The trend of globalization has led to the transformation of almost every aspect of society, that is, it has altered the perception that it is a community, redefined the meaning of cultural identity and civil society, and required a new form of intercultural interaction (Chen & Zhang, 2010). Due to the momentum of new social media, the global trend creates new social networks and activities, redefines political, economic, geographical and other limits of human society, and intensifies and accelerates social exchanges (Steger, 2009).

Nevertheless, the models are essential in the sciences to focus attention on relevant variables and expose predictive relationships, or when possible, causative (Cioffi-Revilla, 2014). The models analyzed in the literature are essential to decompose the communication process into its constituent elements and the lines that represent communication in the various interactions. The history of communication models reveals that as the new models were created, the concept of information environment was expanded, that is, more variables contribute to the communication process (van Ruler, 2018).

Digital communication has been widespread in a great way in previous years, representing the physical transfer of data through the internet communication channel. Digital communication plays a vital role in today's electronic world, and data transfer rate depends on its own characteristics. In its simplest form, a telecommunications system consists of a transmitter, a channel, a receiver and two transducers (Ihlen & Levenshus, 2017).

Mass self-communication is the use of digital media where users can create their own content through chosen software or websites and reach a global audience. The cumulative effect of these actions of many communicators creates an emerging and undirected phenomenon in which society effectively communicates with itself through the coltive actions of its communicators (Castells, 2009). This mass self-communication depends on access to technology-driven communication for users and information as part of a broader network society (Mulgund & Kelly, 2020).

One of the most fundamental consequences of mass self-communication is that the interpretation of reality becomes an individualized experience without great shared narratives. The cognition of an individual in processing power reaches limits in relation to the ability to re-imagine and reassess the environment, and thus begin to reinforce previously understood interpretations (Mulgund & Kelly, 2020; Uysal & Yang, 2013).

Most of the recent literature demonstrates how, among the variety of digital tools available, social media has become central to the functions of communication, marketing in different contexts (Lamberton & Stephen, 2016). While they increasingly use social media to engage with potential customers and create value, companies still implement digital and traditional sales communication tools, and therefore the selection of their modes of communication is fragmented (Müller, Pommeranz, Weisser, & Voigt, 2018).

Other studies address this issue, investigating the integration of different communication tools, considering the effects of social networks and traditional marketing on different customer metrics (Kumar et al., 2016), or in relation to their variable effectiveness in time (De Vries et al. 2017). The social media, telecOomunicaços and information technology industries are going through a period of profound change. It is developments closely related to the growth of digitization, reductions in the cost of computing power, deregulation and market deregulation that have triggered the so-called "digital revolution".

Business success not only requires integration into different social media on the Internet, such as websites, blogs, social networks, applications, but also a digital communication strategy that allows reaching diverse audiences and to ensure the development of the organization's purpose. Of these, the corporate website is the most important primary element to initiate any digital communication, because it is established as an integrating tool that synthesizes the company's strategy effectively (Pedro et al., 2021).

The Safety and Quality of Information in Health Systems

Information is the basis for decision-making. With the high advances in information exchange, information systems have undergone major changes over the years, and taking into account these aspects, health and medical environments need to equip themselves with tools for a rapid and accurate exchange of medical information to improve the entire health system (Jang et al., 2017). These systems harvest, process, store, distribute and share relevant information and are responsible for creating communication, increasing productivity, making decisions and supporting strategic and tactical decisions (Shahbaz et al., 2019).

The success of an information system depends on a clear strategy, proper design and implementation of the system, and to do so, the health system in addition to having a technological structure and hardware and software support, must meet the needs and expectations of system users. In this sense, the successful implementation of an IS leads to organizational processes and work procedures effective at the individual level, which according to DeLone and McLean depends on several factors such as the quality of systems and information, use of SI, user satisfaction and organizational impact (Saghaeiannejad-Isfahani et al., 2015).

Primary Health Care (PHC) is crucial for equitable access to comprehensive, cost-effective health care. The health information system is a fundamental element of PHC for the production of information for managers at all levels of the health system (WHO, 2016). In general, informed decisions, efficient patient care and equity in the distribution of resources in aPA, as the basis of health systems, depend on high-quality data (Gonete et al., 2021). The use of high-quality data is a prerequisite for effective policy making and efficient planning, and provides the necessary knowledge from healthcare professionals. This issue is important because it plays a significant role in the health sector, and decision-making based on these data can mean the difference between life and death (Alharthi, 2018).

High-quality data is the basis of medical research, reduces costs and prevents medical errors, contributes to monitoring the performance of health services, and helps improve the quality of care (Yates et al., 2020). On the contrary, the use of low-quality health data decreases the quality of care, increases costs and privacy concerns, reduces the satisfaction and performance of health professionals (Adamki et al., 2015). In this sense, evaluating data quality dimensions is the first step in the data quality management process.

Measuring data quality from a user's perspective complements objective quality assessment and reflects user needs and experiences (Mboera et al., 2021). The lack of standardized operational procedures is one of the main obstacles in the effective management of health data by health professionals. Therefore, the perceptions of health professionals about data quality play a vital role in the use of data and in the success of information systems (Karami et al., 2019).

The expressions "service" and "Quality" mean "any activity or benefit that a party may offer that is essentially intangible and cannot result in possession of anything." Quality is a strategic tool to achieve operational efficiency and best business performance (Ramya et al., 2019).

Quality of service concerns a service provider's ability to efficiently satisfy the customer, through which it can improve business performance. Similarly, in the service sector quality is an important element for business success, due to the achievement of a positive link with profits, increased market share, and customer satisfaction (Zidarova & Zografos, 2011).

The term quality of service is more difficult to define and judge. Some authors define this term from different perspectives, Philip Kotler and Gary Armstrong defined the quality of service as the ability of a service company to maintain its customer.

Quality of service can be understood as a comprehensive assessment of a particular service to a customer and to the extent that it meets their expectations and provides satisfaction (Agbor, 2011). According to Sharmin et al. (2016) satisfaction is the customer's feeling in relation to the result of an evaluation process that compared what was received from the service and merchandise with expectations.

Satisfaction concerns the customer's judgment on whether goods and services meet expectations and needs and provide a satisfactory level of consumption-related satisfaction. In this respect, Koutsothanassi et al. (2017) examined the conceptual structure linking the links between the two physical services and interactive features and their impact on customer loyalty. In a user-based approach, quality corresponds to satisfaction, i.e. the higher the quality, the better the satisfaction of consumer preferences (Yarimoglu, 2014). Organizations perceive quality of service as a sustainable and competitive advantage.

A Health Information System (SIS) is a set of technical, organizational, behavioral and procedures organized to generate information to improve health management decisions at all levels of the health system (Wijayati et al., 2019). As an example, health care providers collect data on health services, states, and resources. When an SIS produces high quality, timely and reliable data allows health program managers to monitor, evaluate and improve the performance of the health system (Hoxha et al., 2020).

The sources of health data are generally records of services provided, individual medical records, health resource records and prescriptions for customers, which provide information about the clients and the type of treatments and medicines they need. Managers can gather other information about human resources, finance, medicines and supply systems. However, some studies have shown that there is a need for governments and health decision makers to create strategies for developing tools at the hospital, district and national levels to make the best use of health information from routine systems.

The various hospital information systems are currently used by hospitals, which has made decision making easier, whether it is diagnosis or treatment of customers, as well as hospital management functions such as admission management, laboratory, pharmacy. However, a weak SIS is a unique challenge to achieving the health-related Millennium Development Goals because the performance of health systems cannot be properly assessed or monitored when SIS data is incomplete, inaccurate or untimely (Nasir & Marikar, 2018).

The objective of a health system is to optimize the health of the individuals and populations treated and the gold standard for quality measurement will always be the result of health measures. The SIS includes the socio-technical subsystems of a hospital, all information processing systems and associated human or technical actors in their information processing functions (Salahuddin et al., 2020). Thus, the best use of information requires better quality data and products that requires better health information systems.

The performance of the health system is dependent on the production and use of quality health data and information. Routine health information in RHIS systems is defined as systems that provide information at regular intervals of one year or less to meet the predictable needs of information. These systems include paper or electronic health records and management of district facilities and information systems (Hautamäki et al., 2017). In this context, some studies that analyzed health information systems have shown that socio-economic factors affecting safety, including people, technologies, trefas, organization and the environment (Balaraman & Kosalram, 2013).

There is evidence in this context that SIS usability problems, such as customer identification, have caused user errors that have led to safety incidents, and that the behaviors of healthcare professionals can result in unintended consequences for the information system. Knowledge of these contextual issues can help health organizations, health professionals and those responsible for implementing the SIS understand in situ functioning in their use context and help design strategies to reduce the number of unsafe uses and their possible negative consequences (Hautamäki & Kinnunen, 2017).

Sound, computerized or uncomputerized hospital information systems must not present correct and appropriate information to the right people, however, there are plenty of data sources in a hospital with many different functions with mutually complex relationships and many people depend on this information (Kpobi et al., 2018). The study by Sanjuluca et al. (2022) was important for the analysis of this theme, as it aimed to analyze the use of hospital information systems as a tool to support decision-making by the managers of the hospital in Huíla, Angola. The results determined that at least two thirds of the participants reported being dissatisfied or relatively satisfied with each specific resource of the hospital information systems evaluated. More than 50% have rarely or never used the health information system to support decision-making.

The Strategy of Installed IS, International Experiences

In the European context, the study "European Citizens Use of E-Health Services: A Study of Seven Countries" (Andreassen et al., 2006) aimed to compare between the different countries of Europe on the implementation of IS in health, and concluded that of the seven countries considered, the main use given to the Internet is the search for reading information in the context of a unilateral relationship, there is little interaction. This study also highlighted that women are the main users of ICT in health. The authors concluded that the use of the Internet in the health area has significant effects on the doctor-client relationships, mainly through the relationship of complementarity and not the substitution of traditional figures of the health system.

Similarly, the study "The Impact of Health Information on the Internet on the Physician-Patient Relationship: Patient Perceptions" (Murray et al., 2003) aimed to explore the change in the doctor-client relationship in the European context, and the authors mentioned that the issue of access to ICT and the fact that governments need to overcome infoexclusion so that the various aspects of e-health can have an effective application.

The American reality was demonstrated through the study "Health information Online", conducted by Pew Internet (2005), concluded that eight out of ten internet users sought information about online health, especially on topics associated with physical well-being such as diets, experimental treatments and medications. In this respect, the study by Rovost, Perri, Boyer and Baujard (2003), "Opinions and Ehealth Behaviours of Patients and Health Professionals in the U.S.A. and Europe", established a similarity between the American reality and the European context, and concluded that being more widespread in the USA, the use of the internet in the field of health is increasing on both continents.

The value of communication in organizations is critical to success. People have different communication styles, and workplaces with differences between employees, whether in terms of culture or age, is constantly changing, which can somehow create barriers to effective communication (Page, 2020).

According to Díaz-Soloaga (2019), the implementation of communication strategies to successfully transfer the corporate identity to employees and teams, expand information and develop management relationships allows for an improvement in organizational communication. In this sense, effectively communicating the organization's mission, vision, values and objectives promotes understanding of procedures, schedules and other important criteria.

Managers must communicate effectively for their organization to succeed, and one method of building effective communication between employees is to ensure that managers practice the best planning techniques to clarify their ideas and goals.

Digitization describes how IT or digital technologies can be used to change existing business processes (Li et al., 2016). As an example, the creation of new online or mobile communication channels that allow all customers to easily connect with companies by changing their way of interacting (Ramaswamy & Ozcan, 2016). In digitization, IT serves as a basis for taking advantage of new possibilities for communication, distribution or relationship management processes.

Organizational communication connects the social, economic and cultural aspects of the organization (Scott & Lewis, 2017). And when one analyzes the entry of technology in organizations, it is only a reflection of how the forms of communication have changed and improved. Ideally, organizational communication has been shaped by the continuous advancement of technology (Thomas & Dittman, 2016).

The nature of new communication technologies presents a dilemma to organizational communication actors, as this evolution of technologies has been adopted by many people around the world, and this aspect means that customer relationships will be equally different. In this context, the efficiency of an organization is determined by its effectiveness in terms of communication (Langer, 2014). And, it is currently difficult to imagine a work organization without the necessary communication channels, as an example in the marketing area, marketing professionals need to change their communication strategies towards the public (Asano, 2017).

In addition to the digital resources needed to achieve digital transformation, the central issue that must be considered is the organizational changes needed to adapt to digital change, especially the flexible organizational structure for digital change (Eggers & Park, 2018). Some previous studies have argued that digital transformation has implications for organizational structure, favoring a flexible structure made up of separate business units, agile organizational forms and digital functional areas (Venkatraman, 2017).

Digital functional areas are one of the most important features of digital transformation, in association with analytics. The IT function itself needs to transform a line function and focuses on enabling communication or data flows in a more proactive environment, preparing the support role for digital value creation through exploratory responses (He et al., 2016).

By building these strategies into websites, Kent & Taylor noted that organizations could work to fulfill the "dialogic promise" of digital media, and successfully integrate a form of interpersonal dialogue into Web-based communication. And since then, the principles have been adapted to various studies and measures have been developed with the aim of demonstrating the degree to which each principle manifests itself on website platforms (Yang & Taylor, 2010).

These tools allowed researchers to assess the extent to which organizations' websites are dialogic and analyze the connection between the use of dialogic principles and real responsiveness and accessibility (Callison & Seltzer, 2010). These tools have been widely applied in the analysis of organizations' social media communication, using the public-organization relationship building approach. Most of these studies identified that, although social media as platforms demonstrate more dialogic potential than websites, many organizations still fail to fully utilize the potential of social media to be dialogic (Sommerfeldt & Yang, 2018).

THE RELATIONSHIP BETWEEN DIALOGICAL PRINCIPLES

The construction of relationships has become a key component in the practice of organizations' relationships. Studies on public-organization relationships have demonstrated engagement with stakeholders builds better relationships than those that don't. In this respect, Wilcox & Cameron (2009) described mutual exchanges between organizations and stakeholders as dialogical communication.

The emergence of Web 2.0, with participatory websites and social networking systems such as Facebook, Twitter and blogs, in addition to email, online chats and discussion lists, are major challenges for the execution of dialogical communication by organizations. Thus, like other dialogical media with stakeholders, its management is directly associated with the organizational image (Pang et al., 2017).

Despite awareness of the importance of online communication in the implementation of relationships and a positive organizational image, studies suggest that many organizations are not exploiting the full potential of new social media (Shin, Pang and Kim 2015). The main concerns are the inability of an organization to control its messages, to determine the objectives of the public and the challenge of effectively connecting with stakeholders (Pfeffer, Zorbach and Carley 2014).

Dialogical communication refers to "any negotiated exchange of ideas and opinions" (Kent and Taylor, 1998, 325), and includes an organization's efforts to engage in an open, honest and ethical relationship with its audiences and, which provides organizations with opportunities to listen to stakeholders and adapt to their needs (Pang et al., 2019).

The theory of dialogical communication was proposed by Kent & Taylor (1998) as a way to develop and maintain effective relationships between organizations and their audiences. These authors referred to dialogical communication as any negotiated exchange of ideas and opinions (Kent & Taylor, 1998). And, they proposed that by using websites, organizations have the opportunity to build dialogical relationships with audiences. His theory consists of five basic principles that provide guidelines on how to integrate dialogical relations and the internet.

In this sense, the dialogical Loop refers to the offer of opportunities for users to be able to answer questions and get answers from the organization. The second principle, usefulness of information, refers to the provision of information in various formats appropriate to the needs of users. The generation of return visits is related to the extent to which useful and attractive features are used to encourage users to revisit the site regularly. The fourth principle, the ease of the interface refers to the interactivity and navigability of the site and, the conservation of visitors refers to what is being done to encourage users to stay on the page (Haro-De-Rosario, Sáez-Martín, & Gálvez-Rodríguez, 2017).

Figure 2. Five dialogical principles and publications of digital verbal messages by organizations

Organisations' efforts to deal with user attempts to influence organisations through dialogue and reciprocal interaction are not only possible and advisable, but can prevent the potential for stakeholders to organise themselves antagonisticly. In this sense, digital media provide an environment "where negotiation between organizations and public scans can take place" (Kent and Taylor 1998, p.322).

Digital media dialogues enable the public to provide feedback on organizational practices, provide opportunities for organizations to respond to public concerns, and include their opinions. Online interactivity can facilitate the quality of public-organization dialogues and generate positive results, with greater confidence improved product knowledge and increased profits (Sundar, Xu and Dou 2012). In addition to relationships at the organization level, dialogical communication can play a fundamental role in the development and improvement of the organization's image, because although traditional media are useful in image management, digital media have been contextualized as the "new virtual scenario" (Vernuccio 2014, p.214).

While many organizations have some kind of presence in digital media, some studies suggest that they do not fully use interactive online resources to promote their images or products. According to Vernuccio (2014) organizations hesitate to encourage the active participation of stakeholders in the way they communicate their brands and images. And as a consequence, some organizations may miss the opportunity to generate positive results that are often created more effectively by involving social dynamics on the stakeholder side, i.e. some previous research has shown that communication generated organized by digital users creates more value for organizations than communication generated by the organization itself (Schivinski and Dabrowski, 2014).

Corporate communications professionals can use a wide range of digital media to convey business information and interact with stakeholders and the general public, as well as create electronic content to inform and educate online users about their products and services (Köhler & Zerfass, 2019; García García, Carrillo-Durán & Tato Jimenez, 2017). Or on the other hand, they can use digital platforms to communicate about their activities, including corporate social networks, accountability practices and/or real-time user engagement (Camilleri, 2018; 2020).

Institutions and organizations promote their activities or offerings through websites or other social networks, and have responsive designs and different verbal communication formats, vocal and visual content to attract their audiences (Killian & McManus, 2015; Ruehl & Ingenhoff, 2015; Fraustino & ConnollyAhern, 2015).

Although the Scale of Public Dialogical Communication of the Trusted Organization was developed to evaluate the general communication of the public organization as between the government and the public (Yang et al., 2010; Yang, 2015), there is a lack of specific structure for times of crises and optimize the unique priorities of communication to meet the needs of citizens (Houston et al., 2015).

The Relationship Between Dialogical Principles in Communication in the Pharmaceutical Industry

Large international companies, including the pharmaceutical sector, have serious reputational problems related to the challenge of the complex balance between primary purpose and how they address problems (Gallup, 2019). There is recognition that these issues are related to the perception of the public (Caliber's Global Pharma Study, 2020). And, others argue that the needs of people with a particular disease area relationship with the pharmaceutical industry, and the industry uses these customer groups as a channel to communicate with other stakeholders such as governments and the media (Kang et al., 2019).

Pharmaceutical companies are prolific financial donors to patient organizations, and ensure that new drugs that reach the market meet the needs of customers, fulfilling their responsibilities to society (Muller, 2022). The design of long-term and personalized dialogues and relationships with prescribers is very important in the pharmaceutical field, and aims to create links to improve productivity (Marketeer, 2009).

According to Gilpin (2008) the internet is used as a communication vehicle by pharmaceutical companies and these are present online on websites where they provide various information. Its contents and formats show that communication is carried out in a careful manner, and according to Aroso (2013), "companies that provide press releases or press releases on the Internet, we highlight Bial, Roche Portugal, Pfizer" (p. 9).

Pharmaceutical bodies/institutions consider online communication important. APIFARMA highlights its communication department and INFARMED highlights its press office. "INFARMED highlights the Press Office and its advisor, as well as all its contacts and online formats" (Aroso, 2013, p. 9).

The communication process to connect suppliers with pharmacies has less weight than the development of new products, and supplier involvement through information technology infrastructure has proven to be the essential strategy of supplier engagement (Bhimani et al., 2019). According to the authors, the conventional application of social media is encouraged with formal practices in various sectors. However, the use of social media activities remains mostly informal and scarce for business customers in the pharmaceutical industry (Tiwari & Raut, 2019).

Although the various product quality standards are guaranteed in the pharmaceutical industry, the standard for proper quality of service and logistics management for pharmacy employees requires a greater number of investigations. In this sense, strategies should be created based on convenience, time savings and desired level of service (Shokouhyar et al., 2020).

According to Shokouhyar et al. (2020) the Kano model has a unique application to handle customer satisfaction, whether for services or for products. The model points out that the insufficiency of the dimensional quality of a factor transforms happiness into dissatisfaction and, this model requires a highlight in the specific quality factors of the client. Understanding customer satisfaction is more complex for the pharmaceutical industry (Chen et al., 2010). In this sense, it can be assumed that the channels of involvement in the pharmaceutical industry are not very open and easily accessible.

The study by Abedini and Irani (2020) indicated that profit decreases after organizations reach a certain level of quality, and thus, closed channels of involvement and saturation create a dilemma for creating value for pharmaceutical companies and pharmacies. Since the increase in social networks, the various pharmaceutical networks have increased substantially, and have benefited companies by increasing brand awareness, encouraging engagement, generating revenue and significantly increasing sales (Ranta et al., 2020).

The question then arises: how can suppliers stimulate digitisation to improve value proposition and succeed in a fully digitised society? The future of health care and the transformation process may be uncertain, but opening up closed organisations to innovation from a cultural, procedural and structural perspective remains a major challenge, and companies will have to choose the most appropriate operating model for the health environment of the future. To better support pharmaceutical companies in their activities and direct them to a digital future, strategies should be based on understanding the digital objectives of companies and identifying and quantifying the value of specific actions, as well as drawing a clear picture for all stakeholders.

According to Andreas Kaplan and Michael Haenlein (2010: 61), social networks can be defined as "a group of online applications based on the ideological and technological foundations of Web 2.0, and which allow the creation and exchange of user-generated content". The Web 2.0. is, according to Tim O'Reilly (2005) the term used to refer to websites that use technology that goes beyond that used in the initial websites, characterized by static and poorly moldable pages. The pages characterized by Web 2.0. they are interactive and allow the user to collaborate in the creation of content, and contact with other users, generating authentic virtual dialogues, which are often grouped into virtual communities (Lempert, 2006). Currently there is a great diversity of social networks, with different purposes, the best known and most used being Facebook, YouTube, Google +, Twitter, LinkedIn, Instagram and Pinterest.

Social networks are widely used around the world, constituting one of the main contemporary means of communication (Vollmer, 2008). Based on official data, in September 2014, Facebook had around 864 million daily active users. With regard to Twitter, it has 284 million monthly active users, with around 500 million Tweets being sent per day. As for Instagram, the company announced, in December 2014, that it had 300 million monthly active users. Lastly, there are around 330 million users registered on LinkedIn.

The appearance of social networks and the generalization of the Internet has transformed society and the way relationships are established in a community. More than ever, words like "collaboration" and "participation" are used (Djick, 2013). In fact, social networks feed on the content produced by their users and the exchanges established between them (Rashtchy, 2007). Without users, there are no social networks. The word "community" also requires a new meaning, bearing in mind that currently it only takes a few clicks to relate to people with similar interests to ours, forming a sense of community like never before.

It is also interesting to observe how social networks and their development can never appear dissociated from the personal relationships that are established in the offline world (Barker et al., 2012). Since its inception, Facebook has already tested and released dozens of algorithms that try to translate with ever-increasing numbers. The accuracy of personal relationships and the way they are processed. According to official data[1], the main objective is to try to get people to get information from their Newsfeed about their closest friends and who really matters. Thus, they try to translate interpersonal relationships and how they are processed into mathematical formulas and programmatic language (Barker et al., 2012).

The development of interpersonal relationships revolves around developing the ability to relate to others, even in conflict situations. The creation of strategies for resolving these conflicts must build a concept of educational intervention. This relationship may influence the behavior, motivation and emotional state of the sender or receiver.

The field of communication for social change is vast and the models that underpin it are as diverse as the ideologies. Some of them are more traditional, hierarchical and linear, some more participatory and interactive. Most contain elements of both. From an epistemological and ontological perspective, this does not always make sense; but in practice it seems to be a given. Therefore, in general, we see two approaches: one aims to produce a common understanding among all participants in a development initiative, implementing a policy or a development project, ie the top-down model.

The other emphasizes grassroots decision-making that improves their lives, or the bottom-up model. Despite the diversity of approaches, there is a consensus at the beginning of the 21st century on the need for community participation in change at the social and individual levels. Development is shaped and made by people - not for people. For people to do this, they need to understand "How the system works". Therefore, development or social change must be equated with empowerment: the ability of people to influence the wider system and take control of their lives.

It is obvious that people cannot do this alone. It also requires effort on the part of developmental change partners (agencies and agents) to help resolve some of the dysfunctions in the system and create the necessary conditions. This perspective therefore argues that communication needs to be explicitly incorporated into development plans and social change projects to ensure that a mutual sharing/learning process is facilitated. Such communicative sharing is considered the best guarantee for creating successful transformations.

Liberalization has led not only to greater freedom of the press, but also to the emergence of a growing city-centric communications infrastructure, increasingly less interested in the concerns of the poor and rural population. Women and other vulnerable groups continue to experience marginalization and lack of access to communication resources of all kinds. The issue of ensuring access to information and the right to communicate as a precondition for empowering marginalized groups has been addressed by several international meetings and conferences (World Summit on Society and the World Social Forum).

The characteristics of the behaviors may be interrelated with the change in behavior in the close environment of an online or traditional context in terms of communication. Interactions between friends and family have been drastically changed by the introduction of the personal computer and computer-mediated communication (CMC).

Human communications are of the type intrapersonal communication and interpersonal communication. Intrapersonal communication is the communication we have with ourselves, while interpersonal communication is the communication that occurs when interacting with a person with whom he or she has some kind of relationship, it can be both face-to-face and electronically. This is where mediated communication has brought about the understanding that occurs when someone sends a message through some electronic device to a receiver.

REFERENCES

Abedellah, A., Noordin, A. A., & Zaki, A. (2016). Pharmaceutical good manufacturing practice regulatory affairs in Sudan: Continuous debate between regulatory authority and manufacturers Pharmaceut. *Reg. Affairs*, *5*(166), 2.

Abedini, A. A., Irani, H., & Yazdani, H. (2020). Marketing channel problems of herbal medicines from the perspective of pharmaceutical distribution companies. *Payavard Salamat*, *13*, 450–462.

Adamki, M., Asamoah, D., & Riverson, K. (2015). Assessment of data quality on expanded Programme on immunization in Ghana: The case of new Juaben municipality. *Journal of Health & Medical Informatics*, *6*(4), 1–9.

Agbor, J. M. (2011). *Relationship between Customer Satisfaction and Services Quality—A Study of Three Service Sectors in Lemea*. Umea School of Business, Umea University.

Allen, T. D., Golden, T. D., & Shockley, K. M. (2015). How effective is telecommuting? Assessing the status of our scientific findings. *Psychological Science in the Public Interest*, *16*(2), 40–68. doi:10.1177/1529100615593273 PMID:26403188

Alshenqeeti, H. (2016). Are emojis creating a new or old visual language for new generations? A socio-semiotic study. *Advances in Language and Literary Studies*, *7*(6), 56–69.

Anderson, P. (2018). The digitization of the Pharmaceutical Historian archive. *Pharmacy in History, 48*, 2.

Andreassen, H. K., Trondsen, M., Kummervold, P. E., Gammon, D., & Hjortdahl, P. (2006). Patients Who Use E-Mediated Communication With Their Doctor- New Constructions of Trust in the Patient-Doctor Relationship. *Qualitative Health Research, 16*(2), 238–248. doi:10.1177/1049732305284667 PMID:16394212

Anthony, P., & Petersen, S. A. (2021). Examining the digitalisation of virtual enterprises amidst the COVID-19 pandemic: A systematic and meta-analysis Enterprise. *Information Systems, 15*(5), 617–650.

APIFARMA. (2014). *The pharmaceutical industry in Portugal: Know how to invest, know how to innovate, 75 years*. Available in: http://www.apifarma.pt/salaimprensa/Documents/Livro%2075%20anos.pdf

APIFARMA. (2015). *The pharmaceutical industry in numbers.* Available in: http://www.apifarma.pt/publicacoes/ifnumeros/Documents/IF%20em%20N%C3%BAmeros%202015.pdf

Aroso, I. (2013). *The communication strategies of the pharmaceutical industry in Portugal.BOCC.UBI.* University of Beira Interior. https://bocc.ubi.pt/pag/arosoines2013strategiascomunicacaoindustriafarmaceutica.pdf

Auriga. (2016). *Digital Transformation: History, Present, and Future Trends.* Retrieved June 15, 2017, from https://auriga.com/blog/digital-transformation-history-presentand-future-trends/

Bakker, A. B., & Demerouti, E. (2017). Job demands–resources theory: Taking stock and looking forward. *Journal of Occupational Health Psychology, 22*(3), 273–285. doi:10.1037/ocp0000056 PMID:27732008

Balaraman, P., & Kosalram, K. (2013). E-Hospital Management & Hospital Information Systems-Changing Trends. *Int. J. Inf. Eng. Electron. Bus., 1*, 50–58.

Bhimani, H., Mention, A. L., & Barlatier, P. J. (2019). Social media and innovation: A systematic literature review and future research directions. *Technological Forecasting and Social Change, 144*, 251–269. doi:10.1016/j.techfore.2018.10.007

Biel, D., DeLone, M., Gerhardt, W., & Chang, C. (2019). *Radical Interoperability.* Available at: https://www2.deloitte.com/us/en/insights/industry/health-care/ radical-data-interoperability-survey.html

Botan, C. (1993b). A human nature approach to images and ethics in international public relations. *Journal of Public Relations Research, 5*(2), 71–81. doi:10.12071532754xjprr0502_02

Boueé & Schaible. (2015). *The digital transformation of industry*. Roland Berger and BDI.

Bucchi, M. (2022). 'Have we ever been satisfied with Science Communication? Continuity and change'. *Journal of Clinical Outcomes Management, 21*(07), C03.

Buttorff, C., Ruder, T., & Bauman, M. (2017). *Multiple Chronic Conditions in the United States*. RAND Corporation. Available at https://www.rand.org/pubs/tools/TL221.html doi:10.7249/TL221

Caliber's Global Pharma Study. (2020). https://www.aboutfarma.com.br/secaodesktop/novidades/2907/caliber-lanca-estudo-global-inedito-sobre-a-reputacao-da-industria-farmaceutica-antes-e-durante-pandemia

Callison, C., & Seltzer, T. (2010). Influence of responsiveness, accessibility, and professionalism on journalists' perceptions of Southwest Airlines public relations. *Public Relations Review*, *36*(2), 141–146. doi:10.1016/j.pubrev.2010.01.002

Camilleri, M. A. (2018). Unlocking Corporate Social Responsibility Communication through Digital Media. In A. Lindgreen, J. Vanhamme, F. Maon, & R. Watkins (Eds.), Communicating Corporate Social Responsibility in the Digital Era. Academic Press.

Camilleri, M. A. (2020). The market for socially responsible investing: A review of the developments. *Social Responsibility Journal*. https://www.emerald.com/insight/content/doi/10.1108/SRJ-06-2019-0194/full/html

Chen, G.-M., & Zhang, K. (2010). New media and cultural identity in the global society. In R. Taiwo (Ed.), *Handbook of research on discourse behavior and digital communication: Language structures and social interaction* (pp. 801–815). Idea Group. doi:10.4018/978-1-61520-773-2.ch051

Chen, L.-S., Liu, C.-H., Hsu, C.-C., & Lin, C.-S. (2010). C-Kano model: A novel approach for discovering attractive quality elements. *Total Quality Management & Business Excellence*, *21*(11), 1189–1214. doi:10.1080/14783363.2010.529347

Chen, M. (2007). *Membership-based Organizations of the Poor*. Routledge. doi:10.4324/9780203934074

Choudhury, P. R., Foroughi, C., & Larson, B. (2021). Work-from-anywhere: The productivity effects of geographic flexibility. *Strategic Management Journal, 42*(4). doi:10.1002/smj.3251

Davies, A., Tenesa, A., Payton, A., Yang, J., Harris, S. E., Liewald, D., Ke, X., Le Hellard, S., Christoforou, A., Luciano, M., McGhee, K., Lopez, L., Gow, A. J., Corley, J., Redmond, P., Fox, H. C., Haggarty, P., Whalley, L. J., McNeill, G., ... Deary, I. J. (2011). Genome-wide association studies establish that human intelligence is highly heritable and polygenic. *Molecular Psychiatry*, *16*(10), 996–1005. doi:10.1038/mp.2011.85 PMID:21826061

de Vries, L., Gensler, S., & Leeflang, P. S. (2017). Effects of traditional advertising and social messages on brand-building metrics and customer acquisition. *Journal of Marketing*, *81*(5), 1–15. doi:10.1509/jm.15.0178

Delbridge, R., & Sallaz, J. J. (2015). Work: Four Worlds and Ways of Seeing. *Organization Studies*, *36*(11), 1449–1462. Advance online publication. doi:10.1177/0170840615612021

Dingel, J. I., & Neiman, B. (2020). *How Many Jobs Can be Done at Home?* Becker Friedman Institute for Economics at Chicago. Available at: https://github.com/jdingel/DingelNeimanworkathome/blob/master/DingelNeiman-workathome.pdf

Duck, S., & McMahan, D. T. (2009). *The basics of communication – A relational perspective*. Sage.

Eddy, D. M. (1982). Clinical Policies and the Quality of Clinical Practice. *The New England Journal of Medicine*, *307*(6), 343–347. doi:10.1056/NEJM198208053070604 PMID:7088099

Falk, A., Becker, A., Dohmen, T. J., Human, D., & Sunde, U. (2016). *The preference survey module: A validated instrument for measuring risk, time, and social preferences*. Discussion paper 9674, IZA, Institute of Labor Economics.

Faraj, W., Renno, W., & Bhardwaj, A. (2021). Unto the breach: What the COVID-19 pandemic exposes about digitalization. *Information and Organization, 31*(1), 100337. doi:10.1016/j.infoandorg.2021.100337

Fraustino, J. D., & Connolly-Ahern, C. (2015). Corporate associations written on the wall: Publics' responses to Fortune 500 ability and social responsibility Facebook posts. *Journal of Public Relations Research, 27*(5), 452–474. doi:10.1080/1062726X.2015.1098543

Gamble, T. K., & Gamble, M. (2014). *Interpersonal communication: building connections together*. Sage.

García García, M., Carrillo-Durán, M.V. & Tato Jimenez, J.L. (2017). Online corporate communications: website usability and content. *Journal of Communication Management, 21*(2), 140-154.

Gawer, A. (2009). Platform Dynamics and Strategies: From Products to Services. In A. Gawer (Ed.), *Platforms, Markets and Innovation*. Edward Elgar Publishing. doi:10.4337/9781849803311.00009

Ghangurde, A. (2018). *McKinsey executives on expanding the pharmaceutical industry's digital drive, lessons from Amazon*. https://scrip.pharmaintelligence.informa.com/SC141824/McKinsey-Execs-On-Expanding-Pharmas-Digital-Push-Lessons-From-Amazon

Gilpin, D. (2008). Narrating the organizational self: Reframing the role of the news release. *Public Relations Review, 34*(1), 9–18. doi:10.1016/j.pubrev.2007.08.005

Goh, K. H., Wang, L., Yeow, A. Y. K., Poh, H., Li, K., Yeow, J. J. L., & Tan, G. Y. H. (2021). Artificial intelligence in sepsis early prediction and diagnosis using unstructured data in healthcare. *Nature Communications, 12*(1), 711. doi:10.103841467-021-20910-4 PMID:33514699

Gonete, T. Z., Yazachew, L., & Endehabtu, B. F. (2021). Improving data quality and information utilization at Metema Primary Hospital, Amhara national regional state, Northwest Ethiopia 2018: Capstone project. *Health Informatics Journal, 27*(3), 14604582211043160. doi:10.1177/14604582211043160 PMID:34569329

Grossman, R. (2014). *Science Communication: Could You Explain It to Your Granny?* https://www.theguardian.com/science/blog/ 2014/oct/10/science-communicators-quantum-physics-granny

Hariry, R. V., & Barenji, A. (2021). Paradkar From industry 4.0 to pharma 4.0. Handbook of Smart Materias Technologies and Devices, 1-22.

Harkaway, N. (2012). *The blind giant: Being human in a digital world*. John Murray Publishers.

Haro-de-Rosario, A., del Mar Gálvez-Rodríguez, M., Sáez-Martín, A., & Caba-Pérez, C. (2017). Role of the Board of Directors in Business Ethics In Latin American Countries. *RAE-Business Administration Magazine, 57*(5), 426–438.

Hautamäki, E.; Kinnunen, U.-M.; Palojoki, S. (2017). Health information systems usability-related use errors in patient safety incidents. *Finn. J. eHealth eWelfare, 9*, 6.

He, S., Oerman, T., & van de Ven, J. (2016). The sources of the communication gap. *Management Science, 63*(9), 2832–2846. doi:10.1287/mnsc.2016.2518

Holtzhausen, D. R., & Zerfass, A. (2013). *May. Strategic communication: A concept at the center of applied communication?* Paper presented at the Preconference "Strategic communication – A concept at the center of applied communications", International Communication Association, Annual Conference, Boston, MA.

Hoxha, K., Hung, Y. W., Irwin, B. R., & Grepin, K. A. (2020). Understanding the challenges associated with the use of data from routine health information systems in low-and middle-income countries: A systematic review. *The HIM Journal*. PMID:32602368

Ihlen, Ø., & Levenshus, A. (2017). Panacea, placebo or prudence: Perspectives and constraints for corporate dialogue. *Public Relations Inquiry*, *6*(3), 219–232. doi:10.1177/2046147X17708815

Internet, P. (2005). *Health information Online*. Available at: https://www.pewresearch.org/internet/2005/05/17/health-information-online/

Jang, H. J., Choi, Y. D., & Kim, N. H. (2017). Effects and Satisfaction of Medical Device Safety Information Reporting System Using Electronic Medical Record. *Healthcare Informatics Research*, *23*(2), 94–100. doi:10.4258/hir.2017.23.2.94 PMID:28523207

Kastelan Mrak, M., & Sokolic, D. (2017). The Evolution of Work Organization and its Implication for Educational Policies and Managerial Practices. *Proceedings of the 6th International Scientific Symposium Economy of Eastern Croatia - Vision and Growth*, 335-344.

Kelly, C. (2015). *A linguistic study of the understanding of emoticons and emojis in text messages.* Halmstad University.

Kennedy, A. K., & Sommerfeldt, E. J. (2015). A postmodern turn for social media research: Theory and research directions for public relations scholarship. *Atlantic Journal of Communication*, *23*(1), 31–45. doi:10.1080/15456870.2015.972406

Kent, M. L., & Lane, A. B. (2017). A rhizomatous metaphor for dialogic theory. *Public Relations Review*, *43*(3), 568–578. doi:10.1016/j.pubrev.2017.02.017

Kent, M. L., & Taylor, M. (1998). Building dialogic relationships through the World Wide Web. *Public Relations Review*, *24*(3), 321–334. doi:10.1016/S0363-8111(99)80143-X

Killian, G., & McManus, K. (2015). A marketing communications approach for the digital era: Managerial guidelines for social media integration. *Business Horizons*, *58*(5), 539–549. doi:10.1016/j.bushor.2015.05.006

Kitson, G., Marie, G., Francoia, J.-P., Zalesskiy, S. S., Sigerson, R. C., Mathieson, J. S., & Cronin, L. (2018). Digitization of multistep organic synthesis in reactionware for on-demand pharmaceuticals. *Science*, *359*(6373), 314–319. doi:10.1126cience.aao3466 PMID:29348235

Köhler, K. & Zerfass, A. (2019). Communicating the corporate strategy: An international benchmark study in the UK, the USA, and Germany. *Journal of Communication Management, 23*(4), 348-374.

Kottke, T. E., Stiefel, M., & Pronk, N. P. (2016). *"Well-Being in All Policies": Promoting Cross-Sectoral Collaboration to Improve People's Lives. NAM Perspectives.* Discussion Paper, National Academy of Medicine. doi:10.31478/201604c

Koutsothanassi, E., Bouranta, N., & Psomas, E. (2017). Examining the relationships among service features, customer loyalty and switching barriers in the Greek banking sector. *International Journal of Quality and Service Sciences*, *9*(3/4), 425–440. doi:10.1108/IJQSS-02-2017-0013

Kpobi, L., Swartz, L., & Ofori-Atta, A. L. (2018). Challenges in the use of the mental health information system in a resource-limited setting: Lessons from Ghana. *BMC Health Services Research*, *18*(1), 98. doi:10.118612913-018-2887-2 PMID:29422047

Lakshmi, B., &. Patel, P. (2020). *Digital Marketing in Pharmaceutical Industry–An Overview and Assessment*. Academic Press.

Lamberti, M. J., Wilkinson, M., Donzanti, B. A., Wohlhieter, G. E., Parikh, S., Wilkins, R. G., & Getz, K. (2019). A Study on the Application and Use of Artificial Intelligence to Support Drug Development. *Clinical Therapeutics*, *41*(8), 1414–1426. doi:10.1016/j.clinthera.2019.05.018 PMID:31248680

Lamberton, C., & Stephen, A. T. (2016). A Thematic Exploration of Digital, Social Media, and Mobile Marketing: Research Evolution from 2000 to 2015 and an Agenda for Future Inquiry. *Journal of Marketing*, *80*(6), 146–172. doi:10.1509/jm.15.0415

Lamichhane, Y., R. (2016). Non-verbal Skills: Unavoidable in Communication. *Repositioning: The Journal of Business and Hospitality*, *1*(91).

Laurillard, D. (2013). *Rethinking university teaching: A conversational framework for the effective use of learning technologies*. Routledge. doi:10.4324/9781315012940

Lavorgna, L., De Stefano, M., Sparaco, M., Moccia, M., Abbadessa, G., Montella, P., Buonanno, D., Esposito, S., Clerico, M., Cenci, C., Trojsi, F., Lanzillo, R., Rosa, L., Morra, V. B., Ippolito, D., Maniscalco, G., Bisecco, A., Tedeschi, G., & Bonavita, S. (2018). Fake news, influencers and health-related professional participation on the Web: A pilot study on a social-network of people with Multiple Sclerosis. *Multiple Sclerosis and Related Disorders*, *25*, 175–178. doi:10.1016/j.msard.2018.07.046 PMID:30096683

Lee, J., Cameron, I., & Hassall, M. (2019). Improving process safety: What roles for Digitalization and Industry 4.0? *Process Safety and Environmental Protection*, *132*, 325–339. doi:10.1016/j.psep.2019.10.021

Marlow, S. L., Lacerenza, C. N., & Salas, E. (2017). Communication in virtual teams: A conceptual framework and research agenda. *Human Resource Management Review*, *27*(4), 575–589. doi:10.1016/j.hrmr.2016.12.005

Mboera, L. E. G., Rumisha, S. F., Mbata, D., Mremi, I. R., Lyimo, E. P., & Joachim, C. (2021). Data utilisation and factors influencing the performance of the health management information system in Tanzania. *BMC Health Services Research*, *21*(1), 498–506. doi:10.118612913-021-06559-1 PMID:34030696

McGovern, L., Miller, G., & Hughes-Cromwick, P. (2014). *The Relative Contribution of Multiple Determinants to Health Outcomes*. Available at: https://www.rwjf.org/en/library/research/2014/08/the-relative-contribution-of-multiple-determinants-to-healthout.html

McIntyre & Srinivasan. (2017). Networks, platforms, and strategy: Emerging views and next steps. *Strategic Management Journal, Wiley Blackwell*, *38*(1), 141–160.

Mijuk, G. (2018). *Drug development gains momentum in big data analysis*. Novartis. https://www.novartis.com/stories/discovery/drug-development-gets-big-data-analytics-boost

Moglia, M., Hopkins, J., & Bardoel, A. (2021). Telework, hybrid work and the United Nation's Sustainable Development Goals: Towards policy coherence. *Sustainability (Basel)*, *13*(16), 9222. doi:10.3390u13169222

Moorhead, S. A., Hazlett, D. E., Harrison, L., Carroll, J. K., Irwin, A., & Hoving, C. (2013). A new dimension of health care: Systematic review of the uses, benefits, and limitations of social media for health communication. *Journal of Medical Internet Research*, *15*(4), e1933. doi:10.2196/jmir.1933 PMID:23615206

Mulgund, S., & Kelly, M. (2020). *Command and control of operations in the information environment: Leading with information in operational planning, execution, and assessment*. Department of the Air Force.

Müller, J. M., Pommeranz, B., Weisser, J., & Voigt, K. I. (2018). Digital, social media, and mobile marketing in industrial buying: Still in need of customer segmentation? Empirical evidence from Poland and Germany. *Industrial Marketing Management*, *73*, 70–83. doi:10.1016/j.indmarman.2018.01.033

Muller, N. (2022). Perceptions about corporate positioning on controversial sociopolitical issues: Examining big pharma engagement with patient advocacy. *Public Relations Review*, *48*(5), 102261. doi:10.1016/j.pubrev.2022.102261

Murphy, P. (2011). *Contextual distortion: Strategic communication vs. the networked nature of everything*. Paper presented at the International Communication Association 2011 pre-conference Strategic communication - A concept at the centre of applied communications, Boston, MA.

Murphy, P. (2011, August). *Putting the Earth into Global Media Studies*. Academic Press.

Murray, E., Lo, B., Pollack, L., Donelan, K., Catania, J., Lee, K., Zapert, K., & Turner, R. (2003). The impact of health information on the physician-patient relationship. *J Med Internet Res., 5*.

Nagel, P., & Lubinga, E. (2015). Nonverbal communication. In S. Steinberg & G. Angelopulo (Eds.), *Introduction to communication science for Southern African students* (pp. 85–106). Juta.

Nasir, N., & Marikar, K. (2018). ISQUA18-2296Does Adoption of Health Information System (HIS) in Hospital Affect the Compliance to the Hospital Accreditation Program. *International Journal for Quality in Health Care*, *30*(suppl_2), 12–13. doi:10.1093/intqhc/mzy167.15

Ngamvichaikit, A. (2021). Leveraging design thinking for pharmaceutical digital marketing Asian. *Journal of Business Research*, *11*(1).

Olson, R. (2018). *Don't be such a poor storyteller. In Don't Be Such a Scientist*. Springer. doi:10.5822/978-1-61091-918-0

Olson, S. R., & Pollard, T. (2004). The muse pixelipe: Digitalization and media literacy education. *The American Behavioral Scientist*, *48*(2), 248–278. doi:10.1177/0002764204267272

Parida, D., Sjödin, W., & Reim, S. (2019). *Reviewing Literature on Digitalization, Business Model Innovation, and Sustainable Industry*. Past Achievements and Future Promises Multidisciplinary Digital Publishing Institute.

Pavlik, J. V., & Mankintosh, S. (2018). *Converging media: A new introduction to mass communication*. Oxford University Press.

Pereira, T. J., & Puggina, A. C. (2017). Validation of the self-assessment of communication skills and professionalism for nurses. *Revista Brasileira de Enfermagem, 70*(3), 588–594. doi:10.1590/0034-7167-2016-0133 PMID:28562808

Peter, M. K., & Dalla Vecchia, M. (2021). The Digital Marketing Toolkit: A Literature Review for The Identification of Digital Marketing Channels and Platforms Studies in Systems, Decision and Control. Springer.

Petrou, P., & Bakker, A. B. (2016). Crafting one's leisure time in response to high job strain. *Human Relations, 69*(2), 507–529. doi:10.1177/0018726715590453

Pfeffer, T. Z., & Carley, K. M. (2014). Understanding online firestorms: Negative word-of-mouth dynamics in social media networks. *Journal of Marketing Communications, 20*(1-2), 1–2, 117–128. doi :10.1080/13527266.2013.797778

Pfisterer, A. B., Paschke, M., & Pasotti, J. (2019). Communicating science through the media. Zurich-Basel Plant Science Center.

Ramya, N., Kowsalsya, A., & Dharanipriya, K. (2019). Service quality and its dimensions. *EPRA International Journal of Research and Development, 4*(2), 38-41. Retrieved from https://www.eprajournals.com/

Ranta, V., Keränen, J., & Aarikka-Stenroos, L. (2020). How B2B suppliers articulate customer value propositions in the circular economy: Four innovation-driven value creation logics. *Industrial Marketing Management, 87*, 291–30. doi:10.1016/j.indmarman.2019.10.007

Reinhardt, J.C., Oliveira, D.T., & Ring, I.C. (2021). Industry 4.0 and the future of the pharmaceutical industry. *Pharm. Eng.*

Rideout, V., & Robb, M. B. (2018). *Social media, social life: Teens reveal their experiences. Research report*. Common Sense.

Rosenbaum, G. C., Ramírez, G. C., Edwards, K., Kim, J., Campbell, J. M., & Bickle, M. C. (2017). The digitization of health care retailing. *Journal of Research in Interactive Marketing, 11*(4), 432–446. doi:10.1108/JRIM-07-2017-0058

Ross, J. W. (2018). How to develop a great digital strategy January. *MIT Sloan Management Review, 58*(2), 7–9.

Ruehl, C.H., & Ingenhoff, D. (2015), Communication management on social networking sites: Stakeholder motives and usage types of corporate Facebook, Twitter and YouTube pages. *Journal of Communication Management, 19*(3), 288-302.

Saghaeiannejad-Isfahani, S., Saeedbakhsh, S., Jahanbakhsh, M., & Habibi, M. (2015). Analysis of the quality of hospital information systems in Isfahan teaching hospitals based on the DeLone and McLean model. *Journal of Education and Health Promotion*, *4*, 5. doi:10.4103/2277-9531.151883 PMID:25767816

Salahuddin, L., Ismail, Z., Hashim, U. R., Ismail, N. H., Ikram, R. R. R., Rahim, F. A., & Hassan, N. H. (2020). Healthcare practitioner behaviours that influence unsafe use of hospital information systems. *Health Informatics Journal*, *26*(1), 420–434. doi:10.1177/1460458219833090 PMID:30843460

Savage, M., & Warde, A. (1993). *Urban Sociology, Capitalism and Modernity*. Macmillan Publishers Ltd. doi:10.1007/978-1-349-22991-8

Schivinski, B., & Dabrowski, D. (2014). The effect of social media communication on consumer perceptions of brands. *Journal of Marketing Communications, 22*(2).

Schneider, K. (2017). The resurgence of awe in psychology: Promise, hope, and perils. *The Humanistic Psychologist*, *45*(2), 103–108. doi:10.1037/hum0000060

Sehlstedt, N. (2016). Embracing digital health in the pharmaceutical industry Int. *Journal of Healthcare Management*, *9*(3), 145–14.

Shahbaz, M., Gao, C., Zhai, L., Shahzad, F., & Hu, Y. (2019). Investigating the adoption of big data analytics in healthcare: The moderating role of resistance to change. *Journal of Big Data*, *6*(1), 1–20. doi:10.118640537-019-0170-y

Sharmin, S., Tasnim, I., & Shimul, D. (2016). Measuring Customer Satisfaction through SERVQUAL Model: A Study on Beauty Parlors in Chittagong. *European Journal of Business and Management*, *8*, 97–108.

Shearer, E., & Grieco, E. (2019). *Americans Are Wary of the Role Social Media Sites Play in Delivering the News*. Pew Research Center.

Shin, Pang, & Kim. (2015). Building relationships through integrated online media platforms: Analysis of top 100 global brands. *Journal of Business and Technical Communication, 29*(2), 184-220. doi:10.1177/1050651914560569

Shokouhyar, S., Shokoohyar, S., & Safari, S. (2020). Research on the influence of quality factors of after-sales service on customer satisfaction. *Journal of Retailing and Consumer Services*, *56*, 102139. doi:10.1016/j.jretconser.2020.102139

Shrank, W. H., Rogstad, T. L., & Parekh, N. (2019). Waste in the US health care system: Estimated costs and potential for savings. *Journal of the American Medical Association*, *322*(15), 1501–1509. doi:10.1001/jama.2019.13978 PMID:31589283

Smith, B. G. (2010). Socially distributing public relations: Twitter, Haiti, and interactivity in social media. *Public Relations Review*, *36*(4), 329–335. doi:10.1016/j.pubrev.2010.08.005

Solomon, D., & Theiss, J. (2013). *Interpersonal communication – Putting theory into practice, Routledge*. Taylor & Francis Group.

Sommerfeldt, E. J., Kent, M. L., & Taylor, M. (2012). Activist practitioner perspectives of website public relations: Why aren't activist websites fulfilling the dialogic promise? *Public Relations Review*, *38*(2), 303–312. doi:10.1016/j.pubrev.2012.01.001

Stankevičiūtė, Ž., & Kunskaja, S. (2022). Strengthening of work-life balance while working remotely in the context of COVID-19 pandemic. *Human Systems Management*, *41*(2), 221–235. doi:10.3233/HSM-211511

Steger, M. F. (2009). Meaning in life. In S. J. Lopez & C. R. Snyder (Eds.), *Oxford handbook of positive psychology* (pp. 679–687). Oxford University.

Sundar, S. S., Oh, J., Kang, H., & Sreenivasan, A. (2013). How does technology persuade? Theoretical mechanisms for persuasive technologies. In J. P. Dillard & L. Shen (Eds.), *The SAGE handbook of persuasion: Developments in theory and practice* (pp. 388–400). Sage Publications, Inc.

Tiwana, A., & Konsynski, B. (2010). Complementarities between organizational IT architecture and governance structure. *Information Systems Research*, *21*(2), 288–304. doi:10.1287/isre.1080.0206

Tiwari, S., & Raut, C. (2019). Comparing strategic orientation of two online pharmaceutical firms: Cases of netmeds and medplus. SSRN *Electron. J.* doi:10.2139/ssrn.3323452

Turmunkh, U., van den Assem, M. J., & Van Dolder, D. (2019). Malleable lies: Communication and cooperation in a high stakes tv game show. *Management Science*, *65*(10), 47954812. doi:10.1287/mnsc.2018.3159

Turnbull, C. F. (2010). Mom just facebooked me and Dad knows how to text: The influences of computer-mediated communication on interpersonal communication and differences through generations. *Elon Journal of Undergraduate Research in Communications*, *1*(1), 5–16.

Uysal, N., & Yang, A. (2013). The power of activist networks in the mass self-communication era: A triangulation study of the impact of WikiLeaks on the stock value of Bank of America. *Public Relations Review*, *39*(5), 459–469. doi:10.1016/j.pubrev.2013.09.007

Valentini, C. (2015). Is using social media 'good' for the public relations profession? A critical reflection. *Public Relations Review*, *41*(2), 170–177. doi:10.1016/j.pubrev.2014.11.009

van Osch, W., & Coursaris, C. K. (2014). Social media research: An assessment of the domain's productivity and intellectual evolution. *Communication Monographs*, *81*(3), 1–25. doi:10.1080/03637751.2014.921720

van Ruler, D. V., & Sriramesh, K. (2007). Defining strategic communication. *International Journal of Strategic Communication*, *1*(1), 3–35. doi:10.1080/15531180701285244

van Velthoven, M. H., Cordon, G., & Challagalla, C. (2019). Digitization of healthcare organizations: The digital health landscape and information theory. *International Journal of Medical Informatics*, *124*, 49–57. doi:10.1016/j.ijmedinf.2019.01.007 PMID:30784426

Venkatesh, V., Rabah, J., Fusaro, M., Couture, A., Varela, W., & Alexander, K. (2016). Factors impacting university instructors' and students' perceptions of course effectiveness and technology integration in the age of web 2.0. *McGill Journal of Education*, *51*(1), 533–561. doi:10.7202/1037358ar

Venter, E. (2017). Bridging the communication gap between generation Y and the baby boomer generation. *International Journal of Adolescence and Youth*, *22*(4), 497–507. doi:10.1080/02673843.2016.1267022

Vernuccio, M. (2014). Communicating Corporate Brands Through Social Media: An Exploratory Study. *Journal of Business Communication*. http://eds.a.ebscohost.com/

Wijayati, T. A., & Achadi, A. (2019). Factors Affecting the Success of Hospital Management Information System: A Systematic Review. In *Proceedings of the 6th International Conference on Public Health*. Sebelas Maret University.

Wilcox, D., & Cameron, G. T. (2009). *Public Relations: Strategies and Tactics* (9th ed.). Pearson Allyn & Bacon.

Wirtz, J. C., & Zimbres, T. (2018). A systematic analysis of research applying 'principles of dialogic communication' to organizational websites, blogs and social media: Implications for theory and practice. *Journal of Public Relations Research*, *30*(1-2), 5–34. doi:10.1080/1062726X.2018.1455146

Yang, A., & Taylor, M. (2010). Relationship-building by Chinese NGOs' websites: Education, not activation. *Public Relations Review*, *36*(4), 342–351. doi:10.1016/j.pubrev.2010.07.001

Yang, S. U., Kang, M., & Cha, H. (2015). A study on dialogic communication, trust, and distrust: Testing a scale for measuring organization–public dialogic communication (OPDC). *Journal of Public Relations Research*, *27*(2), 175–192. doi:10.1080/1062726X.2015.1007998

Yang, S. U., Kang, M., & Johnson, P. (2010). Effects of narratives, openness to dialogic communication, and credibility on engagement in crisis communication through organizational blogs. *Communication Research*, *37*(4), 473–497. doi:10.1177/0093650210362682

Yarimoglu, E. K. (2014). Turkish retail industry and the relations with Albania. *European Scientific Journal*, *10*(7). Advance online publication. doi:10.19044/esj.2014.v10n7p%p

Yates, M., Bechman, K., Dennison, E. M., MacGregor, A. J., Ledingham, J., Norton, S., & Galloway, J. B. (2020). Data quality predicts care quality: Findings from a national clinical audit. *Arthritis Research & Therapy*, *22*(1), 87. doi:10.118613075-020-02179-y PMID:32303251

Zhou, J. (2013). Digitalization and intelligentization of manufacturing industry. *Advances in Manufacturing*, *1*(1), 1–7. doi:10.100740436-013-0006-5

Zidarova, E. D., & Zografos, K. (2011). Measuring Quality of Service in Airport Passenger Terminals. *Transportation Research Record: Journal of the Transportation Research Board*, *2214*(1), 69–76. doi:10.3141/2214-09

Chapter 12
Communication and Coordination Issues in Managing Distributed Scrum Teams

Fernando Almeida
Polytechnic Institute of Gaya, Portugal

ABSTRACT

Software development companies have progressively been experiencing the need to migrate their traditional development processes to agile environments. Several frameworks have emerged that support this paradigm, and Scrum is one of the most widely adopted on a global scale. However, Scrum was originally designed to work in small, local team environments. The challenge lies in designing its adoption in large-scale environments with geographically distributed teams. This chapter seeks to explore this challenge by identifying communication and coordination issues that may arise when adopting distributed Scrum. Three case studies are considered to allow comparison of different approaches considering structural and contextual factors associated with each organization.

INTRODUCTION

Agile software development methods have acquired great popularity over the past decades. Dissatisfaction with the traditional development model that required a lot of planning and documentation in the early stages of a project, extrapolation of software delivery times, increased costs above initial estimates, and little flexibility regarding changes in requirements along the project are typically pointed out as the reasons for the increase in the number of agile projects in the software industry (Pikkarainen et al., 2008).

At the same time, there is also an increase in distributed software development motivated by the organizational problems faced by companies and the scarcity of highly qualified human resources in software engineering. According to Chakravorty et al. (2014), this model of distributed software development

DOI: 10.4018/978-1-6684-7353-5.ch012

contributes to increasing the development speed through geographically distributed teams. Furthermore, Lee & Xia (2010) report benefits in reducing costs associated with those projects.

Scrum is currently the most agile method used by software companies (Petrova, 2019). Scrum is a simple, lightweight Agile framework used for managing the development of complex products immersed in complex environments. Scrum is empirically based and uses an iterative and incremental approach to deliver value frequently and thereby reduce project risks (Sutherland, 2014). Several studies report its adoption in software development teams (Hajjdiab et al., 2012; Rigby et al., 2016). However, this method was originally designed to be applied in small teams that share the same physical space as recognized in Schwaber & Beedle (2002). Therefore, the adoption of this model in geographically distributed teams is also expected to bring new challenges. Several challenges are pointed out in the literature in areas such as communication between teams, project and process management, knowledge management, and cultural issues (Almeida et al., 2019; Dikert et al., 2016).

Communication and project coordination mechanisms in large-scale environments are more relevant in view of the larger number of developers and their geographical location, which can be quite diverse. In this sense, this study addresses the challenge of exploring the adoption of Scrum methodology in geographically distributed teams through the realization of three case studies within software companies. Firstly, it intends to explore the different levels of team distribution and the causes that led to the choice of the distributed model. Next, an attempt is made to systematize a set of characteristics and practices corresponding to this type of development. Finally, it seeks to identify ways to mitigate the communication and coordination issues that can be found in this distributed model of software development. This work essentially intends to offer practical contributions to software companies that are taking the first steps in the distribution of their development teams. Through this work, these companies will be better prepared to face the challenges posed by the adoption of Scrum in a distributed environment.

The chapter is organized as follows: Initially, a literature review is performed on the software development processes in distributed teams. Next, the methodology and associated methods adopted in this study are presented. It is also in this section that the profile of the software companies participating in this study is presented. After that, the results of the study are presented and discussed considering the relevance of this evidence to the scientific community. Finally, the conclusions of the study are stated. Also, in this section, the theoretical and practical implications, limitations, and some indications of future work are presented.

BACKGROUND

Responsibilities Associated With Project Management

A project manager is a person chosen by the organization to lead the team responsible for the execution to achieve the project objectives. As evidenced by Heagney (2016), the main goal of the project manager is to ensure the success of the project. He/she is responsible for leading the team to achieve the project objectives. He/she is the main link between organizational strategy and project execution so that all efforts are properly directed to meet the project objectives.

The role of a project manager is different from a functional manager or operations manager. As argued by Ibraheem (2018), the functional manager focuses on providing oversight of running a functional or business unit, while operations managers are responsible for the efficiency of business operations. The project manager is responsible for meeting project needs such as tasks, team needs, and individual needs to achieve the purpose and objectives of the project. In this sense, Lent & Pinkowska (2012) and Tahir (2019) argue that the project manager should possess some fundamental behavioral skills such as leadership, creativity, assertiveness, negotiation, results orientation, and a strong appreciation of business ethics.

Managing Distributed Teams

Distributed Scrum teams are teams that have individual members working in different physical locations while working on the same project. The same applies to projects that have different teams, working together in different locations. Team members may never physically meet during the project or have very few interactions (Casey, 2010; Takkunen, 2014). This happens, more and more, in software development, where the different geographical locations and time zones of individual team members, or groups of team members, are a common scenario, leading to "global distributed teams" (Morrison-Smith & Ruiz, 2020). As software projects become more complex, they often require multi-disciplinary teams to develop them. The best-talented people to join the team can be anywhere in the world and are often not available to move to a common location. The developments in Information and Communications Technologies (ICT) enhanced the possibility to work from any place while keeping the connection with others working on the same project and assuring team cohesion. Therefore, distributed teams have become a new trend in workplace development. For software companies, distributed teams are a way to involve the best people in the project, without moving them, lowering the development costs. For team members is a way to avoid displacement, allowing them to work from the place of their choice, and reducing costs in terms of time, money, and stress (Morrison-Smith & Ruiz, 2020). For both teams and companies distributed teams are considered a way to enhance productivity (Bosch-Sijtsema et al., 2009).

Managing distributed teams brings new challenges: if team members are in different time zones, scheduling remote meetings could be difficult. Communication and establishing trust between distributed members can be challenging and members working alone can feel lonely or left behind. Also, team members can have different communication styles, work ethics, and cultural values. With Scrum teams, face-to-face communication is an important issue stated as one of the Agile Manifesto's principles: "the most efficient and effective method of conveying information to and within a development team is face-to-face conversation." (Beck et al., 2001). This principle can be hard to follow with distributed teams.

According to Takkunen (2014), the main challenges that distributed teams face are social and communication issues (lack of informal conversation, loss of non-verbal cues, establishing consensus and shared meaning at distance, fewer opportunities to build strong ties between members, different cultures and different work processes), time zone differences, and inadequate ICT. This view is confirmed by Mundra et al. (2013) by pointing out that Scrum is designed to work with internal teams or teams physically located at the same site. Thus, the study by Mundra et al. (2013) proposes an approach called Scrum of Scrums with the goal of scaling Scrum across large teams and projects. These meetings allow teams to group together to discuss their work, focusing especially on the area of overlap and integration. The meetings aim to align the technical ideas of the teams that are on the same project, as well as address issues that may result in delivery delays. For the meetings held once a week, called the alignment meeting, a team member is chosen to represent them. This choice comes from the team, which recognizes a member of the group capable of giving technical positions about the product and finding solutions for the other teams.

Dikert et al. (2016) pointed out that, when dealing with large-scale development teams, coordination problems arise when teams are distributed on many geographical sites. Besides project management problems, some other issues were stressed, like missing kick-off meetings, lack of a sense of proximity, and difficulty in scheduling meetings when distributed teams operate in different time zones. Although these problems, Dikert et al. (2016) stated that Scrum and distributed teams must still be used together.

Saha (2016) listed some challenges faced by distributed teams during the implementation of scrum processes, namely, rare face-to-face communication, difficulties in managing the product backlog, lack of mutual understanding among teams, over specialism (over-specialized and experienced teams may create additional challenges for other teams), over individualism (less interaction and collaboration from some teams concerning the others), difficulties in tracking progress across teams, and an excess of management interference that can lead to less productivity.

Ockerman (2020) identified communication issues that a Scrum Master must focus on to support distributed teams. One is to check their team members regularly because team members need one-on-one time to express their concerns regarding the project. Concerns that could be dealt during an informal coffee break cannot be solved the same way with distributed teams. Another issue is transparency, meaning that the team must have a full understanding of the project's evolution, goals, decision-making, etc. According to Ockerman (2020), lack of information, or an overload of information cause transparency challenges. Scrum Masters must deal with transparency assuring that the team gets all the needed information. A third issue was the need to address conflict. Scrum Masters must allow team members to engage in conflict productively and creatively. With distributed teams, this issue can be hard to address and requires different techniques.

These challenges have been approached by several researchers and professionals aiming to find how to overcome them and seeking new ways to better manage distributed teams and increase their performance. Some best practices to cope with communication challenges in distributed Scrum teams were discussed by Walimbe (2016). Several case studies were analyzed, and a framework was proposed to deal with a list of issues related to communication within teams: effective use of communication tools, how to manage daily scrum meetings, working under different time zones, overcoming language barriers, and dealing with lack of trust and coordination.

Almeida et al. (2019) addressed several challenges in knowledge management in large-scale Scrum teams by analyzing two projects from a software company. One of the challenges that were addressed was geographically distributed teams since team members were working in the location of the projects' target market and other distinct geographical locations. This study found that challenges in knowledge management increase with the existence of distributed team members. Cultural and time zone differences among team members were also discussed along with the importance of using collaborative digital platforms to manage distributed teams. The study also pointed out the importance of having team members connected to the culture of the project's target market.

Morrison-Smith & Ruiz (2020) conducted a literature review, with 255 relevant studies, most of them in the last two decades, to highlight the collaboration challenges experienced by distributed teams. They also addressed existing mitigation strategies. Those relevant studies primarily focused on technology use. Morrison-Smith & Ruiz (2020) separated challenges into five categories: geographical distance, temporal distance, perceived distance, the configuration of dispersed teams, and diversity of workers. The authors also described four implications for designing groupware that better supports the work of distributed teams to address the research question "How can we design technology for supporting distributed teams?". The first implication was "to assist the creation of common ground and work standards" to cope with team members' different backgrounds. Technology must support conversations to establish a common project-specific technical language, methodologies, and best practices. The second implication was about facilitating communication. Technology must be designed to provide the benefits of face-to-face conversations for both synchronous and asynchronous communication and also for informal communication. Language barriers due to team members that speak different languages should also be addressed. Providing mechanisms for work transparency was the third implication meaning that technology should be designed to provide that transparency. Work transparency allows each team member to feel aware of the others, providing the necessary amount of information, but preserving privacy and limiting distractions. Finally, the last implication was the design of lightweight and familiar technology. Since ICT varies across organizations, some distributed team members may face limitations in accessing sophisticated collaboration technologies. Therefore, the team must use lightweight technology, maximizing the number of potential users. It should also deal with team members' different levels of technical competence.

Another study that explored the reasons for non-effective communication in distributed Scrum teams was developed by Kostin & Strode (2022) who identified that the main reason for the loss of communication quality was the absence of non-verbal communication components such as vocal or body language. This situation is also confirmed by Abu-Arqoub & Alserhan (2019) who highlight barriers to effective intercultural communication and in which only verbal communication prevents team members from understanding the true meaning of messages. Another reason given by Kostin & Strode (2022) for poor communication is the existence of a mismatch of communication preferences within teams, assuming that a local communication pattern works for other geographically distributed teams.

Morrison-Smith & Ruiz (2020) also stressed that temporal distance and perceived distance are distinct concepts from geographical distance. Temporal distance is related not only to different time zones but also to different work patterns that can affect overlapping work hours. Perceived distance is the subjective distance that results from a person's impression about how far another person is. Two team members can be geographically distant, yet they can feel close to each other. This means that more coordination is needed to face temporal and perceived distances that can have a greater impact than geographical distance. Morrison-Smith & Ruiz (2020) pointed out that there is a need for a better understanding of how geographical distance, temporal distance, and perceived distance relate to each other.

Lumseyfai (2020) proposed a model for enabling successful distributed project team performance built around four pillars: governance methodology (the methodology used to govern teams, including practices for ensuring coordination, tracking, and communication across team members), human interaction (practices centered on engaging and motivating team members, fostering a comfortable environment, instilling a sense of purpose, and facilitating collaboration), technology management (dealing with ICT tools used by teams) and organizational environment (factors that can impact team's performance within the organization). Agile techniques were incorporated into this model, particularly Scrum techniques. A research experiment was conducted to evaluate the relationship between each of the four model pillars and distributed teams' performance. The experiment found that there was a significant, positive correlation between those four pillars and the distributed team's performance.

Carter (2020) discussed how to overcome some challenges in distributed Scrum software development teams that result from the 2020 COVID-19 public health crisis. One was to keep the company culture when working at distance since it is more difficult for team members to interpret management communications, often sent by email. To maintain company culture, ICT tools like videoconferencing tools can help mitigate this challenge. A second challenge was to keep the focus on the product vision by wasting time on work not related to it. Carter (2020) points out some strategies to keep the focus on product vision where ICT plays an important role. The third challenge stated the importance of maintaining the integrity of Scrum methodology. This means that the Agile Manifesto elements (Beck et al., 2001) must be followed despite the team is distributed. Some of the manifesto elements are easier to follow with distributed teams than others. Carter (2020) refers that an important aspect is to keep the Scrum master and product owner roles suggesting that each group of team members in the same time zone should have their own Scrum masters and product owners acting as proxies. Managing collaboration was the fourth challenge. It also deals with communication and social issues that arise when team members are not working in the same physical location. Again, ICT tools play an important role to mitigate this challenge. For each challenge, Carter (2020) listed a set of ICT tools that can overcome them.

The literature review demonstrates that distributed Scrum teams face many challenges, and an additional effort must be made to manage and implement them. Some authors even argue that a group of geographically distributed people cannot even be considered a Scrum team (Sabine, 2016). Therefore, the literature review shows that the adoption of the Scrum methodology with distributed teams is a phenomenon that needs to be addressed.

METHODOLOGY, MATERIALS, AND METHODS

This study applies a qualitative approach through the realization of three case studies with software development companies using the Scrum distributed methodology. According to Yin (2017), qualitative analysis has an emphasis on processes and meanings and allows an in-depth analysis of the phenomena in the real environment where they occur. The case study inherits the general properties of the qualitative methodology and enables the use of available theories to explain a given contemporary phenomenon in the business context and in which it becomes useful to explore a situation that is not well defined (Queirós et al., 2017). One of the essential aspects of adopting case studies is to ensure reliability and validity. For this, Yin (2017) considers it essential to look at four perspectives: (i) construction validity; (ii) internal validity; (iii) external validity; and (iv) reliability. In the construction validity dimension, it was ensured the realization of multiple case studies that allow understanding how distributed Scrum is adopted by different companies; as internal validity was considered a framework that allows exploring the way teams and processes are organized in a distributed Scrum environment; as external validity was sought to find case studies that represent different organization structure and distribution of work; and as reliability interviews were conducted with the Product Owner, Scrum Master, and a member of the Scrum Team to include three perspectives on the same phenomenon.

Table 1 briefly presents the profile of the companies involved in the case studies analysis. A total of 8 Portuguese companies in software engineering were contacted for the case studies. However, 4 of them were excluded because they were not available for the interviews under the requested conditions. Another company was also excluded because it presents an identical and redundant profile concerning CS2. In the end, a total of 3 companies in the software solutions and services development area were considered. CS1 is a micro company that develops games for online platforms on social networks. It was a company made up of two colleagues from the MSc. degree course in multimedia. CS2 is a small and medium-sized enterprise (SME) providing services in the IT area that simplifies the process of infrastructure management and reduces expenses associated with equipment and IT staff from the implementation of the Device as a Service (DaaS) model. CS3 is a large company with more than 20 years of experience, and it is dedicated to the development of e-commerce solutions for the African market. The size of the company follows the OECD framework, in which the three different types of companies are considered: (i) micro company: 1 to 9 employees; (ii) SME: 10 to 249 employees; and (iii) large enterprise: 250 employees or more. The distribution level considered the various distribution models of Scrum teams as proposed by Rothman & Kilby (2019), in which the organization of distributed Scrums should be analyzed according to the models of collaboration with remote workers. In CS1, team members share the same physical office, but some members occasionally work in a distributed way; CS2 has two distributed teams but all of them are in compatible time zones (e.g., less than 3 hours difference); and in CS3, 16 out of 23 (close to 70%) of the teams are distributed in quite different time zones, like the development teams in India, Egypt, and Portugal (e.g., between 2 and 6 hours).

Table 1. Profile of the companies

	Case Study I (CS1)	**Case Study II (CS2)**	**Case Study III (CS3)**
Established year	2015	2006	1998
No. of employees	8	121	278
Size	Micro company	SME	Large enterprise
No. of Scrum teams	1	6	23
No. of Distributed Scrum teams	1	2	16
Distribution level	Collocated	Distributed with full overlapping hours	Distributed with partial overlapping hours

Source: Authors

The interviews were conducted between 6th September and 17th December 2020. Due to the restrictions imposed by the COVID-19 pandemic and to avoid potential contagion risks with the presence of people outside the companies, the meetings were held via Google Meet and Zoom. These two video-conferencing platforms were chosen by the participating companies and offer similar conditions for the study. The questions for the interviews were sent 48 hours before each interview. After the interviews, an individual report of each interview was created and then sent by email to each company for validation.

The analysis of the implementation processes of distributed Scrum software engineering teams followed the framework established by Rizvi et al. (2015) in which it is suggested to explore the practices of distribution models according to four dimensions (i.e., contextual, model, challenges, and benefits) as shown in Table 2. A total of eight questions were formulated. From these four dimensions, it is possible to have a sufficiently comprehensive perception of the various practical approaches followed by organizations in the implementation of distributed Scrum teams.

Table 2. Research dimensions

Dimension	Description	Interview Questions
Contextual	The aim is to know the needs of the company to adopt Scrum's distributed model and to explore the composition of these teams considering the profile and experience of the human resources involved.	Q1. What has been the main motivation for distributed adoption of Scrum? Q2. What is the profile of these teams?
Model	This dimension seeks to evidence the distribution model adopted and to understand the reasons for its adoption. It is also important to know whether this model has been reformulated or corrected over time.	Q3. What has been the typology of the Scrum distributed model adopted? Q4. How has this model been defined?
Challenges	The implementation of Scrum distributed team management incorporates a set of risks and limitations that becomes relevant to know. Equally relevant is to explore the mitigation strategies implemented by companies.	Q5. What are the risks and limitations of the adopted model? Q6. What mitigation strategies have been implemented?
Benefits	Benefits also arise from the inclusion of distributed team management models. It becomes relevant to know the good practices implemented by companies and explore the benefits that these approaches can offer.	Q7. What have been the benefits achieved for the company? Q8. What are the good practices that can be identified?

Source: Authors

SOLUTIONS AND RECOMMENDATIONS

The analysis of the results was carried out using thematic analysis. This is an interpretative method of data analysis that through the identification, analysis and description of patterns or themes, allows presenting and organizing the data in a synthetic but rich way. According to Miles et al. (2019), the thematic analysis is flexible by allowing the use of different epistemological positioning and is suitable for different types of qualitative data like interviews and focus groups. The webQDA software was adopted to perform the thematic analysis, which allowed grouping the identified themes by each research dimension. The individual reports of each interview were uploaded to the webQDA and the most cited words were identified. After that, it was analyzed which case studies support each individual theme, and similar themes were aggregated to provide the final list of themes presented in Table 3. The common and specific themes for each case study were identified. Most of the identified themes are common to several case studies. However, some specific to each company emerge, namely in the contextual dimension and that allows us to identify different motivations for the implementation of distributed Scrum. Also, in the "model" dimension, there are notable differences in the models implemented by the participating companies in the case study. This was a strategic decision that resulted from the choice of three companies with different approaches in implementing the distributed Scrum model. There are also remarkable synergies between CS2 and CS3, which result from similar approaches in the implementation of distributed Scrum, despite the size of the teams and the distributed model being more extensive and complex in CS3.

Contextual Dimension

All companies implement the distributed Scrum model in all several development phases of a project (e.g., planning, design, development, quality assurance, testing). This finding is not surprising considering the results of the study conducted by Rizvi et al. (2015) which highlights the difficulties of implementing

Table 3. Findings of the thematic analysis

Dimension	Final Theme
Contextual	All: Involvement in all software development lifecycle (FT1) All: Experience in Scrum (FT2) All: Business needs (FT3) CS2 and CS3: Cost reduction (FT4) CS1: Capture of new talent (FT5) CS3: Knowledge of local market (FT6) CS3: Experience in distributed team structure (FT7)
Model	All: Dynamic adaptation (FT8) CS1: Mostly local teams (FT9) CS2: Distributed in close time zone (FT10) CS3: Distributed in different time zones (FT11)
Challenges	All: Communication, collaboration, and coordination issues (FT12) All: Lack of visibility (FT13) All: Shared components (FT14) All: Keep team spirit (FT15) CS3: Cultural differences (FT16) CS2 and CS3: Regional holidays (FT17)
Benefits	All: Better technological infrastructure (FT18) All: Monitor work progress (FT19) All: Knowledge management (FT20) CS2 and CS3: Creation of cross-functional teams (FT21) CS2 and CS3: Decentralize decision-making (FT22) CS2 and CS3: Documentation of processes (FT23)

Source: Authors

an agile strategy only in a specific area of software engineering. In all companies, employees already had experience in Scrum development. It was mentioned in CS3: "it is necessary that at least part of the group has experience to assist in the implementation and deployment to facilitate the dissemination of knowledge in the teams" (CS3, Product Owner). Therefore, it is evident that in CS3 it is essential the previous practical experience in the involvement in Scrum projects for the integration in distributed and large-scale Scrum teams.

Other reasons did not receive consensus in all companies. Cost reduction was not one of the main reasons for CS1, but the capture of new talent. CS3 identified other reasons such as knowledge of the local market and previous experience in adopting distributed teams. In fact, the needs of the business present themselves as the main factor that led these organizations to adopt a distributed model of software development. CS1 highlights the integration of software engineering professionals from Brazil into their teams due to the existence of new businesses in this market and the difficulties of hiring new talent locally. This seems to be an emerging factor as European companies, particularly from the United Kingdom, seek the Portuguese market for outsourcing their activities in search of talent and less impact on the daily management of their business (Cleverti, 2018). However, in CS2 and CS3 other motivational factors for this paradigm shift are also mentioned, such as cost reduction. As Choudhury et al. (2019) state, information technologies play a key role in the inclusion of distributed work teams. This approach can be a regular structure or serve as an adaptation in a given period, motivated by economic crisis factors. COVID-19 emerges as an external factor that has made companies' digitalization efforts even more relevant (Amankwah-Amoah et al., 2021). CS3 highlights that it had to make an additional investment in its teams in India to ensure acceptable access conditions to its remote test platforms in the face of the exponential increase in traffic.

The composition of the teams follows several principles such as maturity, diversity, and technical skills. In distributed teams, it is essential to value diversity (Hennel & Rosenkranz, 2017; Vergini, 2018). The team must be open-minded and appreciate the differences of ideas, perspectives, origins, and personalities of its members. In CS3 the importance of knowledge of the local market is also mentioned. The e-commerce solutions developed in CS3 are aimed at specific markets with specific convictions and beliefs. For example, in Nigeria, the existence of colorful solutions and alerts that are not acceptable to users in the European market is highly valued. Having team members with knowledge of this reality is essential for the commercial success of the applications. Also, in CS3, knowledge about team distribution practices is valued. Therefore, Scrum masters are chosen with this criterion as a fundamental reference.

Model Dimension

Regardless of the adopted model, in all the case studies the importance of dynamic adaptation to the characteristics of projects and teams was mentioned. In the companies participating in the study, it was reported the existence of Sprints lasting 2 weeks. This is the most used period as mentioned in Weinreich et al. (2015) and it enables us to follow the evolution of the development phase without too many context breaks. However, in CS3, it is also mentioned the existence of Sprints with 3 and 4 weeks in larger projects. However, despite the existing knowledge about large-scale agile frameworks, none of them is adopted because they generate excessive bureaucracy in a process that is intended to be agile. Thus, the adoption of large-scale frameworks does not emerge as a facilitating element for team communication and coordination due to its difficulty of adoption, especially in teams with little maturity in the software industry.

In CS1 most Scrum teams are local, although all members can potentially work in a distributed way. Team members are usually in the same physical location, with some members occasionally working in a distributed way. The exception to this rule was mainly visible in the period from March to May when due to COVID-19 all members were distributed. However, all members were in the same time zone. Even with members of other nationalities (i.e., Brazil) the time zone is not significant to create constraints. Therefore, various Scrum meetings are facilitated (i.e., daily scrums, scrum meetings). The challenges emerge essentially in terms of interactivity since the meetings have to be held by teleconference.

In CS2, there are two teams distributed but in which there is a relatively long and comprehensive period to interact. Daily scrum and sprint planning have a specific slot for their occurrence to allow the participation of all members. The model in CS3 is similar, but the teams are distributed in different time zones. This makes it difficult for employees to interact during working hours. In this regard, the Scrum Master of CS3 states “immediate clarification of work tasks is lost, but they are compensated with technological tools such as Skype and Zoom that allows solving impediments quickly and effectively”.

Challenges Dimension

The main challenges highlighted in the case studies are communication, collaboration, and coordination issues. It has been recognized that to continue obtaining the benefits of Scrum, its practices must be extended and modified, always aiming at improving communication and synchronizing the teams’ work. Hummel et al. (2013) highlight that a crucial issue for Scrum’s success is good communication among those involved, which in the case of geographically distributed teams can become a problem. In this dimension, CS2's Scrum Master highlights that the ideal is to provide a rich communication environment between teams through video conferencing, SMS, e-mail, chats, wikis, forums, etc. This technological diversity is also mentioned by Harris (2020) to ensure that those involved in the project feel closer and have a greater facility to hold the necessary meetings. In line with this vision, slow and unreliable means of communication should be avoided, which could hinder coordination, collaboration, and problem-solving. A collateral effect of this approach was emphasized in CS3. According to the Product Owner in CS3, there has been an increase in the importance of describing user stories that are much richer and more detailed. This is intended to minimize communication efforts to clarify items whose interpretation or available information suggests additional questions or clarification.

The loss of visibility of the project study and the delay of feedback is another problem identified. One way to combat this situation is through the adoption of management structures in which the division of roles is clearer. This does not mean lower levels of collaboration, but only a greater formalization of roles, which will also allow the welcoming of new collaborators. The definition of user stories is a work that assumes greater relevance. It has been accepted in all case studies that the role of the Product Owner in a distributed model has to be re-checked. The client's needs must be clear to the technical team from the beginning of the project, as the necessary clarification and rectification efforts will have a greater effort. CS3 refers to the importance of having a centralized backlog with themes not yet addressed to any of the teams. This backlog should have global access promoted through a backlog management tool that has this functionality. Walimbe (2016) advocates that a centralized backlog is a tool to maintain the overall vision of the project, and should be discussed constantly with the business area, as it can lead to reprioritization or the creation of new teams. Furthermore, it is important to use tools that counteract the discussion of problems (Talukder et al., 2017). However, CS1 states that this more decisive role of the Product Owner does not inhibit developers from coming up with solutions to overcome possible challenges, or even more efficient ways of building a solution. Also, the Product Owner assumes a greater relevance in prioritizing the tasks of the backlog. This task should always be aligned with what the company needs within the strategic planning performed. Furthermore, the correct prioritization of the backlog tasks will allow increasing the visibility on the project development that assumes a greater relevance in distributed environments.

Maintaining the cohesion of the teams is a key element for the success of the projects (Bach-Dabrowska, 2014; Lindsjorn et al., 2016). In Scrum environments, the daily meeting provides a significant contribution for all members to participate and increases the visibility of the project. This approach is a contribution to trust and team spirit (Söderback et al., 2015). However, the alignment of teams according to the same team zone is a factor that helps in building team cohesion. Therefore, CS3 reports difficulties in the teams in which members with significant cultural differences participate. CS3 Product Owner reports the difficulty of some members in accepting the equal participation of women in their teams when visiting clients or in team-building initiatives. The development of more personal relationships emerges as a challenge. CS3 also reported difficulties in aligning working weekdays between Portugal and Egypt, as the beginning of the week in Portugal is on Monday, while in Egypt is on Sunday. There were also difficulties in aligning workdays related to regional holidays that are often not known by the whole team.

Benefits Dimension

The adoption of distributed Scrum teams has contributed to greater support from the top management to the technological infrastructures that proved to be fundamental with the emergence of COVID-19. The Product Owner of CS2 notes that "the companies that bet on distributed Scrum were better prepared for the collaborative efforts of remote work and digitalization that emerged with COVID-19". Work progress monitoring was also an area of greater relevance as it is a key element for increasing team cohesion (Hidalgo, 2019). Furthermore, it was also mentioned in all the cases of study of the attributions given by distributed Scrum for the promotion of knowledge management in organizations. This observation is in accordance with the results of the study conducted by Andriyani et al. (2017) who consider that the Scrum methodology is an appropriate space for knowledge creation and conversion. Moreover, the study conducted by Abdul et al. (2017) and Sjödin et al. (2020) reveals the potential of Scrum as a stimulus for innovation in products and services. It was mentioned in CS3: "I believe that the distributed Scrum methodology adopted in the company stimulates teamwork, collaboration, and the behavior of knowledge" (Scrum Master, CS3). The influence of knowledge management on the use of Scrum arises, because during all processes of execution of the framework ceremonies, the interaction between individuals is the most practiced, which stimulates knowledge exchange. CS1 refers to this level: "the migration to the distributed environment has raised some resistance among our younger employees since they felt inhibited to participate in the project's remote activities" (Scrum Master, CS1). However, this situation does not invalidate the role of knowledge management in distributed Scrum but indicates greater training needs.

Some specific benefits have also been identified in CS2 and CS3. With the adoption of distributed Scrum, the relevance of cross-functional teams becomes more evident. However, people are not necessarily cross-functional but grow with this profile throughout their maturity process. CS3 at this level launches the following recommendation: "start with a team of several talents and then organically build that team to be individually cross-functional" (Scrum Master, CS3). Ideally, all developers should be able to assume all functions. However, this is not always possible, but at least it is intended that each developer should be able to perform some more tasks. Several benefits associated with the adoption of cross-functional teams are greater diversification in the development of solutions, higher quality, and greater learning capacity (De Oliveira et al., 2016; Jeske & Calvard, 2020).

The adoption of distributed Scrum also contributes to the local empowerment of teams through a more decentralized decision process. As stated in the CS2 Scrum Master, the resolution of impediments has become a crucial element to achieve the project goals. Finally, benefits were also identified in the documentation of the processes. This outcome appears to be in contradiction with the principles of agile but is in line with the conclusions of the study conducted by Stapel et al. (2011), in which it is highlighted that projects with distributed human resources may require more documentation to avoid any issues related to misunderstandings of scope.

FUTURE RESEARCH DIRECTIONS

Software companies have been looking for new ways to manage teams in a distributed working environment. Progressively the demand for talent in the software field involves hiring and reorganizing teams in different physical spaces. This process has been accelerated with the COVID-19 pandemic which has reduced local interactions and increased the need to think about new processes and technologies to support remote work (Ma, 2021; Moens et al., 2022). The challenge of Scrum scaling has been studied in the literature especially considering a case study approach since the context in which this activity occurs is crucial to understand its impacts. As reported by Rigby et al. (2016), there are numerous success and failure stories in Scrum scaling. This is a challenge that is still very much present, and in this sense, several frameworks have been launched to support agile activity on a large scale. We highlight the emergence of frameworks such as Scaled Agile Framework (SAFe), Scrum@Scale (SaS), Large Scale Scrum (LeSS), Nexus, Disciplined Agile Delivery (DAD), among others. Furthermore, in the adoption of these frameworks it is reported success stories but difficulties in adjusting the framework to the teams' characteristics and projects' needs. Therefore, one area for future research has been to explore how these frameworks can be effectively built in the organizational context (Beecham et al., 2021; Edison et al., 2022; Marinho et al., 2021). Furthermore, it is recognized that motivational management practices are important to achieve a project management model that meets the organization's challenges. At this level, there have been studies that look at the role of Management 3.0 in the context of distributed and larger teams (Almeida & Espinheira, 2022).

Software development is characterized as a social process in which many different participants are involved. Therefore, an organization cannot just look to its internals, but must think of ways to integrate the knowledge of users, suppliers, external consultants, etc. As Ghobadi & Mathiassen (2016) acknowledge, the integration of this knowledge is critical to achieving project success. Established software development methods offer little help in managing the complex interactions between stakeholders. This integration is often seen as a technical problem rather than a social problem, which is compounded by these social interactions being dynamic. Social interactions are created, sustained, and changed throughout the software development process (Espinosa-Curiel et al., 2018). Therefore, it becomes evident that projects require effective interprofessional and interorganizational cooperation. It can be concluded that the success of projects lies in their ability to integrate diverse knowledge and specialties. The future challenge is to find ways to integrate this knowledge in teams that are geographically dispersed, and in which trust among the various actors is built more slowly. This challenge is increased by the temporary nature of the projects, which makes information processing more vulnerable and introduces barriers to information dissemination.

CONCLUSION

The physical separation of software development teams brings a series of challenges that are typically presented as key factors of Scrum such as direct interaction with the customer and face-to-face communication between teams. Therefore, to continue obtaining the benefits of Scrum, these practices must be extended and modified, always aiming to improve communication and synchronize the teams' work. Several motivational factors emerge in the implementation of Scrum in a distributed environment such as the need for global resources, cost reduction, or the advantage of being close to the global market. There is not a single typology for the application of distributed Scrum model. This study identified three alternatives: (i) teams are collocated and share the same physical space with some exceptions during the project life cycle; (ii) distributed with full overlapping hours, in which the employees have a significant number of hours of the day to interact; and (iii) distributed with partial overlapping hours, in which the existence of more than three hours of difference between the teams makes the interaction during working hours difficult.

Several practical challenges emerge in the implementation of distributed Scrum. Communication, collaboration, and coordination issues stand out due to the geographical dispersion of the team members. Maintaining cohesion and team spirit is a challenge for all members to have a feeling of presence in the project and organization. Risks may also arise from an incorrect, incomplete, or outdated view of the project status. Other challenges may also arise from the location of distributed teams, namely cultural and regional differences and holidays which may also pose new challenges to the joint work of the teams.

The implementation of distributed Scrum brings benefits to organizations and has contributed to the offer of better technological infrastructure and a greater focus on monitoring the work progress so that all team members can have visibility on the development of the project. The distributed environment facilitates the creation of cross-functional teams and the development of knowledge management practices. Furthermore, the decision process becomes more decentralized. Finally, greater importance is given to documentation to reduce the emergence of impediments.

This study offers both theoretical and practical contributions. From the theoretical perspective, this chapter extends the work presented by Walimbe (2016) that discussed the communication issues and propose a set of strategies to mitigate these difficulties. However, that study does not explore the reasons that motivated the organizations to adopt distributed Scrum and the different organization typologies of the distributed Scrum teams. On contrary, this chapter explored different approaches for the implementation of distributed Scrum and realize the difficulties, challenges, and benefits of its adoption. From the practical perspective, the results of this study are relevant mainly for software engineering companies that are taking the first steps of migrating from their traditional Scrum to a distributed environment. Despite being three Portuguese companies, the issues raised can easily be considered in various international contexts, considering that distributed Scrum considers geographically distributed and multicultural teams. This study has some limitations. First, a case study approach is adopted, hence its generalization is difficult considering that software companies and their teams have their own specificities. Initially, it was considered the involvement of eight enterprises, but it was found to be an excessive number due to the redundancy of information between them and also due to the greater difficulty of participation of the companies in academic studies due to the COVID-19 pandemic. In this sense, it is suggested in the future to complement this study with a quantitative analysis that allows exploring the challenges of migration to distributed Scrum considering the size of each organization and the degree of maturity of these teams. Furthermore, the specific challenges of team migration to certain countries were not explored. Consequently, the relevance of the cultural issue would need to be better explored considering several specific markets.

REFERENCES

Abdul, A., Bass, J. M., Ghavimi, H., & Adam, P. (2017). Product Innovation with Scrum: A Longitudinal Case Study. *Proceedings of the International Conference on Information Society (i-Society 2017)*, 1-6. 10.23919/i-Society.2017.8354664

Abu-Arqoub, I. A., & Alserhan, F. A. (2019). Non-verbal barriers to effective intercultural communication. *Utopía y Praxis Latinoamericana*, *24*(5), 307–316.

Almeida, F., & Espinheira, E. (2022). Adoption of Large-Scale Scrum Practices through the Use of Management 3.0. *Informatics (MDPI)*, *9*(1), 1–14. doi:10.3390/informatics9010020

Almeida, F., Miranda, E., & Falcão, J. (2019). Challenges and facilitators practices for knowledge management in large-scale scrum teams. *Journal of Information Technology Case and Application Research*, *21*(2), 90–102. doi:10.1080/15228053.2019.1637087

Amankwah-Amoah, J., Khan, Z., Wood, G., & Knight, G. (2021). COVID-19 and digitalization: The great acceleration. *Journal of Business Research*, *136*, 602–611. doi:10.1016/j.jbusres.2021.08.011 PMID:34538980

Andriyani, Y., Hoda, R., & Amor, R. (2017). Understanding Knowledge Management in Agile Software Development Practice. *Proceedings of the International Conference on Knowledge Science, Engineering and Management*, 195-207. 10.1007/978-3-319-63558-3_17

Bach-Dabrowska, I., & Pawlewski, P. (2014). Optimization model of agile team's cohesion. *Procedia Computer Science*, *35*, 1577–1585. doi:10.1016/j.procs.2014.08.241

Beck, K. (2001). *The Agile Manifesto*. Agile Alliance. Retrieved from http://agilemanifesto.org/

Beecham, S., Clear, T., Lal, R., & Noll, J. (2021). Do scaling agile frameworks address global software development risks? An empirical study. *Journal of Systems and Software*, *171*, 1–30. doi:10.1016/j.jss.2020.110823

Bosch-Sijtsema, P., Ruohomäki, V., & Vartiainen, M. (2009). Knowledge Work Productivity in Distributed Teams. *Journal of Knowledge Management*, *13*(6), 533–546. doi:10.1108/13673270910997178

Carter, J. (2020, June 24). *Virtual Software Development Teams: 4 Challenges to Overcome* [Web log message]. Retrieved from https://techbeacon.com/app-dev-testing/virtual-software-development-teams-4-challenges-overcome

Casey, V. (2010). Virtual software team project management. *Journal of the Brazilian Computer Society*, *16*(2), 83–96. doi:10.1007/13173-010-0013-3

Chakravorty, T., Chakraborty, S., & Jigeesh, N. (2014). Analysis of Agile testing attributes for faster time to Market: Context of Manufacturing sector related IT projects. *Procedia Economics and Finance*, *11*, 536–552. doi:10.1016/S2212-5671(14)00219-6

Choudhury, P. R., Larson, B. Z., & Foroughi, C. (2019). Is It Time to Let Employees Work from Anywhere? *Harvard Business Review*. Retrieved from https://hbr.org/2019/08/is-it-time-to-let-employees-work-from-anywhere

Cleverti. (2018). *Brexit & IT: Why Portugal is Top Outsourcing Choice*. Retrieved from https://www.cleverti.com/blog/brexit-and-it-why-portugal-is-outsourcing-destination-of-choice

De Oliveira, E. A., Pimenta, M. L., Hilletofth, P., & Eriksson, D. (2016). Integration through cross-functional teams in a service company. *European Business Review*, *28*(4), 405–430. doi:10.1108/EBR-01-2016-0014

Dikert, K., Paasivaara, M., & Lassenius, C. (2016). Challenges and success factors for large-scale agile transformations: A systematic literature review. *Journal of Systems and Software*, *119*, 87–108. doi:10.1016/j.jss.2016.06.013

Edison, H., Wang, X., & Conboy, K. (2022). Comparing Methods for Large-Scale Agile Software Development: A Systematic Literature Review. *IEEE Transactions on Software Engineering*, *48*(8), 2709–2731. doi:10.1109/TSE.2021.3069039

Espinosa-Curiel, I. E., Rodríguez-Jacobo, J., Vázquez-Alfaro, E., Fernández-Zepeda, J. A., & Fajardo-Delgado, D. (2018). Analysis of the changes in communication and social interactions during the transformation of a traditional team into an agile team. *Journal of Software (Malden, MA)*, *30*(9), e1946. doi:10.1002mr.1946

Ghobadi, S., & Mathiassen, L. (2016). Perceived barriers to effective knowledge sharing in agile software teams. *Information Systems Journal*, *26*(2), 95–125. doi:10.1111/isj.12053

Hajjdiab, H., Taleb, A. S., & Ali, J. (2012). An Industrial Case Study for Scrum Adoption. *Journal of Software*, *7*(1), 237–242. doi:10.4304/jsw.7.1.237-242

Harris, C. (2020). *Distributed scrum: How to manage a remote scrum team*. Retrieved from https://www.atlassian.com/agile/scrum/distributed-scrum

Heagney, J. (2016). *Fundamentals of Project Management*. Amacom.

Hennel, P., & Rosenkranz, C. (2017). Team Diversity and Performance – How Agile Practices and Psychological Safety Interact. *Proceedings of the International Conference on Information Systems*, 1-12.

Hidalgo, E. S. (2019). Adapting the scrum framework for agile project management in science: Case study of a distributed research initiative. *Heliyon*, *5*(3), 1–32. doi:10.1016/j.heliyon.2019.e01447 PMID:30976706

Hummel, M., Rosenkranz, C., & Holten, R. (2013). The Role of Communication in Agile Systems Development. *Business & Information Systems Engineering*, *5*(5), 343–355. doi:10.100712599-013-0282-4

Ibraheem, A. (2018). *Project and functional managers: Coopetition paradox and leadership impact*. Available at: https://uu.diva-portal.org/smash/get/diva2:1228648/FULLTEXT01.pdf

Jeske, D., & Calvard, T. S. (2020). A review of the literature on cross-functional integration (2010–2020): Trends and recommendations. *The International Journal of Organizational Analysis*.

Josh, L. (2020). A Four-Pillared Holistic Model for Improving Performance in Engineering Virtual Project Teams. *Engineering Management Journal*, *32*(2), 107–119. doi:10.1080/10429247.2019.1672409

Kostin, D., & Strode, D. (2022). Effective communication in globally distributed Scrum teams. *ACIS 2022 Proceedings, 5*, 1-13. https://aisel.aisnet.org/acis2022/5

Lee, G., & Xia, W. (2010). Toward agile: An integrated analysis of quantitative and qualitative field data. *Management Information Systems Quarterly*, *34*(1), 87–114. doi:10.2307/20721416

Lent, B., & Pinkowska, M. (2012). Soft skills needed in the ICT project management – classification and maturity level assessment. *International Journal of Applied Systemic Studies*, *4*(3), 168–185. doi:10.1504/IJASS.2012.051133

Lindsjorn, Y., Sjoberg, D., Dingsoyr, T., Bergersen, G. R., & Dybä, T. (2016). Teamwork quality and project success in software development: A survey of agile development teams. *Journal of Systems and Software*, *122*, 274–286. doi:10.1016/j.jss.2016.09.028

Lumseyfai, J. (2020). A Four-Pillared Holistic Model for Improving Performance in Engineering Virtual Project Teams. *Engineering Management Journal*, *32*(2), 107–119. doi:10.1080/10429247.2019.1672409

Ma, J. (2021). Telework Triggered by Epidemic: Effective Communication Improvement of Telecommuting in Workgroups during COVID-19. *American Journal of Industrial and Business Management*, *11*(2), 202–214. doi:10.4236/ajibm.2021.112013

Marinho, M., Camara, R., & Sampaio, S. (2021). Toward Unveiling How SAFe Framework Supports Agile in Global Software Development. *IEEE Access : Practical Innovations, Open Solutions*, *9*, 109671–109692. doi:10.1109/ACCESS.2021.3101963

Miles, M. B., Huberman, A. M., & Saldana, J. (2019). *Qualitative Data Analysis: A Methods Sourcebook*. SAGE Publications.

Moens, E., Lippens, L., Sterkens, P., Weytjens, J., & Baert, S. (2022). The COVID-19 crisis and telework: A research survey on experiences, expectations and hopes. *The European Journal of Health Economics*, *23*(4), 729–753. doi:10.100710198-021-01392-z PMID:34761337

Morrison-Smith, S., & Ruiz, J. (2020). Challenges and Barriers in Virtual Teams: A Literature Review. *SN Applied Sciences*, *2*(1096), 1–33. doi:10.100742452-020-2801-5

Mundra, A., Misra, S., & Dhawale, C. A. (2013). Practical Scrum-Scrum Team: Way to Produce Successful and Quality Software. *Proceedings of the 13th International Conference on Computational Science and Its Applications*, 119-123. 10.1109/ICCSA.2013.25

Ockerman, S. (2020, June 1). *3 Things Virtual Teams Need from a Scrum Master* [Web log message]. Retrieved from https://www.scrum.org/resources/blog/3-things-virtual-teams-need-scrum-master

Petrova, S. (2019). *Adopting Agile: The Latest Reports About The Popular Mindset*. Retrieved from https://adevait.com/blog/remote-work/adopting-agile-the-latest-reports-about-the-popular-mindset

Pikkarainen, M., Haikara, J., Salo, O., Abrahamsson, P., & Still, J. (2008). The impact of agile practices on communication in software development. *Empirical Software Engineering*, *13*(3), 303–337. doi:10.100710664-008-9065-9

Queirós, A., Faria, D., & Almeida, F. (2017). Strengths and Limitation of Qualitative and Quantitative Research Methods. *European Journal of Education Studies*, *3*(9), 369–387.

Rigby, D. K., Sutherland, J., & Takeuchi, H. (2016). Embracing Agile. *Harvard Business Review*. Retrieved from https://hbr.org/2016/05/embracing-agile

Rizvi, B., Bagheri, E., & Gasevic, D. (2015). A systematic review of distributed Agile software engineering. *Journal of Software (Malden, MA)*, *27*(10), 723–762. doi:10.1002mr.1718

Rothman, J., & Kilby, M. (2019). *From Chaos to Successful Distributed Agile Teams: Collaborate to Deliver*. Practical Ink.

Sabine, D. (2016, December 20). *A Group of Geographically Distributed Staff is NOT a Scrum Team* [Web log message]. Retrieved from https://www.agileadvice.com/2016/12/20/scrum-master/group-geographically-distributed-staff-not-scrum-team/

Schwaber, K., & Beedle, M. (2002). *Agile software development with SCRUM*. Prentice-Hall. Retrieved from https://billlewistraining.com/wp-content/uploads/2017/02/PMP-Agile-Study-Materials.pdf

Shah, S. (2016). *Challenges When Using Scrum in Globally Distributed Teams* [Graduate Thesis]. Harrisburg University of Science and Technology. Retrieved from https://digitalcommons.harrisburgu.edu/

Sjödin, D., Parida, V., Kohtamäki, M., & Wincent, J. (2020). An agile co-creation process for digital servitization: A micro-service innovation approach. *Journal of Business Research*, *112*, 478–491. doi:10.1016/j.jbusres.2020.01.009

Söderback, J., Hrastinski, S., & Öberg, L. M. (2015). *Using Distributed Scrum for Supporting Online Collaborative Learning: A Qualitative Descriptive Study of Students Perceptions*. Retrieved from https://core.ac.uk/display/36346620

Stapel, K., Knauss, E., Schneider, K., & Zazworka, N. (2011). FLOW Mapping: Planning and Managing Communication in Distributed Teams. *Proceedings of the IEEE Sixth International Conference on Global Software Engineering*, 190-199. 10.1109/ICGSE.2011.9

Sutherland, J. (2014). *Scrum: The Art of Doing Twice the Work in Half the Time*. Currency.

Tahir, M. (2019). The effect of project manager's soft skills on success of project in the construction industry. *International Journal of Applied Research in Social Sciences*, *1*(5), 197–203.

Takkunen, M. (2014). *Scrum Implementation in a Virtual Team Environment* [MSc Thesis]. Helsinki Metropolia University of Applied Sciences. Retrieved from https://core.ac.uk/download/pdf/38111804.pdf

Talukder, A., Senapathi, M., & Buchan, J. (2017). Coordination in Distributed Agile Software Development: A Systematic Review. *Proceedings of the Australasian Conference on Information Systems*, 1-12.

Vergini, S. (2018). *Key Factors to Succeed at Managing Distributed Agile Teams*. Retrieved from https://www.knowledgehut.com/blog/agile/key-factors-to-succeed-agile-teams

Walimbe, P. (2016). *To Overcome Communication Challenges in Distributed/Virtual Scrum Teams* [MSc Thesis]. Harrisburg University of Science and Technology. Retrieved from https://digitalcommons.harrisburgu.edu/pmgt_dandt/4

Weinreich, R., Neumann, N., Riedel, R., & Müller, E. (2015). Scrum as Method for Agile Project Management Outside of the Product Development Area. *Proceedings of the IFIP International Conference on Advances in Production Management Systems (APMS)*, 565-572. 10.1007/978-3-319-22756-6_69

Yin, R. K. (2017). *Case Study Research and Applications: Design and Methods*. SAGE Publications.

ADDITIONAL READING

Adelakun, O., & Iyamu, T. (2021). Translation of Activities in a Global Virtual Teams Software Development: Agile vs. Waterfall. *Journal of Cases on Information Technology*, *23*(4), 1–18. doi:10.4018/JCIT.20211001.oa11

Alzoabi, Z. (2014). Agile Software: Body of Knowledge. In I. Management Association (Eds.), Software Design and Development: Concepts, Methodologies, Tools, and Applications (pp. 96-116). IGI Global.

Arumugam, C., & Vaidyanathan, S. (2022). Agile Team Measurement to Review the Performance in Global Software Development. In I. Management Association (Ed.), Research Anthology on Agile Software, Software Development, and Testing (pp. 2015-2025). IGI Global. doi:10.4018/978-1-6684-3702-5.ch096

Gustavsson, T., Berntzen, M., & Stray, V. (2022). Changes to team autonomy in large-scale software development: A multiple case study of Scaled Agile Framework (SAFe) implementations. *International Journal of Information Systems and Project Management*, *10*(1), 29–46. doi:10.12821/ijispm100102

Khalid, A., Butt, S. A., Jamal, T., & Gochhait, S. (2020). Agile Scrum Issues at Large-Scale Distributed Projects: Scrum Project Development At Large. *International Journal of Software Innovation*, *8*(2), 85–94. doi:10.4018/IJSI.2020040106

Ng, P. (2016). Rapid Agile Transformation at a Large IT Organization. In I. Ghani, D. Jawawi, S. Dorairaj, & A. Sidky (Eds.), *Emerging Innovations in Agile Software Development* (pp. 85–102). IGI Global. doi:10.4018/978-1-4666-9858-1.ch005

Salma, F., & Gómez, J. M. (2021). Challenges and Trends of Agile. In M. Mora, J. Gómez, R. O'Connor, & A. Buchalcevová (Eds.), *Balancing Agile and Disciplined Engineering and Management Approaches for IT Services and Software Products* (pp. 189–204). IGI Global. doi:10.4018/978-1-7998-4165-4.ch010

Uludag, Ö., Philipp, P., Putta, A., Paasivaara, M., Lassenius, C., & Matthes, F. (2022). Revealing the state of the art of large-scale agile development research: A systematic mapping study. *Journal of Systems and Software*, *194*, 1–43. doi:10.1016/j.jss.2022.111473

Vogel, J., & Telesko, R. (2020). Derivation of an Agile Method Construction Set to Optimize the Software Development Process. *Journal of Cases on Information Technology*, *22*(3), 19–34. doi:10.4018/JCIT.2020070102

KEY TERMS AND DEFINITIONS

Knowledge Sharing: Degree to which the different groups of project members are well informed about each other's areas of expertise and can disseminate knowledge among them.

Management 3.0: It is a collaborative and humanized management model, which elects the employee as the main asset of an organization in search of better business results.

Project Manager: Professional responsible for the planning, execution, and monitoring of a project.

Risk Management: Defining and implementing procedures to assess the risks faced by an organization, with the goal of taking appropriate preventive measures.

Sponsor: Person or organization that you represent and who has the "last word" (i.e., the main authority of the project). The sponsor provides the financial resources to pay for the project and its execution, as well as resolving problems, scope changes, and approving important deliverables.

Stakeholder: Individuals or groups that have an interest or some aspect of rights or ownership in the project, may contribute to the form of knowledge or support, or may impact or be impacted by the project.

Chapter 13
The Growth of Cyberbullying at Workplace After COVID-19:
The Problems of New Forms of Communication

Blanca Martínez Marcos
Universidad de Salamanca, Spain

ABSTRACT

Internal communication in organizations is one of the fundamental pillars for their correct development. Forms of communication were very scarce until the incorporation of ICTs in the labor market, but the rise of remote work has meant a new opening towards new forms of communication although also the emergence of new risks and problems that can have a very negative impact and that, as of today, have not been eradicated. Communication between the company's interest groups can have many benefits and translate into a large competitive advantage, but these new communication channels have also turned into a new tool through which new forms of harassment can be carried out (cyberbullying). In Spain, as all around the world, there are more and more cases of cyberbullying and very little existing legislation, leading to it becoming a serious problem that still has not been given sufficient visibility.

INTRODUCTION

Organizations, whatever their size, are composed of a series of pillars that are absolutely necessary for such an organization to be able to grow prosperously in the medium/long term: the mission (what the organization wants), the vision (where it is heading) and the values (what are the ideological characteristics of the organization's human capital). These three pillars make up what is known as the organizational culture and are the raison d'être of the organization (Santander Universidades, 2022).

DOI: 10.4018/978-1-6684-7353-5.ch013

On the other hand, organizations are made up of stakeholders (managers, employees, customers, suppliers, shareholders, government, society...). Personal identification and acceptance of the human capital that makes up the organization's stakeholders with the corporate culture is one of the key points for the correct functioning and growth of the organization (González Masip, 2018).

It is logical to think that the purpose of the creation of a for-profit organization is to achieve the greatest economic gain and the greatest possible growth and expansion, however, the practices carried out throughout its history to achieve these objectives are key to achieving stability over time and market leadership.

Financing methods, production processes, technology, management style, geographic location, market niche... are strategies that, with greater or lesser difficulty, can be copied by other organizations. The difference that can turn into a true competitive advantage with respect to others is its human capital and, in order to attract and retain the best human capital, human resources practices must be implemented that are adapted both to the organizational culture and to the main characteristics and demands that arise or may arise from the people that make up the organization (Danvila-del Valle & Sastre-Castillo, 2007, pp. 145-187).

In order to be able to interweave all these variables and be able to anticipate problems or new developments that may arise, one of the most important things that must exist at all levels (both stakeholders and departments in the organization) is communication. Organizations are "living organisms" that need a constant relationship with their stakeholders.

Communication in an organization can be external (mainly aimed at reinforcing and projecting its image with external stakeholders such as: suppliers, customers, investors...) or internal (as its name suggests, it takes place within the company through both formal and informal channels) and that will be the form of communication on which we will focus in this chapter.

Following the Covid-19 pandemic, many organizations were forced to introduce teleworking as a temporary measure - there were already organizations that applied this form of work, but the percentage was very small. The eradication of physical presence in the workplace meant that the forms and channels of communication had to be adapted to this new way of working and, therefore, it was necessary to resort to the use of ICTs in order to have the most efficient communication channels (Pérez Pérez et al., 2004, pp. 11-28).

This research project will carry out a study on internal communication, specifically on certain negative practices (cyberbullying) that have arisen as a result of the increased use of ICTs as the main means of communication, with a special increase during the Covid-19 pandemic and in the post-pandemic period.

BACKGROUND

Communication in the Organization

As mentioned above, communication is one of the most important elements within an organization, if there is good communication, there are many functions that are much easier to perform: assignment of tasks, conflict resolution, anticipation of possible problems, support and rapprochement with the people who make up the organization, generation of a better working environment, etc.

Communication processes allow the organization to maintain coordination between its different parts and thus achieve its essential characteristic: being a system (Katz & Khan, 1986).

It being such an important element, it should also be understood that its variants are practically infinite, both those contemplated within the organizational structure and the new ones that may arise as the organization changes in structure, size, departmental composition, expansion, internationalization or hiring of new employees.

It should be noted that, regardless of the classification set out below, the communications that are carried out may be written or oral.

First of all, a distinction must be made between formal and informal communication. This differentiation is made according to the channels used to carry out any type of communication.

- Formal communication refers to that which is produced using the channels pre-established by the company for communication to take place between the stakeholders of the organization (whether between employees regardless of their hierarchical level, between managers and suppliers, between employees and customers, etc.).
- Informal communication occurs when communication is carried out outside the company's formal channels. It may be information with a solid foundation, a rumor, or a piece of news that is not well verified. Generally, these are communications that can generate uncertainty, and, in addition, are outside of the organization's control, which is the main reason why companies always try to combat this type of communication channels (National Institute of Safety and Hygiene at Work, 2007, pp. 3-5).

A distinction can also be made between external and internal communication: as the name itself indicates, if the communication is carried out within the organization it will be internal communication and, otherwise it is external communication.

Thirdly, we can speak of vertical or horizontal communication:

- Vertical communication can be downward or upward and occurs when communication takes place between people at different hierarchical levels in the organization. If it occurs from a superior to an employee, it will be downward (usually the most common) and if it occurs the other way around the communication is upward.
- Horizontal communication occurs when communication takes place between people at the same hierarchical level (regardless of whether they are in different departments, if the hierarchical level is the same, communication is horizontal) (National Institute of Safety and Hygiene at Work, 2007, p. 4).

In addition to the above classifications, just as organizations must adapt to the changes and developments that arise in their environment, communication must also adapt to these changes to remain effective and efficient (Vallejo Peña & Pardo Molina, 2009, pp. 148-169).

It should be borne in mind that, until relatively recently, the only known form of performing work was physically at the work center assigned to each worker. With the emergence and development of ICT, especially in the last decade (and with an unprecedented increase as a result of the pandemic), remote work has become possible, and some companies even have the option of hybrid work, combining some days of physically being at the workplace and other days of teleworking remotely. Logically, these new ways of performing work activities have also changed the forms of internal communication in the company (Vázquez, 2022).

It is precisely for this reason that, since the entry of ICTs in the workplace, a distinction must also be made between communication that takes place in the physical workplace and that which takes place through ICTs in virtual channels without the people who carry out these communications having to be in the workplace in a physical form.

This "virtualization" of communication has made communication much faster and able to take place from practically any geographical location at any time of the day, but this new forms of communication also present a series of disadvantages and dangers that pose new challenges for organizations to confront (Baeza Botía, 2009).

New forms of Internal Communication Through ICTs

Although ICTs have been present in the workplace for several decades, not all organizations have had the economic capacity, infrastructure, or desire to incorporate them into their business activities.

In particular, with regard to internal company communication, there was greater reluctance to use ICTs. Companies with a presence in several countries or with several headquarters or work centers in the same country were the most likely to use new technologies as a method of internal communication. On the other hand, another type of companies that have also used ICT for many years have been small and medium-sized enterprises dedicated to the export of goods to other countries (Ueki et al., 2005).

Generally, the fastest, most secure, private and efficient way to carry out this type of communication is to create an intranet for the organization.

The intranet is a completely private network that allows to share resources, information, perform tasks and have a constant communication between users belonging to the same organization or linked to it. In most cases, the intranets of the organizations are monitored by the people in charge of them and, in this way, it is possible to prevent cybernetic attacks, improper uses of the same, correct computer errors... (Telefónica Ecuador, 2020).

However, apart from intranets, there are also other new forms of internal communication in some companies, such as instant messaging applications (Whatsapp, Wechat, Telegram...) or social networks (LinkedIn, Facebook, Twitter, Instagram...) (IMF, 2013).

All these forms of communication, from a functional point of view, should only present advantages, however, this is not the case since there are users who do not use these methods of communication properly and even use them for negative purposes such as cyberbullying.

When the Covid-19 pandemic forced to restrict to the maximum the presence in the workplace, there were companies that were already accustomed to the use of this type of tools in their work activity and had no organizational problems (since they already had a structure and technological and economic resources sufficient to adapt to this unforeseen event) but there were many other companies that had to "update" in a very fast and chaotic way without knowing how to use these resources (ElDerecho.com, 2020).

When there is no well-established usage policy and users are not well informed and trained to use this kind of tools, the most serious problems can arise.

On the other hand, although it is not yet widespread among organizations, it is important to highlight the role of artificial intelligence, which, according to some studies, is here to stay.

AI is going to be like the new electricity, said Javier Zamora, a tenured professor in the Department of Information Systems at IESE Business School in Spain. It is a general-purpose technology, that is, it has the ability to radically change the industry. It allows you to do things that were not possible before. More than a threat, from the communication sector we should see it as an ally. (Oxean, 2020)

Some of the benefits it can bring are:

- Make immediate analysis of information and trends.
- Produce better metrics for daily work.
- Perform ultra-targeted communications.
- Train new professionals in scale in best practices.
- Respond quickly to a communication crisis, following established parameters and without the sieve of human emotions

The opportunities offered by AI and big data in communication are many, but so are the challenges. Therefore, in companies it will be increasingly necessary to collaborate between communication, technology and legal departments (Aced, 2022).

MAIN FOCUS OF THE CHAPTER

Violence in the Workplace: Special Mention of Harassment

Violence in the workplace stems from a combination of causes relating to people, the work climate and working conditions, as well as the forms of interaction between the different stakeholders in the company, especially between employees and managers.

It can take two different forms: physical violence or psychological violence. Physical violence seeks, directly or indirectly, to cause physical harm to the victim. Psychological violence is produced when a person or group of people exercise modal or verbal, alternating or continuous recurrent, and sustained mistreatment over time of workers seeking to destabilize, isolate, destroy their reputation, deteriorate their self-esteem and diminish their working capacity in order to degrade him or her and trying to eliminate him or her from the position that person occupies.

Based on this categorization, it is possible to distinguish between workplace harassment, occupational violence (type I, II, III), sexual harassment, harassment based on sex or discriminatory harassment (National Institute of Safety and Health at Work, 2012).

Workplace harassment is one that occurs when there is an exposure to behaviors of psychological violence, directed repeatedly and prolonged over time; towards one or more people by another/s who act fren to that/s from a position of power (not necessarily hierarchical). This exposure occurs within the framework of a working relationship and poses a significant risk to health (National Institute of Safety and Hygiene at Work, 2009, p. 3).

Within the category of occupational violence, we distinguish:

Type I Violence. This group is characterized because those who carry out the violent actions have no legitimate relationship of treatment with the victim.

Type II Violence. In these cases, there is some kind of professional relationship between the perpetrator of the violent act and the victim.

Type III Violence. In this type of violence, the perpetrator of it has some type of labor involvement with the affected place or with a specific worker in that place (Unión Social Obrera, 2020).

With regard to sexual harassment, European Communities Recommendation 92/131 of 27 November 1991 concerning the dignity of women and men at work states that conduct of a sexual nature or other conduct based on sex which affects the dignity of women and men at work, including the conduct of superiors and colleagues, it is unacceptable if:

Such conduct is unwanted, unreasonable and offensive to the person who is the object of it;

- The refusal or subjection of a person to such conduct by employers or employees (including superiors and colleagues) is used explicitly or implicitly as a basis for a decision which has an effect on that person's access to vocational training and employment, on the continuation of such conduct, salary or any other decisions relating to employment and/or;
- Such conduct creates an intimidating, hostile and humiliating work environment for the person being targeted; and that such conduct may, in all circumstances, be contrary to the principle of equal treatment. (National Institute of Safety and Hygiene at Work, 2000, p. 2).

The 1991 Code of Practice on Measures to Combat Sexual Harassment adopted by the Commission of the European Communities covers sexual conduct in a broad sense, noting that conduct of a sexual nature includes verbal or non-verbal or annoying physical conduct.(EUR-Lex, 2007).

The most recent and widespread definition in Spain, according to Law 3/2007, is any behavior, verbal or physical, of a sexual nature that has the purpose or effect of violating the dignity of a person, in particular when it creates an intimidating, degrading or offensive environment (Organic Law 3/2007, art. 7.1).

The behaviors that can be considered sexual harassment can be classified as follows:

Verbal behavior: offensive sexual jokes and comments about the worker's physical appearance or sexual condition; obscene sexual comments; questions, descriptions or comments about sexual fantasies, preferences and abilities/abilities; degrading or obscene ways of addressing people; spreading rumors about people's sex lives; communications (telephone calls, emails, etc...) of sexual content and offensive character; invitations or pressure to arrange dates or sexual encounters; invitations, petitions or demands for sexual favours when they are related, directly or indirectly, to professional career, improvement of working conditions or job retention; Persistent invitations to participate in social or recreational activities, even if the person subject to them has made it clear that they are unwanted and inopportune.

Nonverbal behaviors: use of images, graphics, vignettes, photographs or drawings of sexually explicit or suggestive content; obscene gestures, whistles, gestures or immodest looks; Sexually offensive letters, notes, or emails.

Physical behaviors: deliberate and unsolicited physical contact (pinching, touching, unwanted massage… or excessive or unnecessary physical approach; deliberately cornering or seeking to be alone with the person unnecessarily; intentionally or "accidentally" touching sexual organs (Comisiones Obreras & Delegación del Gobierno Contra la Violencia de Género, 2021, pp. 11-12).

Regarding harassment based on sex, Organic Law 3/2007, defines it as "any behavior carried out on the basis of the sex of a person, with the purpose or effect of violating their dignity and creating an intimidating, degrading or offensive environment" (Organic Law 3/2007, art. 7.2).

Behaviors that can be considered harassment based on sex can be:

Use of discriminatory behavior on the grounds of being a woman or a man; and comments on people taking on tasks that have traditionally been performed by persons of the opposite sex; or in degrading or offensive ways of addressing persons of a certain sex; or the use of sexist humour; ridicule and despise abilities, women's skills and intellectual potential; re-evaluate past behaviors with lesbian, gay, transgender or bisexual people; and value the work of people with disparagement, unfairly or biased, based on their sex or sexual orientation; assign tasks or jobs below the person's professional capacity or competencies (Comisiones Obreras & Delegación del Gobierno Contra la Violencia de Género, 2021, pp. 12-13).

Finally, discriminatory harassment refers to any act whose purpose is to violate the dignity of a person and their moral integrity, violating fundamental rights, specifically: the right to equality and non-discrimination based on racial origin, age, sex, religion, disability, or identity or sexual orientation (Ledesma, 2017).

If we transfer these theoretical data to the real work environment, a report by the Spanish Ministry of Equality states that one out of every five women who suffer sexual harassment in Spain claims that it took place in the context of their work. On sexual harassment and harassment based on sex in the workplace in Spain, it is concluded that this is carried out mostly by men, who are mainly hierarchical superiors (47.4%), people of the same job category (32.4%) and by other people (9.2%) among which are family and friends of the boss (1.8%) and customers (1.5%) (Ministry of Equality, 2021).

In addition, it now warns of the great "invisibility" those episodes of sexual and gender-based harassment have in the work environment. "Not only are they hidden, but they are not shared with other people", which leaves the victims in a situation of great vulnerability because they must "learn to live with and confront" these experiences individually. 72% of women who have suffered harassment practices recognize that they have not given notice or filed a complaint.

It is emphasized that the "reality" shows that it is "very difficult to provide evidence of a conduct that frequently occurs without witnesses, and this discourages many victims from taking appropriate legal action". Without complaints, there is no response from the company and, therefore, cases of harassment go "unpunished".

Another piece of data from the study reflects the extent to which these situations are hushed up. 51.6% of the women did not know if other female colleagues had been victims of harassment.

The profile of the victims tends to be young women. Those who do not have a stable partner, who have a very precarious economic or employment situation, or immigrants, have a "higher risk" of suffering sexual harassment. Also, those who work in masculinized environments or in which a markedly sexist group culture predominates.

Regarding the harassers, the study states that they are mostly men, and range from bosses to colleagues and clients. The women in the sample indicate that the harassment episodes suffered were mainly carried out by hierarchical superiors (47.4%), by people in the same work category (32.4%) and by other people (9.2%), including family members and friends of the boss (1.8%) and clients (1.5%) (Carvajal, 2021).

Concerning harassment at work, also known as mobbing or moral harassment, although there is no legal definition of the concept, it can be defined as a series of behaviors or practices, characterized by a systematic and prolonged psychological pressure, either from a superior or a colleague with the consent and allowance of the superior, which is exerted on a person in the performance of his or her work, seeking to destroy his or her personal reputation and undermine his or her moral dignity in order to achieve psychological damage and a disruption of his or her working life that distances him or her from work, causing his or her self-exclusion (Oulego, 2020).

The types of mobbing that may exist are: horizontal mobbing (between hierarchical equals), vertical mobbing (between different hierarchical levels), strategic mobbing (seeks to make the worker leave the company voluntarily so as not to receive compensation), management mobbing (using threats of dismissal to increase the worker's productivity or to dismiss him/her for different reasons without compensation), disciplinary mobbing (threats are used so that employees work submissively and do not question the decisions and actions of their superiors) and, finally, perverse mobbing (it does not have a work-related purpose, the cause is solely due to the harassing and manipulative personality of the harasser).

The forms of harassment in the workplace, especially as a result of remote work, have also been modified. Some of the examples of mobbing present in telework are:

- Permanent connection.
    - Demanding to be connected outside working hours.
    - Sending emails and receiving several calls a day to monitor your work performance.
    - Being forced to answer messages, calls or video calls outside working hours.
    - Threats of dismissal to those who do not have internet access.
- Not respecting schedules and privacy
    - Not having a schedule for eating and resting because you are "at home".
    - The obligation of turning on the camera without a defined purpose, or asking about the employee's location.
    - Excessive schedules with respect to the working day.
    - Surprising changes in work shifts.
    - Demanding to work without any objective basis.
    - Sexual harassment.
- Measuring Productivity
    - Measuring productivity through the minutes workers spend in front of their screens.
    - Minimization of achievements and efforts.
    - Being treated in a discriminatory manner with respect to your colleagues.
    - Demanding a heavy workload in an unreasonable time frame.
    - Shouting and humiliating the employee in front of colleagues by criticizing performance.
- Ignoring and excluding
    - Deliberately not including a team member in WhatsApp groups.
    - Deliberately not sending invitations to videoconferences where the employee must be present.

Many studies and literature point out that, although anyone can be a victim of violence in the workplace, women are one of the groups most affected by this problem. In Spain in particular, women, people suffering from some type of disability and people of different gender or with a sexual orientation other than heterosexuality are the groups that suffer the most violence in the workplace, especially harassment (Comisiones Obreras & Delegation of the Government Against Gender Violence, 2021, pp. 36–38).

The Proliferation of Teleworking as a Consequence of COVID-19

Covid-19 has been and is still a pandemic that has affected all countries in the world in all areas: economics, politics, health, education and, of course, labor.

The world as it was known up to that time changed drastically and society as a whole had to adapt quickly to this change in an excessively short period of time.

Faced with the compulsory nature of lockdown by most governments, many companies were faced with the problem of how to carry out their productive and labor activity without having to close down (since, in many cases, it would mean absolute ruin), especially considering the uncertainty that existed surrounding when the lockdown and the pandemic would end. By March, more than a third of humanity was in lockdown. At the end of April, more than 1.6 billion workers were seeing their jobs at risk. (Bello, 2020).

Teleworking was a method of working that, in some companies and professions, had already been practiced for some time, however, it was not widespread. Until the pandemic started, there were few companies or workplaces where remote work was used (in some countries it was more widespread than in others), the main advantage of its implementation lies in the fact that this way of working uses ICT as a form of organization to enable distance from the workplace.

Teleworking began in the 70s in the United States, but the lack of development in these technologies meant that its proliferation was very slow and limited (Pérez Pérez et al., 2004b).

With the passage of time and the continuous development of ICT, its use in the workplace (which mainly sought to save money and time), was growing.

Observing that these tools were of great benefit to organizations, growth in their use led to the improvement of existing tools and the creation of new, increasingly specific and sophisticated ones, which led to their further proliferation.

When the pandemic began, governments had to find the most appropriate measures to save the maximum possible number of lives without causing a worldwide stoppage that would cause irreversible damage to the economy, measures that had to guarantee the physical distancing of the population.

At the labor level, teleworking was the measure that the government imposed and extended to all jobs and organizations where it was possible, except for essential services.

To understand the impact it had, one must consider the fact that, before the pandemic, the incidence rate of regular or occasional telework was 30 percent or more in some northern European countries, 10 percent or less in countries such as Greece, Italy, Poland, and the Czech Republic. As the aftermath of the pandemic began to proliferate around the world (early 2020s), and as governments began to report on the measures to be taken, the result was that, in Europe, 4 out of 10 workers began to work remotely. Not surprisingly, in countries where teleworking was more developed before the pandemic, such as Finland, the incidence of teleworking reached 60 percent, and in other northern European countries the incidence was 40 percent. The European average number of people who had never worked remotely before and had to start doing so because of the pandemic was 24 percent (ILO, 2021).

It should be noted that not all countries have the same capacity when it comes to being able to decree telework as a method of work for their population. The level of economic development of the country (economic and occupational structure and the level of access to Internet broadband), as well as the possibility of workers having their own computer equipment that allows them to perform this type of work or the ability of the organization to provide them with one, are decisive factors in being able to develop telework in an appropriate way, therefore, the higher the economic level of the country, the greater the chances of being able to establish telework as an alternative to the development of physical presence at the workplace.

The educational level of the workers also has an influence, since, as mentioned in previous sections, in order to know how the tools and applications provided by ICTs work and how to use them, a minimum level of knowledge and/or training is required. For older people, the mandatory nature of the situation to which they were exposed during the pandemic in terms of teleworking was a major problem, since they were not familiar with the use of the related applications or with remote access to the workplace. In these cases, both the correct development of the work activity and the productivity of the organization can be compromised.

According to a study carried out among more than 1,500 employers and qualified professionals (60% from Spain and 40% from Latin America), 90% of the professionals surveyed say that before the pandemic caused by Covid-19 they never teleworked or did so less than two days a week. They also said that, currently, 82% do it always or more than half of the days. Despite this, the data reveals that 4 out of 10 qualified professionals do not feel qualified to work remotely (Bello, 2020).

Data Protection in Teleworking

Data protection is not an issue that can be considered only in relation to telework, in fact, the Internet of Things and the constant global networking means the concern for data protection is growing worldwide in everything related to the use of personal data through ICT. Exposure to the risks arising from poor protection in this area are now present in practically any day-to-day activity for any person and, both the likelihood of suffering an attack in this regard and its consequences, are unknown to a large number of users. ICTs are not only used for teleworking, in fact, they have been applied to the workplace for a long time, however, several factors must be taken into account: - Its implementation in organizations has been gradual and its development has been a constant which has allowed experimentation, adaptation and maturation of the same, so that, while they were being implemented, they could study the advantages, disadvantages and risks to subsequently develop and implement the necessary tools to alleviate or make these risks and disadvantages disappear.

- Their application was completely voluntary, not all jobs and not all organizations needed the use of ICT or the implementation of teleworking to carry out their activity efficiently.
- Organizations that constantly use ICTs in their centers have their own equipment prepared and equipped with the necessary tools to protect them from cyber-attacks or to detect misuse of the equipment by the worker, since it is equipment that is physically located in the workplace and, on some occasions, can even be monitored to find out what activities are being carried out through it (UNIVE Abogados, 2022).

Among these risks are the privacy and security of the company's information and, especially, of the workers who, having to carry out their work activities telematically, in many cases do so from their own computer equipment and with their own home internet connection.

It is obvious that, during the first months of the pandemic, this adaptation to teleworking had to be done so quickly that there was hardly time for proper planning, however, at presente, it has been two years since the beginning of this situation so that there are already recommendations, advice and applicable legislation to alleviate this new problem.

The Spanish Data Protection Agency (hereinafter AEPD) has published a series of tips to maintain privacy and integrity in teleworking and, for its part, the Government approved Law 10/2021, of July 9, on telecommuting (Law 10/2021, of July 9, on Remote Work, 2021).

The parties involved in this case are both the company and the workers themselves who are going to perform their work telematically. The recommendations for each of the parties are as follows (Grupo Atico34, 2021):

The company must:

- Ensure security when accessing company materials, equipment, and resources from outside the organization (access permissions, storage methods, destruction of stored information, checking the security level of the devices to be accessed...).
- Use duly authorized service providers with a proven reputation (for intra-company messaging services, information storage in the cloud...).
- Provide workers with adequate prior training so that they are clear about their rights, their obligations, the security measures to be taken to be able to work from home, how to act in the event that this security is breached at any time...
- Have a clear and concise structure on permissions and restrictions for access to the organization's information (control who, when, how and from where the data is accessed).
- Carry out a periodic review of the equipment being used for teleworking and monitor the activity of the organization's equipment and networks to be able to detect any unusual activity.
- Ensure that employees have the right to digital disconnection. Despite the fact that it is easier to contact employees via social networks or instant messaging applications, the company has the obligation to respect the right of employees not to be disturbed for work-related matters outside their working hours.

Employees must:

- Respect the company's data protection. Each company will have clear and specific measures applicable to teleworking and employees must comply with them.
- Protect the devices they use for remote access. Through the installation of appropriate antivirus software, use of secure passwords, not downloading programs from outside the company that may contain viruses...
- Not use the same equipment for professional and personal use, as far as possible. In some cases, the company itself will provide employees with equipment for remote access to work, but in cases where this is not the case, the employee should try as far as possible to separate these two spheres.
- Store information related to the business activity in accordance with the company's stipulations so that the security of this data is not compromised by the employee's negligence.
- Have a fluid communication with the company. Especially in cases where the employee believes that the safety of work equipment may have been compromised, so that the company can take appropriate decision (Prevención Integral, 2021).

These are some of the basic measures that can ensure that data protection is not compromised by working physically outside the organization. Of course, they are only a small part of the whole, since, in view of the new scenarios created as a result of the growing implementation of teleworking, there is a broad variety of data protection violation problems, and new problems are arising almost daily.

The main problem lies in the fine line that separates the work and private spheres when the work activity is carried out remotely. When the work activity is carried out in the workplace in a physical form it is easy to delimit these two spheres, as well as place limits on the working hours, however, when the work activity is carried out from the employee's home, it is more difficult to separate the two.

In addition, there are companies that were able to provide their employees with the appropriate technological resources (company laptops, cell phones, tablets...) to be able to use the intranet, instant messaging apps and social networks with exclusively work profiles, but there were others that could not provide this type of resources to their employees, and this compromised their data protection and forced employees to use communication channels of a personal nature (personal Whatsapp, personal social networks...) (Bulnes, 2022).

With the IT equipment provided by the company, the level of data protection is higher, since remote access is secure, they are usually monitored equipment, and the use of applications is restricted., and also, once working hours are over, disconnecting or turning off these devices is enough to disconnect from work, whereas, if employees have provided their personal resources, even if working hours are over, there is the possibility of constant communication by the other members of the company, and this means that the right to digital disconnection (mandatory for all employees by law) can be violated, which, in fact, in Spain is still not respected despite being legislatively regulated (Garvi Carvajal, 2021).

Cyberbullying

In view of what has been explained in the previous sections and the central theme of this research, one of the problems arising from the incorporation of ICTs in the workplace and also linked to the problem of proper data protection is cyberbullying. On many occasions a person begins to suffer cyberbullying at the workplace due to incorrect treatment of personal data, which means that the harasser has access to the data necessary to carry out this type of behavior.

It should be borne in mind that this phenomenon, even though ICTs have been developing and maturing for several decades, is relatively recent and unexplored.

Cyberspace has become a medium where users can interact, and this has meant a great change in terms of personal relationships. Concerning the workplace, cyberspace is not only used to perform the tasks related to each job, but also for the stakeholders in an organization to interact with each other when their job functions require it (customers, employees, suppliers, managers, shareholders...).

Cyberbullying is so called because it refers to the carrying out of harassing actions through digital media.

There are different definitions of what is considered cyberbullying. The first time this term was used, by educator Bill Belsey in 2005, it was conceptualized as "the action involving the use of electronic information and means of communication to harass an individual or group" (Díaz, 2021) .

Subsequently, other authors added in their conceptualization that, "cyberbullying involves the use of information and communication technologies as a platform for intentional, repeated and hostile behavior by an individual or group to harm others" (Ortega et al., 2008, p. 184).

One of the most recent and widespread definitions is provided by the ILO which uses this term "to describe aggressive behavior carried out through information and communication technologies, and may include images/video clips, emails or social networking sites, among others" (De Stefano et al., 2021).

Cyberbullying can be carried out through a large number of behaviors by an individual or a group of bullies:

- Spreading false rumors or socially reprehensible conduct.
- Dissemination of private photographs or videos with sensitive content.
- Impersonation to carry out unlawful conduct (offensive comments, threats, creation of fake identity websites or fake profiles on social networks in order to defame the victim).
- Access to the victim's personal equipment.
- Sending offensive, threatening, and harassing messages.

In short, the possible actions that could be carried out by the harasser against the victim are very broad and, as ICTs evolve, new forms of cyberbullying are also emerging (Barea, 2021).

In any case, it should be borne in mind that, regardless of the cyberbullying activity or activities carried out against the victim, its main manifestations are moral or sexual.

On the other hand, two very important factors that must be considered are, on the one hand, the reiteration of the conduct and, on the other hand, the frequency of the conduct. The specific case of the repetition of the conduct is somewhat more complicated to determine.

The profile of the victim of cyberbullying is not a fixed profile, it can affect any person in the organization regardless of the their hierarchical position, however, women remain a group at greater risk of this type of behavior, and in fact, 70% of victims are women (Álvarez, 2022).

As for the profile of cyberbullies, the same is true as in the case of victims. There is no fixed profile or specific behaviors that facilitate the identification of this type of person.

Cyberbullies can occupy any position in the organization, in fact, there are people who may think that people with senior management positions are more likely to become cyberbullies, but the truth is, as mentioned above, that anyone can carry these behaviors regardless of the position they occupy (same hierarchical level as the victim, higher hierarchical level, lower, even suppliers or customers can develop this type of behavior).

Cyberbullying creates a series of very negative consequences, both for the victim and for the organization.

Some of the preventative measures that can be applied when this type of behavior occurs may be: information, training, inclusion of specific preventative measures in the organization's protocols, disciplinary punishments for people who carry out these activities, and psychological, social, labor and legal support for the victim.

Apart from these measures, it is important to highlight that the Spanish Agency of Data Protection makes a set of recommendations aimed at eradicating workplace harassment and harassment based on sex when this type of conduct occurs in the digital environment (Spanish Agency for Data Protection, 2020), available to any person or organization who wishing to be informed about this topic.

In short, cyberbullying is a new way of carrying out the act of harassment derived from the use of information and communication technologies in the workplace, it is a new phenomenon in the sense that it occurs through new media and that are in constant innovation.

The IVECO Case and Its Repercussions in Spain

Even though cyberbullying at work is a relatively new concept in all over the world, speaking specifically of the Spanish case, for the moment, there is no specific legislative regulation on it, it is important to bear in mind that the latest advances that have been carried out on this topic occurred as a result of one of the cases of cyberbullying at work with most media repercussion in history.

The IVECO case:

Veronica was a 32-year-old mother of two young children who had been working for several years at the IVECO factory in San Fernando de Henares (Madrid, Spain). Company with around 2500 which designs, manufactures and markets a wide range of commercial vehicles.

This woman maintained a romantic relationship with a co-worker before marrying and starting her family. During the time that lasted the relationship with her co-worker, Veronica voluntarily recorded a video in which she had sex with that person and voluntarily sent that recording to her partner at that time.

Free act, which can be considered by some as reckless, for trusting his partner, but which is not a crime, so the victim cannot be blamed at all. This action of recording a video of sexual content and subsequent sending, is called sexting.

After the breakup of the couple, Veronica married and had two children, however, her previous partner continued to communicate with her and let her know that she wanted to continue maintaining a relationship. Faced with Veronica's denial, he began threatening to spread the video of sexual content if she did not have sex with him again. In this case, being faced with an extortion of a sexual nature, the denomination of the behavior is sextortion (Adsuara, 2019).

In April 2019 the video was disseminated, at first in a WhatsApp group of colleagues from the company in which there were 20 people and, subsequently, the colleagues themselves began to forward said video to the rest of the company also through Whatsapp until there came a time when almost all of Veronica's co-workers had the video, around 200 people (Valdés, 2019b).

Although the first dissemination of the video is suspected to have been made by Veronica's ex-partner, the truth is that this fact has not been proven and, the subsequent retransmissions were made by more than 100 workers of the same company, a fact that already constitutes a crime of sexual harassment.

Veronica's colleagues did not stop making fun of her and, the worker, was subjected to all kinds of humiliations since the video began to be broadcast, having to endure insults, jokes, contempt ... by his peers.

The situation reached such an extreme that Veronica, decided to go to the human resources department to request help since she was subjected to very high levels of stress and depression, however, when telling what happened to those responsible for the department, the company considered that it was a personal matter and not a work environment, so they decided not to take action in this regard, simply, from the human resources department they told her to report the facts because it was a crime against privacy, but she refused to do so (Durán et al., 2019).

Veronica faced with this situation suffered several anxiety attacks on consecutive days because she feared that this video would be viewed by her family, for her, going to work had become a real hell since she had to continue enduring the insults and mockery of colleagues and more and more people owned the video.

Finally, on May 25, 2019, Verónica committed suicide at her home in Alcalá de Henares (Madrid, Spain).

An operator says:

That wasn't the first time. A few years ago, those files "already ran." At that moment Veronica "managed to stop him," three colleagues recall. This time, for more than 10 days, laughter resounded through the corridors; the videos jumped from mobile to mobile; And colleagues swirled at her workplace to make sure it was her. "I think none of us really realized how serious what was happening was, it was taken as a joke." (Valdés, 2019)

After the suicide of the victim, the succession of investigations and trials has come to an end with the closure of the case. The Court of Instruction number 5 of Alcalá de Henares has archived the proceedings opened to investigate the origin of the dissemination. The file is produced by "lack of known author" of the crime of discovery and disclosure of secrets investigated.

As a result of this high-profile case, cyberbullying in the workplace began to gain greater visibility and concern on the part of experts and companies, so it can be said that this case was the precedent that began to sow greater awareness and visibility about cyberbullying.

As mentioned in previous sections, the main problem is that most victims do not dare to report the cases, not only of cyberbullying, but also of harassment in the workplace in general. This circumstance makes it very difficult to obtain real statistics on how many cases of cyberbullying at the workplace exist in Spain and, therefore, this invisibility does not help to publicize the depth of the problem (Europa Press, 2022).

Currently there are many companies that have already started to work on the creation and implementation of protocols to prevent cyberbullying, however, these are not sufficient measures as it is a problem that not only is not stopping but continues to grow.

The reality of organizations is that practically all have defined protocols to prevent 'face-to-face' harassment, but for the remote environment they are obsolete. The problem is that the regulations do not help companies either, because they do not contain indications or instructions on how these plans should be. "Cyberbullying is no different in essence, but it does change the way it occurs, without physical or temporal borders" (Del Rosal, 2021).

The cases of cyberbullying already existed previously, however, it has been as a result of the IVECO case when the victims have begun to denounce it, more companies have taken a greater awareness and legal regulation begins to focus its efforts on regulating it more exhaustively and, the trigger for greater concern for this problem has been that thecases of cyberbullying at work during the pandemic, as mentioned above, significantly increased (Rodríguez Molina, 2020).

Since legislative regulation is so scarce, for the time being, the only regulation that Spain can avail itself of is ILO Convention 190 on violence and harassment, which specifically mentions the types of harassment listed above and makes special mention of cyberbullying, although without an in-depth look., it is foreseeable that in the coming years Spain will make a much more exhaustive normative regulation on all these issues since, on 2022, Spain was the 13th ILO Member State to ratify Convention No. 177 (on homework) and the 15th to ratify the aforementioned Convention No. 190 (OIT, 2022).

Broad definitions and discussions of the topic and incorporate views of others (literature review) into the discussion to support, refute, or demonstrate your position on the topic[1].

Issues, Controversies, Problems

The main theme of the book is internal communication in organizations after the Covid-19 pandemic, especially in hybrid work environments. The author of this chapter has wanted to point out the fact that, without underestimating the great advantages that ICTs have brought both for internal communication and for carrying out work in a hybrid way, there are still also problems such as cyberbullying in the workplace which are not receiving the attention they deserve.

Cases of unreported cyberbullying in organizations show, when they occur, obvious internal communication gaps. Firstly, the most important communication gap is on the part of the organization itself, which has not managed to ensure that its employees have the confidence and security to report the situation internally. Secondly, it also shows that the organization's systems for protection and prevention of this type of behavior are either non-existent or ineffective and, finally, the reaction of the victim's coworkers when they are aware that this type of activity is taking place also shows whether the organization has been able to instill good values, adequate communication channels and an appropriate organizational culture.

It is true that, in some cases of cyberbullying, the organization will have direct legal responsibility, although not in all of them, however, the organization as an entity that is part of society, should try to help its workers within its possibilities, even if only by offering moral support or psychological assistance. In the IVECO case mentioned above, despite the fact that the worker informed the human resources department of what was happening, their response was simply that she had to file a police report and, despite the fact that they saw that the victim did not dare to report, they did nothing. This is the kind of behavior that we, as a society, should aspire to, victims should be supported, advised, and helped even if a formal complaint should be made through other channels outside the organization.

SOLUTIONS AND RECOMMENDATIONS

Without prejudice to its subsequent development in the conclusion section, the author would like to highlight the fact that misinformation and lack of training are major problems in social structures when it comes to combating such a serious problem as violence (in any of its manifestations and areas), in this research we speak specifically about violence in the workplace, but the solutions presented as "the foundations" to begin to combat this problem can be applied in other areas.

It would be advisable, in the first place, to start educating about violence from a very early age at home, in schools, high schools and later in universities. Violence is negative but the fact that it is negative does not mean that it does not exist, it is present throughout life in many areas, and trying to hide it does not fix this problem. it is preferable to educate and train people to know how to deal with situations like this (both the person with violent traits who may be a potential aggressor to learn to manage their emotions and control themselves, and the person who in the future may be a victim of an aggression or witness to one so that they are also know how to react).

It is essential to strengthen learning in emotion management, communication, empathy... subjects which are not present in most educational plans in schools and that are very useful tools for human beings.

On the other hand, it is also necessary to give visibility to a reality that exists and that should not be hidden, that visibility can mean that other potential victims are identified and know where to go and what to do to report their situation.

And, of course, it's necessary to develop a specific legal regulation on cyberbullying (both at the workplace and in other areas) at the global level. This will greatly facilitate the delimitation of actions that can be identified as cyberbullying at work, the specific sanctions for each type of criminal behavior, the specific help for victims, the reporting channels they can turn to....

Specifically at an organizational level, from the point of view of human resources, the author considers this department as one of the pillars when it comes to intervening when this behavior occurs in the company. The human resources department is not only dedicated to recruitment and selection, it must also be concerned about the welfare of its workers and this includes its intervention when such cases occur, because the victim feeling protected by their organization can be very important when it comes to deciding to file a complaint.

Undoubtedly, in the absence of specific legislation, both trade unions and companies must work on designing and implementing specific protocols on cyberbullying that are much more effective and that cover the wide range of forms of cyberbullying that currently exist and must clearly delimit which cases can be considered cyberbullying and which ones cannot.

FUTURE RESEARCH DIRECTIONS

As specific legislation on cyberbullying evolves worldwide and as more visibility is given to all the cases that exist, more research can be carried out to determine whether a more specific profile of the bully can be defined, whether the emerging regulations are sufficient, what new ways to prevent cyberbullying may emerge...

CONCLUSION

Communication in organizations, like any strategy on the part of the company whatever the field (productive, financial, competitive, etc.), needs prior planning: analysis, studies, tests, checking for failures and errors, strengthening the strong points and, if necessary, redesigning the plan.

Communication must be a tool that helps the company grow in all aspects, and a company grows when the people who are part of it feel at ease in it, feel that they are listened to, that they are important, that their opinion is taken into account, when they know that if they have a problem they have superiors to turn to for help and that they will get that help.

Employees are the pillar of a company, and if its employees are happy, this is transferred to other areas (production, corporate image, customer service, obtaining more economic benefits...).

However, the fact that there are efficient communication channels in a company and that such communication is good among stakeholders (whether working in person or remotely) does not mean that the company is exempt from problems, although it is very likely that a solution can be achieved in a much more effective way than if there were no efficient communication system.

Especially in cases of harassment in the workplace, the fact that the victim has the certainty that whoever the aggressor is (regardless of the hierarchical level of the company), he/she will get help from the company, would help a lot to encourage more reports of such cases. The main problem today that victims of violence in the workplace face is the lack of confidence that a complaint will help, the lack of information about whether your company has protocols for such cases or whether it has an external channel for complaints to which they can turn. But how can these problems be eradicated?

Through communication: informing all stakeholders of the protocols available in the company, of the rights and obligations they have, training workers to be able to identify if they are being subjected to workplace violence and how they should act in that case, generating empathy so that in the event that the victim is not able to report, it is the colleagues themselves who help stop the situation (contrary to what happened in the IVECO case), generating formal channels of communication that are not only vertical and horizontal, but also the possibility that the victims are able to go to the union or the Labor Inspectorate to make complaints and know these mechanisms.

It is everyone's job to eradicate any type of violence in society, and the workplace is no exception. Workplace violence, like other types of violence such as gender violence or violence in the family, is a problem that affects society as a whole and has dire consequences. It is not only a legislative task and the task of public entities to create tools to punish this type of behavior, but organizations also have to be a part of this fight. We must educate and train in order to prevent any instances, give public visibility to the cases that occur to show what the reality of the situation is, punish them at the time they occur and, above all, help the victims and offer them the maximum possible level of support.

REFERENCES

Abogados, U. N. I. V. E. (2022). *Phishing: Crecen los ciberataques con el aumento del teletrabajo*. https://www.unive.es/893__phishing_crecen_los_ciberataques_con_el_aumento_del_teletrabajo.html?art=1

Aced, C. (2022). Inteligencia artificial y big data: ¿oportunidades o riesgos para la comunicación? *Cristina Aced comunicación*. https://cristinaaced.com/ia-big-data-comunicacion/

Adsuara, B. (2019). Entre todos la matamos y ella sola se suicidó. *La Información*. https://www.lainformacion.com/opinion/borja-adsuara/entre-todos-la-matamos-y-ella-sola-se-suicido/6502632/

Agencia Española de Protección de Datos. (2020). *Recomendaciones para prevención del acoso digital*. https://www.aepd.es/es/prensa-y-comunicacion/blog/recomendaciones-prevencion-acoso-digital

Álvarez, S. (n.d.). *Ciberacoso y ciberviolencia en el mundo del trabajo* (N.º 4) [Audio]. Recuperado 21 de junio de 2022, de https://voices.ilo.org/es-es/podcast/ciberacoso-y-ciberviolencia-en-el-mundo-del-trabajo

Baeza Botía, E. (2009). Tipos de comunicación. *Tiempos Modernos*. https://www.tiemposmodernos.eu/ret-tipos-de-comunicacion/#

Barea, M. (2021). *El ciberacoso laboral como riesgo psicosocial emergente*. AfforHealth. https://afforhealth.com/el-ciberacoso-laboral-como-riesgo-psicosocial/

Bello, E. (2020). A los profesionales les falta formación en teletrabajo. *IEBS*. https://www.iebschool.com/blog/estudio-teletrabajo-rrhh-2-0/

Bulnes, A. (2022). WhatsApp para trabajar: ¿una herramienta útil o una invasión más de la vida personal? *El País*. https://elpais.com/tecnologia/2022-02-22/whatsapp-para-trabajar-una-herramienta-util-o-una-invasion-mas-de-la-vida-personal.html

Carvajal, S. (2021). Siete de cada 10 mujeres que sufren acoso sexual en el trabajo no denuncian por miedo a las represalias. *El Mundo*. https://www.elmundo.es/espana/2021/04/29/608a8ae1fdddffe4458b45f4.html

Comisiones Obreras & Delegación del Gobierno Contra la Violencia de Género. (2021). *El acoso sexual y el acoso por razón de sexo en el ámbito laboral en España*. https://www.ccoo.es/2f7f86bfc8a8105e09b013342bbf9e0d000001.pdf

Danvila-del Valle, I., & Sastre-Castillo, M. Á. (2007). Capital humano y ventaja competitiva sostenible: Un análisis de la relaciónentre la formación y los resultados empresariales. *EsicMarket, 128*, 145-187. https://revistasinvestigacion.esic.edu/esicmarket/index.php/esicm/article/view/73/160

De Stefano, V., Stylogiaannis, C., Wouters, M., & Durri, I. (2021). *"Actualización de las necesidades del sistema":Mejora de la protección frente al ciberacoso y a la violencia y el acoso en el mundo del trabajo posibilitados por las TIC*. https://www.ilo.org/legacy/spanish/intserv/working-papers/wp001/index.html

Del Rosal, P. (2021). Los protocolos contra el ciberacoso, los grandes olvidados en los planes de teletrabajo. *El Confidencial*. https://www.elconfidencial.com/juridico/2021-03-27/protocolos-contra-el-ciberacoso-los-grandes-olvidados_3010040/

Díaz, V. L. (2021). El ciber acoso en el mundo del trabajo: Es suficiente la nueva ley para prevenirlo? *Revista IDEIDES, 61*. http://revista-ideides.com/el-ciber-acoso-en-el-mundo-del-trabajo-es-suficiente-la-nueva-ley-para-prevenirlo/

Durán, L., Fernández García, S., & Núñez Villaveirán, L. (2019). Una empleada de Iveco se suicida tras viralizarse en la empresa un vídeo sexual. *El Mundo*. https://www.elmundo.es/madrid/2019/05/28/5ced493efdddffb0758b48fb.html

El teletrabajo durante la pandemia de Covid-19 y después de ella. (2021). https://www.ilo.org/wcmsp5/groups/public/---ed_protect/---protrav/---travail/documents/publication/wcms_758007.pdf

ElDerecho.com. (2020). *El teletrabajo ha puesto en riesgo a muchas empresas y algunas no son conscientes*. Noticias jurídicas y actualidad. https://elderecho.com/el-teletrabajo-ha-puesto-en-riesgo-a-muchas-empresas-y-algunas-no-son-conscientes

EUR-Lex. (2007). *Código práctico encaminado a combatir el acoso sexual en el trabajo*. https://eur-lex.europa.eu/ES/legal-content/summary/code-of-practice-to-clamp-down-on-sexual-harassment-at-work.html

Europa Press. (2022). Expertos advierten de que solo el 1% de los casos de mobbing o acoso sexual en el ámbito laboral sale a la luz. *epsocial*. https://www.europapress.es/epsocial/igualdad/noticia-expertos-advierten-solo-casos-mobbing-acoso-sexual-ambito-laboral-sale-luz-20220527165041.html

Garvi Carvajal, A. (2021). El derecho a la desconexión laboral sigue sin respetarse. *El País*. https://elpais.com/economia/negocios/2021-11-20/el-derecho-a-la-desconexion-laboral-sigue-sin-respetarse.html

González Masip, J. (2018). Los grupos de interés y su importancia en la propuesta de valor de las empresas. *Boletín Económico de ICE, 3096*, 47-57. https://dialnet.unirioja.es/servlet/articulo?codigo=6381236

Grupo Atico34. (2021). *Protección de datos y teletrabajo: Recomendaciones.* https://protecciondatos-lopd.com/empresas/proteccion-datos-teletrabajo/

IMF. (2013). Las redes sociales en la comunicación interna. *IMF Blog Corporativo.* https://blogs.imf-formacion.com/blog/corporativo/prl/las-redes-sociales-en-la-comunicacion-interna/

Instituto Nacional de Seguridad e Higiene en el Trabajo. (2000). *Acoso sexual en el trabajo.* https://www.insst.es/documents/94886/191756/NTP+507+Acoso+sexual+en+el+trabajo.pdf

Instituto Nacional de Seguridad e Higiene en el Trabajo. (2007). *La comunicación en las organizaciones* (N.º 685; p. 6). https://www.insst.es/documents/94886/326775/ntp_685.pdf

Instituto Nacional de Seguridad e Higiene en el Trabajo. (2009). *Acoso psicológico en el trabajo: Definición* (N.º 854; p. 6). https://www.insst.es/documents/94886/326775/854+web.pdf

Instituto Nacional de Seguridad y Salud en el Trabajo. (2012). *Violencia en el trabajo.* https://www.insst.es/materias/riesgos/riesgos-psicosociales/violencia-en-el-trabajo

Katz, D., & Khan, R. (1986). *Psicología Social de las Organizaciones.* https://www.academia.edu/27894499/Katz_D_Kahn_R_Psicolog%C3%ADa_Social_de_Las_Organizaciones

Ledesma, E. (2017). *¿Qué es el acoso laboral discriminatorio?* Jupsin. https://jupsin.com/jupsin/acoso-discriminatorio/

Ley 10/2021, de 9 de julio, de trabajo a distancia, n.º 164 (2021).

Ley Orgánica 3/2007 de 22 de marzo, para la Igualdad efectiva de mujeres y hombres.

OIT. (2022). España ratifica el Convenio sobre el trabajo a domicilio y el Convenio sobre la violencia y el acoso. *Organización Internacional del Trabajo.* https://www.ilo.org/global/standards/WCMS_847845/lang--es/index.htm#:~:text=190)%20ante%20el%20Director%20General,190.

Ortega, R., Calmastra, J., & Mora, J. (2008). Cyberbullying. *International Journal of Psychology & Psychological Therapy*, *8*(2), 183–192. https://www.redalyc.org/pdf/560/56080204.pdf

Oulego, J. R. (2020). El acoso laboral: Concepto, tipos de acoso y protección jurídica del trabajador. *Adefinitivas.* https://adefinitivas.com/arbol-del-derecho/el-acoso-laboral-concepto-tipos-de-acoso/

Oxean. (2020). Inteligencia artificial en la comunicación corporativa ¿qué podemos esperar? *Oxean comunicaicón cross.* https://oxeancross.com/blog/ia-en-la-comunicacion-corporativa-que-podemos-esperar/

Pérez Pérez, M., Martínez Sánchez, Á., De Luis Carnicer, P., & Vela Jiménez, M. J. (2004a). La adopción del teletrabajo y las tecnologías de la información: Estudio de relaciones y efectos organizativos. *Revista de Economía y Empresa, 22*(52-53), 11-28. https://dialnet.unirioja.es/servlet/articulo?codigo=2274025

Prevención Integral. (2021). *El ciberacoso en el trabajo: Un mal presente en la digitalización empresarial.* https://www.prevencionintegral.com/actualidad/noticias/2021/10/01/ciberacoso-en-trabajo-mal-presente-en-digitalizacion-empresarial

Rodríguez Molina, I. M. (2020). Acoso laboral en tiempo de pandemia. Ciberacoso: Riesgo Psicosocial Emergente. *Gentes Consultores Academy & Consulting*. https://www.linkedin.com/pulse/acoso-laboral-en-tiempos-de-pandemia-ciberacoso-rodriguez-molina/?originalSubdomain=es

Santander Universidades. (2022). Misión, visión y valores de una empresa: Qué son y cómo definirlos. *Santander*. https://www.becas-santander.com/es/blog/mision-vision-y-valores.html

Telefónica Ecuador. (2020). Conoce cómo la intranet ayuda a mejorar la comunicación interna en tu empresa. *Think Big / Empresas*. https://empresas.blogthinkbig.com/intranet-una-manera-efectiva-de-encarar-la-comunicacion-interna/

Ueki, Y., Tsuji, M., & Cárcamo Olmos, R. (2005). Tecnología de la información y las comunicaciones (TIC) para el fomento de las pymes exportadoras en América Latina y Asia Oriental. *Los procesos de comunicación permiten a la organización mantener la coordinación entre sus distintas partes y alcanzar así su característica esencial: la de ser un sistema*. https://core.ac.uk/download/pdf/38671914.pdf

Unión Social Obrera. (2020). *Violencia en el trabajo: Uno de los principales riesgos psicosociales del ámbito laboral*. USO. https://www.uso.es/violencia-en-el-trabajo-riesgo-psicosocial-laboral/

Valdés, I. (2019). Ya no puedo más. *El País*. https://elpais.com/sociedad/2019/06/01/actualidad/1559383749_362348.html

Vallejo Peña, F. A., & Pardo Molina, M. (2009). La Comunicación Vertical: Un acercamiento a su problemática en las organizaciones. *Revista Internacional De Organizaciones*, *2*(2), 149–168. doi:10.17345/rio2.149-168

Vázquez, D. (2022). Teletrabajo: Breve historia en 6 claves de algo más que una moda y algo menos que una revolución laboral. *Business Insider*. https://www.businessinsider.es/historia-teletrabajo-claves-ultima-revolucion-laboral-global-1051091

KEY TERMS AND DEFINITIONS

AI: It refers to systems or machines that mimic human intelligence to perform tasks and can iteratively improve from the information they collect.

Big Data: Data sets or combinations of datasets whose size (volume), complexity (variability), and speed of growth (velocity) make it difficult to capture, manage, process, or analyze them using conventional technologies and tools, such as relational databases and conventional statistics or visualization packages, within the time necessary to make them useful.

Communication: It is the set of processes carried out by an organization in order to transmit its corporate information both internally and externally.

Human Resources: Department within a company that manages everything related to the people who work in it.

ICTs: Information and Communication Technologies are the resources and tools used for the processing, administration, and distribution of information through technological elements, such as computers, telephones, televisions, etc.

ILO: International Labour Organization, is the specialized agency of the UN that deals with labor-related issues in the world.

Organization: An orderly structure where people with different roles, responsibilities or positions coexist and interact to achieve a particular objective.

Spanish Data Protection Agency: Is the independent control authority that ensures compliance with data protection regulations and guarantees and protects the fundamental right to the protection of personal data.

Stakeholders: All those groups that are directly or indirectly affected by the development of the business activity, and therefore also have the capacity to affect its development directly or indirectly.

UN: The United Nations is an international organization founded in 1945 after World War II by 51 countries committed to maintaining international peace and security, fostering friendly relations among nations, and promoting social progress, better standards of living and human rights. Today it has 193 member countries.

ENDNOTE

1 "Through ICTs, individuals can repeatedly access aggressive content that has been posted online on a single occasion. Similarly, a single act could have repeatedly harmed the victim without the perpetrator of the conduct necessarily having intended that result, so that other persons, instead of the principal perpetrator, could have caused the repetition of the offensive conduct" (Barea, 2021).

Compilation of References

Aamodt, M. (2013). *Industrial/organizational psychology, 7e*. Wadsworth.

Abbas, J., & Dogan, E. (2022). The impacts of organizational green culture and corporate social responsibility on employees' responsible behaviour towards the society. *Environmental Science and Pollution Research International*, *29*(40), 60024–60034. doi:10.100711356-022-20072-w PMID:35414156

Abdul, A., Bass, J. M., Ghavimi, H., & Adam, P. (2017). Product Innovation with Scrum: A Longitudinal Case Study. *Proceedings of the International Conference on Information Society (i-Society 2017)*, 1-6. 10.23919/i-Society.2017.8354664

Abedellah, A., Noordin, A. A., & Zaki, A. (2016). Pharmaceutical good manufacturing practice regulatory affairs in Sudan: Continuous debate between regulatory authority and manufacturers Pharmaceut. *Reg. Affairs*, *5*(166), 2.

Abedini, A. A., Irani, H., & Yazdani, H. (2020). Marketing channel problems of herbal medicines from the perspective of pharmaceutical distribution companies. *Payavard Salamat*, *13*, 450–462.

Abogados, U. N. I. V. E. (2022). *Phishing: Crecen los ciberataques con el aumento del teletrabajo*. https://www.unive.es/893__phishing_crecen_los_ciberataques_con_el_aumento_del_teletrabajo.html?art=1

Aboramadan, M., Kundi, Y., & Farao, C. (2021). Examining the effects of environmentally specific servant leadership on green work outcomes among hotel employees: The mediating role of climate for green creativity. *Journal of Hospitality Marketing & Management*, *30*(8), 929–956. Advance online publication. doi:10.1080/19368623.2021.1912681

Abu-Arqoub, I. A., & Alserhan, F. A. (2019). Non-verbal barriers to effective intercultural communication. *Utopía y Praxis Latinoamericana*, *24*(5), 307–316.

Aced, C. (2022). Inteligencia artificial y big data: ¿oportunidades o riesgos para la comunicación? *Cristina Aced comunicación*. https://cristinaaced.com/ia-big-data-comunicacion/

Adamki, M., Asamoah, D., & Riverson, K. (2015). Assessment of data quality on expanded Programme on immunization in Ghana: The case of new Juaben municipality. *Journal of Health & Medical Informatics*, *6*(4), 1–9.

Adams, M. (2020). *The demographic cliff is already here—And it's about to get worse*. Education Advisory Board (EAB). Retrieved from: https://eab.com/insights/expert-insight/enrollment/the-demographic-cliff-is-already-here-and-its-about-to-get-worse/

Adamu, A., & Mohamad, B. (2019). A reliable and valid measurement scale for assessing internal crisis communication. *Journal of Communication Management (London)*, *23*(2), 90–108. doi:10.1108/JCOM-07-2018-0068

Adsuara, B. (2019). Entre todos la matamos y ella sola se suicidó. *La Información*. https://www.lainformacion.com/opinion/borja-adsuara/entre-todos-la-matamos-y-ella-sola-se-suicido/6502632/

Agbor, J. M. (2011). *Relationship between Customer Satisfaction and Services Quality—A Study of Three Service Sectors in Lemea*. Umea School of Business, Umea University.

Agencia Española de Protección de Datos. (2020). *Recomendaciones para prevención del acoso digital*. https://www.aepd.es/es/prensa-y-comunicacion/blog/recomendaciones-prevencion-acoso-digital

Akhter, S. (2022). Key informants' interviews. In M. Islam, N. Khan, & R. Baikady (Eds.), *Principles of social research methodology* (pp. 389–404). Springer Nature. doi:10.1007/978-981-19-5441-2_27

Allen, M. S., Walter, E. E., McDermott, M. S., Kaur, J., & Rosenbaum, D. A. (2014). The effects of mindfulness meditation training on multitasking in a high-stress information environment. *Proceedings of the Human Factors and Ergonomics Society Annual Meeting*, *58*(1), 2296–2300. doi:10.1177/1541931214581445

Allen, T. D. (2017). The work-family role interface: A synthesis of the research from industrial and organizational psychology. In A. M. Rossi, J. Meurs, & T. D. Allen (Eds.), *The work-family interface: An introduction* (pp. 3–26). Routledge.

Allen, T. D., Golden, T. D., & Shockley, K. M. (2015). How effective is telecommuting? Assessing the status of our scientific findings. *Psychological Science in the Public Interest*, *16*(2), 40–68. doi:10.1177/1529100615593273 PMID:26403188

Almatrooshi, B., Singh, S. K., & Farouk, S. (2016). Determinants of organizational performance: A proposed framework. *International Journal of Productivity and Performance Management*, *65*(6), 844–859. doi:10.1108/IJPPM-02-2016-0038

Almeida, F., & Espinheira, E. (2022). Adoption of Large-Scale Scrum Practices through the Use of Management 3.0. *Informatics (MDPI)*, *9*(1), 1–14. doi:10.3390/informatics9010020

Almeida, F., Miranda, E., & Falcão, J. (2019). Challenges and facilitators practices for knowledge management in large-scale scrum teams. *Journal of Information Technology Case and Application Research*, *21*(2), 90–102. doi:10.1080/15228053.2019.1637087

Almeida, L. A. S. (2013). A importância da comunicação interna para a motivação dos colaboradores. *Exedra*, *8*, 91–103.

Almeida, V. (2003). *A Comunicação Interna na Empresa*. Áreas Editora.

Alrowwad, A., Obeidat, B., Tarhini, A., & Aqqad, N. (2017). The impact of transformational leadership on organizational performance via the mediating role of corporate social responsibility: A structural equation modeling approach. *International Business Research*, *10*(1), 199–221. doi:10.5539/ibr.v10n1p199

Alshenqeeti, H. (2016). Are emojis creating a new or old visual language for new generations? A socio-semiotic study. *Advances in Language and Literary Studies*, *7*(6), 56–69.

Al-Swidi, A. K., Gelaidan, H. M., & Redhwan, M. S. (2021). The joint impact of green human resource management, leadership and organizational culture on employees' green behaviour and organisational environmental performance. *Journal of Cleaner Production*, *316*, 1–19. doi:10.1016/j.jclepro.2021.128112

Álvarez, S. (n.d.). *Ciberacoso y ciberviolencia en el mundo del trabajo* (N.º 4) [Audio]. Recuperado 21 de junio de 2022, de https://voices.ilo.org/es-es/podcast/ciberacoso-y-ciberviolencia-en-el-mundo-del-trabajo

Alves, J. C. C. (2012). *A importância da comunicação interna e das atividades de team building*. Lisboa: Instituto Superior de Ciências Sociais e Políticas. Dissertação de Mestrado em Comunicação Social.

Alzahrani, M., & Alghamdi, N. (2016). The negative effects of social media: Anxiety and cognitive capacity. *Journal of King Saud University - Computer and Information Sciences*, *28*(4), 395-400. doi:10.1016/j.jksuci.2015.09.001

Amankwah-Amoah, J., Khan, Z., Wood, G., & Knight, G. (2021). COVID-19 and digitalization: The great acceleration. *Journal of Business Research*, *136*, 602–611. doi:10.1016/j.jbusres.2021.08.011 PMID:34538980

Amnesty International. (2019, February 20). *Respuesta a las Crisis de Amnistía Internacional. Las víctimas ocultas de la represión: cómo pueden activistas y periodistas protegerse del trauma secundario.* Amnesty International. https://www.amnesty.org/es/latest/news/2019/02/how-activists-and-reporters-can-protect-themselves-from-secondary-trauma/

Anderson, S. P., & Gabszewicz, J. J. (2005). The media and advertising: a tale of two-sided markets. In *Handbook of Cultural Economics.* Elsevier Science.

Anderson-Connoly, R., Grunberg, L., Greenberg, S. E., & Moore, S. (2002). Is lean mean? Workplace transformation and employee well-being. *Work, Employment and Society, 16*(3), 389–423. doi:10.1177/095001702762217407

Anderson, P. (2018). The digitization of the Pharmaceutical Historian archive. *Pharmacy in History, 48*, 2.

Andreassen, H. K., Trondsen, M., Kummervold, P. E., Gammon, D., & Hjortdahl, P. (2006). Patients Who Use E-Mediated Communication With Their Doctor- New Constructions of Trust in the Patient-Doctor Relationship. *Qualitative Health Research, 16*(2), 238–248. doi:10.1177/1049732305284667 PMID:16394212

Andriyani, Y., Hoda, R., & Amor, R. (2017). Understanding Knowledge Management in Agile Software Development Practice. *Proceedings of the International Conference on Knowledge Science, Engineering and Management*, 195-207. 10.1007/978-3-319-63558-3_17

Anthony, P., & Petersen, S. A. (2021). Examining the digitalisation of virtual enterprises amidst the COVID-19 pandemic: A systematic and meta-analysis Enterprise. *Information Systems, 15*(5), 617–650.

Anuário da Comunicação Corporativa. (2020). *Mega Brasi*l. Retrieved September, 16, 2022 from, https://portal.megabrasil.com.br/anuario

Anuário da Comunicação Corporativa. (2021). *Mega Brasil.* Retrieved September, 16, 2022 from, https://portal.megabrasil.com.br/anuario

Anuário da Comunicação Corporativa. (2022). *Mega Brasil.* Retrieved September, 16, 2022 from, https://portal.megabrasil.com.br/anuario

APIFARMA. (2014). *The pharmaceutical industry in Portugal: Know how to invest, know how to innovate, 75 years.* Available in: http://www.apifarma.pt/salaimprensa/Documents/Livro%2075%20anos.pdf

APIFARMA. (2015). *The pharmaceutical industry in numbers.* Available in: http://www.apifarma.pt/publicacoes/ifnumeros/Documents/IF%20em%20N%C3%BAmeros%202015.pdf

Appel-Meulenbroek, R. (2015). The physical environment and user behaviour. In P. Forsyth & D. Huguenin (Eds.), *The Routledge Handbook of Transport Economics* (pp. 191–203). Routledge.

Aprigio, M. (2020). *Pesquisa revela que trabalhadores estão mais cansados por causa do home office*. UOL. Retrieved November, 02, 2022 from https://jc.ne10.uol.com.br/economia/2020/05/5609492-pesquisa-revela-que-trabalhadores-estao-mais-cansados-por-causa-de-home-office.html

Aroso, I. (2013). *The communication strategies of the pharmaceutical industry in Portugal.BOCC.UBI.* University of Beira Interior. https://bocc.ubi.pt/pag/arosoines2013strategiascomunicacaoindustriafarmaceutica.pdf

Ateeq, K. (n.d.). *Hybrid Working Method: An Integrative Review. Hybrid Working Method: An Integrative Review.* Retrieved July 24, 2022, from https://ieeexplore.ieee.org/abstract/document/9759041

Atwal, G., & Williams, A. (2009). Luxury brand marketing: The experience is everything! *Journal of Brand Management, 16*(5-6), 16. doi:10.1057/bm.2008.48

Augusto, C. E. (2022). *Vítor Cotovio: a ansiedade pandémica provou a nossa incapacidade para lidar com a incerteza.* Revista Prevenir. Retrieved from. https://www.prevenir.pt/literacia-em-saude/entrevista/vitor-cotovio-a-ansiedade-pandemica-provou-a-nossa-incapacidade-de-lidar-com-a-incerteza/#

Auriga. (2016). *Digital Transformation: History, Present, and Future Trends.* Retrieved June 15, 2017, from https://auriga.com/blog/digital-transformation-history-presentand-future-trends/

Bach-Dabrowska, I., & Pawlewski, P. (2014). Optimization model of agile team's cohesion. *Procedia Computer Science, 35*, 1577–1585. doi:10.1016/j.procs.2014.08.241

Backstrom, K., & Johansson, U. (2017). An exploration of consumers' experiences in physical stores: Comparing consumers' and retailers' perspectives in past and present time. *International Review of Retail, Distribution and Consumer Research, 27*(3), 241–259. doi:10.1080/09593969.2017.1314865

Baeza Botía, E. (2009). Tipos de comunicación. *Tiempos Modernos.* https://www.tiemposmodernos.eu/ret-tipos-de-comunicacion/#

Bakker, A. B. (2021). Job crafting and the COVID-19 pandemic: An opportunity for a new normal. *Work, Aging and Retirement, 7*(1), 23–33. doi:10.1093/workar/waaa027

Bakker, A. B., & Demerouti, E. (2017). Job demands–resources theory: Taking stock and looking forward. *Journal of Occupational Health Psychology, 22*(3), 273–285. doi:10.1037/ocp0000056 PMID:27732008

Balaraman, P., & Kosalram, K. (2013). E-Hospital Management & Hospital Information Systems-Changing Trends. *Int. J. Inf. Eng. Electron. Bus., 1*, 50–58.

Barea, M. (2021). *El ciberacoso laboral como riesgo psicosocial emergente.* AfforHealth. https://afforhealth.com/el-ciberacoso-laboral-como-riesgo-psicosocial/

Baron, R. M., & Kenny, D. A. (1986). The moderator–mediator variable distinction in social psychological research: Conceptual, strategic, and statistical considerations. *Journal of Personality and Social Psychology, 51*(6), 1173–1182. doi:10.1037/0022-3514.51.6.1173 PMID:3806354

Barsham, F., & Al-Zoubi, A. (2021). Cybersecurity and data privacy concerns in remote work during the COVID-19 pandemic. *Journal of Cybersecurity and Information Management, 4*(1), 22–37. doi:10.37380/jcim.2021.4.2

Bawden, D., & Robinson, L. (2020). Information Overload: An Overview. In *Oxford Encyclopedia of Political Decision Making*. Oxford University Press. doi:10.1093/acrefore/9780190228637.013.1360

Beck, K. (2001). *The Agile Manifesto.* Agile Alliance. Retrieved from http://agilemanifesto.org/

Beecham, S., Clear, T., Lal, R., & Noll, J. (2021). Do scaling agile frameworks address global software development risks? An empirical study. *Journal of Systems and Software, 171*, 1–30. doi:10.1016/j.jss.2020.110823

Beheshti, N. (2021). We worked longer hours during the pandemic: Research says we need to work smarter, not harder. *Forbes.* Retrieved from: https://www.forbes.com/sites/nazbeheshti/2021/08/18/we-worked-longer-hours-during-the-pandemic-research-says-we-need-to-work-smarter-not-harder/?sh=627804bb1805

Bello, E. (2020). A los profesionales les falta formación en teletrabajo. *IEBS.* https://www.iebschool.com/blog/estudio-teletrabajo-rrhh-2-0/

Beno, M. (2021, September 5). On-Site and Hybrid Workplace Culture of Positivity and Effectiveness: Case Study from Austria. *Academic Journal of Interdisciplinary Studies.* Retrieved from https://www.richtmann.org/journal/index.php/ajis/article/view/12658

Bertschek, I., & Niebel, T. (2016). *The impact of broadband internet on the economy: Final report for the European Commission*. ZEW-Centre for European Economic Research.

Bhattacharya, S., Sengupta, S., & Sharma, R. (2020). Privacy and security in the era of remote work: A review and research agenda. *Journal of the Association for Information Science and Technology*, *71*(12), 1419–1435. doi:10.1002/asi.24372 PMID:32427189

Bhimani, H., Mention, A. L., & Barlatier, P. J. (2019). Social media and innovation: A systematic literature review and future research directions. *Technological Forecasting and Social Change*, *144*, 251–269. doi:10.1016/j.techfore.2018.10.007

Biel, D., DeLone, M., Gerhardt, W., & Chang, C. (2019). *Radical Interoperability*. Available at: https://www2.deloitte.com/us/en/insights/industry/health-care/ radical-data-interoperability-survey.html

Boarini, M. (2022). Disruptive communication: Challenges and opportunities of the 21st century. In J. G. Andrade (Ed.), *Navigating digital communication and challenges for organizations* (pp. 39–57). IGI Global. doi:10.4018/978-1-7998-9790-3.ch003

Bondarouk, T., & Ruel, H. J. M. (2021). The COVID-19 pandemic as a catalyst for the reinvention of the future of work. *Journal of Business Research*, *122*, 1–8. doi:10.1016/j.jbusres.2020.12.016

Bosch-Sijtsema, P., Ruohomäki, V., & Vartiainen, M. (2009). Knowledge Work Productivity in Distributed Teams. *Journal of Knowledge Management*, *13*(6), 533–546. doi:10.1108/13673270910997178

Botan, C. (1993b). A human nature approach to images and ethics in international public relations. *Journal of Public Relations Research*, *5*(2), 71–81. doi:10.12071532754xjprr0502_02

Boueé & Schaible. (2015). *The digital transformation of industry*. Roland Berger and BDI.

Bousquet, M., & Nelson, C. (2008). *How the university works: Higher education and the low-wage nation*. New York University Press.

Bowen, W., & Tobin, E. (2017). *Locus of authority: The evolution of faculty roles in higher education*. Princeton University Press.

Brandão, H. P., Borges-Andrade, J. E., & Guimarães, T. A. (2012). Desempenho organizacional e suas relações com competências gerenciais, suporte organizacional e treinamento. *Revista de Administração (São Paulo)*, *47*(4), 523–539. doi:10.5700/rausp1056

Brandt, M. (2020). Why focus on is wellbeing? In E. Kim & B. Lindeman (Eds.), *Wellbeing* (pp. 11–19). Springer., doi:10.1007/978-3-030-29470-0_2

Bridges, L. E. (2018). Flexible as freedom? The dynamics of creative industry work and a case study of the editor in publishing. *New Media & Society*, *4*(4), 1303–1319. doi:10.1177/1461444816688920

Bronfenbrenner, U. (1979). *The Ecology of Human Development*. Harvard University Press.

Brower, A. M. (2021). *The challenges of creating and maintaining company culture during the pandemic*. Society for Human Resource Management. https://www.shrm.org/resourcesandtools/hr-topics/employee-relations/pages/the-challenges-of-creating-and-maintaining-company-culture-during-the-pandemic.aspx

Brown, L. W., Manegold, J. G., & Marquardt, D. J. (2020). The effects of CEO activism on employee's person-organization ideological misfit: A conceptual model and research agenda. *Business and Society Review*, *125*(1), 119–141. doi:10.1111/basr.12196

Brum, A. M. (2010). *Endomarketing de A a Z: como alinhar o pensamento das pessoas à estratégia da empresa, 4ª edição*. Integrate.

Bucchi, M. (2022). 'Have we ever been satisfied with Science Communication? Continuity and change'. *Journal of Clinical Outcomes Management*, *21*(07), C03.

Büchi, M. (2021). Digital well-being theory and research. *New Media & Society*. Advance online publication. doi:10.1177/14614448211056851

Budhwar, P., & Cumming, D. (2020). New Directions in Management Research and Communication: Lessons from the COVID-19 Pandemic. *British Journal of Management*, *31*(3). doi:10.1111/1467-8551.12426

Bulhões, J., & Renault, D. (2016). A precarização da prática jornalística: uma revisão bibliográfica sobre o impacto das condições de trabalho na saúde e qualidade de vida do jornalista. *Parágrafo, 4*(2), 164-175. https://revistaseletronicas.fiamfaam.br/index.php/recicofi/article/view/414

Bulnes, A. (2022). WhatsApp para trabajar: ¿una herramienta útil o una invasión más de la vida personal? *El País*. https://elpais.com/tecnologia/2022-02-22/whatsapp-para-trabajar-una-herramienta-util-o-una-invasion-mas-de-la-vida-personal.html

Burke, W. (2017). Organization change: Theory and practice (5th ed.). New York, NY: SAGE.

Bussy, N. M., Ewing, M. T., & Pitt, L. F. (2003). Stakeholder theory and internal marketing communications: A framework for analysing the influence of new media. *Journal of Marketing Communications*, *9*(3), 147–161. doi:10.1080/1352726032000129890

Buttorff, C., Ruder, T., & Bauman, M. (2017). *Multiple Chronic Conditions in the United States*. RAND Corporation. Available at https://www.rand.org/pubs/tools/TL221.html doi:10.7249/TL221

Cabra, M. (2022, April 10). El fin de la productividad: así pierdes horas sin darte cuenta. *Tecnosaludables*. https://blogs.alimente.elconfidencial.com/bienestar/tecnosaludables/2021-04-10/teletrajo-productividad-reducida-horas-conocimiento-covid_3028024/

Cain, N., & Gradisar, M. (2010). Electronic media use and sleep in school-aged children and adolescents: A review. *Sleep Medicine*, *11*(8), 735–742. doi:10.1016/j.sleep.2010.02.006 PMID:20673649

Caliber's Global Pharma Study. (2020). https://www.aboutfarma.com.br/secaodesktop/novidades/2907/caliber-lanca-estudo-global-inedito-sobre-a-reputacao-da-industria-farmaceutica-antes-e-durante-pandemia

Callison, C., & Seltzer, T. (2010). Influence of responsiveness, accessibility, and professionalism on journalists' perceptions of Southwest Airlines public relations. *Public Relations Review*, *36*(2), 141–146. doi:10.1016/j.pubrev.2010.01.002

Camilleri, M. A. (2018). Unlocking Corporate Social Responsibility Communication through Digital Media. In A. Lindgreen, J. Vanhamme, F. Maon, & R. Watkins (Eds.), Communicating Corporate Social Responsibility in the Digital Era. Academic Press.

Camilleri, M. A. (2020). The market for socially responsible investing: A review of the developments. *Social Responsibility Journal*. https://www.emerald.com/insight/content/doi/10.1108/SRJ-06-2019-0194/full/html

Campbell, R. J. (2004). *Campbell's psychiatric dictionary*. Oxford University Press.

Capoano, E. & Barros, V. T. (2020). Jovem, dedicado, confinado e prejudicado: perfis, rotinas e processos jornalísticos durante a pandemia de Covid-19. *Pauta Geral - Estudos em Jornalismo*, *7*, 1-15. doi:10.5212/RevistaPautaGeral.v.7.17267.229

Capoano, E., & Costa, P. R. (2021). Emotions, morals and resilience: The consumption of news in Ibero-America during the covid-19 pandemic. In D.M. Berube (Eds.), Pandemic communication and resilience. Risk, systems and decisions (pp. 331-345). Springer. https:// doi:10.1007/978-3-030-77344-1_20

Capoano, E., Costa, P. R., Galhardi, R., & Barros, V. T. (2021). Tristeza, medo, raiva e vergonha: Das emoções ao neuroticismo estimulado pelo consumo de notícias sobre covid-19. In R. C. Oliveira, D. Christino, & E. V. Machado Júnior (Eds.), *Covid-19 e a Comunicação* (pp. 255-277). Cegraf - UFG. https://hdl.handle.net/1822/73640

Capoano, E., Martini, M. R., & de Alencar, V. (2021). Identidades, perfiles y procesos: elementos que componen los periodistas de la Agência Mural Jornalismo das Periferias. In J. M. Valero Pastor (Ed.), *Plataformas, consumo mediático y nuevas realidades digitales. Hacia una perspectiva integradora* (pp. 334–353). Dykinson. https://hdl.handle.net/1822/75482

Cappellano, T., & Carramenha, B. (2020). *Trabalho remoto e isolamento social – Primeira onda*. Banco Original. 4CO. Retrieved November, 02, 2022 from https://4co.com.br/wp-content/uploads/2022/01/Trabalho_remoto_v2.2.pdf

Cappellano, T., Carramenha, B. (2020). *Trabalho remoto e isolamento social – Segunda onda*. Banco Original. 4CO. Retrieved November, 02, 2022 from file:///D:/Users/OneDrive/%C3%81rea%20de%20Trabalho/ACADEMIA/ARTIGOS%20E%20EVENTOS/REVISTAS%20ARTIGOS/IGI%20GLOBAL%20Z%C3%89%20GABRIEL/2022-2023/MATERIAL%20DE%20APOIO/PESQUISA%204CO%20%20%20TRABALHO%20REMOTO%202a%20ONDA.pdf

Cardoso, G., Baldi, V., Paisana, M., & Quintanilha, T. L. (2020). *Pandemia e consumos mediáticos*. OberCom - Observatório da Comunicação.

Carlisle, S., Henderson, G., & Hanlon, P. (2009). 'Wellbeing': A collateral casualty of modernity? *Social Science & Medicine*, *69*(10), 1556–1560. doi:10.1016/j.socscimed.2009.08.029 PMID:19765875

Carter, J. (2020, June 24). *Virtual Software Development Teams: 4 Challenges to Overcome* [Web log message]. Retrieved from https://techbeacon.com/app-dev-testing/virtual-software-development-teams-4-challenges-overcome

Carvajal, S. (2021). Siete de cada 10 mujeres que sufren acoso sexual en el trabajo no denuncian por miedo a las represalias. *El Mundo*. https://www.elmundo.es/espana/2021/04/29/608a8ae1fdddffe4458b45f4.html

Casey, V. (2010). Virtual software team project management. *Journal of the Brazilian Computer Society*, *16*(2), 83–96. doi:10.100713173-010-0013-3

Cavallini, M. (2021, August 20). Volta ao trabalho presencial será "difícil e estranha para os profissionais", diz pesquisa. *G1*. https://g1.globo.com/economia/concursos-e-emprego/noticia/2021/08/01/volta-ao-trabalho-presencial-sera-dificil-e-estranha-para-os-profissionais-diz-pesquisa.ghtml&gt

Cecchinato, M. E., Rooksby, J., Hiniker, A., Munson, S., Lukoff, K., Ciolfi, L., Thieme, A., & Harrison, D. (2019, May 2). Designing for digital wellbeing: A research & practice agenda. *Conference on Human Factors in Computing Systems - Proceedings*. https://doi.org/10.1145/3290607.3298998

Cennamo, C., & Santoro, G. (2020). The digital transformation of firms during the COVID-19 pandemic. *Journal of Business Research*, *116*, 276–283. doi:10.1016/j.jbusres.2020.07.042

Chakravorty, T., Chakraborty, S., & Jigeesh, N. (2014). Analysis of Agile testing attributes for faster time to Market: Context of Manufacturing sector related IT projects. *Procedia Economics and Finance*, *11*, 536–552. doi:10.1016/S2212-5671(14)00219-6

Chamorro-Premuzic, T. (2021). The Essential Components of Digital Transformation. *Access on*, 20.

Chamorro-Premuzic, T. (2021). Why hybrid work is the future of work. *Harvard Business Review*, *99*(1), 18–20.

Chandra, K., Arafah, W., & Basri, Y. Z. (2021). Analysis of the Effect of Green Organizational Culture on Organizational Performance and Competitive Advantages of Green through Green Innovation in Manufacturing Industries. *Hunan Daxue Xuebao. Shehui Kexue Ban*, *48*(6), 112–121.

Chao-Hung, W. (2019). How organizational green culture influences green performance and competitive advantage: The mediating role of green innovation. *Journal of Manufacturing Technology Management*, *30*(4), 666–683. doi:10.1108/JMTM-09-2018-0314

Charmaz, K. (2014). *Constructing grounded theory* (2nd ed.). Sage.

Chatman, J. A. (2020, December 9). Building corporate culture in a remote-work world. *Harvard Business Review*. https://hbr.org/2020/12/building-corporate-culture-in-a-remote-work-world

Chawla, N., Sarkar, S., & Sharma, I. (2020). Work from Home and Inter-role Conflict: A Study of Indian Working Women. *Journal of Work and Organizational Psychology*, *36*(2), 135–143.

Chen, G.-M., & Zhang, K. (2010). New media and cultural identity in the global society. In R. Taiwo (Ed.), *Handbook of research on discourse behavior and digital communication: Language structures and social interaction* (pp. 801–815). Idea Group. doi:10.4018/978-1-61520-773-2.ch051

Chen, L.-S., Liu, C.-H., Hsu, C.-C., & Lin, C.-S. (2010). C-Kano model: A novel approach for discovering attractive quality elements. *Total Quality Management & Business Excellence*, *21*(11), 1189–1214. doi:10.1080/14783363.2010.529347

Chen, L., Wang, Y., & Cui, Y. (2020). How do firms promote digital wellness in the workplace? The role of top management support and participative management. *International Journal of Environmental Research and Public Health*, *17*(14), 5019. doi:10.3390/ijerph17145019 PMID:32668635

Chen, M. (2007). *Membership-based Organizations of the Poor*. Routledge. doi:10.4324/9780203934074

Chen, Y. R., Chen, M. Y., & Chen, C. W. (2021). The effect of remote work on job performance: Evidence from the COVID-19 pandemic. *Sustainability*, *13*(15), 8545. doi:10.3390u13158545

Chinapaw, M. J. M., Proper, K. I., Brug, J., van Mechelen, W., & Singh, A. S. (2010). Relationship between young peoples' sedentary behaviour and biomedical health indicators: A systematic review of prospective studies. *Obesity Reviews*, *11*(8), 621–632. doi:10.1111/j.1467-789X.2009.00678.x PMID:21438990

Choudhury, P. R., Foroughi, C., & Larson, B. (2021). Work-from-anywhere: The productivity effects of geographic flexibility. *Strategic Management Journal*, *42*(4). doi:10.1002/smj.3251

Choudhury, P. R., Larson, B. Z., & Foroughi, C. (2019). Is It Time to Let Employees Work from Anywhere? *Harvard Business Review*. Retrieved from https://hbr.org/2019/08/is-it-time-to-let-employees-work-from-anywhere

Choudhury, S. R. (2020). Remote work is here to stay. Benefits and challenges. *Financial Times*. https://www.ft.com/content/4b0fe724-67d9-11ea-a3c9-1fe6fedcca75

Chowdhury, D. (2009). *Structured approach to improve passive aggressive organizational behavior of ABC Technologies: An empirical research* [Dissertation]. Lulu.com. Retrieved from: https://www.google.com/books/edition/Structured_Approach_to_Improve_Passive_A/L28h-OPPl1sC?hl=en&gbpv=0

Christofoletti, R., & Torres, R. J. (2018). Jornalistas expostos e vulneráveis: Ataques digitais como modalidade de risco profissional. *Famecos*, *25*(3), 29210. Advance online publication. doi:10.15448/1980-3729.2018.3.29210

Clarke, S. (2021). *How Luxury Brands Create Exclusive Digital Experiences*. https://www.publicissapient.com/insights/how-luxury-brands-create-exclusive-digital-experiences

Clarke, V., & Braun, V. (2017). Thematic analysis. *The Journal of Positive Psychology, 12*(3), 297–298. doi:10.1080/17439760.2016.1262613

Clemen, P. (2015). *Como implantar uma área de comunicação interna.* Mauad Editora.

Cleverti. (2018). *Brexit & IT: Why Portugal is Top Outsourcing Choice.* Retrieved from https://www.cleverti.com/blog/brexit-and-it-why-portugal-is-outsourcing-destination-of-choice

Comisiones Obreras & Delegación del Gobierno Contra la Violencia de Género. (2021). *El acoso sexual y el acoso por razón de sexo en el ámbito laboral en España.* https://www.ccoo.es/2f7f86bfc8a8105e09b013342bbf9e0d000001.pdf

Cordeiro, P. (2010). *A Rádio e as Indústrias culturais. Estratégias de Programação na transição para o digital.* Livros Horizonte.

Corrêa, E. S. (2005). Comunicação digital: Uma questão de estratégia e de relacionamento com públicos. *Organicom, 2*(3), 94–111. doi:10.11606/issn.2238-2593.organicom.2005.138900

Crane, A. (1995). Rhetoric and Reality in the Greening of Organisational Culture. *Greener Management International, 12*, 49–62.

Curvello, J. J. A. (2012). Comunicação interna e cultura organizacional (2ª ed.). Brasília: Casa das Musas.

Cvenkel, N. (2020). *Well-being in the workplace: governance and sustainability insights to promote workplace health.* Springer Nature. doi:10.1007/978-981-15-3619-9

Cvenkel, N. (2020). *Well-Being in the Workplace: Governance and Sustainability Insights to Promote Workplace Health.* Springer.

Daily, B., Bishop, J., & Govindarajulu, N. (2009). A conceptual model for organizational citizenship behavior directed toward the environment. *Business & Society, 48*(2), 243–256. doi:10.1177/0007650308315439

Danvila-del Valle, I., & Sastre-Castillo, M. Á. (2007). Capital humano y ventaja competitiva sostenible: Un análisis de la relaciónentre la formación y los resultados empresariales. *EsicMarket, 128*, 145-187. https://revistasinvestigacion.esic.edu/esicmarket/index.php/esicm/article/view/73/160

Davies, A., Tenesa, A., Payton, A., Yang, J., Harris, S. E., Liewald, D., Ke, X., Le Hellard, S., Christoforou, A., Luciano, M., McGhee, K., Lopez, L., Gow, A. J., Corley, J., Redmond, P., Fox, H. C., Haggarty, P., Whalley, L. J., McNeill, G., ... Deary, I. J. (2011). Genome-wide association studies establish that human intelligence is highly heritable and polygenic. *Molecular Psychiatry, 16*(10), 996–1005. doi:10.1038/mp.2011.85 PMID:21826061

Davis, M., & Prince, M. (2005). Dynamics of trust between clients and their advertising agencies: Advanced in performanced theory. *Academy of Marketing Review, 11*, 1–32.

De Oliveira, E. A., Pimenta, M. L., Hilletofth, P., & Eriksson, D. (2016). Integration through cross-functional teams in a service company. *European Business Review, 28*(4), 405–430. doi:10.1108/EBR-01-2016-0014

de Sousa, V., Capoano, E. & Paganotti, I. (2022). ¿La Covid-19 ha infectado las noticias? Cómo los periodistas, las audiencias y los procesos de producción son alterados por las pandemias. *Universitas-XXI, 37*, 19-41. doi:10.17163/uni.n37.2022.01

De Stefano, V., Stylogiaannis, C., Wouters, M., & Durri, I. (2021). *"Actualización de las necesidades del sistema": Mejora de la protección frente al ciberacoso y a la violencia y el acoso en el mundo del trabajo posibilitados por las TIC.* https://www.ilo.org/legacy/spanish/intserv/working-papers/wp001/index.html

de Vries, L., Gensler, S., & Leeflang, P. S. (2017). Effects of traditional advertising and social messages on brand-building metrics and customer acquisition. *Journal of Marketing*, *81*(5), 1–15. doi:10.1509/jm.15.0178

Deery, S., Walsh, J., Zatzick, C. D., & Hayes, A. F. (2017). Exploring the relationship between compressed work hours satisfaction and absenteeism in front-line service work. *European Journal of Work and Organizational Psychology*, *26*(1), 42–52. doi:10.1080/1359432X.2016.1197907

Del Rosal, P. (2021). Los protocolos contra el ciberacoso, los grandes olvidados en los planes de teletrabajo. *El Confidencial*. https://www.elconfidencial.com/juridico/2021-03-27/protocolos-contra-el-ciberacoso-los-grandes-olvidados_3010040/

Delbridge, R., & Sallaz, J. J. (2015). Work: Four Worlds and Ways of Seeing. *Organization Studies*, *36*(11), 1449–1462. Advance online publication. doi:10.1177/0170840615612021

Dermol, V., & Širca, N. (2018). Communication, Company Mission, Organizational Values, and Company Performance. *Procedia - Social and Behavioral Sciences, 238*, 542-551. doi:10.1016/j.sbspro.2018.04.034

Desilver, D. (2020, April 24). *Unemployment rose higher in three months of COVID-19 than it did in two years of the Great Recession*. Pew Research Center. https://www.pewresearch.org/fact-tank/2020/04/24/unemployment-rose-higher-in-three-months-of-covid-19-than-it-did-in-two-years-of-the-great-recession/

Deuze, M. (2006). O jornalismo e os novos meios de comunicação social. *Comunicação e Sociedade*, *9*, 15–37. doi:10.17231/comsoc.9(2006).1152

Devesa, L. M. (2016). *A importância da comunicação organizacional no contexto organizacional*. Instituto Politécnico de Setúbal. Tese de Mestrado em Ciências Empresariais.

Díaz, V. L. (2021). El ciber acoso en el mundo del trabajo: Es suficiente la nueva ley para prevenirlo? *Revista IDEIDES, 61*. http://revista-ideides.com/el-ciber-acoso-en-el-mundo-del-trabajo-es-suficiente-la-nueva-ley-para-prevenirlo/

Dictionary, O. E. (1993). *Oxford English Dictionary*. OUP.

Dikert, K., Paasivaara, M., & Lassenius, C. (2016). Challenges and success factors for large-scale agile transformations: A systematic literature review. *Journal of Systems and Software*, *119*, 87–108. doi:10.1016/j.jss.2016.06.013

Dingel, J. I., & Neiman, B. (2020). *How Many Jobs Can be Done at Home?* Becker Friedman Institute for Economics at Chicago. Available at: https://github.com/jdingel/DingelNeimanworkathome/blob/master/DingelNeiman-workathome.pdf

Duarte, A., & Dias, P. (2021). TikTok: Usos e motivações entre adolescentes em Portugal. *Chasqui, Revista Latino-americana de Comunicación*, *1*(147), 81–103. doi:10.16921/chasqui.v1i147.4419

Duarte, J. (2015). Entrevista em profundidade. In J. Duarte (Ed.), *Métodos e técnicas de pesquisa em comunicação* (2nd ed., pp. 62–83). Ed. Atlas.

Duck, S., & McMahan, D. T. (2009). *The basics of communication – A relational perspective*. Sage.

Durán, L., Fernández García, S., & Núñez Villaveirán, L. (2019). Una empleada de Iveco se suicida tras viralizarse en la empresa un vídeo sexual. *El Mundo*. https://www.elmundo.es/madrid/2019/05/28/5ced493efdddffb0758b48fb.html

Ebersberger, B., & Kuckertz, A. (2021). Hop to it! The impact of organization type on innovation response time to the COVID-19 crisis. *Journal of Business Research*, *124*, 126–135. doi:10.1016/j.jbusres.2020.11.051 PMID:36540106

Ecklebe, S., & Löffler, N. (2021). A question of quality: Perceptions of internal communication during the COVID-19 pandemic in Germany. *Journal of Communication Management (London)*, *25*(3), 214–232. doi:10.1108/JCOM-09-2020-0101

Eddy, D. M. (1982). Clinical Policies and the Quality of Clinical Practice. *The New England Journal of Medicine, 307*(6), 343–347. doi:10.1056/NEJM198208053070604 PMID:7088099

Edison, H., Wang, X., & Conboy, K. (2022). Comparing Methods for Large-Scale Agile Software Development: A Systematic Literature Review. *IEEE Transactions on Software Engineering, 48*(8), 2709–2731. doi:10.1109/TSE.2021.3069039

Eggcellentwork.com. (2022). *Manager title without direct reports—Is it good or bad?* Retrieved from: https://eggcellentwork.com/manager-title-without-direct-reports/

Ekman, E. & Ekman, P. (2013). Cultivating emotional balance: Structure, Research, and implementation. *Compassion: Bridging practice and science*, 398-414.

El teletrabajo durante la pandemia de Covid-19 y después de ella. (2021). https://www.ilo.org/wcmsp5/groups/public/---ed_protect/---protrav/---travail/documents/publication/wcms_758007.pdf

ElDerecho.com. (2020). *El teletrabajo ha puesto en riesgo a muchas empresas y algunas no son conscientes*. Noticias jurídicas y actualidad. https://elderecho.com/el-teletrabajo-ha-puesto-en-riesgo-a-muchas-empresas-y-algunas-no-son-conscientes

Endresen, J. (2020). *COVID-19's impact of work, workers, and the workplace of the future*. Cornell Business. Retrieved from: https://business.cornell.edu/hub/2020/09/25/covid-19s-impact-work-workers-workplace-future/

Erat, S., Kitapci, H., & Comez, P. (2017). The effect of organizational loads on work stress, emotional commitment, and turnover intention. International Journal of Organizational Leadership, 6, 221-231. doi:10.19236/IJOL.2017.02.07

Espinosa-Curiel, I. E., Rodríguez-Jacobo, J., Vázquez-Alfaro, E., Fernández-Zepeda, J. A., & Fajardo-Delgado, D. (2018). Analysis of the changes in communication and social interactions during the transformation of a traditional team into an agile team. *Journal of Software (Malden, MA), 30*(9), e1946. doi:10.1002mr.1946

Essenfelder, R., Sant'Anna, E., & Coca, A. P. (2021, October). *Reconfiguração das Redações brasileiras durante a pandemia de Covid-19* [Paper presentation]. 4° Congresso Internacional Media Ecology and Image Studies-Reflexões sobre o ecossistema midiático pós pandemia. Annual Congress, Brazil.

EUR-Lex. (2007). *Código práctico encaminado a combatir el acoso sexual en el trabajo*. https://eur-lex.europa.eu/ES/legal-content/summary/code-of-practice-to-clamp-down-on-sexual-harassment-at-work.html

Eurofound. (2020). *Living, working and COVID-19*. Luxemburgo: Publications Office of the European Union. Retrieved in May 25th, 2022, from: https://www.eurofound.europa.eu/sites/default/files/ef_publication/field_ef_document/ef20059en.pdf

Eurofound. (2020). *Living, working and COVID-19*. Publications Office of the European Union.

Europa Press. (2022). Expertos advierten de que solo el 1% de los casos de mobbing o acoso sexual en el ámbito laboral sale a la luz. *epsocial*. https://www.europapress.es/epsocial/igualdad/noticia-expertos-advierten-solo-casos-mobbing-acoso-sexual-ambito-laboral-sale-luz-20220527165041.html

Evans, E. (1977). *Radio. A Guide to Broadcasting Techniques*. Barrie & Jenkins.

Falk, A., Becker, A., Dohmen, T. J., Human, D., & Sunde, U. (2016). *The preference survey module: A validated instrument for measuring risk, time, and social preferences*. Discussion paper 9674, IZA, Institute of Labor Economics.

Farahat, S., Amin, O., Hamdy, H., & Fouad, M. (2021). The impact of work-related stress of the cognition domain of executive functioning of health care workers during the COVID-19 pandemic. *International Archives of Occupational and Environmental Health*. Advance online publication. doi:10.100700420-021-01814-8 PMID:34734341

Faraj, W., Renno, W., & Bhardwaj, A. (2021). Unto the breach: What the COVID-19 pandemic exposes about digitalization. *Information and Organization*, *31*(1), 100337. doi:10.1016/j.infoandorg.2021.100337

Fardouly, J., Diedrichs, P. C., Vartanian, L. R., & Halliwell, E. (2018). Social comparisons on social media: The impact of Facebook on young women's body image concerns and mood. *Body Image*, *26*, 38–45. doi:10.1016/j.bodyim.2018.06.003 PMID:25615425

Fernández, E., Junquera, B., & Ordiz, M. (2003). Organizational culture and human resources in the environmental issue: A review of the literature. *International Journal of Human Resource Management*, *14*(4), 634–656. doi:10.1080/0958519032000057628

Ferrari, P. (2020). *Como sair das bolhas*. Educ.

Fevereiro. (2022). https://hbr.org/2021/11/the-essential-components-of-digital-transformation

Figaro, R. (2014). Jornalismos e trabalho de jornalistas: desafios para as novas gerações no século XXI. *Parágrafo, 2*(2), 23-37. https://www.eca.usp.br/acervo/producao-academica/002672767.pdf

Figaro, R., Marques, A. F., Camargo, C. A., Rebechi, C. N., de Oliveira, D. F., Kinoshita, J. O., . . . Santana, Y. A. (2021). Os comunicadores no contexto de um ano da pandemia de Covid-19. *Líbero*, (49), 61-89. https://seer.casperlibero.edu.br/index.php/libero/article/view/1621/1310

Figaro, R. (2011). A abordagem ergológica e o mundo do trabalho dos comunicadores. *Trabalho, Educação e Saúde*, *9*(suppl 1), 285–297. doi:10.1590/S1981-77462011000400014

Figaro, R., & Silva, A. F. M. D. (2020). A comunicação como trabalho no Capitalismo de plataforma: O caso das mudanças no jornalismo. *Contracampo*, *39*(1), 101–115. doi:10.22409/contracampo.v39i1.38566

Finkel, R., Jones, D., Sang, K., & Russel, D. S. (2017). Diversifying the creative: Creative work, creative industries, creative identities. *Organization*, *24*(3), 281–288. doi:10.1177/1350508417690167

Fishenden, J. (1997, April). Managing intranets to improve business process. *Aslib Proceedings*, *49*(4), 90–96. doi:10.1108/eb051454

Flamholtz, E. (1996). *Effective managerial control: Theory and practice*. Kluwer Academic Publishers. doi:10.1007/978-1-4613-1359-5

Fleming, C. (2010). *The Radio Handbook*. Routledge.

Flood, J., & Leap, T. (2018). *Managing risk in high-stakes faculty employment decisions*. ILR Press. doi:10.7591/cornell/9781501728952.001.0001

Formica, S., & Sfodera, F. (2022). The Great Resignation and Quiet Quitting paradigm shifts: An overview of current situation and future research directions. *Journal of Hospitality Marketing & Management*, *31*(8), 899–907. doi:10.1080/19368623.2022.2136601

Fornells-Ambrojo, M., Davenport, T., & Auton, J. (2020). Digital well-being: A comprehensive framework for health and well-being in the digital age. *Internet Interventions : the Application of Information Technology in Mental and Behavioural Health*, *21*, 100327. doi:10.1016/j.invent.2020.100327

Forni, J. J. (2021). *Gestão de Crises e Comunicação*. Atlas. Edição do Kindle.

Fraustino, J. D., & Connolly-Ahern, C. (2015). Corporate associations written on the wall: Publics' responses to Fortune 500 ability and social responsibility Facebook posts. *Journal of Public Relations Research*, *27*(5), 452–474. doi:10.1080/1062726X.2015.1098543

Fuglsang, L. (2001). Three Perspectives in STS in the Policy Context. In S. Cutcliffe & C. Mitcham (Eds.), *Visions of STS: Counterpoints in Science, Technology, and Social Studies* (pp. 35–49). State University of New York Press.

Gamble, T. K., & Gamble, M. (2014). *Interpersonal communication: building connections together*. Sage.

García García, M., Carrillo-Durán, M.V. & Tato Jimenez, J.L. (2017). Online corporate communications: website usability and content. *Journal of Communication Management, 21*(2), 140-154.

Gardner, L. (2023). Flagships prosper, while regionals suffer: Competition is fierce and the gap is widening. *Chronicle of Higher Education*. Retrieved from: https://www.chronicle.com/article/flagships-prosper-while-regionals-suffer

Garvi Carvajal, A. (2021). El derecho a la desconexión laboral sigue sin respetarse. *El País*. https://elpais.com/economia/negocios/2021-11-20/el-derecho-a-la-desconexion-laboral-sigue-sin-respetarse.html

Gawer, A. (2009). Platform Dynamics and Strategies: From Products to Services. In A. Gawer (Ed.), *Platforms, Markets and Innovation*. Edward Elgar Publishing. doi:10.4337/9781849803311.00009

Ghangurde, A. (2018). *McKinsey executives on expanding the pharmaceutical industry's digital drive, lessons from Amazon*. https://scrip.pharmaintelligence.informa.com/SC141824/McKinsey-Execs-On-Expanding-Pharmas-Digital-Push-Lessons-From-Amazon

Ghobadi, S., & Mathiassen, L. (2016). Perceived barriers to effective knowledge sharing in agile software teams. *Information Systems Journal, 26*(2), 95–125. doi:10.1111/isj.12053

Gibson, C. B., & Gibbs, J. L. (2006). Unpacking the concept of virtuality: The effects of geographic dispersion, electronic dependence, dynamic structure, and national diversity on team innovation. *Administrative Science Quarterly, 51*(3), 451–495. doi:10.2189/asqu.51.3.451

Gibson, J. J. (1979). *The Theory of Affordances. The Ecological Approach to Visual Perception*. Taylor & Francis.

Gill, A., Ahmad, B., & Kazmi, S. (2021). The effect of green human resource management on environmental performance: The mediating role of employee eco-friendly behavior. *Management Science Letters, 11*, 1725–1736. doi:10.5267/j.msl.2021.2.010

Gilpin, D. (2008). Narrating the organizational self: Reframing the role of the news release. *Public Relations Review, 34*(1), 9–18. doi:10.1016/j.pubrev.2007.08.005

Giruge, F. V., & Vanessa, S. (2020). *How Working from Home during COVID-19 Affects Parental Stress*. Social Science Research Network.

Goh, K. H., Wang, L., Yeow, A. Y. K., Poh, H., Li, K., Yeow, J. J. L., & Tan, G. Y. H. (2021). Artificial intelligence in sepsis early prediction and diagnosis using unstructured data in healthcare. *Nature Communications, 12*(1), 711. doi:10.103841467-021-20910-4 PMID:33514699

Gonete, T. Z., Yazachew, L., & Endehabtu, B. F. (2021). Improving data quality and information utilization at Metema Primary Hospital, Amhara national regional state, Northwest Ethiopia 2018: Capstone project. *Health Informatics Journal, 27*(3), 14604582211043160. doi:10.1177/14604582211043160 PMID:34569329

González Masip, J. (2018). Los grupos de interés y su importancia en la propuesta de valor de las empresas. *Boletín Económico de ICE, 3096*, 47-57. https://dialnet.unirioja.es/servlet/articulo?codigo=6381236

Google Digital Wellbeing. (n.d.). *What is Digital Wellbeing?* https://bit.ly/2sEOjE0

Government Emergency Ordinance no. 132/2020, on support measures for employees and employers in the context of SARS-COV2-pandemic, as well as for stimulating employment growth in force since August 2020, https://www.pwc.ro/en/tax-legal/alerts/law-no--153-2020-entering-into-force-on-24-july-2020--amending-a1.html

Gratton, L. (2019). Agile working: How to do it. *Strategic HR Review*, *18*(3), 151–156. doi:10.1108/SHR-02-2019-0025

Greenhaus, J. H., & Beutell, N. J. (1985). Sources of conflict between work and family roles. *Academy of Management Review*, *10*(1), 76–88. doi:10.2307/258214

Griep, Y., Vranjes, I., van Hooff, M. M., Beckers, D. G., & Geurts, S. A. (2021). Technology in the workplace: Opportunities and challenges. In C. Korunka (Ed.), *Flexible Working Practices and Approaches: Psychological and Social Implications* (pp. 93–116). Springer. doi:10.1007/978-3-030-74128-0_6

Grieve, R., Indian, M., Witteveen, K., Tolan, G. A., & Marrington, J. (2013). Face-to-face or Facebook: Can social connectedness be derived online? *Computers in Human Behavior*, *29*(3), 604–609. doi:10.1016/j.chb.2012.11.017

Griffis, H. (2022, June 2). *What Is a Hybrid Work Model, and How Do We Make It Work?* Built In. https://builtin.com/remote-work/hybrid-work-model

Grossman, R. (2014). *Science Communication: Could You Explain It to Your Granny?* https://www.theguardian.com/science/blog/ 2014/oct/10/science-communicators-quantum-physics-granny

Grupo Atico34. (2021). *Protección de datos y teletrabajo: Recomendaciones*. https://protecciondatos-lopd.com/empresas/proteccion-datos-teletrabajo/

Gui, M., Fasoli, M., & Carradore, R. (2017). Digital well-being. Developing a new theoretical tool for media literacy research. *Italian Journal of Sociology of Education*, *9*(1), 155–173. doi:10.14658/pupj-ijse-2017-1-8

Hajjdiab, H., Taleb, A. S., & Ali, J. (2012). An Industrial Case Study for Scrum Adoption. *Journal of Software*, *7*(1), 237–242. doi:10.4304/jsw.7.1.237-242

Halford, S. (2005). Hybrid workspace: Re-spatialisation of work, organisation and management. *New Technology, Work and Employment*, *20*(1), 19–33. doi:10.1111/j.1468-005X.2005.00141.x

Hao, K. (2018). How to Promote Digital Well-being at Work. *Harvard Business Review*. https://bit.ly/3UbkGpC

Hare, N. (2022). What is quiet quitting and how should leaders respond? *Forbes*. Retrieved from: https://www.forbes.com/sites/allbusiness/2022/09/01/what-is-quiet-quitting-and-how-should-leaders-respond/?sh=20f6b7ae6de0

Hariry, R. V., & Barenji, A. (2021). Paradkar From industry 4.0 to pharma 4.0. Handbook of Smart Materias Technologies and Devices, 1-22.

Harkaway, N. (2012). *The blind giant: Being human in a digital world*. John Murray Publishers.

Haro-de-Rosario, A., del Mar Gálvez-Rodríguez, M., Sáez-Martín, A., & Caba-Pérez, C. (2017). Role of the Board of Directors in Business Ethics In Latin American Countries. *RAE-Business Administration Magazine*, *57*(5), 426–438.

Harris, C. (2020). *Distributed scrum: How to manage a remote scrum team*. Retrieved from https://www.atlassian.com/agile/scrum/distributed-scrum

Harris, L. C., & Crane, A. (2002). The greening of organizational culture - management views in the depth, degree and diffusion of change. *Journal of Organizational Change Management*, *15*(3), 214–234. doi:10.1108/09534810210429273

Hartmann, F., Kraus, K., Nilsson, G., Anthony, R., & Govindarajan, V. (2020). Management control systems (2nd ed.). Boston, MA: McGraw-Hill.

Hautamäki, E.; Kinnunen, U.-M.; Palojoki, S. (2017). Health information systems usability-related use errors in patient safety incidents. *Finn. J. eHealth eWelfare, 9*, 6.

Heagney, J. (2016). *Fundamentals of Project Management*. Amacom.

Health & Human Services. (2022). *Mental Health*. U.S. Department of Health & Human Services. https://www.mentalhealth.gov/

Heloani, J. R. (2005). Mudanças no mundo do trabalho e impactos na qualidade de vida do jornalista. *FGV EAESP – Gvpesquisa,* 1-92. http://hdl.handle.net/10438/3098

Heloani, R. (2006). O trabalho do jornalista: Estresse e qualidade de vida. *Interações*, (22), 171–198. https://www.redalyc.org/articulo.oa?id=35402208

Heloani, R., & Silva, E. P. (2021). Reflexões teóricas e metodológicas sobre pesquisas no campo da saúde mental e trabalho. *Cadernos CERU, 32*(1), 62–82. doi:10.11606/issn.2595-2536.v32i1p62-82

Henderson, L., & Knight, T. (2012). Integrating the hedonic and eudaimonic perspectives to more comprehensively understand wellbeing and pathways to wellbeing. *International Journal of Wellbeing, 2*(3), 196–221. doi:10.5502/ijw.v2i3.3

Hennel, P., & Rosenkranz, C. (2017). Team Diversity and Performance – How Agile Practices and Psychological Safety Interact. *Proceedings of the International Conference on Information Systems*, 1-12.

He, S., Oerman, T., & van de Ven, J. (2016). The sources of the communication gap. *Management Science, 63*(9), 2832–2846. doi:10.1287/mnsc.2016.2518

Hesketh, I., & Cooper, C. L. (2017). Why wellbeing, why now? In C. L. Cooper & I. Hesketh (Eds.), *Managing health and wellbeing in the public sector: A guide to best practice* (pp. 19–32). Routledge. doi:10.4324/9781315681344-3

Hickman, A. (2020). *Corporate PR requires renewed focus on internal comms post Covid-19*. Retrieved in March 20th, 2022, from: https://www.prweek.com/article/1691759/corporate-pr-requires-renewed-focus-internal-comms-post-covid-19-survey-finds?utm_content=137192127&utm_medium=social&utm_source=linkedin&hss_channel=lcp-29812&fbclid=IwAR1C-HsO3Pk-lMep7gFgIE-0ZZfaNqhWO_sstqJnsQPv3dL

Hidalgo, E. S. (2019). Adapting the scrum framework for agile project management in science: Case study of a distributed research initiative. *Heliyon, 5*(3), 1–32. doi:10.1016/j.heliyon.2019.e01447 PMID:30976706

Hoffman, M., Litzky, B. E., & Jain, A. (2020). *Workforce Reduction and Remote Work: Implications for Job Quality and Income Inequality*. Social Science Research Network.

Holliday, M. (2021). *10 causes of employee turnover & how to prevent/reduce them*. Oracle NetSuite. Retrieved from: https://www.netsuite.com/portal/resource/articles/human-resources/employee-turnover-causes.shtml

Holmqvist, J., Wirtz, J., & Fritze, M. (2020). Luxury in the digital age: A multi-actor service encounter perspective. *Journal of Business Research, 121*, 747–756. doi:10.1016/j.jbusres.2020.05.038

Holt, E., & Munday, I. (2020). Cyberbullying in remote work: The mediating roles of social support and communication frequency. *Journal of Business and Psychology, 35*(4), 519–533. doi:10.100710869-019-09644-w

Holtzhausen, D. R., & Zerfass, A. (2013). *May. Strategic communication: A concept at the center of applied communication?* Paper presented at the Preconference "Strategic communication – A concept at the center of applied communications", International Communication Association, Annual Conference, Boston, MA.

Hoxha, K., Hung, Y. W., Irwin, B. R., & Grepin, K. A. (2020). Understanding the challenges associated with the use of data from routine health information systems in low-and middle-income countries: A systematic review. *The HIM Journal*. PMID:32602368

Hummel, M., Rosenkranz, C., & Holten, R. (2013). The Role of Communication in Agile Systems Development. *Business & Information Systems Engineering*, *5*(5), 343–355. doi:10.100712599-013-0282-4

Huta, V., & Ryan, R. M. (2010). Pursuing Pleasure or Virtue: The Differential and Overlapping Well-Being Benefits of Hedonic and Eudaimonic Motives. *Journal of Happiness Studies*, *11*(6), 735–762. doi:10.100710902-009-9171-4

Ibraheem, A. (2018). *Project and functional managers: Coopetition paradox and leadership impact*. Available at: https://uu.diva-portal.org/smash/get/diva2:1228648/FULLTEXT01.pdf

Ihlen, Ø., & Levenshus, A. (2017). Panacea, placebo or prudence: Perspectives and constraints for corporate dialogue. *Public Relations Inquiry*, *6*(3), 219–232. doi:10.1177/2046147X17708815

IMF. (2013). Las redes sociales en la comunicación interna. *IMF Blog Corporativo*. https://blogs.imf-formacion.com/blog/corporativo/prl/las-redes-sociales-en-la-comunicacion-interna/

Instituto Nacional de Seguridad e Higiene en el Trabajo. (2000). *Acoso sexual en el trabajo*. https://www.insst.es/documents/94886/191756/NTP+507+Acoso+sexual+en+el+trabajo.pdf

Instituto Nacional de Seguridad e Higiene en el Trabajo. (2007). *La comunicación en las organizaciones* (N.º 685; p. 6). https://www.insst.es/documents/94886/326775/ntp_685.pdf

Instituto Nacional de Seguridad e Higiene en el Trabajo. (2009). *Acoso psicológico en el trabajo: Definición* (N.º 854; p. 6). https://www.insst.es/documents/94886/326775/854+web.pdf

Instituto Nacional de Seguridad y Salud en el Trabajo. (2012). *Violencia en el trabajo*. https://www.insst.es/materias/riesgos/riesgos-psicosociales/violencia-en-el-trabajo

Internet, P. (2005). *Health information Online*. Available at: https://www.pewresearch.org/internet/2005/05/17/health-information-online/

Ishtiaque, F. & Habib, L. (2016). Impact of Internal Communication on Organizational Development. *International Journal of Trend in Research and Development, 3*, 242-247.

Jackson, S., Schuler, R., & Werner, S. (n.d.). Managing human resources (11th ed.). Mason, OH: South-Western.

Jacobs, J., & Gerson, K. (2005). *The time divide: Work, family, and gender inequity*. Harvard University Press.

Jang, H. J., Choi, Y. D., & Kim, N. H. (2017). Effects and Satisfaction of Medical Device Safety Information Reporting System Using Electronic Medical Record. *Healthcare Informatics Research*, *23*(2), 94–100. doi:10.4258/hir.2017.23.2.94 PMID:28523207

Jean-Victor, A., Bendavid, Y., Fouksman, O., & Milgrom, E. (2020). The cross-country shift to home-based work and its implications for the future of work. *Journal of Public Economics*, *189*, 104270. doi:10.1016/j.jpubeco.2020.104270

Jeske, D., & Calvard, T. S. (2020). A review of the literature on cross-functional integration (2010–2020): Trends and recommendations. *The International Journal of Organizational Analysis*.

Josh, L. (2020). A Four-Pillared Holistic Model for Improving Performance in Engineering Virtual Project Teams. *Engineering Management Journal*, *32*(2), 107–119. doi:10.1080/10429247.2019.1672409

Kapferer. J.N., Kemstock, J., Brexendorf. T., & Powell, S. (2017). Advances in Luxury Brand Management. *Journal of Brand Management.*

Kaplin, W., & Lee, B. (2006). *The law of higher education: A comprehensive guide to legal implications of administrative decision-making*. Jossey-Bass.

Karhawi, I. (2021). Comunicação organizacional e influenciadores digitais: aproximações e conflitos. In *Comunicação organizacional: práticas, desafios e perspectivas digitais* (pp. 141–153). Summus Editorial.

Kastelan Mrak, M., & Sokolic, D. (2017). The Evolution of Work Organization and its Implication for Educational Policies and Managerial Practices. *Proceedings of the 6th International Scientific Symposium Economy of Eastern Croatia - Vision and Growth*, 335-344.

Katz, D., & Khan, R. (1986). *Psicología Social de las Organizaciones.* https://www.academia.edu/27894499/Katz_D_Kahn_R_Psicolog%C3%ADa_Social_de_Las_Organizaciones

Kelly, C. (2015). *A linguistic study of the understanding of emoticons and emojis in text messages.* Halmstad University.

Kemp, N. (2018). *Is the advertising industry doing enough to protect and promote the mental wellbeing of employees?* https://www.campaignlive.co.uk/article/advertising-industry-doing-enough-protect-promote-mental-wellbeing-employees/1495437

Kennedy, A. K., & Sommerfeldt, E. J. (2015). A postmodern turn for social media research: Theory and research directions for public relations scholarship. *Atlantic Journal of Communication*, *23*(1), 31–45. doi:10.1080/15456870.2015.972406

Kent, M. L., & Lane, A. B. (2017). A rhizomatous metaphor for dialogic theory. *Public Relations Review*, *43*(3), 568–578. doi:10.1016/j.pubrev.2017.02.017

Kent, M. L., & Taylor, M. (1998). Building dialogic relationships through the World Wide Web. *Public Relations Review*, *24*(3), 321–334. doi:10.1016/S0363-8111(99)80143-X

Keyes, C. L. M. (1998). Social Well-Being. *Social Psychology Quarterly*, *61*(2), 121–140. doi:10.2307/2787065

Keyes, C. L. M. (2005). Mental illness and/or mental health? Investigating axioms of the complete state model of health. *Journal of Consulting and Clinical Psychology*, *73*(3), 539–548. doi:10.1037/0022-006X.73.3.539 PMID:15982151

Killian, G., & McManus, K. (2015). A marketing communications approach for the digital era: Managerial guidelines for social media integration. *Business Horizons*, *58*(5), 539–549. doi:10.1016/j.bushor.2015.05.006

Kim, J., Jung, S., Seok, B., & Choi, H. (2022). The Relationship among Four Lifestyles of Workers amid the COVID-19 Pandemic (Work–Life Balance, YOLO, Minimal Life, and Staycation) and Organizational Effectiveness: With a Focus on Four Countries. *Sustainability (Basel)*, *14*(21), 14059. Advance online publication. doi:10.3390u142114059

Kim, J., & Lee, J. (2019). Digital well-being: Concept, measurement, and future directions. In S. S. Sundar (Ed.), *The Oxford handbook of digital well-being* (pp. 3–22). Oxford University Press. doi:10.1093/oxfordhb/9780190932590.013.1

Kim, Y., Kim, W., Choi, H., & Phetvaroon, K. (2019). The effect of green human resources management on hotel employees' eco-friendly behavior and environmental performance. *International Journal of Hospitality Management*, *76*, 83–93. doi:10.1016/j.ijhm.2018.04.007

King, N. (2004). Using interviews in qualitative research. In C. Cassell & G. Symon (Eds.), *Essential Guide to Qualitative Methods in Organizational Research* (pp. 11–22). Sage. https://legislatie.just.ro/Public/DetaliiDocument/199418

Kirkman, B. L., Gibson, C. B., & Kim, K. (2012). Across borders and technologies: Advancements in virtual teams research. *Advances in Global Leadership*, *7*, 251–288. doi:10.1093/oxfordhb/9780199928286.013.0025

Kirkman, B. L., & Mathieu, J. E. (2005). The dimensions and antecedents of team virtuality. *Journal of Management, 31*(5), 700–718. doi:10.1177/0149206305279113

Kirschner, P. A., & Karpinski, A. C. (2010). Facebook and academic performance. *Computers in Human Behavior, 26*(6), 1237–1245. doi:10.1016/j.chb.2010.03.024

Kissflow. (2020). 4 cross-departmental collaboration challenges and how to overcome them. *Kissflow*. Retrieved from: https://kissflow.com/digital-workplace/collaboration/challenges-in-cross-departmental-collaboration/

Kitson, G., Marie, G., Francoia, J.-P., Zalesskiy, S. S., Sigerson, R. C., Mathieson, J. S., & Cronin, L. (2018). Digitization of multistep organic synthesis in reactionware for on-demand pharmaceuticals. *Science, 359*(6373), 314–319. doi:10.1126cience.aao3466 PMID:29348235

Klaus, P. (2020). The End of The World as We Know It? The Influence of Online Channels on the Luxury Customer Experience. *Journal of Retailing and Consumer Services, 57*, 102248. doi:10.1016/j.jretconser.2020.102248

Knight, R. (2021). *Hybrid workforces are the future. Here's how to make them successful*. World Economic Forum. https://www.weforum.org/agenda/2021/03/hybrid-workforces-are-the-future-heres-how-to-make-them-successful/

Knowles, J. (2020). *3 tough challenges PR pros are facing amid COVID-19 uncertainty*. Retrieved in March 18th, 2022 from: https://www.prdaily.com/3-tough-challenges-pr-pros-are-face-amid-covid-19-uncertainty/?fbclid=IwAR3JjOOr9B8la7GnfEQ7y58mjr9flKuU53q8SEhvb3PS90fc4hO-EAeWZvQ

Koenig, K. (2021). Did students really take pandemic gap years? *EdSurge*. Retrieved from: https://www.edsurge.com/news/2021-11-08-did-students-really-take-pandemic-gap-years

Koetsier, J. (2020, April 6). 4 ways remote work is changing tech salaries. *Forbes*. Retrieved from https://www.forbes.com/sites/johnkoetsier/2020/04/06/4-ways-remote-work-is-changing-tech-salaries/?sh=4c4d46261f0f

Köhler, K. & Zerfass, A. (2019). Communicating the corporate strategy: An international benchmark study in the UK, the USA, and Germany. *Journal of Communication Management, 23*(4), 348-374.

Kooij, D. T., Kanfer, R., Betts, M., & Rudolph, C. W. (2021). Future of work: Implications for individual well-being, organizational performance, and societal prosperity. *Work, Aging and Retirement, 7*(1), 3–22. doi:10.1093/workar/waaa026

Kossek, E. E., & Lautsch, B. A. (2012). Work–life flexibility for whom? Occupational status and work–life inequality in upper, middle, and lower level jobs. *The Sociological Quarterly, 53*(3), 282–314. doi:10.1111/j.1533-8525.2012.01248.x

Kostin, D., & Strode, D. (2022). Effective communication in globally distributed Scrum teams. *ACIS 2022 Proceedings, 5*, 1-13. https://aisel.aisnet.org/acis2022/5

Kotler, P., Kartajaya, H., & Setiawan, I. (2021). *Marketing 5.0: Tecnology for Humanity* (1st ed.). Wiley.

Kottke, T. E., Stiefel, M., & Pronk, N. P. (2016). *"Well-Being in All Policies": Promoting Cross-Sectoral Collaboration to Improve People's Lives. NAM Perspectives*. Discussion Paper, National Academy of Medicine. doi:10.31478/201604c

Koutsothanassi, E., Bouranta, N., & Psomas, E. (2017). Examining the relationships among service features, customer loyalty and switching barriers in the Greek banking sector. *International Journal of Quality and Service Sciences, 9*(3/4), 425–440. doi:10.1108/IJQSS-02-2017-0013

Kpobi, L., Swartz, L., & Ofori-Atta, A. L. (2018). Challenges in the use of the mental health information system in a resource-limited setting: Lessons from Ghana. *BMC Health Services Research, 18*(1), 98. doi:10.118612913-018-2887-2 PMID:29422047

Kreiner, G. E., Hollensbe, E. C., & Sheep, M. L. (2009). Balancing borders and bridges: Negotiating the work-home interface via boundary work tactics. *Academy of Management Journal*, *52*(4), 704–730. doi:10.5465/amj.2009.43669916

Kreps, G. L. (1995). *La comunicación en las organizaciones*. Addison-Wesley Iberoamericana.

Kunsch, M. M. K. (2003). *Planejamento de Relações Públicas na Comunicação Integrada*. Summus Editorial.

Kunsch, M. M. K. (2007). Comunicação organizacional na era digital: Contextos, percursos e possibilidades. *Signo y Pensamiento*, *26*(51), 38–51.

Kunsch, M. M. K. (2016). A comunicação nas organizações: dos fluxos lineares às dimensões humana e estratégica. In M. M. K. Kunsch (Ed.), *Comunicação organizacional estratégica: aportes conceituais e aplicados* (pp. 37–58). Summus Editorial.

Laato, S., Islam, A. N., Islam, M. N., Whelan, E., & Talukder, S. (2021). What drives unproductive smartphone usage at work? Roles of self-control, autonomy, relatedness, and work engagement. *Sustainability*, *13*(5), 2815. doi:10.3390u13052815

Lakshmi, B., &. Patel, P. (2020). *Digital Marketing in Pharmaceutical Industry–An Overview and Assessment*. Academic Press.

Lamberti, M. J., Wilkinson, M., Donzanti, B. A., Wohlhieter, G. E., Parikh, S., Wilkins, R. G., & Getz, K. (2019). A Study on the Application and Use of Artificial Intelligence to Support Drug Development. *Clinical Therapeutics*, *41*(8), 1414–1426. doi:10.1016/j.clinthera.2019.05.018 PMID:31248680

Lamberton, C., & Stephen, A. T. (2016). A Thematic Exploration of Digital, Social Media, and Mobile Marketing: Research Evolution from 2000 to 2015 and an Agenda for Future Inquiry. *Journal of Marketing*, *80*(6), 146–172. doi:10.1509/jm.15.0415

Lamichhane, Y., R. (2016). Non-verbal Skills: Unavoidable in Communication. *Repositioning: The Journal of Business and Hospitality, 1*(91).

Laurillard, D. (2013). *Rethinking university teaching: A conversational framework for the effective use of learning technologies*. Routledge. doi:10.4324/9781315012940

Lavorgna, L., De Stefano, M., Sparaco, M., Moccia, M., Abbadessa, G., Montella, P., Buonanno, D., Esposito, S., Clerico, M., Cenci, C., Trojsi, F., Lanzillo, R., Rosa, L., Morra, V. B., Ippolito, D., Maniscalco, G., Bisecco, A., Tedeschi, G., & Bonavita, S. (2018). Fake news, influencers and health-related professional participation on the Web: A pilot study on a social-network of people with Multiple Sclerosis. *Multiple Sclerosis and Related Disorders*, *25*, 175–178. doi:10.1016/j.msard.2018.07.046 PMID:30096683

Law no. 296/2020 amending and completing the fiscal code, https://www.pwc.ro/en/tax-legal/alerts/law-no--296-2020-amending-and-completing-the-fiscal-code-.html

Leavy, P. (2017). *Research design: quantitative, qualitative, mixed methods, arts-based, and community-based participatory research approaches*. The Guilford Press. Retrieved in May 1st, 2022, from: https://r2.vlereader.com/Reader?ean=9781462530038

Ledesma, E. (2017). *¿Qué es el acoso laboral discriminatorio?* Jupsin. https://jupsin.com/jupsin/acoso-discriminatorio/

Lee Yohn. (2021). Culture is not a campaign. *Forbes*. https://www.forbes.com/sites/leeyohn/2021/03/30/culture-is-not-a-campaign/?sh=1f6469a37481

Lee, G., & Xia, W. (2010). Toward agile: An integrated analysis of quantitative and qualitative field data. *Management Information Systems Quarterly*, *34*(1), 87–114. doi:10.2307/20721416

Lee, I., Cameron, I., & Hassall, M. (2019). Improving process safety: What roles for Digitalization and Industry 4.0? *Process Safety and Environmental Protection*, *132*, 325–339. doi:10.1016/j.psep.2019.10.021

Lee, R. M., & Robbins, S. B. (2019). Digital well-being: A framework for research and practice. In S. S. Sundar (Ed.), *The Oxford handbook of digital well-being* (pp. 23–35). doi:10.1093/oxfordhb/9780190932590.013.2

Lent, B., & Pinkowska, M. (2012). Soft skills needed in the ICT project management – classification and maturity level assessment. *International Journal of Applied Systemic Studies*, *4*(3), 168–185. doi:10.1504/IJASS.2012.051133

Ley 10/2021, de 9 de julio, de trabajo a distancia, n.º 164 (2021).

Ley Orgánica 3/2007 de 22 de marzo, para la Igualdad efectiva de mujeres y hombres.

Liang, Y., Wu, X., Liu, J., & Zhu, L. (2021). How digital technology induces technostress: A review and synthesis of the literature. *International Journal of Information Management*, *57*, 102–282. doi:10.1016/j.ijinfomgt.2020.102282

Lima, C. A. R., Fechine, Veloso, A., Melo, P. R., & Dantas, I. H. (2021). O rádio expandido no enfrentamento à pandemia de COVID-19: A experiência da Rádio Universitária Paulo Freire. *Radiofonias – Revista de Estudos em Mídia Sonora, Mariana-MG, 12*(1), 58-90.

Lima, S. P., & Mick, J. (2013). Sindicalização e identidade política dos jornalistas brasileiros. *Estudos em Jornalismo e Mídia*, *10*(1), 4–24. doi:10.5007/1984-6924.2013v10n1p4

Lindsjorn, Y., Sjoberg, D., Dingsoyr, T., Bergersen, G. R., & Dybä, T. (2016). Teamwork quality and project success in software development: A survey of agile development teams. *Journal of Systems and Software*, *122*, 274–286. doi:10.1016/j.jss.2016.09.028

Lin, L. Y., Sidani, J. E., Shensa, A., Radovic, A., Miller, E., Colditz, J. B., & Primack, B. A. (2018). Association between social media use and depression among US young adults. *Depression and Anxiety*, *35*(9), 818–826. doi:10.1002/da.22714

Lin, L. Y., Sidani, J. E., Shensa, A., Radovic, A., Miller, E., Colditz, J. B., & Primack, B. A. (2019). Association between social media use and empathy among US young adults. *The Journal of Adolescent Health*, *65*(6), 703–711. doi:10.1016/j.jadohealth.2019.06.003

Liu, X., & Lin, K.-L. (2020). Green Organizational Culture, Corporate Social Responsibility Implementation, and Food Safety. *Frontiers in Psychology*, *11*, 1–7. doi:10.3389/fpsyg.2020.585435 PMID:33240175

Livingstone, S., & Helsper, E. (2010). Balancing opportunities and risks in teenagers' use of the internet: The role of online skills and internet self-efficacy. *New Media & Society*, *12*(2), 309–329. doi:10.1177/1461444809342697

Lok, P., & Crawford, J. (2004). The effect of organisational culture and leadership style on job satisfaction and organisational commitment: A cross-national comparison. *Journal of Management Development*, *23*(4), 321–338. doi:10.1108/02621710410529785

Lonsdale, C. (Ed.). (2022). Taking Care. A Report on Mental Health, Well-Being & Trauma among Canadian Media Workers. In *Forum on Violence and Trauma.* Canadian Journalism. https://www.journalismforum.ca/taking-care-report

Lopes, F., Santos, C. A., Peixinho, A. T., Magalhães, O. E., & Araújo, R. (2021). COVID-19: Uma pandemia que reconfigura o jornalismo? *Media & Jornalismo*, *21*(39), 57–75. doi:10.14195/2183-5462_39_3

Lovelock, C., & Wirtz, J. (2011). *Services Marketing: People, Technology*. Pearson.

Lussier, R., & Hendon, J. (2016). Human resource management: Functions, application, and skill development (2nd ed.). Thousand Oaks, CA: Sage.

MacDonald, J. B., Hodgins, G., Saliba, A. J., & Metcalf, D. A. (2023). Journalists and depressive symptoms: A systematic literature review. *Trauma, Violence & Abuse*, *24*(1), 86–96. doi:10.1177/15248380211016022 PMID:33998329

Macintosh, N., & Daft, R. (1987). Management control systems and department interdependencies: An empirical study. *Accounting, Organizations and Society*, *12*(1), 49–61. doi:10.1016/0361-3682(87)90015-8

Magistretti, S., Trabucchi, D., Dell'Era, C., & Buganza, T. (2019). A new path toward a hybrid model: Insights from PwC's Italian experience Centre. *Research Technology Management*, *62*(5), 30–37. doi:10.1080/08956308.2019.1638223

Ma, J. (2021). Telework Triggered by Epidemic: Effective Communication Improvement of Telecommuting in Workgroups during COVID-19. *American Journal of Industrial and Business Management*, *11*(2), 202–214. doi:10.4236/ajibm.2021.112013

Mäkiniemi, J. P., & Kinnunen, U. (2020). Promoting digital well-being at work: The roles of job resources and personal resources. *International Journal of Environmental Research and Public Health*, *17*(7), 2516. doi:10.3390/ijerph17072516 PMID:32272647

Malhotra, N. K., Rocha, I., Laudisio, M. C., Altheman, É., Borges, F. M., & Taylor, R. B. (2005). *Introdução à pesquisa de marketing*. Academic Press.

Marinho, M., Camara, R., & Sampaio, S. (2021). Toward Unveiling How SAFe Framework Supports Agile in Global Software Development. *IEEE Access : Practical Innovations, Open Solutions*, *9*, 109671–109692. doi:10.1109/ACCESS.2021.3101963

Markman, A. (2021, January 27). How to weigh the benefits and drawbacks of working from home. *Harvard Business Review*. https://hbr.org/2021/01/how-to-weigh-the-benefits-and-drawbacks-of-working-from-home

Marlow, S. L., Lacerenza, C. N., & Salas, E. (2017). Communication in virtual teams: A conceptual framework and research agenda. *Human Resource Management Review*, *27*(4), 575–589. doi:10.1016/j.hrmr.2016.12.005

Marr, B. (2018). *Data-driven HR: How to use analytics and metrics to drive performance*. Kogan Page.

Martinez-Ramon, J., Morales-Rodriguez, F., & Perez-Lopez, S. (2021). Burnout, resilience, and COVID-19 among teachers: Predictive capacity of an artificial neural network. *Applied Sciences*, *11*, 8206. doi:10.3390/app11178206

Maslach, C., & Jackson, S. (1984). Burnout in organizational settings. *Applied Social Psychology Annual*, *5*, 133–153.

Mateus Steffens, C., & Rojas Gualdrón, D. F. (2009). *Del tratamiento moral de las enfermedades mentales a la salud mental comunitaria. Una aproximación histórico-epistemológica al concepto de salud mental durante el periodo de higiene mental* [Doctoral dissertation]. Universidad Autónoma de Bucaramanga, Colômbia. http://hdl.handle.net/20.500.12749/17629

Matteson, M., & Ivancevich, J. (2014). Merger and acquisition stress: fear and uncertainty at mid-career. In R. Hess (Ed.), *Career stress in changing times*. Routledge.

Maxwell, J. (2005). *Qualitative Research Design: An Interactive Approach. Social Science.*

Mayrhofer, W., & Brewster, C. (2007). European human resource management: Researching developments over time. In R. Schuler & S. Jackson (Eds.), Strategic human resource management (2nd ed.). Malden, MA: Blackwell.

Mboera, L. E. G., Rumisha, S. F., Mbata, D., Mremi, I. R., Lyimo, E. P., & Joachim, C. (2021). Data utilisation and factors influencing the performance of the health management information system in Tanzania. *BMC Health Services Research*, *21*(1), 498–506. doi:10.118612913-021-06559-1 PMID:34030696

McCarthy, J. (1998). What Is Artificial Intelligence? Stanford University.

McClure, P. K. (2018). "You're fired," says the robot: The rise of automation in the workplace, technophobes, and fears of unemployment. *Social Science Computer Review*, *36*(2), 139–156. doi:10.1177/0894439317698637

McCullough, G., Huebner, E. S., & Laughlin, J. E. (2000). Life Events, Self-Concept, and Adolescents' Positive Subjective Well-Being. *Psychology in the Schools*, *37*(3), 281–290. doi:10.1002/(SICI)1520-6807(200005)37:3<281::AID-PITS8>3.0.CO;2-2

McGovern, L., Miller, G., & Hughes-Cromwick, P. (2014). *The Relative Contribution of Multiple Determinants to Health Outcomes*. Available at: https://www.rwjf.org/en/library/research/2014/08/the-relative-contribution-of-multiple-determinants-to-healthout.html

McIntyre & Srinivasan. (2017). Networks, platforms, and strategy: Emerging views and next steps. *Strategic Management Journal, Wiley Blackwell*, *38*(1), 141–160.

McKinsey & Company. (2022, May 27). *COVID-19: Implications for business*. https://www.mckinsey.com/business-functions/risk-and-resilience/our-insights/covid-19-implications-for-business

Medeiros, T. (2016). Retrieved November, 02, 2022 from https://drauziovarella.uol.com.br/infectologia/virus/

Men, R., & Bowen, S. (2017). *Excellence in internal communication management*. Business Expert Press.

Meske, C., Leicht-Deobald, U., & Schütte, M. (2021). The Effects of Home Office on Digital Distraction, Work Engagement, and Exhaustion. *Journal of Business and Psychology*, 1–18. doi:10.100710869-021-09703-x

Mijuk, G. (2018). *Drug development gains momentum in big data analysis*. Novartis. https://www.novartis.com/stories/discovery/drug-development-gets-big-data-analytics-boost

Miles, M. B., Huberman, A. M., & Saldana, J. (2019). *Qualitative Data Analysis: A Methods Sourcebook*. SAGE Publications.

Minot State. (2009). *Registrar's office: Minimum class size policy*. Minot State University. Retrieved from: https://www.minotstateu.edu/records/pages/policy-minimum-class-size.shtml

Moens, E., Lippens, L., Sterkens, P., Weytjens, J., & Baert, S. (2022). The COVID-19 crisis and telework: A research survey on experiences, expectations and hopes. *The European Journal of Health Economics*, *23*(4), 729–753. doi:10.100710198-021-01392-z PMID:34761337

Moglia, M., Hopkins, J., & Bardoel, A. (2021). Telework, hybrid work and the United Nation's Sustainable Development Goals: Towards policy coherence. *Sustainability (Basel)*, *13*(16), 9222. doi:10.3390u13169222

Moorhead, S. A., Hazlett, D. E., Harrison, L., Carroll, J. K., Irwin, A., & Hoving, C. (2013). A new dimension of health care: Systematic review of the uses, benefits, and limitations of social media for health communication. *Journal of Medical Internet Research*, *15*(4), e1933. doi:10.2196/jmir.1933 PMID:23615206

Morin, E. (2021). *É hora de mudarmos de via: As lições do coronavírus*. Bertrand Brasil. Edição do Kindle.

Morrison-Smith, S., & Ruiz, J. (2020). Challenges and Barriers in Virtual Teams: A Literature Review. *SN Applied Sciences*, *2*(1096), 1–33. doi:10.100742452-020-2801-5

Mukherjee, S. P. (2019) *A Guide to Research Methodology: An Overview of Research Problems, Tasks and Methods*. Taylor & Francis Group. Retrieved in May 1st, 2022, from: https://ebookcentral.proquest.com/lib/uwestlon/reader.action?docID=5890625

Mulgund, S., & Kelly, M. (2020). *Command and control of operations in the information environment: Leading with information in operational planning, execution, and assessment*. Department of the Air Force.

Müller, J. M., Pommeranz, B., Weisser, J., & Voigt, K. I. (2018). Digital, social media, and mobile marketing in industrial buying: Still in need of customer segmentation? Empirical evidence from Poland and Germany. *Industrial Marketing Management*, *73*, 70–83. doi:10.1016/j.indmarman.2018.01.033

Muller, N. (2022). Perceptions about corporate positioning on controversial sociopolitical issues: Examining big pharma engagement with patient advocacy. *Public Relations Review*, *48*(5), 102261. doi:10.1016/j.pubrev.2022.102261

Mundra, A., Misra, S., & Dhawale, C. A. (2013). Practical Scrum-Scrum Team: Way to Produce Successful and Quality Software. *Proceedings of the 13th International Conference on Computational Science and Its Applications*, 119-123. 10.1109/ICCSA.2013.25

Murphy, P. (2011). *Contextual distortion: Strategic communication vs. the networked nature of everything.* Paper presented at the International Communication Association 2011 pre-conference Strategic communication - A concept at the centre of applied communications, Boston, MA.

Murphy, P. (2011, August). *Putting the Earth into Global Media Studies*. Academic Press.

Murray, E., Lo, B., Pollack, L., Donelan, K., Catania, J., Lee, K., Zapert, K., & Turner, R. (2003). The impact of health information on the physician-patient relationship. *J Med Internet Res., 5*.

Musthofa, W. S., Farida, N., & Ngatno, N. (2017). Effect of entrepreneurial orientation on business performance. *International Journal of Civil Engineering and Technology*, *8*, 82–90.

Nadwarny, E. (2021). College enrollment plummeted during the pandemic. This fall, it's even worse. *NPR Morning Edition*. Retrieved from: https://www.npr.org/2021/10/26/1048955023/college-enrollment-down-pandemic-economy

Nagel, L. (2020). The influence of the COVID-19 pandemic on the digital transformation of work. *The International Journal of Sociology and Social Policy*, *40*(9/10), 861–875. doi:10.1108/IJSSP-07-2020-0323

Nagel, P., & Lubinga, E. (2015). Nonverbal communication. In S. Steinberg & G. Angelopulo (Eds.), *Introduction to communication science for Southern African students* (pp. 85–106). Juta.

Nasir, N., & Marikar, K. (2018). ISQUA18-2296Does Adoption of Health Information System (HIS) in Hospital Affect the Compliance to the Hospital Accreditation Program. *International Journal for Quality in Health Care*, *30*(suppl_2), 12–13. doi:10.1093/intqhc/mzy167.15

Neveu, E. (2010). As notícias sem jornalistas: Uma ameaça real ou uma história de terror? *Brazilian Journalism Research*, *6*(1), 29–57. doi:10.25200/BJR.v6n1.2010.246

Neveu, E. (2019). O desafio de pensar ecologicamente. *Jornalismo*, *20*(1), 198–201. doi:10.1177/1464884918808139

Ngamvichaikit, A. (2021). Leveraging design thinking for pharmaceutical digital marketing Asian. *Journal of Business Research*, *11*(1).

Nguyen, M. H. (2021). Managing Social Media Use in an "Always-On" Society: Exploring Digital Wellbeing Strategies That People Use to Disconnect. *Mass Communication & Society*, *24*(6), 795–817. doi:10.1080/15205436.2021.1979045

Nicoletti, J., & Mick, J. (2018). Influências da precarização na qualidade jornalística: construção de uma matriz de indicadores. *Passagens, 9*(1), 127-141. http://www.repositorio.ufc.br/handle/riufc/38547

Nikolova, I., & Devinney, T. M. (2021). The long-term effects of COVID-19 on employee well-being: Implications for HRM research and practice. *The Academy of Management Perspectives*, *35*(4), 457–462. doi:10.5465/amp.2021.0184

Nilles, J. M. (1994). The geography of telecommuting. In J. Fulk & C. Steinfield (Eds.), *Organizations and communication technology* (pp. 243–264). Sage.

Nowell, L. S., Norris, J. M., White, D. E., & Moules, N. J. (2017). Thematic Analysis: Striving to Meet the Trustworthiness Criteria. *International Journal of Qualitative Methods*, *16*(1), 1–13. doi:10.1177/1609406917733847

O'Leary, M. B., & Cummings, J. N. (2007). The spatial, temporal, and configurational characteristics of geographic dispersion in work teams. *Management Information Systems Quarterly*, *31*(3), 433–452. doi:10.2307/25148802

Ockerman, S. (2020, June 1). *3 Things Virtual Teams Need from a Scrum Master* [Web log message]. Retrieved from https://www.scrum.org/resources/blog/3-things-virtual-teams-need-scrum-master

OIT. (2022). España ratifica el Convenio sobre el trabajo a domicilio y el Convenio sobre la violencia y el acoso. *Organización Internacional del Trabajo*. https://www.ilo.org/global/standards/WCMS_847845/lang--es/index.htm#:~:text=190)%20ante%20el%20Director%20General,190.

Olson-Buchanan, J., Boswell, W. R., & Morgan, B. B. (2016). The future of work: The role of technology in reshaping the nature of work. In P. L. Perrewé, J. R. B. Halbesleben, & C. C. Rosen (Eds.), *The role of technology in workplace stress, health, and well-being* (pp. 9–36). Emerald Group Publishing Limited.

Olson, R. (2018). *Don't be such a poor storyteller. In Don't Be Such a Scientist*. Springer. doi:10.5822/978-1-61091-918-0

Olson, S. R., & Pollard, T. (2004). The muse pixelipe: Digitalization and media literacy education. *The American Behavioral Scientist*, *48*(2), 248–278. doi:10.1177/0002764204267272

Ordonanța de urgență nr. 36 din 5 mai 2021, privind utilizarea semnăturii electronice avansate sau semnăturii electronice calificate, însoțite de marca temporală electronică sau marca temporală electronică calificată și sigiliul electronic calificat al angajatorului în domeniul relațiilor de muncă, și pentru modificarea și completarea unor acte normative [Government Emergency Ordinance No.36/ 5 May 2021 regarding the use of the advanced or qualified electronic signature accompanied by the electronic temporary marc or by qualified electronic temporary mark and the qualified electronic seal of the employer in the field of work relationships, and for modifying and filling of some normative acts]. https://legislatie.just.ro/Public/DetaliiDocumentAfis/242068

Ordonanța de Urgență nr. 72 din 30 mai 2022 pentru modificarea și completarea Ordonanței de urgență a Guvernului nr. 63/2022 privind unele măsuri temporare pentru acordarea de sprijin material categoriilor de persoane aflate în situații de risc de deprivare materială și/sau risc de sărăcie extremă, suportate parțial din fonduri externe nerambursabile, precum și unele măsuri de distribuire a acestuia [Government Emergency Ordinance No. 72/ 30 May 2022 regarding the modification and completion of the Government Emergency Ordinance No. 63/2020 regarding some temporary measures for the grant of material support to categories of citizens under risks of material deprivation and/or in risk of extreme poverty, supported partially from external non-refundable funds, as well as some measures of fund this distribution]. https://legislatie.just.ro/Public/DetaliiDocumentAfis/255838

Ortega, R., Calmastra, J., & Mora, J. (2008). Cyberbullying. *International Journal of Psychology & Psychological Therapy*, *8*(2), 183–192. https://www.redalyc.org/pdf/560/56080204.pdf

Osmann, J., Selva, M., & Feinstein, A. (2021). How have journalists been affected psychologically by their coverage of the COVID-19 pandemic? A descriptive study of two international organizations. *BMJ Open*, *11*(7), e045675. Advance online publication. doi:10.1136/bmjopen-2020-045675 PMID:34253664

Oulego, J. R. (2020). El acoso laboral: Concepto, tipos de acoso y protección jurídica del trabajador. *Adefinitivas*. https://adefinitivas.com/arbol-del-derecho/el-acoso-laboral-concepto-tipos-de-acoso/

Oxean. (2020). Inteligencia artificial en la comunicación corporativa ¿qué podemos esperar? *Oxean comunicaicón cross*. https://oxeancross.com/blog/ia-en-la-comunicacion-corporativa-que-podemos-esperar/

Paasonen, S. (2021). *Dependent, Distracted, Bored: Affective Formations in Networked Media*. MIT Press. doi:10.7551/mitpress/11903.001.0001

Pan, C., Abbas, J., Álvarez-Otero, S., Khan, H., & Cheng, C. (2022). Interplay between corporate social responsibility and organizational green culture and their role in employees' responsible behavior towards the environment and society. *Journal of Cleaner Production*, *366*, 1–8. doi:10.1016/j.jclepro.2022.132878

Parida, D., Sjödin, W., & Reim, S. (2019). *Reviewing Literature on Digitalization, Business Model Innovation, and Sustainable Industry*. Past Achievements and Future Promises Multidisciplinary Digital Publishing Institute.

Parker, K., & Horowitz, J. (2022). Majority of workers who quit a job in 2021 cite low pay, no opportunities for advancement, feeling disrespected. *Pew Research Center*. Retrieved from: https://www.pewresearch.org/fact-tank/2022/03/09/majority-of-workers-who-quit-a-job-in-2021-cite-low-pay-no-opportunities-for-advancement-feeling-disrespected/

Pasquale, P. P., Neto, C. L., & Gomes, C. L. C. C. (2012). *Comunicação Integrada de Marketing: a teoria na prática*. Elsevier.

Pavlik, J. V., & Mankintosh, S. (2018). *Converging media: A new introduction to mass communication*. Oxford University Press.

Penteado, R. Z., & Gastaldello, L. M. (2016). Saúde e qualidade de vida de jornalistas: Estudo de revisão. *Revista Brasileira em Promoção da Saúde*, *29*(2), 295–304. doi:10.5020/18061230.2016.p295

Pereira, T. J., & Puggina, A. C. (2017). Validation of the self-assessment of communication skills and professionalism for nurses. *Revista Brasileira de Enfermagem*, *70*(3), 588–594. doi:10.1590/0034-7167-2016-0133 PMID:28562808

Pérez Pérez, M., Martínez Sánchez, Á., De Luis Carnicer, P., & Vela Jiménez, M. J. (2004a). La adopción del teletrabajo y las tecnologías de la información: Estudio de relaciones y efectos organizativos. *Revista de Economía y Empresa*, *22*(52-53), 11-28. https://dialnet.unirioja.es/servlet/articulo?codigo=2274025

Peter, M. K., & Dalla Vecchia, M. (2021). The Digital Marketing Toolkit: A Literature Review for The Identification of Digital Marketing Channels and Platforms Studies in Systems, Decision and Control. Springer.

Petrou, P., & Bakker, A. B. (2016). Crafting one's leisure time in response to high job strain. *Human Relations*, *69*(2), 507–529. doi:10.1177/0018726715590453

Petrova, S. (2019). *Adopting Agile: The Latest Reports About The Popular Mindset*. Retrieved from https://adevait.com/blog/remote-work/adopting-agile-the-latest-reports-about-the-popular-mindset

Pettigrew, A. (1979). Studying organizational culture. *Administrative Science Quarterly*, *24*(4), 570–581. doi:10.2307/2392363

Pfeffer, T. Z., & Carley, K. M. (2014). Understanding online firestorms: Negative word-of-mouth dynamics in social media networks. *Journal of Marketing Communications*, *20*(1-2), 1–2, 117–128. doi:10.1080/13527266.2013.797778

Pfisterer, A. B., Paschke, M., & Pasotti, J. (2019). Communicating science through the media. Zurich-Basel Plant Science Center.

Pikkarainen, M., Haikara, J., Salo, O., Abrahamsson, P., & Still, J. (2008). The impact of agile practices on communication in software development. *Empirical Software Engineering*, *13*(3), 303–337. doi:10.100710664-008-9065-9

Pimpão, A. C. P. (2013). A importância da comunicação interna numa empresa – aplicada ao caso Timwe. Lisboa. Business School. Tese de Mestrado em Gestão.

Pinto, E., & Heloani, R. (2007). Aspectos teóricos e metodológicos da pesquisa em saúde mental e trabalho: Reflexões a partir de uma análise comparativa do estresse em jornalistas e guardas municipais. *Cadernos de Psicologia Social do Trabalho, 10*(1), 105–120. doi:10.11606/issn.1981-0490.v10i1p105-120

Pio, D. (2017). *A força transformadora da comunicação interna.* Simplissimo Livros.

Pontes, F. S., & Lima, S. P. (2019). Impactos do mercado jornalístico na vida de seus trabalhadores: Um estudo sobre indicadores de saúde dos jornalistas brasileiros. *Famecos, 26*(2), e31729–e31729. doi:10.15448/1980-3729.2019.2.31729

Pool, S., & Pool, B. (2007). A management development model: Measuring organizational commitment and its impact on job satisfaction among executives in a learning organization. *Journal of Management Development, 26*(4), 353–369. doi:10.1108/02621710710740101

Portwood-Stacer, L. (2013). Media refusal and conspicuous non-consumption: The performative and political dimensions of Facebook abstention. *New Media & Society, 15*(7), 1041–1057. doi:10.1177/1461444812465139

Posetti, J., Bell, E., & Brown, P. (2020). El periodismo y la pandemia: una instantánea global de su impacto. *ICJF/Tow Center for Digital Journalism.* https://www.icfj.org/sites/default/files/2020-11/Journalism%20and%20the%20Pandemic%20Project%20Report%201%202020_Spanish2.pdf

Premeaux, S. F., Adkins, C. L., & Brasington, D. M. (2021). It's the little things that matter: Remote work and well-being during COVID-19. *Journal of Business and Psychology, 36*(5), 687–702. doi:10.100710869-021-09790-3

Prevención Integral. (2021). *El ciberacoso en el trabajo: Un mal presente en la digitalización empresarial.* https://www.prevencionintegral.com/actualidad/noticias/2021/10/01/ciberacoso-en-trabajo-mal-presente-en-digitalizacion-empresarial

Price Waterhouse Coopers. (2021). *It's time to reimagine how and where work will get done: PwC's US remote work survey.* PwC. Retrieved from: https://www.pwc.com/us/en/services/consulting/business-transformation/library/covid-19-us-remote-work-survey.html

Putnam, L. (2015). *Workplace wellness that works: 10 steps to infuse well-being and vitality into your organisation.* Wiley. doi:10.1002/9781119154839

Putnam, L. L., & Mumby, D. K. (2016). *Organizations and Organizing: Rational, Natural and Open Systems Perspectives.* Routledge.

Queirós, A., Faria, D., & Almeida, F. (2017). Strengths and Limitation of Qualitative and Quantitative Research Methods. *European Journal of Education Studies, 3*(9), 369–387.

Ramya, N., Kowsalsya, A., & Dharanipriya, K. (2019). Service quality and its dimensions. *EPRA International Journal of Research and Development, 4*(2), 38-41. Retrieved from https://www.eprajournals.com/

Ranta, V., Keränen, J., & Aarikka-Stenroos, L. (2020). How B2B suppliers articulate customer value propositions in the circular economy: Four innovation-driven value creation logics. *Industrial Marketing Management, 87*, 291–30. doi:10.1016/j.indmarman.2019.10.007

Rawlins, B. L. (2008). Give the emperor a mirror: Toward developing a stakeholder measurement of organizational transparency. *Journal of Public Relations Research, 21*(1), 71–99. doi:10.1080/10627260802153421

Reinartz, W., Wiegand, N., & Imschloss, M. (2018). The impact of digital transformation on the retailing value chain. *International Journal of Research in Marketing.*

Reinecke, L., & Trepte, S. (2014). Authenticity and well-being on social network sites: A two-wave longitudinal study on the effects of online authenticity and the positivity bias in SNS communication. *Computers in Human Behavior*, *30*, 95–102. doi:10.1016/j.chb.2013.07.030

Reinhardt, J.C., Oliveira, D.T., & Ring, I.C. (2021). Industry 4.0 and the future of the pharmaceutical industry. *Pharm. Eng.*

Renard, K., Cornu, F., Emery, Y., & Giauque, D. (2021). The Impact of New Ways of Working on Organizations and Employees: A Systematic Review of Literature. *Administrative Sciences*, *11*(2), 38. doi:10.3390/admsci11020038

Richard, P., Devinney, T., Yip, G., & Johnson, G. (2009). Measuring organizational performance: Towards methodological best practice. *Journal of Management*, *35*(3), 718–804. doi:10.1177/0149206308330560

Rideout, V., & Robb, M. B. (2018). *Social media, social life: Teens reveal their experiences. Research report*. Common Sense.

Riel, C. B. M. v. (2013). *Reputação*. Campus.

Rigby, D. K., Sutherland, J., & Takeuchi, H. (2016). Embracing Agile. *Harvard Business Review*. Retrieved from https://hbr.org/2016/05/embracing-agile

Rizvi, B., Bagheri, E., & Gasevic, D. (2015). A systematic review of distributed Agile software engineering. *Journal of Software (Malden, MA)*, *27*(10), 723–762. doi:10.1002mr.1718

Robbins, S. P., & Sanghi, S. (2007). *Organizational Behavior*. Pearson Education.

Rodríguez Molina, I. M. (2020). Acoso laboral en tiempo de pandemia. Ciberacoso: Riesgo Psicosocial Emergente. *Gentes Consultores Academy & Consulting*. https://www.linkedin.com/pulse/acoso-laboral-en-tiempos-de-pandemia-ciberacoso-rodriguez-molina/?originalSubdomain=es

Roffarello, A. M., & de Russis, L. (2019, May 2). The race towards digital wellbeing: Issues and opportunities. *Conference on Human Factors in Computing Systems - Proceedings*. 10.1145/3290605.3300616

Rondon, C. (2020). *A hora da retomada*. Anuário da Comunicação Corporativa 2020. Mega Purilub. Tamanho de um vírus. Retrieved November, 02, 2022 from https://www.purilub.com.br/blog/tamanho-de-um-virus/65

Rosenbaum, G. C., Ramírez, G. C., Edwards, K., Kim, J., Campbell, J. M., & Bickle, M. C. (2017). The digitization of health care retailing. *Journal of Research in Interactive Marketing*, *11*(4), 432–446. doi:10.1108/JRIM-07-2017-0058

Rosengren, S., Eisend, M., Koslow, S., & Dahlen, M. (2020). A Meta-analysis of when and how advertising creativity works. *Journal of Marketing*, *84*(6), 39–56. doi:10.1177/0022242920929288

Rosen, L. D., Whaling, K., Carrier, L. M., Cheever, N. A., & Rokkum, J. (2013). The media and technology usage and attitudes scale: An empirical investigation. *Computers in Human Behavior*, *29*(6), 2501–2511. doi:10.1016/j.chb.2013.06.006 PMID:25722534

Rosen, L. D., Whaling, K., Rab, S., Carrier, L. M., & Cheever, N. A. (2019). Is Facebook creating “iDisorders”? The link between clinical symptoms of psychiatric disorders and technology use, attitudes and anxiety. *Computers in Human Behavior*, *84*, 183–190. doi:10.1016/j.chb.2018.02.033

Ross, J. W. (2018). How to develop a great digital strategy January. *MIT Sloan Management Review*, *58*(2), 7–9.

Rothman, J., & Kilby, M. (2019). *From Chaos to Successful Distributed Agile Teams: Collaborate to Deliver*. Practical Ink.

Ruão, T. (1999). A Comunicação Organizacional e a gestão de Recursos Humanos: Evolução e actualidade. Comunicação e Sociedade 1. *Cadernos do Noroeste, 12*(1-2), 179-194. Retrieved February, 18, 2023 from https://repositorium.sdum.uminho.pt/bitstream/1822/60017/1/1999_Ruao_Comunicacao-organizacional.pdf

Ruck, K., & Welch, M. (2012). Valuing internal communication; management and employee perspectives. *Public Relations Review, 38*(2), 294-302. doi:10.1016/j.pubrev.2011.12.016

Ruck, K., & Men, L. R. (2021). Guest editorial: Internal communication during the COVID-19 pandemic. *Journal of Communication Management (London), 25*(3), 185–195. doi:10.1108/JCOM-08-2021-163

Rudisill, J., Edwards, J., Hershberger, P., Jadwin, J., & McKee, J. (2010). Coping with job transitions over the work life. In T. Miller (Ed.), *Handbook of stressful transitions across the lifespan* (pp. 111–132). Springer. doi:10.1007/978-1-4419-0748-6_6

Ruehl, C.H., & Ingenhoff, D. (2015), Communication management on social networking sites: Stakeholder motives and usage types of corporate Facebook, Twitter and YouTube pages. *Journal of Communication Management, 19*(3), 288-302.

Ryff, C. D. (1989). Happiness Is Everything, or Is It? Explorations on the Meaning of Psychological Well-Being. *Journal of Personality and Social Psychology, 57*(6), 1069–1081. Advance online publication. doi:10.1037/0022-3514.57.6.1069

Saad, E. (2021). Comunicação organizacional e transformação digital: novos cenários, novos olhares. In Comunicação organizacional. São Paulo: Summus Editorial.

Sabine, D. (2016, December 20). *A Group of Geographically Distributed Staff is NOT a Scrum Team* [Web log message]. Retrieved from https://www.agileadvice.com/2016/12/20/scrum-master/group-geographically-distributed-staff-not-scrum-team/

Saghaeiannejad-Isfahani, S., Saeedbakhsh, S., Jahanbakhsh, M., & Habibi, M. (2015). Analysis of the quality of hospital information systems in Isfahan teaching hospitals based on the DeLone and McLean model. *Journal of Education and Health Promotion, 4*, 5. doi:10.4103/2277-9531.151883 PMID:25767816

Sahu, N., Deng, H., & Mollah, A. (2018). Investigating The Critical Success Factors Of Digital Transformation For Improving Customer Experience. *International Conference on Information Resources Management.*

Salahuddin, L., Ismail, Z., Hashim, U. R., Ismail, N. H., Ikram, R. R. R., Rahim, F. A., & Hassan, N. H. (2020). Healthcare practitioner behaviours that influence unsafe use of hospital information systems. *Health Informatics Journal, 26*(1), 420–434. doi:10.1177/1460458219833090 PMID:30843460

Salaverría, R. (2015). Mídia e Jornalistas, um futuro em comum? *Parágrafo, 3*(1), 79-84. https://revistaseletronicas.fiamfaam.br/index.php/recicofi/article/view/297

Sampasa-Kanyinga, H., & Lewis, R. F. (2016). Sleep duration and screen time among children and adolescents: A systematic review. *Journal of Sleep Research, 25*(5), 556–567. doi:10.1111/jsr.12436 PMID:27178659

Santander Universidades. (2022). Misión, visión y valores de una empresa: Qué son y cómo definirlos. *Santander*. https://www.becas-santander.com/es/blog/mision-vision-y-valores.html

Sassenberg, K., Greving, H., & Fetterman, A. K. (2019). Individual differences in the experience of digital stress. In S. S. Sundar (Ed.), *The Oxford handbook of digital well-being* (pp. 125–138)., doi:10.1093/oxfordhb/9780190932590.013.8

Satchell, C., & Dourish, P. (2009). Beyond the User: Use and Non-Use in HCI. *OZCHI '09: Proceedings of the 21st Annual Conference of the Australian Computer-Human Interaction Special Interest Group: Design: Open 24/7*, 9–16.

Savage, M., & Warde, A. (1993). *Urban Sociology, Capitalism and Modernity*. Macmillan Publishers Ltd. doi:10.1007/978-1-349-22991-8

Scaria, D., Brandt, M. L., Kim, E., & Lindeman, B. (2020). What is wellbeing? In E. Kim & B. Lindeman (Eds.), *Well-being* (pp. 3–10). Springer. doi:10.1007/978-3-030-29470-0_1

Schein, E. H. (1992). Organizational culture and leadership (2ª ed.). São Francisco: Jossey-Bass Publishers.

Schivinski, B., & Dabrowski, D. (2014). The effect of social media communication on consumer perceptions of brands. *Journal of Marketing Communications, 22*(2).

Schneider, K. (2017). The resurgence of awe in psychology: Promise, hope, and perils. *The Humanistic Psychologist, 45*(2), 103–108. doi:10.1037/hum0000060

Schroeder, R. (2021). A second demographic cliff adds urgency for change. *Inside Higher Education*. Retrieved from: https://www.insidehighered.com/digital-learning/blogs/online-trending-now/second-demographic-cliff-adds-urgency-change

Schuster, J., & Finkelstein, M. (2008). *The American faculty: The restructuring of academic work and careers*. The Johns Hopkins University Press.

Schwaber, K., & Beedle, M. (2002). *Agile software development with SCRUM*. Prentice-Hall. Retrieved from https://billlewistraining.com/wp-content/uploads/2017/02/PMP-Agile-Study-Materials.pdf

Schwab, K. (2016). *A Quarta Revolução Industrial*. Edipro.

Scully-Russ, E., & Torraco, R. (2020). The changing nature and organization of work: An integrative review of the literature. *Human Resource Development Review, 19*(1), 66–93.

Seely, N. (2019). Journalists and mental health: The psychological toll of covering everyday trauma. *Newspaper Research Journal*, *40*(2), 239–259. doi:10.1177/0739532919835612

Seetharaman, P. (2020). Business models shifts: Impact of Covid-19. *International Journal of Information Management, 54*, 102173. doi:10.1016/j.ijinfomgt.2020.102173 PMID:32834338

Sehlstedt, N. (2016). Embracing digital health in the pharmaceutical industry Int. *Journal of Healthcare Management, 9*(3), 145–14.

Sequesseque, R. M. A. C. (2019). *Motivação para o desempenho profissional: caso de estudo* (Doctoral dissertation).

Serra, P., & Bergamoba, A. (2020). Sociologia do Jornalismo: Por uma agenda de pesquisa. *Plural: Revista de Ciências Sociais.*, *27*(2), 5–21. doi:10.11606/issn.2176-8099.pcso.2020.179833

Shah, N., Engineer, S. Bhagat, N., Chauhan, H. & Shah, M. (2020). Research trends on the usage of machine learning and Artificial Intelligence. *Advertising Augmented Human Research*, *5*(19), 1–15.

Shah, S. (2016). *Challenges When Using Scrum in Globally Distributed Teams* [Graduate Thesis]. Harrisburg University of Science and Technology. Retrieved from https://digitalcommons.harrisburgu.edu/

Shahbaz, M., Gao, C., Zhai, L., Shahzad, F., & Hu, Y. (2019). Investigating the adoption of big data analytics in healthcare: The moderating role of resistance to change. *Journal of Big Data*, *6*(1), 1–20. doi:10.118640537-019-0170-y

Shah, S. M. A., Jiang, Y., Wu, H., Ahmed, Z., Ullah, I., & Adebayo, T. S. (2021). Linking Green Human Resource Practices and Environmental Economics Performance: The Role of Green Economic Organizational Culture and Green Psychological Climate. *International Journal of Environmental Research and Public Health*, *18*(20), 1–17. doi:10.3390/ijerph182010953 PMID:34682698

Shahzadi, I., Javed, A., Pirzada, S. S., Nasreen, S., & Khanam, F. (2014). Impact of employee motivation on employee performance. *European Journal of Business and Management*, *6*(23), 159–166.

Sharma, M. K., Sunil, S., Anand, N., Amudhan, S., & Ganjekar, S. (2021). Webinar fatigue: Fallout of Covid-19. *The Journal of the Egyptian Public Health Association*, *96*(9), 9. Advance online publication. doi:10.118642506-021-00069-y PMID:33861363

Sharmin, S., Tasnim, I., & Shimul, D. (2016). Measuring Customer Satisfaction through SERVQUAL Model: A Study on Beauty Parlors in Chittagong. *European Journal of Business and Management*, *8*, 97–108.

Shearer, E., & Grieco, E. (2019). *Americans Are Wary of the Role Social Media Sites Play in Delivering the News*. Pew Research Center.

Shin, Pang, & Kim. (2015). Building relationships through integrated online media platforms: Analysis of top 100 global brands. *Journal of Business and Technical Communication, 29*(2), 184-220. doi:10.1177/1050651914560569

Shockley, K. M., & Clark, M. A. (2020). Psychological safety in remote teams: The role of task complexity. *Journal of Business and Psychology*, *35*(6), 761–774. doi:10.100710869-019-09647-z

Shokouhyar, S., Shokoohyar, S., & Safari, S. (2020). Research on the influence of quality factors of after-sales service on customer satisfaction. *Journal of Retailing and Consumer Services*, *56*, 102139. doi:10.1016/j.jretconscr.2020.102139

Shrank, W. H., Rogstad, T. L., & Parekh, N. (2019). Waste in the US health care system: Estimated costs and potential for savings. *Journal of the American Medical Association*, *322*(15), 1501–1509. doi:10.1001/jama.2019.13978 PMID:31589283

Sianoja, M., Syrek, C. J., & Korpela, K. (2019). Digitalization and work–life boundaries. *International Journal of Environmental Research and Public Health*, *16*(19), 3698. doi:10.3390/ijerph16193698 PMID:31581430

Silverstone, R., & Haddon, L. (1996). Design and the Domestication of Information and Communication Technologies: Technical Change and Everyday Life. In R. Silverstone & R. Mansell (Eds.), *Communication by Design. The Politics of Information and Communication Technologies* (pp. 44–74). Oxford University Press.

Singh, J., & Singh, J. (2020). *COVID-19 and its impact on society. Electronic Research Journal of Social Sciences and Humanities*, 2.

Sjödin, D., Parida, V., Kohtamäki, M., & Wincent, J. (2020). An agile co-creation process for digital servitization: A micro-service innovation approach. *Journal of Business Research*, *112*, 478–491. doi:10.1016/j.jbusres.2020.01.009

Smith, B. G. (2010). Socially distributing public relations: Twitter, Haiti, and interactivity in social media. *Public Relations Review*, *36*(4), 329–335. doi:10.1016/j.pubrev.2010.08.005

Smith, M. L., & Anderson, C. M. (2019). From remote to hybrid work: Challenges and opportunities. *Journal of Business and Psychology*, *34*(6), 681–687. doi:10.100710869-019-09640-y

SNS24. (2022). *COVID-19*. Retrieved in April 1st, 2022, from: https://www.sns24.gov.pt/tema/doencas-infecciosas/covid-19/

Sobel, M. E. (1982). Asymptotic Confidence Intervals for Indirect Effects in Structural Equation Models. *Sociological Methodology*, *13*, 290–321. doi:10.2307/270723

Söderback, J., Hrastinski, S., & Öberg, L. M. (2015). *Using Distributed Scrum for Supporting Online Collaborative Learning: A Qualitative Descriptive Study of Students Perceptions*. Retrieved from https://core.ac.uk/display/36346620

Solomon, D., & Theiss, J. (2013). *Interpersonal communication – Putting theory into practice, Routledge*. Taylor & Francis Group.

Sommerfeldt, E. J., Kent, M. L., & Taylor, M. (2012). Activist practitioner perspectives of website public relations: Why aren't activist websites fulfilling the dialogic promise? *Public Relations Review*, *38*(2), 303–312. doi:10.1016/j.pubrev.2012.01.001

SousaV.CostaP. R.CapoanoE.PaganottiI. (2020). Riscos, dilemas e oportunidades: atuação jornalística em tempos de Covid-19. *Estudos em Comunicação*, (31), 1-33. https://doi.org/ doi:10.25768/20.04.03.31.01

Stabile, D. (2007). *Economics, competition, and academia: An intellectual history of sophism versus virtue*. Edward Elgar Publishing. doi:10.4337/9781847207166

Stanier, J., Li, M., & Anderson, J. (2022, March 16). What Great Hybrid Cultures Do Differently. *Harvard Business Review*. https://hbr.org/2022/03/what-great-hybrid-cultures-do-differently

Stankevičiūtė, Ž., & Kunskaja, S. (2022). Strengthening of work-life balance while working remotely in the context of COVID-19 pandemic. *Human Systems Management*, *41*(2), 221–235. doi:10.3233/HSM-211511

Stapel, K., Knauss, E., Schneider, K., & Zazworka, N. (2011). FLOW Mapping: Planning and Managing Communication in Distributed Teams. *Proceedings of the IEEE Sixth International Conference on Global Software Engineering*, 190-199. 10.1109/ICGSE.2011.9

Steger, M. F. (2009). Meaning in life. In S. J. Lopez & C. R. Snyder (Eds.), *Oxford handbook of positive psychology* (pp. 679–687). Oxford University.

Stewart, D. (2010). *Growing the Corporate Culture*. https://www.wachovia.com/foundation/v/index.jsp?vgnextoid

Stich, J.-F. (2021). Flexible working and applicant-attraction: A person-job fit approach. *Personnel Review*, *50*(1), 358–378. doi:10.1108/PR-12-2019-0672

Storm, H., Crowley, J., Berrie, A., & Mamo, E. (2022, April). Managing our mental health: A guide for journalists and media professionals. In *Headlines/Mind*. Google News Initiative. https://www.mind.org.uk/media/12403/managing-our-mental-health-guide.pdf

Sundar, S. S., Oh, J., Kang, H., & Sreenivasan, A. (2013). How does technology persuade? Theoretical mechanisms for persuasive technologies. In J. P. Dillard & L. Shen (Eds.), *The SAGE handbook of persuasion: Developments in theory and practice* (pp. 388–400). Sage Publications, Inc.

Supiano, B. (2023). Course correction: Students expect total flexibility in the pandemic-era classroom. But is that what they really need? *Chronicle of Higher Education*. Retrieved from: https://www.chronicle.com/article/course-correction

Sutherland, J. (2014). *Scrum: The Art of Doing Twice the Work in Half the Time*. Currency.

Suwana, F., Pramiyanti, A., Mayangsari, I., Nuraeni, R., & Firdaus, Y. (2020). Digital Media Use of Gen Z During COVID-19 Pandemic. *Jurnal Sosioteknologi*, *19*(3), 327–340. doi:10.5614ostek.itbj.2020.19.3.2

Tahir, M. (2019). The effect of project manager's soft skills on success of project in the construction industry. *International Journal of Applied Research in Social Sciences*, *1*(5), 197–203.

Tahir, R., Athar, M. R., Faisal, F., Shahani, N., & Solangi, B. (2019). Green organizational culture: A review of literature and future research agenda. *Annals of Contemporary Developments in Management & HR*, *1*(1), 23–38. doi:10.33166/ACDMHR.2019.01.004

Takkunen, M. (2014). *Scrum Implementation in a Virtual Team Environment* [MSc Thesis]. Helsinki Metropolia University of Applied Sciences. Retrieved from https://core.ac.uk/download/pdf/38111804.pdf

Talevi, D., Socci, V., Carai, M., Carnaghi, G., Faleri, S., Trebbi, E., di Bernardo, A., Capelli, F., & Pacitti, F. (2020). Mental Health Outcomes of the Covid-19 Pandemic. *Rivista di Psichiatria*, *55*(3), 137–144. doi:10.1708/3382.33569 PMID:32489190

Talukder, A., Senapathi, M., & Buchan, J. (2017). Coordination in Distributed Agile Software Development: A Systematic Review. *Proceedings of the Australasian Conference on Information Systems*, 1-12.

Tandon, A., Dhir, A., Almugren, I., AlNemer, G. N., & Mantymaki, M. (2021). Fear of Missing Out (FOMO) among social media users: A systematic literature review, synthesis and framework for future research. *Internet Research*, *31*(3), 782–821. doi:10.1108/INTR-11-2019-0455

Telefónica Ecuador. (2020). Conoce cómo la intranet ayuda a mejorar la comunicación interna en tu empresa. *Think Big / Empresas*. https://empresas.blogthinkbig.com/intranet-una-manera-efectiva-de-encarar-la-comunicacion-interna/

Terra, C.F. (2021). *Marcas influenciadoras digitais*. São Caetano do Sul: Difusão Editora.

Tiwana, A., & Konsynski, B. (2010). Complementarities between organizational IT architecture and governance structure. *Information Systems Research*, *21*(2), 288–304. doi:10.1287/isre.1080.0206

Tiwari, S., & Raut, C. (2019). Comparing strategic orientation of two online pharmaceutical firms: Cases of netmeds and medplus. SSRN *Electron. J.* doi:10.2139/ssrn.3323452

Traquina, N. (2002). Uma comunidade interpretativa transnacional: a tribo jornalística. *Media e Jornalismo*, *1*(1), 45-64. http://fabricadesites.fcsh.unl.pt/polocicdigital/wp-content/uploads/sites/8/2017/02/mj_1.pdf#page=45

Turmunkh, U., van den Assem, M. J., & Van Dolder, D. (2019). Malleable lies: Communication and cooperation in a high stakes tv game show. *Management Science*, *65*(10), 47954812. doi:10.1287/mnsc.2018.3159

Turnbull, C. F. (2010). Mom just facebooked me and Dad knows how to text: The influences of computer-mediated communication on interpersonal communication and differences through generations. *Elon Journal of Undergraduate Research in Communications*, *1*(1), 5–16.

Twenge, J. M., Martin, G. N., & Campbell, W. K. (2021). Decreases in psychological well-being among American adolescents after 2012 and links to increased digital media use. *Emotion (Washington, D.C.)*, *21*(6), 1132–1142. doi:10.1037/emo0000927

Ueki, Y., Tsuji, M., & Cárcamo Olmos, R. (2005). Tecnología de la información y las comunicaciones (TIC) para el fomento de las pymes exportadoras en América Latina y Asia Oriental. *Los procesos de comunicación permiten a la organización mantener la coordinación entre sus distintas partes y alcanzar así su característica esencial: la de ser un sistema*. https://core.ac.uk/download/pdf/38671914.pdf

UNESCO. (2020). *The effect of COVID-19 on journalists' mental health*. Reuters Institute for the Study of Journalism e pela University of Toronto. https://www.unesco.org/en/world-media-trends/effect-covid-19-journalists-mental-health

Unión Social Obrera. (2020). *Violencia en el trabajo: Uno de los principales riesgos psicosociales del ámbito laboral*. USO. https://www.uso.es/violencia-en-el-trabajo-riesgo-psicosocial-laboral/

USC Annenberg Center for Public Relations. (2022). *The future of Corporate Activism*. Global Communication Report. https://annenberg.usc.edu/research/center-public-relations/global-communication-report

Uysal, N., & Yang, A. (2013). The power of activist networks in the mass self-communication era: A triangulation study of the impact of WikiLeaks on the stock value of Bank of America. *Public Relations Review*, *39*(5), 459–469. doi:10.1016/j.pubrev.2013.09.007

Valadares, G. N. (2020, December 15). Jornalismo compassivo: e se a saúde emocional dos repórteres virar prioridade nas redações em 2021? *Abraji/Farol Jornalismo.* https://medium.com/jornalismo-no-brasil-em-2021/jornalismo-compassivo-e-se-a-sa%C3%BAde-emocional-dos-rep%C3%B3rteres-virar-prioridade-nas-reda%C3%A7%C3%B5es-em-2021-b7dae2698a73

Valdés, I. (2019). Ya no puedo más. *El País.* https://elpais.com/sociedad/2019/06/01/actualidad/1559383749_362348.html

Valentini, C. (2015). Is using social media 'good' for the public relations profession? A critical reflection. *Public Relations Review, 41*(2), 170–177. doi:10.1016/j.pubrev.2014.11.009

Vallejo Peña, F. A., & Pardo Molina, M. (2009). La Comunicación Vertical: Un acercamiento a su problemática en las organizaciones. *Revista Internacional De Organizaciones, 2*(2), 149–168. doi:10.17345/rio2.149-168

van den Abeele, M. M. P. (2021). Digital Wellbeing as a Dynamic Construct. *Communication Theory, 31*(4), 932–955. doi:10.1093/ct/qtaa024

van Dijck, J., Poell, T., & de Waal, M. (2018). *The Platform Society: Public Values in a Connective World.* Oxford University Press. doi:10.1093/oso/9780190889760.001.0001

van Osch, W., & Coursaris, C. K. (2014). Social media research: An assessment of the domain's productivity and intellectual evolution. *Communication Monographs, 81*(3), 1–25. doi:10.1080/03637751.2014.921720

van Ruler, D. V., & Sriramesh, K. (2007). Defining strategic communication. *International Journal of Strategic Communication, 1*(1), 3–35. doi:10.1080/15531180701285244

van Velthoven, M. H., Cordon, G., & Challagalla, C. (2019). Digitization of healthcare organizations: The digital health landscape and information theory. *International Journal of Medical Informatics, 124*, 49–57. doi:10.1016/j.ijmedinf.2019.01.007 PMID:30784426

Vázquez, D. (2022). Teletrabajo: Breve historia en 6 claves de algo más que una moda y algo menos que una revolución laboral. *Business Insider.* https://www.businessinsider.es/historia-teletrabajo-claves-ultima-revolucion-laboral-global-1051091

Venkatesh, V., Rabah, J., Fusaro, M., Couture, A., Varela, W., & Alexander, K. (2016). Factors impacting university instructors' and students' perceptions of course effectiveness and technology integration in the age of web 2.0. *McGill Journal of Education, 51*(1), 533–561. doi:10.7202/1037358ar

Venter, E. (2017). Bridging the communication gap between generation Y and the baby boomer generation. *International Journal of Adolescence and Youth, 22*(4), 497–507. doi:10.1080/02673843.2016.1267022

Verghese, A. K. (2017). Internal communication: practices and implications. *SCMS Journal of Indian Management*, 103-113.

Vergini, S. (2018). *Key Factors to Succeed at Managing Distributed Agile Teams.* Retrieved from https://www.knowledgehut.com/blog/agile/key-factors-to-succeed-agile-teams

Vernuccio, M. (2014). Communicating Corporate Brands Through Social Media: An Exploratory Study. *Journal of Business Communication.* http://eds.a.ebscohost.com/

Walimbe, P. (2016). *To Overcome Communication Challenges in Distributed/Virtual Scrum Teams* [MSc Thesis]. Harrisburg University of Science and Technology. Retrieved from https://digitalcommons.harrisburgu.edu/pmgt_dandt/4

Walther, J. B., & Bunz, U. (2005). The rules of virtual groups: Trust, liking, and performance in computer-mediated communication. *Journal of Communication, 55*(4), 828–846. doi:10.1111/j.1460-2466.2005.tb03025.x

Wang, S., Abbas, J., Sial, M. S., Álvarez-Otero, S., & Cioca, L. (2022). Achieving green innovation and sustainable development goals through green knowledge management: Moderating role of organizational green culture. *Journal of Innovation & Knowledge*, *7*(4), 1–9. doi:10.1016/j.jik.2022.100272

Wang, Y., Zhou, Y., Li, S., & Zhang, L. (2019). The effects of digital media on children's empathy: A meta-analysis. *Journal of Educational Computing Research*, *57*(8), 1999–2025. doi:10.1177/0735633118797999

Wassell, E., & Dodge, R. (2015). A multidisciplinary framework for measuring and improving wellbeing. *International Journal of Sciences, Basic and Applied Research*, *21*(2), 97–107.

Weinreich, R., Neumann, N., Riedel, R., & Müller, E. (2015). Scrum as Method for Agile Project Management Outside of the Product Development Area. *Proceedings of the IFIP International Conference on Advances in Production Management Systems (APMS)*, 565-572. 10.1007/978-3-319-22756-6_69

Whicker, M., Kronenfeld, J., & Stricker, R. (1993). *Getting tenure (Survival skills for scholars).* Sage.

WHO. (n.d.). *COVID-19.* Retrieved in May 23rd, 2022, from: https://www.who.int/emergencies/diseases/novel-coronavirus-2019/situation-reports

Wijayati, T. A., & Achadi, A. (2019). Factors Affecting the Success of Hospital Management Information System: A Systematic Review. In *Proceedings of the 6th International Conference on Public Health.* Sebelas Maret University.

Wilcox, D., & Cameron, G. T. (2009). *Public Relations: Strategies and Tactics* (9th ed.). Pearson Allyn & Bacon.

Wirtz, J. C., & Zimbres, T. (2018). A systematic analysis of research applying 'principles of dialogic communication' to organizational websites, blogs and social media: Implications for theory and practice. *Journal of Public Relations Research*, *30*(1-2), 5–34. doi:10.1080/1062726X.2018.1455146

Wood, S. (2008). Job characteristics, employee voice and wellbeing in Britain. *Industrial Relations Journal*, *39*(2), 153–168. doi:10.1111/j.1468-2338.2007.00482.x

Work Better. (2021, January 11). *Steelcase*. www.steelcase.com. https://www.steelcase.com/research/articles/work-better/?utm_source=forbes&utm_medium=tb-article&utm_campaign=work-better&utm_term=work-better-article

Workforce Hub. (n.d.). Churn rate. *Workforce Hub.* Retrieved from: https://www.workforcehub.com/glossary/churn-rate/

Workplace, Q. (2021). *The Impact of COVID-19 on Employee Engagement.* Retrieved in April 1st, 2022, from: https://www.quantumworkplace.com/impact-of-covid-19-on-employee-engagement

World Health Organization. (2020). *Digital health.* https://bit.ly/3zl3y73

World Health Organization. (2021). *Mental Health Atlas 2020.* World Health Organization. https://www.who.int/publications-detail-redirect/9789240036703

World Health Organization. (2022, June 17). *Mental health: Strengthening our response*. World Health Organization. https://www.who.int/news-room/fact-sheets/mental-health-strengthening-our-response

Yang, A., & Taylor, M. (2010). Relationship-building by Chinese NGOs' websites: Education, not activation. *Public Relations Review*, *36*(4), 342–351. doi:10.1016/j.pubrev.2010.07.001

Yang, S. U., Kang, M., & Cha, H. (2015). A study on dialogic communication, trust, and distrust: Testing a scale for measuring organization–public dialogic communication (OPDC). *Journal of Public Relations Research*, *27*(2), 175–192. doi:10.1080/1062726X.2015.1007998

Yang, S. U., Kang, M., & Johnson, P. (2010). Effects of narratives, openness to dialogic communication, and credibility on engagement in crisis communication through organizational blogs. *Communication Research*, *37*(4), 473–497. doi:10.1177/0093650210362682

Yarimoglu, E. K. (2014). Turkish retail industry and the relations with Albania. *European Scientific Journal*, *10*(7). Advance online publication. doi:10.19044/esj.2014.v10n7p%p

Yates, M., Bechman, K., Dennison, E. M., MacGregor, A. J., Ledingham, J., Norton, S., & Galloway, J. B. (2020). Data quality predicts care quality: Findings from a national clinical audit. *Arthritis Research & Therapy*, *22*(1), 87. doi:10.118613075-020-02179-y PMID:32303251

Yin, R. K. (2017). *Case Study Research and Applications: Design and Methods*. SAGE Publications.

Zhou, J. (2013). Digitalization and intelligentization of manufacturing industry. *Advances in Manufacturing*, *1*(1), 1–7. doi:10.100740436-013-0006-5

Zidarova, E. D., & Zografos, K. (2011). Measuring Quality of Service in Airport Passenger Terminals. *Transportation Research Record: Journal of the Transportation Research Board*, *2214*(1), 69–76. doi:10.3141/2214-09

Zuboff, S. (2019). *The Age of Surveillance Capitalism: The fight for a human future at the new frontier of power*. PublicAffairs.

Zucker, J. (2021, March 2). The next big thing in employee benefits: Flexibility. *Forbes*. Retrieved from: https://www.forbes.com/sites/forbeshumanresourcescouncil/2021/03/02/the-next-big-thing-in-employee-benefits-flexibility/?sh=31c5588e2105

About the Contributors

Alexandre Duarte, with a PhD in Communication Sciences from University of Minho, a Master degree in Communication & Image and a Bachelor in Marketing & Advertising by IADE, is an Assistant Professor in Universidade NOVA de Lisboa, researcher at ICNOVA, and invited Professor in Universidade Católica Portuguesa, where coordinates the Post-Graduation Courses in Advertising & Creativity and Service Design. Throughout his career, Alexandre worked in several multinational advertising agencies such as TBWA, Saatchi & Saatchi, Ogilvy, W/Portugal, W/Brazil, Lowe & Partners, or Brandia Central as a Senior Creative Copywriter. Author of many seminars on strategic and creative communication, regularly participates in conferences and lectures in both business and academic contexts. Between 2012 and 2014, was the Tutor of the EUROBEST Young Marketers Academy and in the beginning of 2014, was appointed CEO of RESTART, an Institute of Creativity, Arts and New Technologies. In 2019 was re-elected member of the Directors Board of EDCOM, and in 2023 elected member of the Research Committee.

Patrícia Dias is Assistant Professor of the Faculty of Human Sciences (FCH) at the Catholic University of Portugal (UCP), where she coordinates the Post-graduate course Social Brands – Communication and Marketing in the Digital Environment. She is a member of the Executive Board of the Research Centre on Peoples and Cultures (CEPCEP), integrated researcher at the Research Centre for Communication and Culture (CECC), and collaborator at the Católica Research Centre on Psychological, Family and Social Wellbeing. Holding a PhD in Communication Sciences, her research interests are the use of digital media by children and families, mobile communication, digital marketing and communication strategies, and emergent technologies within the scope of the Internet of Things. She is the author of "Smarketing - How Mobile Marketing is Changing Portugal" (2020), "Living in the Digital Society" (2014) and of "The Mobile Phone and Daily Life" (2008).

Teresa Ruão is senior lecturer in the Communication Sciences Department at the University of Minho and Pro-Rector for Institutional Communication, since 2021. She has a PhD in Communication Sciences (2008) from the University of Minho and researches on Organizational and Strategic Communication. Develops teaching activities in the field of Organizational Communication and Public Relations. She has held several positions within the University of Minho over the years. Notably, she served as Vice-President of the Institute of Social Sciences and President of the Pedagogical Council between 2010 and 2019; and was Vice-Head of the Communication and Society Research Centre from 2019 to 2021. She is a member of the Portuguese Communication Sciences Association (Sopcom) and was a board member of its Organizational Communication Work Group for 10 years. She has been an evaluator for the Portuguese Foundation for Science and Technology, since 2017, and for in the Portuguese Agency for Assessment and Accreditation of Higher Education, since 2018. As a researcher, she has been a member of several research projects, has published numerous books, papers, scientific reports and was a speaker in several national and international congresses.

José Gabriel Andrade is a researcher and professor on media, marketing and communication at the University of Minho. José holds a European PhD in Communication Sciences from the Catholic University of Portugal with the support of the Portuguese Foundation for Science and Technology, Fundação para a Ciência e a Tecnologia (FCT) and a Master in Communication Sciences: Communication, Organisation and New Technologies from the Portuguese Catholic University, Universidade Católica Portuguesa - UCP, with the support of the high level scholarship Program of the European Union for Latin America (Alban). He coordinated the master's degree on Digital Communication and integrated the structure responsible for quality management, internships, communication and interface with the community at the University, actively participating in the professional and personal development of the students.

* * *

Fernando Luís Almeida has a Ph.D. in Computer Science Engineering from the Faculty of Engineering of University of Porto (FEUP). He also holds an MSc in Innovation and Entrepreneurship and in Informatics Engineering from FEUP. He has around 10 years of teaching experience at higher education levels in the field of computer science and management. He has also worked for 15 years in several positions as a software engineer and project manager for large organizations and research centers like Critical Software, CICA/SEF, INESC TEC, and ISR Porto. He is a founder member of the International Association of Innovation Professionals and he is involved in the development of the US TAG group for ISO 56000 (Innovation Management). His current research areas include innovation policies, entrepreneurship, software development, and decision support systems.

Amilcar Barreto is a visiting lecturer in Marketing Communication and strategy at the Catholic University of Portugal (Instituto de Ciências da Saúde). Mr. Barreto's main research interests are digital communication, namely the pharmaceutical digital communication, and consumer digital communication and omnichannel. Amilcar shares his time working in global positions in a big Pharma company where he is responsible for multichannel & digital communication in neuroscience and rare disease and researcher in Universidade Católica Portuguesa, where he is finishing his PhD in Communication Sciences. Mr. Barreto is a team leader and an active player in different teams creating integrated strategies. He has been working for almost two decades in different positions in marketing communications in the pharmaceutical industry and fast moving consumer goods, in companies such as J&J, Roche and Novartis.

Margareth Boarini holds a doctorate in intelligence technologies and digital design from the Pontifical Catholic University of São Paulo (PUC-SP) and a master's degree in social communication from the Methodist University of São Paulo. She teaches post-graduate courses in corporate communication and leadership (FAAP Digital), and is a researcher focused on the impacts of new technologies in the universe of communication (big data, artificial intelligence, social networks, among others). A consultant in the area of corporate communication, she is a member of research groups Comunidata (PUC-SP) and Influcom (Faculdade Cásper Líbero). She is a post-doctoral fellow in intelligence technologies and digital design (PUC-SP) with a focus on humans and non-humans.

Edson Capoano is a researcher at Communication and Society Study Centre – CECS, at University of Minho, Portugal, about journalism, social media and audiences' participation. Currently, is researching relations between emotions and communication.

Pedro Coelho has a degree in Creativity and Business Innovation from Politécnico do Porto, Vilniaus Kolegija and Eesti Ettevõtluskõrgkool Mainor, and is currently specialising in Digital Communication. Working in the area of Communication and Marketing since he obtained his degree in June, he has integrated several ERASMUS+ projects in countries such as Bulgaria, Estonia and Italy, Lithuania.

Rita Curvelo is an Assistant Professor at the Human Sciences Faculty of Portuguese Catholic University, and researcher at CECC - Research Centre for Communication and Culture. PhD in Media and journalism studies at The Social and Human Sciences Faculty of Nova University in Lisbon. Main research interests include Cultural marketing, Radio studies, Publics and audiences Interpersonal and Organizational communication. Communications professional at Group Renascença Multinedia, between 1998 and 2015, with specialization in all areas of Radio Communication. Book Author of Marketing das Artes em Direto (Lisbon, 2009), and A Rádio Musical no panorama ibérico: estratégias e dinâmicas de comunicação (Porto, 2021).

Renato Essenfelder is a Brazilian journalist, professor, and Ph.D. researcher in Communication Sciences at the LabCom Research Unit - Portugal. Professor at the University Fernando Pessoa (Porto, Portugal), with particular interest in the application of innovative technologies in communications.

Daniel Roque Gomes is Professor at the School of Education, of the Polytechnic University of Coimbra. He holds a Post-doc by SOCIUS - ISEG Lisbon School of Economics & Management, and a PhD In Psychology with specialization in Work and Organizational Psychology by ISCTE-IUL. He was the Administrator of the Polytechnic University of Coimbra from 2017-2021 and is currently Vice-President of the Polytechnic University of Coimbra in charge of the Quality Management, Sport, and the Academic Affairs of the institution. His research focuses broadly on human resources management, organizational behavior and Internal Communication.

Gabriela Gomes has a degree in Human Relations and Organizational Communication, a Master in Management and she is post graduated in Human Resources Management. She is currently a PhD student in Business Management at the Faculty of Economics, University of Coimbra. She was a research fellow at the Centre of Applied Research in Management and Economics (CARME) at the Polytechnic of Leiria. Her areas of interest are Human Resources Management, Burnout and Organizational Behavior.

Alexandra Leandro was born in Oporto in 1975. Since 2002, has been a member of the faculty of the Polytechnic of Coimbra (School of Higher Education) as a professor of Communication Sciences, Organizations and Media. Usually teaches curricular units of Marketing, Advertising and Public Relations. Previously, Alexandra has had the opportunity to work in several Marketing departments, mainly in the Food Industry. In 1998, graduated in Social Communication (specialization in Advertising) by the

University of Minho. Afterwards, Alexandra post-graduated in Communication Law (Faculty of Law of the University of Coimbra), has become an MBA in Marketing and concluded the master's degree in Management (Porto Business School, University of Porto). In 2017, has successfully concluded her Doctoral degree in the University of Minho. Alexandra's PhD dissertation was entitled: "The communication of socially responsible organizations: an analysis of CSR reports."

Orlando Manuel Lima Rua is Assistant Professor of Management at the Porto School of Accounting and Business (ISCAP) of the Polytechnic of Porto (Portugal). Researcher at Center for Organisational and Social Studies of the Polytechnic of Porto (CEOS.PP), Portugal. Researcher at the Research Center for Business Sciences (NECE), University of Beira Interior, Portugal. Applied Management Research Unit (UNIAG) of the Association of Polytechnic Institutes of Northern Portugal.

Mădălina Moraru is Associate Professor Ph.D. at the Faculty of Journalism and Communication Studies, Course Director of the Advertising and Digital Communication Master programme and researcher at the University of Bucharest, Romania. Her main interests are the anthropological and narrative approaches on national and international advertising. She has been teaching classes related to the advertising field for more than 10 years (Advertising agency, Storytelling in advertising and Introduction to advertising). As a member of the Edcom –EACA, ECREA, and ESA, she aims to be active and stay in touch with cutting-edge research worldwide. Mrs Moraru has been recently elected as a board member of the European Institute for Commercial Communications Education (Edcom) and re-elected in the Research Committee of the same organization, which is a hub for education and training opportunities in the creative industries founded by EACA. From 2010 to 2013 she received postdoctoral fellowships as visiting professor from The University of Oklahoma, United States, and Staffordshire University and Buckinghamshire New University, United Kingdom. From October 2010 to March 2013 she conducted the strategic European grant POSDRU/89/1.5/S/62259, entitled Glocalization in Romanian Advertising-Archetypes and Themes of Popular Culture for Building the Local Identity of National and Multinational Brands. During her activity, she authored many chapters, over 20 research articles, as well as two books entitled "Myth and Advertising" (Bucharest, Nemira Publishing House, 2009) and "Advertising Stories. From Inspiration to Strategy" (Bucharest, Tritonic Publishing House, 2015).

Eduardo Ortega has a degree in Business Management and a Master in Marketing Management. He is currently a PhD candidate in Business Management at the Faculty of Economics, University of Coimbra. He was a research fellow at the Centre of Applied Research in Management and Economics (CARME) at the Polytechnic of Leiria. His areas of interest are Marketing, with emphasis on Marketing and Human Resources Management.

Neuza Ribeiro is professor of human resources management and organizational behavior at the School of Technology and Management, Polytechnic University of Leiria and researcher of CARME - Center of Applied Research in Management and Economics. She received a Post-doc in Management and a Doctorate in Industrial Management with a specialization in Organizational Behavior from Aveiro University (2010). Her research focuses broadly on human resources management and organizational behavior.

Mallika Sankar is an assistant professor in the School of Business and Management at the Christ University in Bangalore, India. She received her Ph.D. in management from Bharathiar University, MBA from Pondicherry University and undergraduate studies at Mahatma Gandhi University. She has collaborated actively with researchers in several other disciplines of business management, published articles and co-authored a book in research methodology. She is preferred as a resource person in several faculty development programs, conferences, workshops. She has also served as trainer in the programs organized by AICTE and an invited speaker in many public events and academic institutions. She has also served in industry at various administrative positions for over 12 years. Her areas of teaching include research methodology, business analytics and strategic management at the post graduate, graduate and undergraduate levels.

Romina Surugiu is Associate Professor of Journalism and Media Studies, and Vice Dean of the Faculty of Journalism and Communication Studies, University of Bucharest. She holds a PhD in Philosophy from the University of Bucharest (2006), and worked as a postdoctoral researcher in Communication Studies at the University of Bucharest (2010-2013), and at the Uppsala University (2012). She has published/coordinated research on journalism practice and specialist journalism, on the dynamics of work and gender in the media, and on the history of the European television. She served as a board member of Romanian Public Television. She was a management committee member of the EU COST Action on the Dynamics of Virtual Work IS 1202 (2012-2016, chair: Professor Ursula Huws).

Michael C. Zalot, Ph.D., is currently Director of Graduate Business Programs and Assistant Professor at Cedar Crest College in Allentown, PA, USA. He earned his doctorate at New York University in Media, and then an MBA in Information Systems Management elsewhere, following his industry work in multimedia development. Dr. Zalot publishes at the intersection of culture and media technologies, with an eye toward business applications as well. He teaches courses on business application software, business communication, and strategic leadership, among other topics, and directs both the Master of Business Administration and the innovative Modular Master of Science programs at Cedar Crest.

Index

www.ingramcontent.com/pod-product-compliance
Lightning Source LLC
LaVergne TN
LVHW062155300926
849161LV00010B/2667

9781668473535